T0360881

THE
WASHINGTON CONSENSUS

A Critical Evaluation of the Principles and Implications for Economic Development

THE

WASHINGTON CONSENSUS

A Critical Evaluation of the Principles and Implications for Economic Development

Imad A. Moosa

Ton Duc Thang University, Vietnam

 **World Scientific**

NEW JERSEY · LONDON · SINGAPORE · BEIJING · SHANGHAI · HONG KONG · TAIPEI · CHENNAI · TOKYO

Published by

World Scientific Publishing Co. Pte. Ltd.

5 Toh Tuck Link, Singapore 596224

USA office: 27 Warren Street, Suite 401-402, Hackensack, NJ 07601

UK office: 57 Shelton Street, Covent Garden, London WC2H 9HE

Library of Congress Cataloging-in-Publication Data
Names: Moosa, Imad A., author.
Title: The Washington consensus : a critical evaluation of the principles and implications for
    economic development / Imad A Moosa, Ton Duc Thang University, Vietnam.
Description: New Jersey : World Scientific, [2021] | Includes bibliographical references and index.
Identifiers: LCCN 2021012078 | ISBN 9789811236402 (hardcover) |
    ISBN 9789811236785 (ebook for institutions) | ISBN 9789811236792 (ebook for individuals)
Subjects: LCSH: International Monetary Fund. | World Bank. | Globalization--Economic
    aspects--Developing countries. | Economic development--Political aspects. |
    International finance. | Developing countries--Economic policy.
Classification: LCC HC59.7 .M5767 2021 | DDC 338.9009172/4--dc23
LC record available at https://lccn.loc.gov/2021012078

British Library Cataloguing-in-Publication Data
A catalogue record for this book is available from the British Library.

For any available supplementary material, please visit
https://www.worldscientific.com/worldscibooks/10.1142/12260#t=suppl

Desk Editors: Balasubramanian Shanmugam/Lum Pui Yee

Typeset by Stallion Press
Email: enquiries@stallionpress.com

Printed in Singapore

To Nisreen, Danny, Ryan and Ivy

Preface

In 2019, I published a book entitled *Eliminating the IMF: An Analysis of the Debate to Keep, Reform or Abolish the Fund*, in which I argued that the IMF had been inflicting so much damage on humanity that it ought to be abolished. Chapter 2 of that book was about the Washington Consensus, the set of principles that govern the conditionality and structural adjustment programs imposed on developing countries in return for loans from international financial institutions. In the same chapter, I discussed each one of the ten principles, which I called the ten commandments, and related them to IMF operations.

A year later, I thought that I could write a whole book on the Washington Consensus, a book in which a whole chapter is devoted to each one of the ten commandments. The outcome has been this book, which falls into 14 chapters. The book starts with an overview of the Consensus, followed by a chapter on IMF conditionality and how they are related. Since the Consensus is inherently neoliberal, Chapter 3 is devoted to a critique of the free market doctrine and the concept of economic freedom as seen by right-wing commentators. The ten commandments are divided into four groups: fiscal reform, interest and exchange rate policies, liberalization of trade and foreign direct investment, and privatization and deregulation (including property rights).

The book is written in the normative tradition of what ought to be as opposed to the positive tradition of what is. The underlying issues are so vital and involve so much injustice that one cannot pretend to be neutral for the sake of neutrality. This may invite accusations of being a "polemic", but this is a price worth paying for dismantling a set of principles that are effectively used to loot developing countries. One cannot possibly be neutral about slavery or fascism because that is immoral, to say the least.

The book was written during the period April–November 2020, when we lived under lockdown as a result of COVID-19. This is why Covid-related themes appear frequently. For example, the issue of free market pricing versus fair pricing is discussed with reference to the pricing of a COVID-19 vaccine. It is also argued that the very prevalence of the Washington Consensus is threatened by the pandemic as international relations will not be the same in a post-Covid world.

Writing this book would not have been possible without the help and encouragement I received from family, friends and colleagues. My utmost gratitude must go to my wife, Afaf, who bore most of the opportunity cost of writing this book and used her skills to draw the diagrams shown therein. I would also like to thank my colleagues and friends, including John Vaz, Kelly Burns, Vikash Ramiah, Mike Dempsey, Liam Lenten, Brien McDonald and Nirav Parikh.

In preparing the manuscript, I benefited from the exchange of ideas with members of the Table 14 Discussion Group, and for this reason, I would like to thank Bob Parsons, Greg O'Brien, Greg Bailey, Bill Breen, Paul Rule, Peter Murphy, Bob Brownlee, Jim Reiss and Tony Pagliaro. In particular, I would like to thank Greg Bailey who read the whole manuscript and provided a large number of insightful comments.

My thanks also go to friends and former colleagues who live far away but provide help via means of telecommunication, including Kevin Dowd (to whom I owe an intellectual debt), Razzaque Bhatti, Ron Ripple, Bob Sedgwick, Sean Holly, Dan Hemmings, Ian Baxter and Basil Al-Nakeeb. I should also mention my dear friend, Sulaiman Al-Jassar, who passed away in August 2020 after contracting COVID-19. Last, but not least, I would like to thank Ms Pui Yee Lum, the Commissioning Editor at World Scientific who encouraged me to write this book.

Naturally, I am the only one responsible for any errors and omissions that may be found in this book. It is dedicated to my daughter, Nisreen, my son, Danny, my grandson, Ryan and my granddaughter, Ivy.

Imad A. Moosa
May 2021

About the Author

Imad Moosa currently holds the position of adjunct professor of finance at Ton Duc Thang University (TDTU), Vietnam. Previously, he held professorial positions at RMIT, Monash University and La Trobe University. He has published extensively in the fields of international finance, financial markets, macroeconomics and energy economics. His most recent books include *Econometrics as a Con Art, Publish or Perish: Perceived Benefits versus Unintended Consequences, The Economics of War* and *Controversies in Economics and Finance*. He has also written for professional magazines such as the prestigious *Euromoney*.

Contents

List of Figures

List of Tables

List of Abbreviations/Acronyms

ABIR	Anglo-Belgian India Rubber Company
ACCC	Australian Competition and Consumer Commission
AIDS	Acquired Immunodeficiency Syndrome
APR	Annual Percentage Rate
ASCE	American Society of Civil Engineers
AT&T	American Telephone and Telegraph
BBC	British Broadcasting Corporation
BC	Before Christ
BEER	Behavioural Equilibrium Exchange Rate
BEPS	Base Erosion and Profit Shifting
BIS	Bank for International Settlements
BIS	Bureau of Industry and Security
BJC	Beijing Consensus
BLS	Bureau of Labor Statistics
BP	British Petroleum
BRI	Belt and Road Initiative
BRICS	Brazil, Russia, India, China and South Africa
BSAC	British South Africa Company
CARES	Coronavirus Aid, Relief, and Economic Security
CBO	Congressional Budget Office
CBS	Columbia Broadcasting System
CDO	Collateralized Debt Obligation
CEO	Chief Executive Officer
CEP	Centre for Economic Performance
CEPR	Centre for Economic and Policy Research

CGD	Center for Global Development
CIA	Central Intelligence Agency
CIGI	Centre for International Governance Innovation
CNN	Cable News Network
COMAC	Commercial Aircraft Corporation of China
COVID	Coronavirus Disease
CPI	Consumer Price Index
CSIS	Center for Strategic and International Studies
DC	District of Columbia
DEA	Drug Enforcement Administration
DEER	Desired Equilibrium Real Exchange Rate
DHS	Department of Homeland Security
DoD	Department of Defense
EAR	Export Administration Regulations
EPI	Economic Policy Institute
EPS	Economic and Private Sector
EU	European Union
FBI	Federal Bureau of Investigation
FCIC	Financial Crisis Inquiry Commission
FDA	Food and Drug Administration
FDI	Foreign Direct Investment
FDIC	Federal Deposit Insurance Corporation
FEER	Fundamental Equilibrium Exchange Rate
GDP	Gross Domestic Product
ICU	International Clearing Union
IEO	Independent Evaluation Office
IFAC	International Federation of Accountants
IGM	Initiative on Global Markets
IMF	International Monetary Fund
IMFC	International Monetary and Financial Committee
IP	Intellectual Property
IQ	Intelligence Quotient
ISI	Import Substitution Industrialization
ISIS	Islamic State in Iraq and Syria
ITMEER	Intermediate-Term Model-Based Equilibrium Exchange Rate
ITO	International Trade Organization
KBR	Kellogg Brown & Root
LOP	Law of One Price

MA	Massachusetts
MC	Mondragon Corporation
MIT	Massachusetts Institute of Technology
NAFTA	North American Free Trade Area
NASA	National Aeronautics and Space Administration
NATO	North Atlantic Treaty Organization
NATREX	Natural Real Equilibrium Exchange Rate
NBER	National Bureau of Economic Research
NPR	National Public Radio
NSA	National Security Agency
NSSM	National Security Study Memorandum
NTM	Non-Tariff Measure
OECD	Organisation for Economic Co-operation and Development
OTC	Over the Counter
PEER	Permanent Equilibrium Exchange Rate
PERI	Political Economy Research Institute
PMSC	Private Military and Security Company
PNAC	Project for the New American Century
PPP	Purchasing Power Parity
RBA	Reserve Bank of Australia
RIC	Regional Investment Corporation
R&D	Research and Development
RMB	Renminbi
SC	South Carolina
SEMAPA	Sociedade de Investimento e Gestão
SIPRI	Stockholm International Peace Research Institute
SPS	Sanitary and Phytosanitary
TAFE	Technical and Further Education
TB	Treasury Bill
TB	Tuberculosis
TRIP	Travel, Logistics & Transport Infrastructure
UK	United Kingdom
UN	United Nations
UNCTAD	United Nations Conference on Trade and Development
UNICEF	United Nations Children's Fund
US	United States
VA	Virginia
WTO	World Trade Organization

Chapter 1

The Washington Consensus: An Overview

1.1 Origin and Evolution

The term "Washington Consensus" was coined by John Williamson in 1989 when he was examining the principles of development economics that had guided economic policy in Latin America since the 1950s. By choice or otherwise, the vintage Latin American principles were being swept aside by an alternative set of principles that had been accepted as appropriate in the Anglo-American world since the resurgence of the free market doctrine in the early 1970s (see, for example, Williamson, 1990). The Consensus is a set of ten policy prescriptions or principles promoted by institutions based in Washington DC—primarily, the International Monetary Fund (IMF), the World Bank and the US Treasury. In this book, the ten principles are referred to as the "ten commandments", with lower case letters to distinguish them from the Ten Commandments, the set of biblical principles relating to ethics and worship.

The ten commandments of the Washington Consensus are preached to, or imposed on, developing countries by leading them to believe that the commandments are the way to prosperity or by threatening them with deprivation from financial aid and dismissal from the "international community". The preachers (and imposers) of the Consensus include "political" Washington, which comprises the US Congress and Administration, and "technocratic" Washington of the IMF, World Bank and right-wing think tanks. Technocratic Washington provides intellectual justification for corporate Washington to loot the preached countries, aided and abetted by political Washington.

Cohen-Setton (2016) describes the Washington Consensus by saying that "John Williamson provided a list of ten policies that more or less everyone in Washington agreed were needed more or less everywhere in Latin America". The Washingtons are aided and abetted by the rest of the "West", typically former and resurgent imperialist countries that are nostalgic to the good old days when they looted their colonies with impunity (and fought over them every now and then). Thus, the term "preachers", as used in this book, covers the Washingtons and former imperialist countries (hence the "preaching countries").

Williamson (1990) uses the phrase "setting their houses in order" in reference to Latin American countries contemplating loans from the Washington-based institutions, which are effectively run by the US Treasury. Williamson (2000) describes the Consensus as "the lowest common denominator of policy advice being addressed by the Washington-based institutions to Latin American countries as of 1989". At least for the critics, the Consensus is seen as synonymous with "neoliberalism" and "globalization". In this respect, Williamson (2002) refers to "audiences the world over" who "seem to believe that this [the Consensus] signifies a set of neoliberal policies that have been imposed on hapless countries by the Washington-based international financial institutions and have led them to crisis and misery". He also refers to "people who cannot utter the term without foaming at the mouth". This is perhaps why at a later stage, Williamson tried to put a humanitarian face to the Consensus and to distance it (or himself) from strict neoliberal, extreme free-market prescriptions. Despite claims of different versions of the Consensus and misunderstanding, the Consensus is what the IMF has been following in its dealings with developing countries.

1.2 The Ten Commandments and Their Implications

In his original formulation, Williamson (1990) specified the ten commandments as follows. The first commandment is fiscal discipline, the rationing of government borrowing and avoidance of large fiscal deficits relative to the size of the economy (measured by Gross Domestic Product (GDP)). The second commandment is reordering public expenditure priorities by redirecting financial resources from subsidies (particularly "indiscriminate subsidies", whatever that means) toward broad-based provision of key pro-growth, pro-poor services such as primary education, primary healthcare and infrastructure investment. The third is tax reform involving the broadening of the tax base and the adoption of moderate marginal tax rates. Therefore, the first three commandments fall under "fiscal reform".

The fourth commandment is the liberalization of interest rates by making them market determined (rather than determined by the monetary authorities) and the preservation of positive (but moderate) real interest rates. Number five is the adoption of a competitive exchange rate, meaning an exchange rate that makes exports cheap in foreign currency terms (hence, competitive). Therefore, the fourth and fifth commandments are about interest rate and exchange rate policies.

The sixth and seventh commandments are about trade and foreign direct investment (FDI), which are related because the underlying objective is for corporate Washington to find markets, cheap labor and cheap (or free) natural resources. The sixth commandment is trade liberalization, with particular emphasis on the elimination of trade barriers, such as tariffs and quotas. Number seven is the liberalization of inward foreign direct investment, which means allowing foreign investors to take control of any sector of the domestic economy.

The last three commandments are about privatization, deregulation and property rights, which are related because deregulation often leads to privatization and facilitates the operations of privatized enterprises in the pursuit of profit maximization. Property rights, on the other hand, give legitimacy to the looting by corporate Washington of public assets in developing and transition countries. The eighth commandment is the privatization of state enterprises by selling them at bargain prices. Number nine is deregulation, the abolition of regulations that impede market entry or restrict competition (except for those justified on the grounds of safety, environmental and consumer protection, and prudential oversight of financial institutions). Last, but not least, the tenth commandment is the establishment of legal security for property rights.

Figure 1.1 shows the structure of the Washington Consensus, where the ten commandments are classified under four pillars: fiscal reform, interest and exchange rate policies, liberalization, and privatization-deregulation. The core of the benefits to corporate Washington lies in three words: "liberalize, deregulate and privatize", which are covered by commandments 5–10. The other commandments contribute to the core benefits, for example, tax reform invariably involves reducing the corporate tax rate under the alleged pretext of "boosting growth and

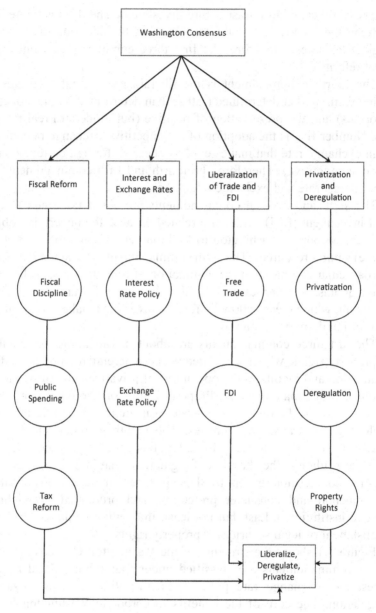

Figure 1.1:   The Washington Consensus: Structure and Outcomes

employment". Low interest rates and competitive exchange rates make it cheaper for multinationals to acquire privatized assets.

The whole structure is based on undermining the role of the state and glorifying the role of the market. Lechini (2008) argues that "one of the most important consequences of the introduction of the policies of the Washington Consensus has been the undermining of the state, an institution that was relentlessly demonized and attacked, and multiple efforts were made to de-legitimise it as a player in the development process". More disturbing, according to Lechini (2008), are "the systematic erosion of effective policy making and policy capacities and the relocation of key macro-economic decision making levers in the markets and in the hands of foreign international financial institutions, jeopardizing both democratic consolidation and development in the South".

A quick look at these principles reveals the hypocrisy behind them. This is not necessarily what Williamson intended but hypocrisy is conspicuous in the implementation, particularly as reflected in the provisions of the IMF's conditionality and structural adjustment programs. Washington, the chief preacher, is the least fiscally disciplined, which means that the preacher is not qualified to preach fiscal discipline. The intention behind fiscal discipline, as preached to developing countries, is the deliberate reduction in the size of the public sector. Redirecting public expenditure to pro-poor, health and education sounds noble, but it is ludicrous as ample evidence exists to show that IMF operations are detrimental to social expenditure because available financial resources are directed mainly to ascertain that the underlying country can pay off its debt. No one can determine what a competitive exchange rate is because exchange rates tend to be misaligned—in any case, exchange rates are supposed to be determined by the market. Competitive exchange rates mean that foreign investors should get a double whammy: cheap public assets, as a result of privatization, made even cheaper by an undervalued currency. The rest of the principles are designed to benefit foreign investors and perhaps the local oligarchy supported by the custodians of the Washington Consensus (primarily the Anglo-American alliance). All of these points will be discussed in detail in the following chapters.

Developing countries are told by the preachers and enforcers of the Washington Consensus that it is in their own interest to cut tax for the rich and corporations, open up their financial systems, remove any trade protection so that foreign corporations have access to new markets and secure the rights of foreign investors to buy (or loot) public assets. These are supposed to be pro-growth policies that will make everyone happy, a win–win situation. The question that arises here is the following: if these policies are that good for growth and prosperity, why is it that when the countries preaching the Consensus did not do the same to boost growth when they were at the same level of development as the countries that are expected to follow the rules now? America grew to be the super power it is now by being highly protective of its industries—so protective that a major reason for the Civil War, in addition to slavery, was the tariffs imposed by the industrial north against the wishes of the agricultural south.

The Consensus is associated with neoliberal policies and the free market doctrine, which encourage a diminishing role for the government in economic activity. It is supposed to provide rules about what a poor country should do to become rich and prosperous. The general ideas derived from the Washington Consensus had a huge influence on the so-called "economic reform" in so many countries. The preaching countries (the beneficiaries) use carrots and sticks to impose "reform": carrots by conveying the message that this is the way to economic prosperity and sticks by threatening deprivation of the financial resources provided by the IMF and World Bank. Ostry *et al.* (2016) argue that the neoliberal agenda underpinning the Consensus rests on two main planks: (i) boosting competition through deregulation and the opening up of domestic markets, including financial markets, to foreign competition and (ii) a smaller role for the state, achieved through privatization and the imposition of limits on the ability of governments to run fiscal deficits and accumulate debt.

One can only ask who the beneficiaries would be of the opening up of domestic markets to foreign competition and privatization that necessarily means reducing the size of the government. To answer this question, Basu (2019) refers to the "neoliberal form of globalisation propagated by the Washington Consensus and applied by the World Bank, International Monetary Fund (IMF) and World Trade Organisation (WTO)", which has benefited "rich countries and transnational corporations at the expense of ordinary people everywhere, and especially in the Global South". Glennie (2011) argues that while developing countries did not benefit from neoliberal ideology, rich countries most certainly did. Measures such as the unimpeded flow of capital, the prohibition of protecting infant industries, and the current intellectual property rights regime ensure that the dominance of businesses based in rich countries is maintained at the expense of other countries' businesses, which struggle to enter the market.

The Consensus has been described as a "wonkish moniker" by Naim (1999) who wonders how and why it became so popular. To start with, the timing was great as the Consensus was "invented" at a time to fill an ideological vacuum as communism was falling apart. The formulation of the Washington Consensus in the late 1980s coincided with the sudden collapse of the Soviet system and its ideological apparatus. At that time, there was widespread revolt against socialist ideas and central planning, hence the search was on for an alternative set of ideas to organize economic and political life. It was relatively simple for politicians with little intellectual power or common sense to understand and use in speeches to promote neoliberalism as the path to heavens. It provided a practical action plan with specific goals, for example, the efficiency associated with privatization and deregulation. It had the endorsement of prestigious institutions and individuals such as economists who could mobilize popular interest. It was adopted by a group that later became the Mont Pèlerin Society, which included Ludwig von Mises, Friedrich von Hayek and Milton Friedman. Perhaps more important is the fact that the Consensus promised the milk and honey provided by multilateral institutions and foreign investors.

Naim (1999) argues that the appeal of the Washington Consensus "was helped by its self-assured tone ('the Consensus'), its prescriptive orientation, its directional message, and its origin in Washington, the capital of the victorious empire". And we should not forget the stick: the pressure put by the IMF and the World Bank on borrowing countries by making their loans conditional upon the adoption of Consensus-inspired policy "reforms". Politicians and policy makers in the borrowing countries are typically apprehensive about the possibility that failure to comply with the instructions coming from Washington is indicative of their lack of "political will". The commandments were presented by the beneficiaries (corporate and political Washington) as "reasonable" changes, inspired by "lessons of experience", most notably as, it seems, the lessons learned from 18th and 19th century imperialism.

The original ten policy principles of the Washington Consensus remained unchallenged only for a short time. Changes in the international economic and political environment and new domestic realities in the borrowing countries created problems that the architects of the Consensus did not envision or encompass, thus forcing the search for new answers. For example, why is it that the adoption of the Consensus by East European countries in the 1990s led to total collapse of output, particularly in Russia?

Williamson (1993) acknowledged that not all of the original ten principles enjoyed the same degree of consensus. According to his assessment at the time, consensus was established in five of the ten policy prescriptions, whereas three of them (financial and trade liberalization and deregulation) were still controversial in a non-ideological way, implying that the emergence of a consensus was just a matter of time requiring technical reconciliation of the differences that still existed even among the proponents of the Consensus. The remaining two, changing public budget priorities and according the same treatment to foreign and domestic firms, were, in Williamson's (1993) view, always bound to be controversial because of their inherent political nature.

Williamson has repeatedly gone to great lengths to qualify very carefully what he really meant when he coined the term "Washington Consensus". He often sought to correct those who misinterpreted the approach and made repeated attempts at clarifying the nuances of his conceptual framework. However, Naim (1999) argues that Williamson's efforts at clarifying the meaning and implication of the Washington Consensus were not adequate to compensate for the distortions resulting from the term's global popularity and its frequent misuse. Subsequently, the Washington Consensus acquired a life of its own, becoming a brand name known worldwide and used quite independently of its original intent and even of its content, in the sense that the term is used without knowledge of the ten commandments.

Naim (1999) goes on to say that since the beginning, advocates of the Washington Consensus have been greatly divided about the pace and sequence of the "reforms" (meaning the implementation of the commandments). Profound differences quickly emerged about the need or desirability of what came to be known as the application of a "shock therapy" (some sort of a "big bang") approach to policy reforms. This approach requires the implementation of as many of the commandments as quickly as possible. The so-called "shock therapy" was tried with disastrous effects in Russia, except for the beneficiaries of privatization. It was almost tried in occupied Iraq on recommendation from the IMF (for the sake of the prosperity of the Iraqi people of course).

Williamson (2002) argues that the term has commonly been used with a different meaning from his original description. He opposes the alternative use of the term, which became common after his initial formulation, to cover a broader market fundamentalism or "neoliberal" agenda. Thus, he states as follows:

I of course never intended my term to imply policies like capital account liberalization (... I quite consciously excluded that), monetarism, supply-side economics, or a minimal state (getting the state out of welfare provision and income redistribution), which I think of as the quintessentially neoliberal ideas. If that is how the term is interpreted, then we can all enjoy its wake, although let us at least have the decency to recognize that these ideas have rarely dominated thought in Washington and certainly never commanded a consensus there or anywhere much else.

In a way, therefore, Williamson was defending a trade mark or a brand name. However, the fact of the matter is that there is no alternative use of the term. The Consensus represents the collection of policies recommended by the IMF over decades. Nothing less than the neoliberal agenda would have commanded consensus in Washington. Perhaps Williamson should have used the term "Williamson Consensus" to describe his collection.

Williamson (2000) argues that the first three of his ten prescriptions are uncontroversial in the economic community (which is debatable), while admitting that the others have evoked some controversy. However, he never discussed the issue of why the first three commandments have never been followed by Washington and most of its allies. He argues that one of the least controversial prescriptions (the redirection of spending to infrastructure, healthcare and education) has often been neglected, but he does not say who neglected a prescription that makes a lot of sense. He also argues that, while the prescriptions were focused on reducing certain functions of the government (for example, using privatization to reduce the role of the government as an owner of productive enterprises), they would also strengthen the government's ability to undertake other actions such as supporting education and health. There seems to be some contradiction between reducing the size of the government and enhancing its ability to support health and education.

This attempt to put a humanitarian face on the Consensus is mere rhetoric because in reality the IMF does not encourage spending on health and education, as we are going to find out. Williamson says that he does not endorse market fundamentalism and believes that the Consensus prescriptions, if implemented correctly, would benefit the poor. It is refreshing to hear that market fundamentalism does not benefit the poor, if this is truly what he means, but any "reform" package suggested by the IMF smells of market fundamentalism. Williamson (2003) laid out an expanded reform agenda, emphasizing crisis-proofing of economies, "second-generation" reforms, and policies addressing inequality and social issues. These are not ideas that Technocratic Washington believes in.

In spite of Williamson's declared reservations, the term "Washington Consensus" has been used more broadly to describe the general shift toward free market policies that followed the displacement of Keynesianism in the 1970s. In this broad sense, the Washington Consensus is sometimes considered to have begun around 1980—see, for example, Skidelsky (2009) who talks about the rise, fall and rise of Keynesian economics in the aftermath of the global financial crisis. Many commentators see the Consensus, in the broader sense of the term, as having been at its strongest during the 1990s. Some have argued that the Consensus in this sense came to an end at the turn of the century, or at least that it became less influential after about the year 2000. For example, Birdsall *et al.* (2010) present an assessment of what went wrong with the Washington Consensus-style reform agenda, using a taxonomy of views that put the blame on the following: (i) shortfalls in the implementation of reforms combined with impatience regarding their expected effects; (ii) fundamental flaws in the design, sequencing, or basic premises of the reform agenda; and (iii) incompleteness of the agenda that left out crucial reform needs, such as volatility, technological innovation, institutional change and inequality.

However, this intellectual exchange has not changed the facts on the grounds that the preached countries are still told to do the usual: liberalize, deregulate and privatize. Therefore, it is not clear how the Washington Consensus became less influential since 2000 because nothing has happened in the last 20 years. The Washington technocrats still peddle the same ideas, and one indicator that nothing has changed is that IMF riots still erupt in response to the implementation of the ten commandments. Finding excuses to justify the failure of these policies is immoral.

More commonly, commentators have suggested that the Consensus in its broader sense survived until the advent of the 2008 global financial crisis. Following the strong intervention undertaken by governments in response to market failures, a number of journalists, politicians and senior officials from global institutions, such as the World Bank, began saying that the Washington Consensus was dead. For example, Painter (2009) declared that the Washington Consensus was dead in April 2009 (presumably as a result of the Great Recession triggered by the global financial crisis). Following the 2009 G-20 London summit, former British Prime Minister Gordon Brown declared that "the old Washington Consensus is over" (Sky News, 2009). In April 2009, Williamson was asked by the Washington Post (2009) whether he agreed with Gordon Brown that the Washington Consensus was dead. He responded as follows:

> It depends on what one means by the Washington Consensus. If one means the ten points that I tried to outline, then clearly it's not right. If one uses the interpretation that a number of people—including Joe Stiglitz, most prominently—have foisted on it, that it is a neoliberal tract, then I think it is right.

The facts on the ground tell us that the so-called "reform" in accordance with the ten commandments of the Washington Consensus (in broad, narrow or whatever sense) has not worked and it will not work. Ostry *et al.* (2016) argue that the benefits of some policies based on the neoliberal agenda appear to have been somewhat overplayed. They suggest that in the case of financial openness, some capital flows, such as foreign direct investment, do appear to confer the benefits claimed for them (this is also doubtful, as we are going to see). In the case of fiscal consolidation, they argue, the short-run costs (in terms of lower output and welfare and higher unemployment) have been underplayed, and the desirability for countries with ample fiscal space of simply living with high debt and allowing debt ratios to decline organically through growth is underappreciated.

Weldon (2016) believes that the IMF is questioning elements of the "neoliberal agenda" and that the Ostry *et al.* article is really just the latest in a series of moves from the Fund that can be seen as a step away from the pre-2008 vintage Washington Consensus. He refers in particular to the change in tone found in the output of the IMF's research department. However, it will take more than the change of heart within the research department to move away from the liberalize, deregulate and privatize culture because this is what corporate Washington wants, and it is corporate Washington that calls the shots. A brilliant economist called Joseph Stiglitz lost his job at the World Bank because he questioned the benefits for the preached countries of the core of the Washington Consensus: liberalize, deregulate and privatize. Stiglitz (2004) notes that "if there is consensus today about what strategies are likely to help the development of the poorest countries, it is this: there is no consensus except that the Washington consensus did not provide the answer".

1.3 Arguments Against the Washington Consensus

Arguments against the Washington Consensus rest on several pillars. Some of the principles are not supported by good economics but rather by the stereotyped, ideologically driven argument that economic efficiency can be enhanced by reducing government intervention in the economy and that the benefits accruing to a minority will trickle down to the rest of the society. Some of the principles imposed on developing countries are not practiced by the preaching countries either in the past (such as free trade) or at the present (such as free trade, competitive exchange rates, positive real interest rates and fiscal discipline). Some of the principles are stated but never put in practice, for example, pro-growth policies. In essence, the principles are designed to loot developing countries in need of financial assistance. The whole of this book is about a critical evaluation of the principles of the Washington Consensus. What follows in this section and the following one is simply a brief preview.

Free trade is not always in the best interest of developing economies. A strict adoption of free trade and the principle of comparative advantage exposes developing countries to the Dutch Disease as they specialize in the production and export of primary products with volatile prices. The promotion of new industries may require both selective tariffs on cheap imports and government subsidies. Brazil would not have become successful in aircraft manufacturing if it were not for government's support of Embraer, which has become an aerospace conglomerate that produces commercial, military, executive and agricultural aircraft and provides aeronautical services. In this respect, Glennie (2011) tells the following story about a question-and-answer session at the 2003 World Bank annual meetings:

> I had talked approvingly of state protection of certain industries to help them compete in a difficult international market. The reply from the panel (I think it was Nick Stern, then the World Bank's chief economist)

was dismissive, something like, "Oh god, you aren't still going on about the infant industry argument are you". Another time I asked a leading World Bank economist how he could explain why South Korea and other countries (including today's developed countries) that had protected their fledgling industries had done so well. I received the reply: "They would have done even better if they hadn't protected them." I am not making this up.

This is the kind of mentality held by the economists preaching the Washington Consensus to developing countries—they tend to make arguments that are not remotely related to good economics. Another argument against the Consensus is that the adoption of strict fiscal rules can cause unnecessary economic hardship as the government may cut spending at an inappropriate time (for example, when the economy is already going down). It is true that structural borrowing must be kept at manageable levels in the long run, but spending cuts at the wrong time can hit welfare support programs, consequently aggravating poverty and inequality. Needless to say, the proponents of the Washington Consensus could not care less about poverty and inequality.

The Chinese approach to dealing with developing countries seems to be working. This has led to the emergence of a comparison between the Washington Consensus and the Beijing Consensus, a term that has been coined by Ramo (2004). It has little in common with Washington's model. Instead of prescribing rigid recommendations for the problems of distant nations, the Beijing Consensus is pragmatic—much like China in the post-1979 world—and recognizes the need for flexibility in solving multifarious problems. It is inherently focused on innovation, while simultaneously emphasizing ideals such as equitable development and a "peaceful rise" (Ramo, 2004).

In recent years, Chinese firms have invested substantial sums in African and Latin American developing countries. The Chinese approach involves substantial investment in infrastructure and public sector assets. The implications of China's growing investments linked to the Belt and Road Initiative (BRI), its ambitious global infrastructure and connectivity program, are increasingly watched by the Anglo-American alliance. Without the Washington Consensus, China has managed to raise more than 700 million people out of absolute poverty since the country's reform and opening period began in the late 1970s. Over four decades, the country has transformed itself from a major recipient of foreign aid into a critical and global provider of investment and development resources. In this respect, Harper (2019) says the following:

> The Chinese economic model, commonly known as the 'Beijing Consensus', has been seen by many developing nations as an alternative to the more established model of the Washington Consensus. It is the Chinese model and its wider appeal that has played a notable role in furthering China's influence in the African states.

Harper also points out that the Chinese economic model represents the latest phase of the East Asian model of state capitalism. This approach played a notable role in the modernization of Japan during the Meiji Restoration of the mid-19th and early 20th centuries and also in the post-war economic boom. China's development model can also be characterized by "neo-Confucian state capitalism". These policies have enabled China (and East Asia in general) to become one of the engines of the global economy. They have also attracted the attention of the developing world, which has become dissatisfied with the free-market policies promoted by Washington. Neo-Confucianism is a social and ethical philosophy using metaphysical ideas as its framework. Unlike the Washington Consensus, neo-Confucianism is humanistic and rationalistic, with the belief that the universe could be understood through human reason and that it is up to humanity to create a harmonious relationship between the universe and the individual (see, for example, Craig, 1998).

The Chinese model is further examined by McKinnon (2010) who reviews the books of Brautigam (2009), Foster *et al.* (2009) and Halper (2010), comparing between the Washington Consensus and the Beijing Consensus as implemented in Africa. He points out that "for China, foreign aid, investment and trade are not really distinct categories". Brautigam (2009) notes that these parts are bound together by intricate financial arrangements under China's Export–Import Bank with other commercial arrangements orchestrated by the Ministry of Commerce, within which the Department of Foreign Aid is nested.

The Chinese model works on the basis of "quasi-barter" such that Chinese construction and engineering companies receive funding directly from the China Export–Import Bank. In return, the host country agrees to repay the Bank over several years in commodity terms, such as oil and iron ore, whose production and marketing may be facilitated by the construction project itself. This is vastly different from the "Western" model, which starts by sending the air force to bomb the host country back to the Stone Age. Subsequently, the resources of the bombed country are confiscated to cover the cost of bombs and rockets (Syria is the latest example). It is not clear, therefore, why Halper describes the Chinese model as "authoritarian", but he admits that it will dominate in the 21st century.

Even though the second commandment of the Consensus, as put forward by Williamson, calls for the redirection of public spending toward public sector initiatives like primary education, primary healthcare and infrastructure investment, this is no more than ink on paper. The Consensus-based conditionality imposed by the IMF on developing countries leads to reduction in social expenditure. The truth is that the Washington Consensus, at least as implemented by the IMF, aims at reducing the size of the public sector, which implicitly means privatization and directing resources to debt service. The facts on the ground show that this is the case. These policies have typically led to what has become known as the "IMF riots" and to economic ruins.

Post-Keynesian economists have their share of opposition to the Washington Consensus. Davidson (2007) argues that the term "Washington Consensus" means different things to different people and even different things to Williamson at different times. However, it seems that the common theme of all versions of the Consensus is the most damaging and the one that is pursued by the IMF for the benefit of corporate and political Washington. That theme is "liberalize, deregulate and privatize". Davidson goes on to summarize the ten commandments in three policy objectives: macroeconomic discipline, a market economy, and openness to the world (the last two account for the trio of liberalize, deregulate and privatize). However, he starts by directing his criticism at the first three commandments that can be lumped under "fiscal discipline". He argues that fiscal discipline will neither avoid the possibility of current account crises, nor produce a fully employed economic system. Then he suggests that a combination of fiscal discipline, the liberalization of financial markets, and the free market competitive exchange rate has created some severe problems for Latin America (and other developing countries for that matter). He then wonders "why intelligent economists such as John Williamson have gone so wrong on their demand for fiscal discipline, financial liberalization, and actively pursuing a competitive exchange rate policy". The answer is simple: it is ideology and the desire to serve corporate interests.

It has become evident in the aftermath of the global financial crisis and the crises of the 1990s that free markets create instability and high unemployment and that financial deregulation has the potential to instil financial instability. Gorton (2010) suggests that the global financial crisis shows that we got slapped in the face by the invisible hand and that it was private decisions made over a long period of time that created the shadow banking system, which was vulnerable to a banking panic.

1.4 Arguments for the Washington Consensus

The arguments used to defend the Washington Consensus, and its underlying principles, are put forward by the enablers and beneficiaries (technocratic Washington, political Washington and corporate Washington) as well as die-hard free marketeers and right-wing economists. Most of the arguments are based on the beauty of the market and how it can solve all of the problems faced by humanity.

Proponents of the Consensus argue that the ten commandments have considerable economic validity and can be justified in terms of "good" economics. For example, it is argued that broadening the tax base, investment in education, sustainable government borrowing, and flexible exchange rates can boost economic welfare. However, broadening the tax base is typically intended to enable the cutting of taxes for rich individuals and corporations, which amounts to a transfer of wealth from the poor to the rich. Yes, investment in education is conducive to growth because it boosts the quality of human capital, but the Washington Consensus, at least as practiced by the IMF, does not encourage spending on health and education. Sustainable government borrowing is a good idea but strict limits on spending at any time, which is preached by the IMF, leads to poverty and inequality. As for whether or not flexible exchange rates boost welfare, the jury is still out, even though it is widely accepted that flexible exchange rates are not suitable for developing countries. By the way, the proponents of the Consensus attribute the problems of the EU to the difficulties of managing a single currency and suggest that a return to competitive exchange rates would be the way out.

It is also claimed that privatization and free trade produce economic benefits, but this proposition is not supported by the facts on the ground. Privatization and free trade are intended to benefit multinationals, not the countries advised or forced to adopt the Washington Consensus. It seems to me that those who advocate free trade (which is typically free in one direction only) should advocate fixed rather than flexible exchange rates because it has been established that exchange rate volatility has an adverse effect on the volume of trade. This was one of the justifications for establishing the European Monetary Union.

Glennie (2011), who argues that the Washington Consensus served rich country interests, is very critical of the arguments put forward to defend the Consensus. However, he senses a change of heart and return to reason among economists. This is what he says:

> The world of global development has seen the return of an important quality in people working on issues this complicated: humility. From the 1980s up to the early 2000s, hubris ruled. It was fairly common for people to be sure about the answer to growth and poverty reduction and to seek to impose it. But while there are still some true believers in the Washington consensus, the majority of development experts are now far more circumspect about making grand claims.

Glennie is particularly critical of Dambisa Moyo, the author of *Dead Aid: Why Aid Makes Things Worse and How There is Another Way for Africa*, whom he describes as "an exception" because she regularly claims that "we know what works" (even though this sounds less arrogant than "I know what works"). Moyo, an African economist, blames the poor for being poor just like those who claim that homeless people are homeless because they did not work hard. In her book, Moyo (2010) argues that millions of Africans get poorer because of aid. Glennie (2009) notes that Moyo is "very prone to exaggeration", suggesting that her book is "not a serious analytical study but an anti-aid polemic of the kind common in the conservative media in the US". Coming from an African economist, who would be aware of the devastation inflicted by IMF operations on African countries, these views are insensitive, to say the least. However, it suffices to say that she currently serves on the boards of Chevron Corporation and the 3M Company and previously she was on the staff of the World Bank and Goldman Sachs. It has become a common practice to employ Africans to demonize Africa and Muslims to demonize Islam.

At this stage, it may be appropriate to demonstrate how the custodians of the Washington Consensus look at Africa and its citizens. In a 1991 internal memo, the then chief economist of the World Bank, Larry

Summers, made the following comment on pollution and prostate cancer in Africa (Ismi, 2004):

> Just between you and me, shouldn't the World Bank be encouraging more migration of the dirty industries to the LDCs [less-developed countries]?... I think the economic logic behind dumping a load of toxic waste in the lowest wage country is impeccable and we should face up to that...I've always thought that underpopulated countries in Africa are vastly under-polluted, their air quality is probably vastly inefficiently low compared to Los Angeles or Mexico City...The concern over an agent that causes a one in a million change in the odds of prostate cancer is obviously going to be much higher in a country where people survive to get prostate cancer than in a country where under 5 mortality is 200 per thousand.

When the memo became public in February 1992, Jose Lutzenburger, Brazil's Secretary of the Environment at the time, wrote to Summers to say the following:

> Your reasoning is perfectly logical but totally insane... Your thoughts [provide] a concrete example of the unbelievable alienation, reductionist thinking, social ruthlessness and the arrogant ignorance of many conventional economists' concerning the nature of the world we live in... If the World Bank keeps you as vice president it will lose all credibility. To me it would confirm what I often said... the best thing that could happen would be for the Bank to disappear.

What happened subsequently was rather amazing: Jose Lutzenburger was fired, soon after writing the letter to Summers, for daring to question a racist attitude toward Africa and the developing world in general. Summers, on the other hand, was promoted to top ranks in the Washington establishment.

The proponents of free trade claim that the Washington Consensus is criticized when things go wrong but never praised when things go right. In this respect, let us look at two specific cases discussed by two Consensus enthusiasts. The first is Worstall (2011) who refers to a graph used by Rodrik (2011) to demonstrate that developing countries had an exceptionally good decade before the global financial crisis struck. Worstall uses the same graph to show that the Consensus works, suggesting that the turning point in the growth of developing countries occurred around 1990, coinciding with the Consensus, which he describes as the "list of basic things that developing countries ought to do". He refers to "correlation between people preaching that Washington Consensus and the economic growth we've all been hoping for in the developing economies".

The graph used by Rodrik and Worstall to convey two different messages is a time series plot of the growth rates of developed and developing countries with superimposed nonlinear trends. Figure 1.2 displays the same picture showing (according to figures provided by the IMF) that developing countries have been growing faster than developed countries. Between 1990 and 2007, developing countries grew at 5.3% compared to 2.9% for developed countries. The global financial crisis made the divergence even bigger as the growth rates during the period 2008–2019 were 4.9% versus 1.5%.

Worstall claims that growth has been faster in developing countries because they adopted the principles of the Washington Consensus in 1990. This is nonsense for a number of reasons. First, the average growth of a

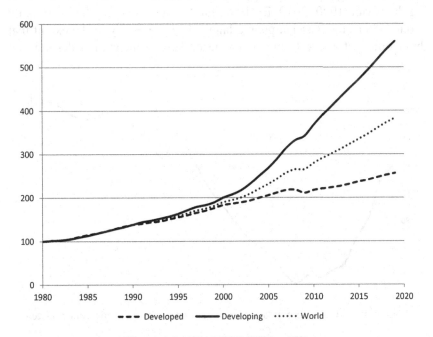

Figure 1.2:　Real GDP (1980 = 100)

number of heterogeneous economies cannot be attributed to one factor, be it the Washington Consensus or anything else. This is casual empiricism coupled with ideological bias (a lethal combination). Second, even if the Washington Consensus is conducive to growth, the process takes time. Growth of developing economies cannot pick up in 1990 just because Williamson came up with his list around that time. Third, the principles of the Washington Consensus had been forced on developing countries by the IMF and World Bank long before Williamson made his collection. Conditionality based on the principles of the Washington Consensus had been imposed on developing countries long before 1990. Fourth, why is it that growth in developed countries benefited from the principles of the Washington Consensus but not developed countries that started liberalizing, privatizing, deregulating, freeing, etc. long before 1990?

The proof is in the pudding. If, as Worstall claims, the Washington Consensus boosts growth, then this should show in the growth figures of individual countries that have adopted the Consensus and otherwise. We know very well that Yeltsin's Russia adopted the Washington Consensus enthusiastically in the early 1990s when the sale of the century involving public assets took place. In Figure 1.3, we can see Russia's real GDP during the period 1990–2019. By 1998, the Russian economy had shrunk by about 43% as the Russian people languished in poverty to the extent that they could not afford to bury their dead. This happened not despite, but

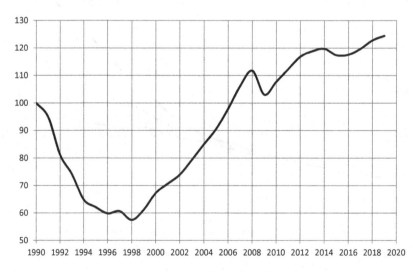

Figure 1.3:   Russia's Real GDP (1990 = 100)

because of, the Washington Consensus. The massive fraudulent privatiza-tion program overseen by Yeltsin and his cronies was the reason why millions of Russians lost their jobs and access to healthcare while billions of dollars were smuggled out of the country. Interestingly, the Russian economy started to recover when Vladimir Putin took over following the resignation of Yeltsin. Putin reversed some of the changes introduced under Yeltsin, including the renationalization of some privatized firms. No wonder that Washington and its allies dislike Putin.

Compare the situation in Russia, with the situation in China which was never "blessed" by the Washington Consensus. The Chinese had adopted a system of state capitalism where, contrary to the principles of the Washington Consensus, the government takes part in economic activity and regulates the private sector. Figure 1.4 displays GDP per capita in China during the period 1960–2019. We can see the spectacular growth that pulled about 700 million people out of poverty. This feat was achieved without the Consensus—more precisely because the Consensus was rejected by the Chinese.

Let us now move to Venezuela. Hausmann (2016) claims that "Venezuela's current catastrophe is a reminder of what can happen when all orthodoxy is tossed out the window". He talks about the conventional wisdom that was ignored by the rulers of Venezuela: market-determined prices and incentives. The first aspect of this conventional wisdom means

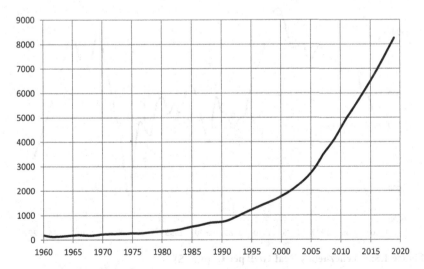

Figure 1.4: China's Real GDP per Capita ($)

that anyone who cannot pay for healthcare should die. The other aspect is that the providers of healthcare should be given a free hand to condemn to death those who cannot pay for healthcare. According to Hausman, the rulers of Venezuela "disregarded that wisdom and went on an expropriation binge", and this happened because Hugo Chavez decided to channel oil revenue to provide healthcare and education to the poor—hence "productivity collapsed". If that had not happened and if Chavez had adopted the principles of the Washington Consensus then, according to Hausman, nothing of this would have happened.

We can check the facts and figures as depicted in Figure 1.5, which shows Venezuela's real GDP per capita in US dollars. It is not that Venezuela was a shining example of economic success before the advent of Hugo Chavez, when the country was run by an oligarchy that was sympathetic to the Washington Consensus. We can, however, observe the progress made under Chavez during the period 2003–2008 before the progress came to an end as a result of the global financial crisis that was caused by the principles of the Washington Consensus.

The collapse that started in 2015 came in response to Venezuela's refusal to be a puppet state and follow the Washington Consensus by surrendering natural resources to corporate Washington. Of course, none of the Consensus gurus would say anything about the economic embargo

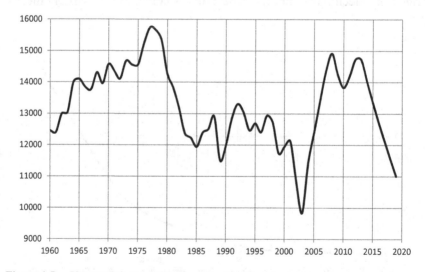

Figure 1.5:   Venezuela's Real GDP per Capita ($)

*Data for 2015–2019 are the author's estimates.

and attempts at regime change to install a regime led by Juan Guido, who is sympathetic to the Consensus and the demands of corporate Washington. A report, published by the Centre for Economic and Policy Research (CEPR) and co-authored by Jeffrey Sachs reveals that "as many as 40,000 people may have died in Venezuela as a result of US sanctions that made it harder for ordinary citizens to access food, medicine and medical equipment" (Buncombe, 2019).

Kiger (2019) describes the situation in Venezuela now and then as follows:

> It wasn't that long ago that Venezuela, which possesses the world's largest crude oil reserves, was a relatively stable democracy with one of Latin America's fastest-rising economies....
>
> But starting in 2014, the South American nation began suffering a startling collapse. With Venezuela's gross domestic product plummeting even more than the United States during the Great Depression, many of its nearly 32 million inhabitants became unable to afford food, and resource-starved hospitals did not have enough soap and antibiotics.

It is no surprise that Venezuela's GDP plummeted even more than the US during the Great Depression because the US was not under sanctions and siege. How can Maduro provide soap and antibiotics when his finance ministry is prevented from paying for them by US-imposed sanctions and when the Bank of England is refusing to release Venezuelan gold?

As a free market enthusiast, Hausmann (2016) suggests that "to achieve social goals, it is better to use—rather than repress—the market". He dismisses the notion of "just" prices by arguing that "economics has shown that this is a really bad idea, because prices are the information system that creates incentives for suppliers and customers to decide what and how much to make or buy". Making prices "just", he argues, "nullifies this function, leaving the economy in perpetual shortage". This means that if the COVID-19 vaccine costs $1,000 a shot, it should be given only to those who can afford it, allowing those who cannot afford it to infect each other. It means that anyone who cannot pay $200,000 for an operation (which not many people can afford) should die. It means that those who cannot afford to pay rent should be left to sleep on the street. What has happened to the magical word "compassion" and the other magical word "ethics"? There is no place for these words in neoclassical economics and consequently in the Washington Consensus.

1.5 Concluding Remarks

According to Williamson (2004), the term "Washington Consensus" was originally used to describe a list of ten reforms that he argued were practically universally agreed in Washington to be desirable in most Latin American countries as of 1989. Williamson's ten commandments fall under four headings: (i) fiscal "reform"; (ii) interest and exchange rate policies; (iii) liberalization of trade and FDI; and (iv) privatization and deregulation. He suggests that the Consensus acquired alternative meanings over the years, one of which encompassed the policies preached to developing countries by the Washington-based international financial institutions (IFIs), and another of which was what critics imagined the policies of those institutions to be (a list that tends to consist of policies that never did command a consensus, even in Washington).

Furthermore, Williamson (2000) argues that the term "Washington Consensus" is used in several different senses, causing a great deal of confusion. He distinguishes between his original meaning as a "summary of the lowest common denominator of policy advice addressed by the Washington-based institutions (including the World Bank) and subsequent use of the term to signify neoliberal or market-fundamentalist policies". The fact of the matter is that irrespective of the underlying version, the Consensus is all about liberalization, privatization and deregulation for the benefit of corporate Washington. Surely, this is the core of the advice given by the Washington-based international financial institutions to the countries that are unfortunate enough to need their help.

Williamson (2003) tries to distance himself from propaganda as follows: "Had my intention been to make propaganda for reform in Latin America, the last city in the world that I would have associated with the cause of reform is Washington". However, Marangos (2014) argues that "it is quite obvious who forms and imposes policies in the developing world, as funds needed for development come with strings attached", identifying the strings as "the neoliberal policies associated with the Washington consensus, analogous to the domestic policies in the USA". Likewise, Stiglitz (2004) suggests that "whatever, its original content and intent, the term 'Washington Consensus', in the minds of most people around the world, has come to refer to development strategies focusing around privatization, liberalization, and macro-stability" and that it is a "set of policies predicated upon a strong faith—stronger than warranted—in unfettered markets and aimed at reducing, or even minimizing, the role of government".

Williamson (1990) argues that "it is generally assumed, at least in technocratic Washington, that the standard economic objectives of growth, low inflation, a viable balance of payments, and an equitable income distribution should determine the disposition of such policy instruments"—by "such" he means the policy instruments embodied in the Washington Consensus. I doubt very much that an equitable income distribution is on the agenda of Washington, whether it is in Washington itself or the countries advised by Washington on the way to economic prosperity. Williamson adds that Washington has a number of other concerns in its relationship with other countries, besides furthering their economic well-being, including "the promotion of democracy and human rights, suppression of the drug trade, preservation of the environment, and control of population growth". One needs to remember a few examples how the US promoted democracy and human rights in other countries, including Iraq and Afghanistan. I must say, however, that the "liberation" of Iraq and Afghanistan had not happened when Williamson wrote his piece. However, he must have been aware of the "liberation" of Iran in 1952 and Chile in 1973.

Even though free marketeers claim that democracy and the free market system are intertwined, the high priests of the free market have demonstrated that if fascism is the price to be paid for the free market doctrine to prevail, then let it be. On 11 September 1973, General Augusto Pinochet overthrew the Chilean democratically elected government of Salvadore Allende, in the process committing massive crimes against humanity. Allende was accused of introducing "socialist" policies (that is, the policies were inconsistent with the Washington Consensus), which were reversed by the Pinochet regime, opting instead for extreme free market policies.

On that occasion, the free market system went hand in hand with fascism (which was also the case in Nazi Germany and Fascist Italy in the 1930s). According to Meadowcroft (2019), Milton Friedman, Friedrich von Hayek and James Buchanan are "alleged to have given explicit, tacit or covert support to the regime"—meaning that they did give explicit, tacit or covert support to the regime. Enthusiastic support for the Pinochet regime came from von Hayek, who (in the name of freedom) supported other authoritarian governments of the time. For Hayek, democracy does not have any intrinsic value—rather, it is valuable because of its consequences. For him, democracy is important as a peaceful means of removing an unpopular or ineffective government (meaning a government that does not pursue free market policies), but no special value should be attributed to a decision because it happened to reflect the will of a numerical majority of the voting population.

Williamson (1990) admits that "Political Washington is also, of course, concerned about the strategic and commercial interests of the United States". He used the wrong word, "also", when he should have used the word "primarily". But then he argues that the interests of the US are best furthered by prosperity in the liberated countries. In the most recent case of Venezuela, it seems that the US interests are best served by the removal of Nicholas Maduro and replacing him with Juan Guido, who promised US oil companies milk and honey. I doubt very much that Guido will contribute to the prosperity of the Venezuelan people, except perhaps his cronies, the oligarchs and the one-percenters.

Chapter 2

The Washington Consensus and IMF Conditionality

2.1 Introduction

The IMF was established in July 1944 as a product of the Bretton Woods conference, which was held to formulate and implement monetary arrangements, pertaining to exchange rates and international payment mechanisms, for the post-war period. In 1971, the Bretton Woods system of fixed exchange rates collapsed when the US abolished the convertibility of the dollar into gold. The IMF should have been abolished then. Instead, the Fund re-emerged as something else, actually more than one something else: a financial and macroeconomic advisor, a trade promoter, and a development agency (let alone an instrument for corporate Washington and a strong communicator of ideology). However, it was not until 2012 that the Fund's mandate was upgraded officially to give it more responsibilities to deal with international macroeconomic and financial stability—in the process, the Fund became more intrusive in the local affairs of borrowing countries.

The loans granted by the IMF to developing countries are governed by the provisions of conditionality, which are based on the principles of the Washington Consensus: liberalizing, deregulating, and privatizing. While conditionality precedes the invention of the term "Washington Consensus", the Consensus is a collection of the principles governing the provisions of conditionality. These provisions are used to hit two birds with one stone: (i) making sure that borrowing countries pay their debt and (ii) providing lucrative opportunities for corporate Washington. In this chapter, the provisions of conditionality are examined against the ten commandments of the Washington Consensus.

2.2   The Nature of IMF Operations

The 1944 Bretton Woods conference materialized as a result of the work of John Maynard Keynes (representative of the British Treasury) and Harry Dexter White (representative of the US Treasury) on the development of ideas pertaining to the post-war international monetary system. White held the view that the IMF should function like a bank, making sure that borrowers would not default and pay their dues on time. Keynes, on the other hand, proposed the idea that the IMF would be a cooperative fund upon which member states could draw to maintain economic activity and employment through periodic crises. At that time, America was the rising power while the British Empire was paling into insignificance, which is why White prevailed and the IMF became what it is now. The underlying arrangement eventually led to the formulation and use of the conditionality provisions to make sure that borrowing countries repay their debt and to hold them hostages.

The IMF uses a formal system of surveillance to monitor economic policies and indicators on national, regional and global levels, with the declared objective of maintaining stability and avoiding crises. The function of surveillance involves annual visits to member countries to enable the IMF staff to meet government and central bank officials for the purpose of conducting "discussions" about economic affairs and "structural reforms". The visits also involve meetings with members of the legislature and representatives from the business community, labor unions, and civil society. These meetings, however, are not held between equal partners—rather, they are forums where the visiting IMF delegation tells the officials of the host countries what to do (or else).

A typical IMF mission to a country requesting a loan starts by lecturing the officials of the poor country on the benefits of liberalization, deregulation and privatization (the essence of the Washington Consensus), which those officials must indulge in to be part of the "free and civilized world". The helpless officials of the poor country are preached on the blessings that will be bestowed upon the people of that country by the almighty market, the very reason for peace and prosperity in "Western" countries. They are then handed documents to sign, declaring allegiance to the almighty market and promising to follow the principles of the Washington Consensus without the slightest deviation. While the IMF delegation is on its way back to Washington, the citizens of the country they have just left are told, by their minister of finance, that the price of bread will quadruple while wages and pensions will be cut in half, all in the name of "reform". A riot ensues but is quelled swiftly by the police and national guard. Two years later, the IMF delegation visits to check allegiance to the almighty market and recommends the privatization of all hospitals. The vicious circle continues.

Not everyone sees the IMF as the Fund portrays itself. Rickards (2016) describes the IMF as "an autonomous part of an emerging scheme of global governance accountable only to small elite of central bankers, finance ministers and heads of state". He goes on to say the following:

> The IMF has a convoluted governance structure in which the highest decision-making body, the Board of Governors, has little power because the votes are weighted in favor of the largest economies, such as the U.S. Actual power rests with the blandly named International Monetary and Financial Committee, the IMFC. Everything about the IMF is designed to make it difficult for outsiders like you to have any idea what is going on. The insiders like that arrangement just fine.

With reference to the book of Ahamed (2014), *Money and Tough Love: On Tour with the IMF*, Richards talks about "IMF missions as they monitor large and small governments around the world", suggesting that "these missions are the key to forcing governments to conform to the rules of the game as established by the global monetary elites". The book suggests that the IMF is just as powerful as the military and Central Intelligence Agency (CIA) when it comes to forcing regime change in countries that do not follow US orders. It is a very hierarchical and undemocratic organization.

2.3 The Origin of Conditionality

Conditionality is much older than Williamson's Washington Consensus. In 1952, a decision was taken by the Executive Board of the IMF to introduce conditionality, requiring any country seeking financial assistance to abide by certain conditions. Typically, these conditions are based on *laissez-faire* free market economics and the ideology of neoliberalism in the spirit of the ten commandments of the Washington Consensus or variants thereof. Until the early 1980s, IMF conditionality largely focused on macroeconomic policies. Following the expansion of the scope of the IMF operations to cover low-income and transition countries, the guidelines on conditionality were revised in 2002. In March 2009, the IMF revised the conditionality framework with the objective of preventing and resolving crises. In 2012, the Executive Board discussed staff papers reviewing the guidelines on conditionality, emphasizing the need to "draw lessons from previous crises and provide better targeted and flexible lending".

According to the IMF (2016), conditionality is described as follows:

> Conditionality in its broad sense covers both the design of IMF-supported programs—that is, the macroeconomic and structural policies—and the specific tools used to monitor progress toward the goals outlined by the country in cooperation with the IMF. Conditionality helps countries solve balance of payments problems without resorting to measures that are harmful to national or international prosperity. At the same time, the measures are meant to safeguard IMF resources by ensuring that the country's balance of payments will be strong enough to permit it to repay the loan. All conditionality under an IMF-supported program must be either critical to the achievement of macroeconomic program goals or for monitoring implementation, or necessary for the implementation of specific provisions under the IMF's Articles of Agreement and policies thereunder.

The most bizarre statement in this description is that "conditionality helps countries solve balance of payments problems without resorting to measures that are harmful to national or international prosperity". Conditionality invariably leads to riots as the cost of living soars, which cannot be conducive to national prosperity. As for "international prosperity", which invariably means prosperity in "Western" countries, it is not clear how subsidizing flour in a poor African country affects the prosperity of the people living in Washington or London. However, if "international prosperity" refers to the prosperity of multinationals and the oligarchy, then affordable bread in a poor country is certainly bad. If a country chooses not to comply with conditionality by refusing to privatize public assets, such an action will have a negative impact on the profit and hence the prosperity of multinationals and the oligarchy—for this act, that country must be punished.

Compliance with conditionality is enforced by disbursing funds in installments that are linked to demonstrable policy actions (such as liberalization, deregulation and privatization), which is an act of brutal blackmail. The IMF assesses the underlying situation periodically to determine whether or not modifications are necessary for achieving the underlying objectives (for example, the removal of subsidies to boost "efficiency"). Compliance with the policy commitments agreed upon with the borrowing country is monitored by observing the following indicators: (i) actions that the borrowing country agrees to take before the approval of financing; (ii) quantitative performance criteria pertaining to macroeconomic indicators; (iii) indicators of progress toward the achievement of objectives; and (iv) structural benchmarks, which refer to "reform" measures needed to accomplish the objectives. Expanding the scope of conditionality (from monetary, fiscal and exchange policies into fields that previously had been largely outside the IMF's jurisdiction) has led to a decline in the rate of compliance.

To make their economies more market-oriented, borrowing countries are required to adopt "stabilization policies", which often turn out to be "destabilization policies", based on the ten commandments of the Washington Consensus and variants thereof. In the following section, those modifications and restatements of the ten commandments are examined critically.

2.4 The Conditionality Provisions

In this section, we discuss currency devaluation, austerity, restructuring of foreign debt, free market pricing, improving governance and fighting corruption, enhancing the rights of foreign investors, and financialization. Some or all of these policy prescriptions are typically recommended by the IMF as components of the so-called "structural adjustment programs".

2.4.1 *Currency devaluation*

Currency devaluation is linked to the Washington Consensus principle of maintaining competitive exchange rates (the fifth commandment). Devaluation is prescribed to reduce or eliminate a balance of payments deficit. It is ironic, however, that the preaching countries (the UK and US in particular) come on top in terms of the current account deficit as a percentage of GDP, having far greater external deficits than those of some impoverished countries such as Nepal, Madagascar and Papua New Guinea. This is more of a puzzle because the US and UK have significant surpluses from the export of arms, which requires the promotion of armed conflict all around the world.

That aside, currency devaluation works only under very strict conditions that are rarely met in reality. For the process to work, the demand for exports and imports must be elastic—the Marshall–Lerner condition must be satisfied, such that that the sum of the elasticities of demand for exports and imports is greater than one. Another condition for the process to work is that the currency of invoicing must be the currency of the underlying country, which is typically not the case for developing countries that tend to use the US dollar for that purpose. Yet another condition for the process to work, external demand for domestic products must be strong, which is unlikely to be the case now that developed countries are experiencing anemic growth. And for the process to work, competitiveness must depend on prices only or predominantly, which is not always the case as perceived quality and consumer loyalty are other determining factors. These conditions will be examined in detail in Chapter 9.

In reality, the motivation for urging borrowing countries to devalue their currencies, as in the Washington Consensus, is to make it cheaper for multinationals to acquire assets and operate in an environment characterized by low running costs, particularly the cost of labor. Currency devaluation is beneficial for multinationals but not for the devaluing developing countries. While it is unlikely to have a positive effect on the balance of payments, it leads to imported inflation. As the prices of imported goods rise, the cost of living rises, and the standard of living of the people living in the devaluating country declines. Devaluation is recommended only because the IMF is more concerned with the profit of multinationals than the welfare of the people it is supposed to help. Stiglitz (2002) suggests that the IMF "was not participating in a conspiracy, but it was reflecting the interests and ideology of the Western financial community".

2.4.2 *Austerity*

Austerity is intended to reduce the budget deficit by cutting public spending (including subsidies) and raising taxes. It is, therefore, linked to the

Washington Consensus principles of fiscal policy discipline, reducing public spending and tax "reform" (the first, second and third commandments). Stiglitz (2002) argues that prescribing fiscal austerity is effectively reverting to Herbert Hoover's economics whereby austerity is imposed when the economy is in deep recession. Under these conditions, fiscal tightness makes things worse.

The casualties of austerity are often social programs. Cuts in spending on health and education aggravate poverty in the short run and hurt economic growth in the long run as the quality of human capital deteriorates. For example, Rowden (2009) suggests that austerity has hindered investment in public health infrastructure, leading to dilapidated health infrastructure, inadequate numbers of health personnel, and demoralizing working conditions that have fueled the "push factors" driving the brain drain of nurses migrating from poor countries to rich ones. The *New York Times* has found evidence indicating that the rise in tuberculosis is linked to IMF loans (Bakalar, 2008). Hertz (2004) suggests that conditionality retards social stability and leads to an increase in poverty in recipient countries. More will be said about the effect of IMF operations on social expenditure later in this chapter.

2.4.3 *Restructuring of foreign debt*

Debt restructuring is a process that allows a private or public company (or a sovereign country facing cash flow problems and financial distress) to reduce and reschedule its delinquent debts to improve or restore liquidity, so that it can continue its operations. Debt restructuring, which involves a reduction of debt and an extension of payment terms, is usually a less expensive alternative to bankruptcy. It can be done by using debt–equity swap, whereby creditors agree to cancel some or all of the debt in exchange for equity in the company or public assets. Haley (2017) describes sovereign debt restructuring as follows:

> Sovereign debt restructurings can be messy. In the most egregious cases, they result in protracted negotiations during which the debtor country loses access to capital markets, forcing an abrupt adjustment of consumption, investment and government expenditures. This reduction in "absorption" and the resulting compression of imports simply reflect the fact that the balance of payments accounts must "balance". But this adjustment can lead to output losses and higher unemployment that frays the social fabric.

Debt restructuring involves negotiations between a strong party (the creditor) and a weak party (the debtor). Indebted developing countries typically mortgage their assets to creditors. With debt restructuring, more concessions are given to creditors and more public assets are mortgaged. If restructuring involves debt–equity swap, the creditor might end up owning public assets that could not be obtained otherwise.

2.4.4 *Free market pricing*

Free market pricing is related to the second commandment of the Washington Consensus, which requires the elimination of food subsidies and raising the prices of public services. The rationale is to obey the market because it is always right. A full chapter will be devoted to the criticism of the free market doctrine. It suffices to say that free market pricing means that people who cannot afford a private hospital bed should die and that those who cannot afford private schools should condemn their children to illiteracy.

Those who call for free market pricing do not believe in rent control and minimum wages on the grounds that they represent obstruction of the price mechanism. Rent control, the argument goes, leads to shortage of rental properties, but non-affordable rent leaves people on the street. That is fine if the government acts to accommodate the homeless, but this is not desirable because it can only happen in a "nanny state". Minimum wages are not good because they create unemployment, even though the minimum wage is truly minimal. That is fine if the government subsidizes the minimum wage through welfare payments, but that is not allowed except in a "nanny state". Market pricing is more efficient than fair pricing, which is fine if the government subsidizes the underlying product, particularly if it is a necessity or a product with a low elasticity of demand. But again that is not allowed except in a "nanny state". In the name of efficiency and to give the CEO of a pharmaceutical company a bonus of $30 million, the COVID-19 shot should cost $2,000— bad luck to those who cannot afford it. They should die in the name of the survival of the fittest in an efficient economy and the jungle of the free market.

Debate on free market pricing versus fair pricing often arises with respect to the prices of prescription drugs, which have low elasticity of demand. This is how Emanuel (2019) describes the situation:

We don't talk about the fair price of a car, or fair prices of restaurant meals, or fair prices for smartphones. But we do think there should be fair prices for drugs. That's because drugs prolong or improve our quality of life, or at least decrease our side effects. Like food and housing, many but not all drugs are basic goods necessary to lead a decent life.

Then he adds:

If someone's drowning in a lake, and you come out and say, "I'm willing to save you, but you just have to pay me $100,000", it's called exploitation. How different is that from when someone is dying of cancer, and we say, "I'm willing to save you—but that will be $140,000, please?"

At the end of September 2020, the US House of Representatives Oversight and Reform Committee held a hearing with current and former executives of major pharmaceutical companies on the high cost of prescription drugs in the US. The typical excuse used by pharmaceutical companies to justify exorbitant drug prices is that drug development is risky and expensive in the sense that the majority of drugs that enter human clinical trials fail. The fact of the matter is that pharmaceutical companies use extortionist pricing to cover the obscene amounts they pay their executives as well as wasteful advertising expenditure. Horowitz (2013) correctly argues that "it's odd for an actor being paid by a pharmaceutical company to tell you what medicine to take" and that "the implication is that despite having no medical experience, you should be advising your doctor on how you should be treated". Emanuel (2019) responds to the claims made by the drug companies by saying that "drug prices are excessive and unjust, and R&D costs don't explain the high drug prices in the U.S.".

A common free market, price-related (mal)practice is price gouging, particularly during emergencies, such as the present COVID-19 emergency. Price gouging occurs when a seller charges more than usual for a good or service that is in short supply. This sounds like the free price–fair price argument, but price gouging may involve a price that is above equilibrium, which can be achieved by hoarding. In a survey of leading economists, only 8% of the participants agreed with a proposal to prohibit "unconscionably excessive" price gouging during natural disasters. Those opposing the proposal (51%) put forward the free market argument that such legislation would lead to a misallocation of resources and lead to lower supply and greater scarcity of the resources (Initiative on Global Markets (IGM), 2012). If anything, this shows how popular the free market doctrine is among "leading economists"—saying otherwise would only come from an "outcast" who is most likely a "socialist" or even a "communist". Price gouging became rampant during the COVID-19 pandemic, covering goods ranging between toilet paper and meat. Yet, the free market prevailed in the sense that this activity is justified even by regulators. For example, in April 2020, the Australian Competition and Consumer Commission (ACCC) declared the following: "The ACCC cannot prevent or take action to stop excessive pricing, as it has no role in setting prices" (Guirguis and Howarth, 2020). This sounds like five-star consumer protection in the spirit of the free market. It is the status quo: regulators are deregulators and consumer protectors are corporate protectors.

The world will be a dangerous place if price gouging is applied to a COVID-19 vaccine. I wonder if, for a vital product like this, a free price will be better than a fair price. A free price in this case is the one that enables the producing company to pay the CEO a bonus of $30 million, even though the CEO has nothing to do with the production of the vaccine. A fair price is the price that keeps the world safe, and the world will not be safe until each of us (members of the human species) is vaccinated. A fair price, which should be set at a level that enables the company to cover the cost of its development, including the sunk cost associated with the development of vaccines that do not come to fruition. In August 2020, CureVac, one of the pharmaceutical groups developing a potential vaccine for COVID-19, ruled out selling its vaccine at cost, arguing instead for an "ethical margin" for shareholders. On the other hand, AstraZeneca and J&J have said they would not seek to profit from their vaccines at least during the pandemic (Mancini and Henderson, 2020). Let us hope that the "ethical margin" will be below the margin associated with free market pricing. I wonder what free marketeers would say about this issue.

Free market pricing is not only about the prices of goods and services but also about the price of labor (wages and salaries). Obscene payments to some executives are typically justified in terms of free market pricing. The CEO of a particular airline gets paid $25 million in annual salary because, allegedly, this is what the market says. The question is the following: If that CEO dies tomorrow, will people stop taking flights with that airline? If it is justified in terms of the supply of and demand for "talent", this particular CEO does not strike anyone as being talented, and he would have got the job through connections. The CEO of a major investment bank that collapsed in 2008, because of sheer incompetence and arrogance on his part, had a net worth of $500 million (out of salaries and bonuses) when he lost his job. The CEO of another investment bank that collapsed in 2008 because of sheer incompetence and arrogance was awarded a $160 million as a golden parachute. In corporatized universities, CEOs (otherwise known as vice chancellors or presidents) get paid seven figure salaries while the competent professors, who do the work that brings in revenue, get paid "peanuts" in comparison. How is this disparity in pay justified in terms of free market pricing and the "law" of supply and demand when, with a few exceptions, people holding influential positions in the corporate sector get there through connections?

2.4.5 *Governance and corruption*

The Washington preachers tell developing countries to reduce the level of corruption that takes mostly the shape of exchanging a favor for an envelope containing a few thousand dollars. In the preaching countries, banksters and Wall Streeters defraud the general public of billions of dollars and get away with it—as a matter of fact, they are rewarded with big bonuses for defrauding people. Kaufman (2009) describes as a myth the proposition that "corruption is a challenge mainly for public officials in developing countries and that it is unrelated to the current global crisis". He argues strongly that "corruption is not unique to developing countries, nor has it declined on average". The difference may be trivial: in a developing country, a corrupt official may be paid for his services by receiving an envelope full of cash; in a developed country, the payment is more subtle, for example, a promise of a lucrative job in the future.

Corruption in the developed world is seen most vividly in the financial sector. Transparency International (2015) suggests that "corruption in the banking sector has manifested itself in many scandals involving money laundering, rate rigging and tax evasion, all of which undermine the public's trust in financial institutions. Excessive risk taking with other peoples' money is fraud. As Dewatripont and Freixas (2012) put it, "it has been noted that risk taking is intrinsically involved in the business of banking and that this can lead to unethical conduct at the expense of the public interest". The extent of corruption on Wall Street is best described by Snyder (2010) as follows:

> If you ask most Americans, they will agree that the financial system is corrupt. It is generally assumed that just like most politicians, most big bankers are corrupt by nature. But the truth is that the vast majority of Americans have no idea just how corrupt the US financial system has become. The corruption on Wall Street has become so deep and so vast that it is hard to even find the words to describe it. It seems that the major financial players will try just about anything these days as long as they think they can get away with it. But in the process they are contributing to the destruction of the greatest economic machine that the planet has ever seen.

Wray (2011) puts a very strong case for the role of fraud in the global financial crisis. He refers to a small time bank robber, Willy Sutton, who responded to the question why he robbed banks by saying "because that's where the money is". Wray describes the global financial crisis as "the biggest scandal in human history", but then he qualifies his statement as follows:

> It is apparent that fraud became normal business practice. I have compared the home finance food chain to Shrek's onion: every layer was not only complex, but also fraudulent, from the real estate agents to the appraisers and mortgage brokers who overpriced the property and induced borrowers into terms they could not afford, to the investment banks and their subsidiary trusts that securitized the mortgages, to the credit ratings agencies and accounting firms that validated values and practices, to the servicers and judges who allow banks to steal homes, and on to CEOs and lawyers who signed off on the fraud. To say that this is the biggest scandal in human history is an understatement. And the fraudsters are still running the institutions.

The worst and most damaging form of corruption is regulatory capture, which is rampant in the preaching countries—political Washington is captured by corporate Washington. Baxter (2011) presents a working definition of capture as follows: "regulatory capture [is] present whenever a particular sector of the industry, subject to the regulatory regime, has acquired persistent influence disproportionate to the balance of interests envisaged when the regulatory system was established". Regulatory capture played a big role in the advent of the global financial crisis. According to Kaufman (2009), capture was the main reason for the systemic failure of oversight, regulation and disclosure in the financial sector. Furthermore, regulatory capture is the cause of what Johnson and Boone (2010) call the "doomsday cycle".

London has become the world capital of financial fraud, and New York is not that far behind. Roberto Saviano, an Italian investigative journalist, is quoted by Carrier (2016) as saying that "the financial services industry based in the City of London facilitates a system that makes the UK the most corrupt nation in the world". He adds:

> If I asked what is the most corrupt place on Earth, you might say it's Afghanistan, maybe Greece, Nigeria, the south of Italy. I would say it is the UK. It's not UK bureaucracy, police, or politics, but what is corrupt is the financial capital. Ninety per cent of the owners of capital in London have their headquarters offshore.

In reference to the secretive offshore markets of Jersey and the Caymans, Saviano describes them as the "access gates to criminal capital in Europe and the UK is the country that allows it". These offshore financial centers serve what he calls "criminal capitalism", arguing that most financial companies that reside offshore are exactly like the Mafia and organized crime that do not abide by the rule of law.

It is ludicrous that the corrupt advises against corruption. While fighting corruption sounds good, the implementers of conditionality are not serious about it because corruption is good for business—it works in the interest of corporate Washington.

2.4.6 *Enhancing the rights of foreign investors vis-à-vis national law*

The conditionality provision of enhancing the rights of foreign investors *vis-à-vis* national law is consistent with the tenth commandment of the Washington Consensus. There have been cases where foreign investors demand compensation for the host government's decisions to introduce new environmental and public health measures, as well as tax increases, changes to the regulatory regime governing utility pricing and alleged mistreatment by the judiciary of the host country.

The rationale for the ultra-generous treatment of foreign investors rests on two assumptions: (i) additional FDI inflows are beneficial from the perspective of the host country, which is not always the case and (ii) the absence of a level playing field between domestic and foreign investors. The fact of the matter is that the claim that foreign investors receive inferior treatment can be used to make a case for putting them above the law, particularly in developing countries. The perpetrators of the December 1984 Bhopal disaster got away with mass murder, the killing of thousands of Indian villagers by "chemical weapons". The main cause of the disaster was underinvestment in safety, which created a dangerous working environment. Specific factors include the filling of tanks beyond recommended levels, poor maintenance and switching off safety systems to save money. In Chapter 13, the tenth commandment of property rights will be discussed, where we will find out about the atrocities committed by foreign investors or invaders who have or claim property rights.

2.4.7 *Financialization*

The financialization of developing economies comes under various labels such as "creating new financial institutions" and the "opening of domestic stock markets for the purpose of boosting the stability of investment and supplementing FDI". While a sound financial sector is essential, the financialization of the economy could turn out to be a very bad idea, particularly if it is taken too far. Krishnan (2016) considers the implementation of neoliberal policies and the acceptance of neoliberal economic theories in the 1970s to be the root of financialization, with the financial crisis of 2007–2008 being one of the ultimate results.

Financialization is a term that describes the dominance of the financial sector over other sectors of the economy, including manufacturing industry and agriculture. It refers to "the increasing importance of financial markets, financial motives, financial institutions, and financial elites in the operation of the economy and its governing institutions, both at the national and international levels" (Epstein, 2002). Komlik (2015) describes financialization simply as "the ascendancy of finance", suggesting that it represents "the capturing impact of financial markets, institutions, actors, instruments and logics on the real economy, households and daily life". Financialization represents regulatory and political capture. David Stockman, a former Director of the Office of Management and Budget, once described financialization as "corrosive", arguing that it had turned the economy into a "giant casino" where banks skim an over-size share of profits (Bartlett, 2013).

Numerous studies have demonstrated the adverse consequences of financialization, particularly the retardation of growth and intensification of inequality, which are arguably related in the sense that inequality itself retards growth. For example, Bartlett (2013) suggests that "financialization is also an important factor in the growth of income inequality, which is also a culprit in slow growth". Cushen (2013) explores the means whereby the workplace outcomes associated with financialization render employees insecure and angry. Black (2011) lists the ways in which the financial sector harms the real economy, describing its functions as "the sharp canines that the predator state uses to rend the nation". The adverse effects of financialization have been widely recognized as being mostly related to the accumulation of debt, which leads to a diversion of increasing portions of the financial resources of the corporate and house-hold sectors to debt service.

Financialization has adverse effects on living standards, capital accumulation, consumption, productivity, aggregate demand, value added, income distribution, employment, wages, tax revenue, asset price inflation, financial stability, and the opacity and complexity of the financial sector. It is intuitive to suggest that some of these effects imply adverse consequences for aggregate output and economic growth. Other mechanisms include competition with the real sector for resources, the brain drain inflicted by the financial sector on the real sector, the Dutch disease explanation, and the dominance of a mentality of trading for short-term gains. However, financialization is useful for multinationals operating in developing countries because it is conducive to fraud and tax evasion. It goes well with most of the ten commandments of the Washington Consensus.

2.5 Arguments Against Conditionality

Perhaps it is a good idea to start with a description of the implementation of conditionality as put forward by Joe Stiglitz when he was interviewed by Greg Palast for *The Guardian* in 2001 (Palasat, 2001). Stiglitz described the four-step process that any country seeking financial assistance must go through. Step 1 is the privatization of state-owned industries and assets, particularly electricity and water companies, a process that involves a significant element of corruption. Step 2, which involves a "hot money cycle", is capital market liberalization or deregulation. This is meant to allow capital flows to come in and go out without any impediment. Step 3 involves the so-called "market-based pricing", as the elimination of subsidies forces the prices of food and other essential consumer items upwards. This is followed by Step 3.5, an IMF-caused riot that Stiglitz describes as "peaceful demonstrations dispersed by bullets, tanks and tear gas". Step 4 involves the imposition of free trade agreements (governed by the rules of the World Trade Organization) for the benefit of multinationals. Stiglitz likens the imposition of free trade to the Opium Wars, which were also for the noble cause of "opening markets".

Palast (2001) refers to a "cache of documents" marked "confidential" and "restricted", obtained from "sources unnameable (not Stiglitz)". One of these documents is entitled a "country assistance strategy", proclaiming "an assistance strategy for every poorer nation, designed..... after careful in-country investigation". According to Stiglitz, however, "investigation" involves "little more than close inspection of five-star hotels". Stiglitz went on to say that the "investigation" concludes with a meeting with a "begging finance minister", who is handed a "restructuring agreement" pre-drafted for "voluntary" signature. The begging finance minister eventually receives the "same four-step programme". The show comes to an end with smiles and firm handshakes in front of the camera. Soon afterwards, the poor people of that country start to feel the pinch—as a result, they revolt because they have nothing to lose.

Conditionality is justified on the grounds that it is a means to ensure that the borrowing country will be able to repay the IMF and that it will not attempt to solve its balance of payment problems in a way that would have an adverse effect on the international economy. Another justification is that conditionality is a means for reassuring that the borrowed funds are used for the stated purpose, typically to rectify macroeconomic and structural imbalances. Khan and Sharma (2001) use historical conjecture to justify IMF conditionality, arguing that the conditionality attached to sovereign lending has a long history. Ferguson (1998) recalls a case from 1818 when Prussia, effectively bankrupted by the Napoleonic wars, approached Nathan Rothschild for a loan. From the onset of negotiations, Rothschild argued that "any loan would have to be secured by a mortgage on Prussian royal domains guaranteed by the Stande (parliament) of the domains concerned". It is ironic that Nathan Rothschild is viewed as a role model, given that as he made his fortune by financing two warring parties. However, lending with collateral is more merciful than lending with IMF conditionality because the former means that the borrower loses the collateral only in the case of default. Lending with IMF conditionality means that the borrowing country loses public assets even if it does not default.

Conditionality has been criticized on several grounds. To start with, it undermines domestic political institutions and stability. The recipient governments sacrifice policy autonomy in exchange for funds, which can lead to public resentment of the local leadership for accepting and enforcing the IMF conditions. A country may be compelled to accept conditions that it would not accept if it were not for a financial crisis. Stiglitz (2002) argues that conditionality is not just the typical requirements that anyone lending money might expect the borrower to fulfill in order to ensure that the money will be paid back. Rather, he argues, "conditionality refers to more forceful conditions, ones that often turn the loan into a policy tool". Dreher (2006) suggests that IMF conditionality is ineffective and that the evidence does not support the proposition that it makes success more likely.

IMF economists always recommend ideologically driven policies without having any knowledge of unique domestic circumstances, which may make the recommended policies difficult to carry out, unnecessary, and even counterproductive. According to Stiglitz (2002), the economists of the IMF recommend a "one-size-fits-all" policy based on their academic training, which focuses on economic models with unrealistic assumptions about how real-life economies work. They do not specialize in the economies of the countries whose policies they oversee, they do not live in those countries, but rather in Washington, and they have little appreciation for the political circumstances under which governments operate. For these economists, political, social and ethical considerations are irrelevant.

Minimizing the ability of the government to regulate the domestic economy opens the door for multinational companies to come in and extract cheap resources. Jahn (2005) argues that while agreements with the IMF are "voluntary", they are for all intents and purposes "imposed", and that "voluntary" signatures do not signify consent to the details of the agreement, but rather desperate need. The policies typically take the form of "shock therapy" designed to move the economy from one extreme to another.

In May 2003, the IMF recommended the transformation of the economy of occupied Iraq to pure capitalism overnight by removing (with immediate effect) all subsidies, charging market prices for government provided goods and services, and privatizing everything under the sun. The same shock therapy was used in Russia in the early 1990s with disastrous effects. The policies are implemented all at once, rather than in an appropriate sequence. According to Stiglitz (2002), this is a result of the IMF's "market fundamentalism", a blind faith in the free market that ignores the facts on the ground. Privatization is advocated in the name of efficiency, but the immediate consequence is invariably massive redundancies. Stiglitz (2002) points out that if a country's unemployment program and other social safety nets are not sufficiently developed, those losing their jobs will have no way to support their families.

Beware of the word "reform" because reform should be voluntary rather than imposed by those wielding a big stick. "Reform" is sometimes imposed, not by the stick or even the sword, but rather by the tank or through a covert action that leads to regime change, a favorite hobby of political Washington.

2.6 The Consequences of Conditionality: Riots and Civil Unrest

The implementation of IMF Conditionality has led to the rise of the term "IMF riots", which was coined to describe the waves of protests witnessed by developing countries as a result of the policies demanded by the IMF. Marshall (2014) defines the term "IMF riots" by referring to "dozens of nations around the world that experienced waves of protests in response to the IMF/World Bank programs of the 1980s and 1990s, which plunged them into crisis through austerity measures, privatization and deregulation all enforced under so-called structural adjustment programs". This does mean that the riots have stopped, given that nothing has changed as far as IMF operations in developing countries are concerned. With particular reference to the IMF (and World Bank), Woodroffe and Ellis-Jones (2000) describe "protests and demonstrations organized by the southern poor", which are "aimed at policies that hurt their livelihoods and, in some cases, undermine the democratic foundations of their countries". They add the following:

> Teachers, civil servants, priests, farmers, students, doctors, trade-union activists, indigenous peoples and women's groups have called on their

governments to halt the introduction of economic reforms which have by-passed their national democratic institutions, and have been foisted on them by the IMF and World Bank. These are poor people, in a desperate situation, who are striving for respect, dignity and a sense of pride in their lives and countries. Their voices deserve to be heard. But they're not. Developing countries are still locked into a dependent relationship with the international financial institutions and donor governments. Despite the rhetoric of poverty reduction, debt relief and economic-stabilization, these countries must still implement liberalisation policies which hurt the poor.

Ryan (1998) refers to "frequent correlation" between the IMF adjustment programs and "political instability and unrest", using this association to explain why "the International Monetary Fund (IMF) has long remained one of the most controversial institutions on the world stage". While the IMF may be viewed favorably as representing a key source of financial survival, it is, in Ryan's words, a "hated and powerful economic overseer akin to a thuggish loan shark". Ryan remarks that "it is the latter more pejorative image of the IMF that seems to resonate more clearly with the general public throughout Africa, Latin America, Asia and the Middle East". The negative image of the IMF can be attributed largely to "the social and political costs associated with economic adjustment".

The arguments put forward by Woodroffe and Ellis-Jones (2000) and Ryan (1998) are shared by Marshall (2014) who refers to "social unrest and revolution emanating from the world's major international financial institutions like the IMF and World Bank, as well as the world's major consulting firms that provide strategic and investment advice to corporations, banks and investors around the world". With respect to the IMF, Marshall (2014) argues that "as IMF austerity programs spread across the globe, poverty followed, and so too did protests and rebellion". He cites figures showing that between 1976 and 1992, 146 protests erupted against IMF-sponsored programs in 39 different countries around the world characterized by "violent state repression of the domestic populations". He further writes the following:

These same programs by the IMF and World Bank facilitated the massive growth of slums, as the policies demanded by the organizations forced countries to undertake massive layoffs, privatization, deregulation, austerity and the liberalization of markets amounting, ultimately, to a new system of social genocide. The new poor and displaced rural communities flocked to cities in search of work and hope for a better future, only to be herded into massive urban shantytowns and slums.

Oxfam (2002) attributes the food crisis in southern Africa to the failure of IMF-designed agricultural policies. These policies are designed without carrying out a full assessment of their likely impact on poverty and food security. The riots and protests are initiated by the poor because they are the victims of IMF policies. While the policies are portrayed as being good for the poor—because they have positive effects on growth, employment, productivity, and social welfare—they are designed to benefit predatory foreign investors, multinationals and the local oligarchs.

2.7 The Consequences of Conditionality: Social Expenditure

Social expenditure is public spending on education and health, although it is reasonable to think that it also covers expenditure on such things as child care. The IMF has been criticized for promoting policies that weaken social protection, by academics, civil society organizations and international organizations. The ability of ordinary people to access healthcare and education can be affected adversely by three factors: (i) direct reduction in public social spending; (ii) poverty and inequality, which affect the ability of people to access private healthcare and education and their ability to meet out-of-pocket payments; and (iii) the mix of health and education providers between public and private. IMF operations have implications for all of these aspects of access to healthcare and education.

The ten commandments of the Washington Consensus are not conducive to boosting social expenditure. The first commandment of fiscal policy discipline, the second commandment of redirecting public spending, and the eighth commandment of the privatization of public enterprises are bound to have negative effects on social expenditure. Likewise, the imposition of conditionality provisions produces an adverse effect on public expenditure on health and education as well as access and affordability. The provision of currency devaluation makes imported medical equipment and medicines more expensive. The provision of austerity implies reduction in public expenditure in general and aggravation of poverty, with diminished ability of people to meet out-of-pocket medical expenses. The provision of restructuring of foreign debt may involve debt–equity swap, ending with foreign investors owning healthcare facilities. The provision of free market pricing puts health and education beyond the affordability of ordinary people. The provision of the enhancement of the "rights" of foreign investors *vis-à-vis* national law undermines the ability of locals to access the health and education facilities run by predatory foreign investors who operate above the local law. The provision of financialization aggravates inequality, affects adversely employment in the productive sectors of the economy, and inflicts brain drain on those sectors.

Against common sense and the facts on the ground, Gupta and Shang (2017) reiterate the IMF declared attitude toward social spending, arguing that "over the past few decades, protecting social programs and spending on health has been a cornerstone of the IMF's support for countries". They cite a number of studies reaching the conclusion that IMF support for countries' "reforms", on average, either preserve or boost public health spending. The rationale is that without "reform", a country's economy could collapse, along with its public healthcare system. While they admit that IMF operations may impede spending on public health in more than one way, this effect is offset by "other important factors through which the IMF's support for a country positively affects public health spending". They argue that the economic and financial stability promoted by IMF-prescribed policies can help governments raise revenue to finance healthcare and that IMF support is conducive to receiving more financing from other donors, which boosts the resources available to finance priority spending on health and other social programs. They also argue that IMF-prescribed tax reform boosts government revenue and that improving the overall efficiency of spending can help governments finance spending on health and education.

In its mild (and diplomatic) criticism of the IMF, the Center for Global Development (2007) suggests that "the IMF has not done enough to explore a full range of fiscal policy options, including more ambitious but still feasible paths for higher government spending, including on health", suggesting that the IMF is in favor of domestic debt reduction or external reserve increases over additional spending even when macroeconomic conditions are quite favorable. It is also argued that "wage bill ceilings have been overused in IMF programs, especially in Africa".

The Center for Global Development (CGD) report suggests that although IMF programs have not imposed ceilings on wages or hiring in health (or education), attempts by the IMF to accommodate hiring for these sectors within aggregate wage bill ceilings have failed. To remedy the situation, the Center makes several recommendations—most importantly, the Fund should be more transparent and proactive in discussing the rationale for its policy advice and the assumptions underlying its programs.

Critics are plentiful on the other side of the debate. Writing in *The Guardian*, Kentikelenis *et al.* (2016) accuse the IMF of not living up to its own hype on social protection, making the unfounded claim that it helps governments to protect and even boost social spending. Stubbs and Kentikelenis (2017) suggest that the IMF's policy proposals do not always yield positive results for the countries it purports to help. In October 2017, the Global Coalition for Social Protection Floors (2017) wrote to the IMF to suggest that "the IMF's approach towards social protection has been principally oriented around the desire to reduce social protection coverage and contain expenditure, rather than ensuring adequate levels of protection for all". In general, the critics contend that adequate investment in health is hampered by pressure to meet rigid fiscal deficit targets and by diverting funds away from the health sector to repay debt or boost reserves (Kentikelenis, 2015; Kentikelenis *et al.*, 2015a, 2015b, 2016; Ooms and Schrecker, 2005; Stuckler and Basu, 2009; Stuckler *et al.*, 2008, 2011). If, as the evidence indicates, IMF-prescribed policies depress economic growth, the resources available to fund healthcare shrink (Barro and Lee, 2005; Dreher, 2006; Przeworski and Vreeland, 2000). Furthermore, these policies are not conducive to the attraction of health aid (Stubbs *et al.*, 2016). Jensen (2004) demonstrates that countries having IMF agreements, *ceteris paribus*, attract 25% less FDI inflows than countries not under IMF agreements, a result that should be valid for development aid.

IMF policies often go beyond spending conditionality to foster a more active reshaping of the health sector, including the enhancement of the role played by the private sector in healthcare provision (Benson, 2001; Gupta *et al.*, 2000; Loewenson, 1995; Turshen, 1999), the introduction of cost-sharing for the use of health services (Independent Evaluation Office (IEO), 2003; Pitt, 1993; Sen and Koivusalo, 1998), and the decentralization of health services (Kentikelenis *et al.*, 2014). Kentikelenis *et al.* (2015b) argue that while it is possible that the revenue generated from patients or hospital privatization may be reinvested in the healthcare system (thus raising spending), the proceeds may be diverted to other areas of spending. The enhancement of the role of the private sector can hardly be a substitute for public health expenditure as private healthcare is beyond the means of the vast majority of people, particularly in low-income countries. What is not clear here is how the proceeds of the privatization of public hospitals are invested in the "health system", given that privatization means putting an end to public healthcare.

IMF operations have an adverse effect on public spending on health and education because the Fund demands spending cuts and redirection. These measures have an adverse effect on the ability of people to pay for private healthcare through austerity, poverty and the rising cost of healthcare resulting, for example, from currency devaluation and the practices of predatory private suppliers of healthcare. IMF operations cause riots and pollution, giving rise to injury and deteriorating health, which require more spending on healthcare. Through both supply and demand factors, IMF operations reduce per capita consumption of healthcare. Last, but not least, IMF operations worsen income and wealth inequality (for example, via privatization and financialization), giving rise to inequality with respect to the consumption of healthcare.

2.8 Concluding Remarks

IMF conditionality consists of some policies, principles, reforms, recommendations, etc., that borrowing countries must follow or else. The ten commandments of the Washington Consensus were formulated (or assembled) by John Williamson on the basis of those policy recommendations that were blessed by technocratic Washington, political Washington and, more importantly, corporate Washington. Naturally, a consensus has been found among the parties that either loot, or enable the looting of, developing countries that are unfortunate enough to need IMF loans.

Opposition to IMF policies is not evident only in the riots caused by the IMF's draconian recommendations. It is also evident in the revolt of the intellectual South, not only against the IMF but also against other international financial institutions such as the World Bank and the World Trade Organization, as well as regional development banks, such as the Inter-American Development Bank, the Asian Development Bank and the African Development Bank. These institutions, according to Lechini (2008), "played a dual role of paramount influence in domestic political processes". This is how Lechini (2008) describes the roles played by these institutions:

> On the one hand, an economic role, forcefully promoting and imple-
> menting—sometimes even contributing with their own staff to the state
> bureaucracies in charge—the neoliberal policies in a whole range of
> markets and economic institutions; and on the other hand, a political
> role, helping to "discipline and align" resistant national governments
> within the narrow limits established by the Washington Consensus.

These international institutions, according to Lechini, "became critical avenues for the advancement of an international hegemonic structure—led by global dominant economic and political forces—into the policy-making and the domestic agenda of supposedly sovereign states, determining new forms of subordination and control".

Other intellectuals voice concern about the neoliberal "show". Gandásegui (2008) refers to the ever expanding capitalist system and the possibilities for political organizations in the countries of the South to act independently, with reasonable margins of autonomy. Bond (2008) contends that Africa is getting progressively poorer and that its integration into the world economy has not generated wealth but has rather improved the globalization and the Washington Consensus mechanisms through which the outflow of wealth is secured. With reference to the case of Ethiopia, Muchie (2008) argues that the main weakness of the structural adjustment approach sponsored by the Washington-based financial institutions is the rupture of the economy from politics and the disembedded-ness of the economy from society. In this process, autonomy and accountability, growth and redistribution, and consensus and inclusive-ness moved in opposite or bifurcated directions. And there is more where these came from (see Lechini, 2008).

The policies and reforms designed by the IMF and other international financial institutions for the benefit of corporate Washington are given glamorous names, but they mean something else, something more sinister. Labor reform means giving multinationals and oligarchs the ability to hire and fire as they wish. Fiscal reform means cutting social expenditure while leaving military expenditure intact. Structural reform means providing better environment for predatory foreign investors. Social security reform means abolishing unemployment benefits and pensions. Downsizing the public sector means firing government employees without compensation. Opening the economy means allowing multi-nationals a free access to domestic markets without any restrictions. Allowing a greater role for foreign investors means giving them the opportunity to buy high-quality public assets at fire-sale prices. Wage restraint means freezing nominal wages, leading to falling real wages. Macroeconomic reform means adopting "Western" style market-oriented macroeconomic policies. Civil service reform means firing government employees. Transition to a private-led economy means selling public assets to oligarchs and predatory foreign investors. Enhancing efficiency means cutting corners, irrespective of environmental and other consider-ations. And reducing the minimum wage means allowing multinationals to pay workers one dollar a day in wages. Naturally, these policies are portrayed as reform at its best for the benefit of the people.

Chapter 3

The Free Market Doctrine and Economic Freedom

3.1 Introduction

The Washington Consensus and IMF conditionality are based on the neoliberal notions of free market and economic freedom, calling for the exclusion of government from economic activity, that is, the government should not participate in, regulate or supervise economic activity. These notions can be traced back to the concept of *laissez-faire*, a French term that means "leave us alone", where "us" refers to the oligarchy or corporate interests. The term emerged in an answer that Jean-Baptiste Colbert (Comptroller General of Finance under King Louis XIV) received when he asked the oligarchs what the government could do to help them.

The doctrine of *laissez-faire* became increasingly popular in the 19th century as the Industrial Revolution gained momentum. John Stuart Mill (1848) put forward arguments for and against the role of the government in economic activity. The popularity of *laissez-faire* reached its peak around 1870, but by the late 19th century, the fundamental changes that occurred as a result of industrial growth and the adoption of mass production cast some doubt on the soundness of *laissez-faire* as a guiding philosophy. In the wake of the Great Depression of the 1930s, *laissez-faire* was largely replaced by Keynesian economics. Unlike *laissez-faire*, Keynesian economics calls for a big role for the government in the economy on the grounds that the economy does not have the tendency to return automatically to full employment (which is a presumption of neoclassical economics). In the 1970s, the free market doctrine was brought back to life by right-wing economists, such as Milton Friedman and Friedrich von Hayek. The underlying principles were accepted by political leaders on both sides of the Atlantic as Freidman and von Hayek inspired both Margaret Thatcher and Ronald Reagan. Their thoughts provided the "intellectual" rationale for the waves of privatization and deregulation that took place consequently. What followed was a bonanza for the oligarchy. It is interesting that von Hayek managed to do what his teacher, Ludwig von Mises, failed to do in the 1920s as he was dismissed as a "reactionary apologist for big business" (Somers and Block, 2014).

Advocates of the free market doctrine base their arguments on the concept of efficiency, implying always that the private sector is more efficient than the public sector and that people who work for the private sector are smart whereas those working for the government have lower IQs and are less efficient. In his introduction to the 2020 edition of the Heritage Foundation's annual publication on economic freedom, James (2020) writes the following:

> While we have clearly seen what happens when people and economies are unleashed from the chains of excessive government control, we must practice constant vigilance so that our nations do not fall prey to the false promises of the ever-present statists. Statists push bigger government and socialist and collectivist policies that are wrapped in deceptive emotional appeals to things like social justice and equality—yet their policies deliver none of it.

For free marketeers, everything is about the individual and nothing about the society or any kind of collective. For them, everything is about private costs and revenues, and nothing about social costs and benefits. There is no place for compassion and altruism, and selfishness is considered a virtue. Thus, a polluter may pollute to maximize profit and those who cannot afford the free market prices of health, education and housing should be condemned to death, illiteracy and homelessness.

3.2   Arguments for and Against the Free Market Doctrine

A free market implies a structure whereby the production, distribution and pricing of goods and services are coordinated by the market forces of supply and demand, unhindered by regulation, and this is why free marketeers believe that the government has no place in economic activity. A free market is the opposite of a regulated market, where the government intervenes (through regulatory measures) in the setting of prices and determination of the production and distribution of goods and services. In a free market, the maestro is the "invisible hand" that slaps and punches us every now and then. Bailey (2000) uses the following description of the free market:

> A minimum definition of a free market is that it embodies an imaginary structure consisting of the combined flow of desires and decisions of a collection of buyers and sellers operating at any given time, of the commodity about which these intellectual attitudes are held and of an institutional arrangement (either formal or informal, or both) facilitating the exchange of information required of the buyers and sellers.

Free marketeers tell us that we face economic problems because no country has a truly free market. By moving to that ideal situation, they argue, all of our problems will disappear and we will all be healthy, wealthy and wise. The facts on the ground show otherwise: significant damage has been inflicted on humanity by the partial move toward that "ideal". According to free marketeers, we should be guided by market forces and accept the tyranny of the invisible hand for the following reasons: (i) a free market acts as a coordinator of independent production and consumption decisions of millions of people; (ii) no one has to understand how the market performs the function of coordinating decisions; (iii) the market determines a distribution of the total income it generates; and (iv) it creates a product life cycle, leading to regular emergence of new products. Free marketeers contend that the market is the best coordinator, that it is a producer of growth, that it reduces coercion by decentralizing power, and that market-determined prices are related to costs. The formal case for a free market is that it would lead to an optimal allocation of resources and hence efficiency in the sense that no one can be made better off without simultaneously making someone else worse off. In reality, the market is not a perfect communicator of a huge number of buy and sell decisions, at least because the assumption of perfect knowledge never holds, no matter how much we are bombarded by advertising.

Yes, the market has a role to play in the economy, but we should not accept every market outcome and refrain from doing anything about it. We cannot refrain from doing anything about homelessness and inequality just because the market says these are by products of the drive to achieve efficiency. We cannot accept, just because the market dictates, the practice of paying incompetent CEOs thousands of times the amounts paid to the actual producers of goods and services, the bakers, janitors and health workers. Yes, the market is a producer of growth, but it is also a producer of economic crises. The market decentralizes power but only in the sense that power moves from elected officials, who are accountable to voters, to oligarchs, who are not accountable to anyone. Market-determined prices are related to cost, more specifically, private cost because the social cost of production is not taken into account (given that decisions should be motivated by individualism and selfishness). The social costs of unemployment are not taken into account when workers are laid off. The market does not lead to a situation where no one can be made better off without simultaneously making someone else worse off. How much does it cost to house all of the homeless as a fraction of the net worth of any member of the 1%? The homeless can be made better off with the loose change of the 1% that will not make them worse off.

The origin of the concept of a free market is traced by Gray (2009) to mid-19th century England where a "far-reaching experiment in social engineering" was conducted. The objective, according to Gray, was to "free economic life from social and political control" by instituting the idea of free market, which required the breaking up of the socially rooted markets that had existed in England for centuries. Gray, who is a critic of free market ideology, argues that "the free market created a new type of economy in which prices of all goods, including labor, changed without regard to their effects on society". It is not obvious therefore why free marketeers complain about government intervention when it was this very intervention that created the free market. Today, the free market system is maintained by pro-business laws, as the executive and legislative bodies are captured by the corporate sector. Today, the corporate sector is supported by government consumption (particularly arms) subsidies, bail-outs and bail-ins. The oligarchs tell the government to leave them alone, but when they are in trouble they demand bail-outs and use fear mongering to accomplish that end, arguing that without bail-out the economy will be in tatters. Like parrots, government officials repeat the rhetoric, aspiring for well-paid private-sector jobs when they leave public service.

The economist who more than anyone else popularized the concept of free market and sold it successfully to politicians (and to the public at large through popular media) was Milton Friedman who went as far as declaring that "underlying most arguments against the free market is a lack of belief in freedom itself" (Friedman, 1962). In a piece written with his wife, the following is stated (Freidman and Friedman, 1979):

A society that puts equality—in the sense of equality of outcome— ahead of freedom will end up with neither equality nor freedom. The use of force to achieve equality will destroy freedom, and the force, introduced for good purposes, will end up in the hands of people who use it to promote their own interests.

Naturally, Friedman did not define freedom to include freedom from disease and poverty. It is the Freidman type of freedom, allowing oligarchs to do as they please and indulge in activities that erode freedom from disease and poverty. Friedman also articulated the proposition that economic freedom is a precondition for political freedom. Freedom of expression, he argued, is not possible when the means of production are under government control and individuals lack the economic means to sustain themselves and their points of view. Sirico (2012) echoes this view by warning that "you cannot have freedom without a free economy". But again a free economy, *a la* Freidman and Sirico, deprives the majority from the freedom to have a decent life. As for "economic freedom is a precondition for political freedom", we need only to remember the people who were slaughtered when the free market was imposed on the people of Chile by a dictator in 1973. Friedman and his fellow free marketeers blessed the move. We should also recall that the Nazis believed firmly in the notion of the free market as they embarked on a massive privatization program prior to World War II.

Another prominent advocate of the notion of free market is Friedrich von Hayek, who established "Neoliberal International", a transatlantic network of academics, businessmen, journalists and activists. Hayek is quoted by Petsoulas (2001) as saying that market economies allow "spontaneous order", that is, "a more efficient allocation of societal resources than any design could achieve". According to this view, sophisticated business networks operating in market economies are formed to produce and distribute goods and services throughout the economy. This network, the argument goes, has not been designed, but emerged as a result of decentralized individual economic decisions. This is not true: the free market system would not have emerged if it were not for government action, and currently it is maintained by support from "pro-business" politicians. The language used by free marketeers is simply rhetoric designed to conceal the extent to which the free market is a government construct.

While free marketeers claim that democracy and the free market system are intertwined, Freidman, von Hayek and James Buchanan supported the fascist regime of Augusto Pinochet who seized power in a violent *coup d'état*, sometimes referred to as "the other 9/11" or "Chile's 9/11". Pinochet overthrew the democratically elected government of Salvadore Allende, in the process committing massive crimes against humanity. Allende was accused of introducing "socialist" policies, which were reversed by the Pinochet regime, opting instead for extreme free market policies. According to Meadowcroft (2019), Milton Friedman, Friedrich von Hayek and James Buchanan are "alleged to have given explicit, tacit or covert support to the regime" (read without the word "alleged"). Enthusiastic support for the Pinochet regime came from von Hayek, who (in the name of freedom) supported other authoritarian governments of the time. According to Meadowcroft (2019), Hayek believed in "transitional dictatorship" that could use authoritarian methods to set a country on the path toward economic liberalism and limited government and that short-lived dictatorship might be justified to curb the excesses of majoritarian rule that threatened economic freedom. For Hayek, if democracy does not bring about good outcomes (meaning a market economy), then it is desirable to dispense with it temporarily (where "temporarily" could mean 10 years and half a million lives lost). Naturally, the three of them were awarded the Nobel Prize in economics, presumably for services to humanity.

Contradiction between the free market system and democracy was recognized a long time ago by Rothschild (1947) who wrote the following:

> When we enter the field of rivalry between [corporate] giants, the traditional separation of the political from the economic can no longer be maintained... Fascism...has been largely brought into power by this very struggle in an attempt of the most powerful oligopolists to strengthen, through political action, their position in the labour market and vis-à-vis their smaller competitors, and finally to strike out in order to change the world market situation in their favor.

If free market policies are associated with democracy, how do we explain the observation that governments pursuing these policies are becoming increasingly autocratic, using "national security" as a pretext to infringe on people's democratic rights and civil liberties? Signs of fascism are conspicuous in the US and other "Western" countries, including nationalism, disregard for human rights, identification of "enemies" as a unifying cause, supremacy of the military, controlled mass media, obsession with national security, religion becoming intertwined with the government, protection of corporate power, suppression of labor power, obsession with crime and punishment, rampant cronyism and corruption, and fraudulent elections. Democracy has been weakened by unfettered capitalism because corporate interests invest ever greater sums in lobbying, public relations, and even bribes and kickbacks, seeking and extracting favorable laws, in the process drowning out the voices of ordinary citizens.

Opponents of the free market doctrine contend that the government has to intervene in economic activity occasionally to maintain competition in large and important industries. While free marketeers argue that only a free market can create healthy competition (and therefore more business and reasonable prices), a free market in its purest form is likely to produce the opposite of the desired outcome. It is plausible to suggest that mergers and acquisitions and the privatization of public enterprises give rise to monopolies (or oligopolies) requiring government intervention to force competition and reasonable prices. Free markets do not create perfect competition, neither do they boost market competition in the long run. Government intervention is necessary to remedy market failure that is held to be an inevitable result of absolute adherence to free market principles.

Unlike the claim made by Clark and Lee (2011) that markets promote morality, Falk and Sczech (2013) suggest that markets erode morals. What is moral about considering inequality and homelessness as non-issues? What is moral about refusing to treat an injured person because he or she cannot pay up-front? What is moral about putting the concepts of freedom and anti-protectionism at the service of vested wealthy interests, allowing them to attack labor laws and the rules providing protection for the majority? What is moral about the empowerment of corporations to exploit and loot? What is moral about allowing the pharmaceutical and insurance industries to hold sick children hostage while their parents bankrupt themselves trying to save their sons or daughters? What is moral about allowing banks to burden people with student loans that cannot be forgiven by declaring bankruptcy? What is moral about bailing out failed corporations by transferring to them taxpayers' money, some of which is used to pay bonuses to the CEOs and their cronies? What is moral about bailing in failed banks by confiscating depositors' money for no fault of the latter? What is moral about loan sharks charging double or triple-digit interest rates on cash advances to those in desperate need of cash? What is moral about price gouging in the midst of a pandemic and rampant unemployment?

I suppose that even criminal activity can be justified in terms of the free market. I believe, however, that no free marketeer would dare advocate drug and sex trafficking, which involve consensual exchange at market-determined prices. Jeffrey Epstein was conducting market transactions when he took advantage of children to satisfy his insatiable appetite for young girls. Furthermore, one truly criminal activity has been advocated by the man himself (Milton Friedman)—that activity is insider trading. It is invariably the case that insider trading is illegal (hence subject to the ultimate form of regulation, prohibition) because it is unfair to other investors who do not have access to insider information. Yet, free marketeers put forward arguments for deregulating insider trading (hence the legalization of a criminal activity) and allowing it to thrive because it is good for market efficiency.

Milton Friedman advocated insider trading by saying that "you want more insider trading, not less" and that "you want to give the people most likely to have knowledge about deficiencies of the company an incentive to make the public aware of that" (Harris, 2003). Friedman did not believe that the trader should be required to make his trade known to the public because the buying or selling pressure itself is information for the market. Other proponents argue that insider trading is a "victimless act": a willing buyer and a willing seller agree to trade a property which the seller rightfully owns, with no prior contract having been made between the parties to refrain from trading if there is asymmetric information. McArdle (2011) describes the process as "arguably the closest thing that modern finance has to a victimless crime". I suppose that Jeffrey Epstein would have described his dealings with "service providers" as victimless free market transactions because no coercion was involved. I wonder if Milton Friedman would have agreed with such a proposition.

Some free marketeers argue that the free market system leads to peace while alternative systems lead to war. This proposition is inconsistent with the history of imperialism and the atrocities committed by the East India

Company in the name of free trade. Energized by the free market doctrine, Biddle (2014) identifies the factors that lead to war and those that lead to peace by contrasting two states of the world: statism versus capitalism, collectivism versus individualism, and altruism versus egoism. For Biddle, war is caused by statism, collectivism and altruism whereas peace is produced by capitalism, individualism and egoism. He argues that capitalism is a cause of peace and that "on the premise of capitalism, initiating war is immoral and absurd". However, for war profiteers acting on the free market doctrine, killing without being killed goes hand in hand with living (happily) without letting others live. For them, the death of others is necessary for the continuation of the extravaganza of their lives. Biddle uses the example of Nazi Germany to support his argument that statism causes war and capitalism causes peace. He overlooks the fact that the Nazis supported German capitalism, initially through privatization and subsequently through the provision of slave labor.

By the same token, Biddle distinguishes between collectivism as a cause of war and individualism as a source of peace. However, if collectivism refers to the whole community, then Biddle's argument is not valid. Ordinary people do not want war because they end up being the losers. It is typically a small cabal of industrialists and financiers who love war because it is a profitable enterprise. On the premise of individualism, initiating war is immoral, selfless, and absurd. If this is the case, how do we explain the fact that one individual, Cecil Rhodes, got Britain to enter the vicious Boer War, during which concentration camps were invented by the victor? And how do we explain the annihilation of the Congolese people as a result of the desire of an individual, King Leopold, to enrich himself? Throughout history, wars have been initiated by individuals or small cabals seeking economic gains in the name of the free market.

In the spirit of the free market doctrine, Biddle (2014) describes altruism as "the primary moral cause of war" whereas egoism is considered a conduit to peace. Thus, if you do something to help other people without realizing any material gain, you are a war monger. However, if you take advantage of people to realize economic gain, you are a person of peace. Biddle seems to overlook reality and speaks out of false idealism. Langness (2016) argues that "self-interest is at the bottom of every war". Dictators and emperors are egoistic, yet they start wars. The military–industrial complex is egoistic, yet the people behind it love war. War profiteers are egoistic, but for them war is a means whereby they can boost their net worth. Surely, Hitler was not altruistic, neither was Genghis Khan. Those who see bombs as a source of revenue rather than killing tools are not altruistic—they represent a manifestation of egoism.

Karl Polanyi, who opposed the free market orthodoxy of Ludwig von Mises in the 1920s, has gained belated recognition as one of the most important thinkers of the 20th century. His anti-market argument is that a self-regulating economic system is a completely imaginary construction that is impossible to achieve or maintain (even though the imaginative resonances are very powerful for many). Polanyi contended that government action is not some kind of "interference" in economic activity and that no economy exists without government. Government action provides not only the infrastructure but also (among other things) the employment system, the arrangements for buying and selling real estate, and the money supply, all of which are constructed and sustained through the exercise of government's coercive power. Accordingly, Somers and Block (2014) suggest that "free market rhetoric is a giant smokescreen designed to hide the dependence of business profits on conditions secured by government". As examples, they use pharmaceutical firms which have successfully resisted any government limits on their price-setting ability while relying on the government-run patent system to maintain monopolistic power. And we should not forget that the compliance of employees with the demands of their managers is maintained by the police, judges and legal rules.

The free market ideology has been dealt a big blow by the global financial crisis because deregulation is seen as a major cause of the crisis. This is not to say that free marketeers are no longer outspoken—they have kept the same rhetoric while ignoring the facts on the ground. Motivated by the crisis, Stiglitz (2010) argues for a restoration of the balance between government and markets, suggesting that the (free market) system is broken and that it can be fixed only by "examining the underlying theories that have led us into this new bubble capitalism". Martinez (2009) contends that the proposition that the activities related to distributing resources and economic growth are better left to the "invisible hand" seems "tragically misguided in the wake of the 2008 market collapse and bailout". He goes on to describe how "the flawed myth of the 'invisible hand' distorted our understanding of how modern capitalist markets developed and actually work". Harcourt (2011) argues that "our faith in 'free markets' has severely distorted American politics".

It is bewildering that belief in the healing power of the free market is still firm despite the devastation inflicted by the global financial crisis on the world economy. Some free marketeers go as far as blaming the global financial crisis on regulation rather than deregulation. For example, Allison (2012) points out that "financial services is a very highly regulated industry, probably the most regulated industry in the world", hence "it is not surprising that a highly regulated industry is the source of many of our economic problems". The fact of the matter is that if, prior to the crisis, there were adequate regulations of leverage, liquidity, underwriting standards and the trading of over-the-counter (OTC) derivatives, the crisis would not have happened or at least it would have been less devastating.

The fact of the matter is that government intervention in economic activity is needed, particularly when something big goes wrong. A person cutting himself shaving does not need the intervention of a surgeon, as the body can heal itself from a minor mishap like cutting oneself shaving. However, a person who gets shot and survives the shooing needs the intervention of a surgeon, otherwise, he will die.

3.3 Rebuttal of Free Marketeers

In this section, we examine the propositions put forward by some die-hard free marketeers in defense of the free market doctrine. One die-hard free marketeer defines a free market as follows (Brook, 2016):

A free market is a market free of government control, regulations, coercion and force. A free market means freedom to act without coercion in the pursuit of the values we need in order to live and to thrive and to flourish and to prosper. In a free market, people can act without force in order to produce economic values, create and produce wealth. In a free market, the only job of government is to catch crooks, to protect people from fraud, to help arbitrate disputes using a justice system. Government has to define property rights, to make them clear: intellectual property rights, physical property rights. But other than that, the government has no role, no economic policy—it leaves the market alone.

He adds:

The only job of government in a free market should be to protect individuals: our freedoms, our ability to go out into the world and do what we want to do in pursuit of the values that we need in order to live and to thrive. So the government is there to protect individual rights. That is the ideal government, the government that only protects individual rights and does not regulate, does not control, does not tell us what to do in our bedroom, does not tell us what to do in business. A system like that is to protect people who are rational and who want to use their minds in order to live the best. The free market idea says that the more constraints society or government places on you, the more limited scientific research is, the more limited entrepreneurship is, the more limited human beings' ability to pursue the things that they think are necessary for their lives is.

It is true that value and wealth can be created under capitalism, but the created wealth, and the power that goes with it, is highly concentrated. Free marketeers assume that a free market begins from a blank canvas where everyone has identical abilities and opportunities. In truth, those who benefit from the free market (as a historical modification of a more regulated system) already possess wealth in a concentrated form. The freedom that Brook talks about is the freedom of the oligarchs to generate profit by any means for the purpose of satisfying an insatiable appetite for wealth accumulation because "greed is good". It is certainly not about ordinary people being free from poverty, illness, homelessness and illiteracy. For free marketeers, freedom is corporate freedom from regulation which, according to Romer (2020), provides leeway for companies to "generate a profit even if they did pervasive harm in the process".

Brook wants governments to stop regulating so that the oligarchs can make profit without bounds by abusing human rights and destroying the environment. He also defends greed and selfishness as human virtues because they are conducive to efficiency, and condemns altruism, morality and ethics. This is why I am not sure why some free marketeers claim that morality comes with the free market. Brook calls on the government to catch crooks, choosing to ignore the fact that the free market provides the right environment for crooks to thrive. But then I think that what he means by crooks are people like someone who was caught and murdered by the Minneapolis police for attempting to use a counterfeit $20 note. He condemns a government that tells us what to do in our bedrooms, implying that the government should not take action against "innovative" entrepreneurs disposing of toxic waste in rivers and lakes because this is inconsistent with the noble cause of profit maximization.

Brook (2016) condemns regulation because it interferes with the working of the "law" of supply and demand, which (he argues) always holds, just like the law of gravity. This is preposterous because economics is not physics, hence economic laws are at best empirical regularities. Laws must be universal, the law of gravity is universal but the "law" of supply and demand is not a law in any sense. Economists talk about "inferior" and "Giffen" goods that do not obey the law of supply and demand. He suggests that governments must protect us but otherwise leave us alone, forgetting that governments should not only protect us from criminals, terrorists, and invaders but also from corporate entities that maximize profit by polluting the environment and use modern-day slave labor. Akerlof and Shiller (2015) argue that "the economic system works as well as it does not just because of individual incentives, but also because a whole raft of individual heroes, social agencies and government regulation puts limits on this downside of markets to phish us for phools".

Free marketeers like Brook tell us that a free market offers the benefit of the freedom to innovate, as if innovation is a monopoly of the profit-driven private sector (it was NASA, not a private company, that took astronauts to the moon). In a free market, it is claimed, the customer is a king as customers drive choices. Against that, Akerlof and Shiller (2015) argue that "free markets, as bountiful as they may be, will not only provide us with what we want, as long as we can pay for it; they will also tempt us into buying things that are bad for us, whatever the costs". As long as profit can be made, corporate entities will deceive us, manipulate us and prey on our weaknesses, to make us buy things that we do not need and reap profit in the process. Akerlof and Shiller (2015) conclude that "markets are not benign forces working for the greater good but instead are filled with businesses that 'phish' by exploiting our weaknesses to get us to buy their products".

Yet another alleged advantage is that a free market economy benefits the society through competition, which provides a wide selection of goods and services at lower prices. This may be true under the ideal system of perfect competition, but in reality competition leads to the "survival of the fittest", turning a competitive industry into oligopoly or monopolistic completion where a huge amount of resources goes into wasteful advertising and manipulation of consumers. The markets for healthcare and higher education are oligopolistic, producing rising prices for deteriorating product quality. Low-quality university degrees have become rather expensive as a result of the corporatization of universities in the spirit of the free market.

Brook (2016) glorifies the free market system by saying the following:

> It is hard to imagine the world with a completely free market. People would be much richer. We would have such advanced technology. We would live to be a hundred and fifty or older, because biotechnology has the capacity, if freed up from regulations and freed up from state control, to really extend human life dramatically. We might have rocket ships going to Mars, we might be colonizing Mars. More importantly than that, there would be no poor people in the world.

I must agree with the proposition that it is hard to imagine the world with a completely free market. Under the kind of environment that Brook aspires for, some people would be much richer but the majority of people would barely survive. In fact, poor people would become richer, or less poor, if we move in the opposite direction and tackle massive inequality. As for living longer under a free market system, Brook seems to be unaware of the fact that privatization killed more Russians than vodka in the dark years of Boris Yeltsin. As for going to Mars, we will have to wait and see if Elon Musk beats NASA in this endeavor—I will bet on NASA.

Another die-hard free marketeer tells us that we should be grateful to the free market system, describing it as "the most powerful, nonreligious force for good in the history of the world" (Dorfman, 2016). According to him, it is because of the free market system that median income is rising, but median income means nothing to the poor, unemployed and homeless. The most successful poverty reduction exercise happened in China under strict government control. Under a free market system, Dorfman suggests, failed businesses are punished and economic growth accelerates. The failed businesses that caused the global financial crisis were not punished but rather rewarded with taxpayers' money, and on that occasion, growth did not accelerate as the economy experienced the Great Recession—thanks to those operating according to the free market doctrine. Naturally, we should thank the free market system for "freedom", the freedom of pharmaceutical to charge $10,000 for one pill and the freedom of a corporatized university to charge $50,000 a year for a piece of paper that undermines the ability of the holder to get a job.

In his *Wealth of Nations*, Adam Smith wrote the following (Smith, 1776):

> It is not from the benevolence of the butcher, the brewer, or the baker that we expect our dinner, but from their regard to their own self-interest. We address ourselves not to their humanity but to their self-love, and never talk to them of our own necessities, but of their advantages.

Nash (1993) makes a similar point:

> Most of us lack the ability to make or provide most of the goods and services we want. How then do we persuade others to do all these nice things for us?... People do all these wonderful things for me because of their prospect of receiving something in return, usually money. And where do I get the money I use to pay all these people? I receive it from still other people who pay me for performing some service or providing some good for them. Reflecting about the market in this way helps us better understand the extent to which we depend upon other people. All of us need other people to supply the goods and services we have come to depend on. But we also need people who will pay us for the goods and services that we can supply, thus providing the money we require to pay those who supply our wants.

No one who opposes the free market doctrine expects something for free from the butcher, the brewer, or the baker, as Smith said, or from "people who do all these wonderful things", as Nash said. We should also, either privately or through the government, pay the inventors of a COVID-19 vaccine. However, when they start hoarding, particularly in crises, to drive up prices, then they should be regulated. This is exactly what war profiteers do in times of war, acting in the name of the free market.

The problem is not with the individual butcher, the brewer, or the baker or with "people who do all these wonderful things", but rather with industries characterized by monopoly, oligopoly or oligopolistic competition where competition that drives down prices for the benefit of consumers no longer exists. Nash actually describes the aspects of a free market that exposes a fundamental contradiction in a profit-centered free market system: people are both providers of labor and consumers, using the wages they receive from employers to buy the goods and services produced by employers (rather, by them in the process of working for employers). To maximize profit, employers may seek to minimize wages, which means that those employees cannot buy the quantity of output that is required for profit maximization. This is the fundamental contradiction that explains why firms during the Industrial Revolution sought overseas markets and with that came imperialism, which involves coercion, a word that is disliked by free marketeers.

Nash goes on to outline important functions of the market, that it allows specialization and provides information via changes in relative prices. This is something that we all agree upon. He also makes the point that the government has several important roles to play in a market economy by setting up a stable system of rules within which exchanges can take place. This view means the market and the people who trade in the market need protection from actions that hinder or prevent free exchange, which is a function of the government. But the government, according to free marketeers, must not take part in economic activity or interfere with business decisions. The government should not interfere, by providing public health, when people die because private hospitals charge $200,000 for an operation. And the government should not provide burial services (which are provided free of charge by the Ministry of Health in some countries) but rather force people who cannot afford a $25,000 burial to burden themselves in debt to bury a loved one, or dump the body somewhere. Markets may be efficient, but they are immoral, tyrannical and brutal.

3.4 The Concept of Economic Freedom

The Heritage Foundation produces an annual publication reporting updates of the economic freedom index, taking the opportunity to demonstrate how economic freedom is the means of salvation and the conduit to prosperity and happiness. The Foundation puts the view that economic freedom makes an economy grow and prosper and that the free market system, which is rooted in economic freedom, "has fueled unprecedented economic growth and development around the world" (Miller *et al.*, 2020). Peet (1992), on the other hand, sees a myth in the concept of freedom as envisaged by those holding "mainstream market liberal political–economic viewpoint" who believe that freedom is entirely an economic construct, which exists in an unfettered market. In this sense, freedom is related to choice, the availability of alternatives.

For the Heritage Foundation, freedom is the freedom (of the privileged) to do things without being hindered by government intervention. It is freedom from restrictions that prevent the oligarchy from doing what it takes to accumulate wealth. The opposite view put forward by Peet is that for most people in society, freedom has entirely different meanings, such as freedom from hunger, freedom of speech, freedom of association, freedom from arbitrary constraints and freedom to be creative and artistic. While deregulation is conducive to freedom, as the Heritage Foundation sees it, it has led to deterioration in freedom from poverty, freedom of speech and association, freedom from arbitrary constrains, and freedom to be creative and artistic. Freedom from COVID-19 is not fought by deregulation but rather by massive government intervention.

The economic freedom index of the Heritage Foundation (reported in Miller *et al.*, 2020) assumes values in the range of 0–100 where 100 implies ultimate economic freedom. The index is calculated from scores assigned to four components, each of which has three sub-components. The four components of the index are the rule of law, government size, regulatory efficiency and market openness. Each one of these components has three sub-components, which are described in the following section. Accordingly, countries are classified into free, mostly free, moderately free, mostly unfree and repressed. Table 3.1 shows the classification with some examples.

The economic freedom index bears striking resemblance to the ten commandments of the Washington Consensus. In Figure 3.1, we can see how the components of the economic freedom index are related to the ten commandments. The fiscal reform commandments are related very

Table 3.1: Classification of Countries by the Economic Freedom Index

Classification	Index Range	Number of Countries	Top of Group	Bottom of Group
Free	80–100	6	Singapore	Ireland
Mostly Free	70–79.9	31	UK	Cyprus
Moderately Free	60–69.9	62	Romania	Madagascar
Mostly Unfree	50–59.9	62	Greece	Chad
Repressed	0–49.9	19	Congo	North Korea

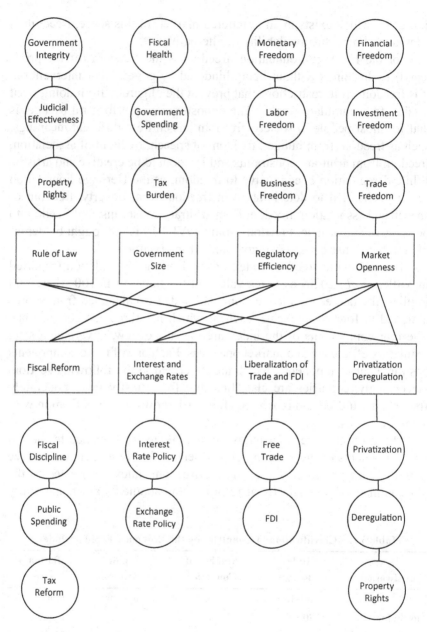

Figure 3.1:   Economic Freedom in Relation to the Washington Consensus

closely to the government size component of the index. Even the names are similar: the Washington Consensus has fiscal discipline, public spending and tax reform, whereas the economic freedom index has fiscal health, government spending and tax burden. The fiscal reform commandments are related to the regulatory framework component because one of the objectives of fiscal discipline is to have a small government that spends less, leaving economic activity for the private sector. Naturally, the ninth commandment of deregulation is related very closely to the regulatory efficiency index. The sixth, seventh, eighth and ninth commandments are related very closely to the index of market openness. It is apparent that the philosophy behind the economic freedom index and the thinking of the Heritage Foundation is very much free market neoliberalism. It follows that Williamson's Washington Consensus is based on neoliberalism even though he tends to suggest otherwise, just to give it a humanitarian face.

3.5 The Sub-Components of the Economic Freedom Index

Figure 3.1 shows the three sub-components of each of the four components of the economic freedom index. In this section, these sub-components are described and commented on in turn.

3.5.1 *Property rights*

According to the Heritage Foundation, the ability to accumulate private property and wealth in a functioning market economy is a "central motivating force for workers and investors". Since when does a worker living on the minimum wage accumulate wealth? It is true that the recognition of private property rights and an effective rule of law to protect them are vital for economic activity, which is probably why the Industrial Revolution started in England, not in China. The problem here is extending the concept of property right to the control of public assets such as land, mineral resources and public assets. This kind of property rights creates the 1–99% divide by aggravating inequality, which is a non-issue for free marketeers.

As a matter of fact, the Foundation refers to natural resources by arguing that property rights with respect to natural resources are a "primary factor in the accumulation of capital for production and investment".

Therefore, it is argued that societies should avoid the "tragedy of the commons" on the grounds that it "leads to the degradation and exploitation of property that is held communally and for which no one is accountable". Thus, public ownership of natural resources should be banned, and these resources should be given to a few oligarchs to sell for private profit without paying taxes. Again, just recall what happened in Russia in the 1990s when natural resources were grabbed by few oligarchs and multinationals with connections to Boris Yeltsin.

3.5.2 *Judicial effectiveness*

Well-functioning legal frameworks protect the rights of all citizens against infringement of the law by others, including the governments and powerful parties. As an essential component of the rule of law, judicial effectiveness requires efficient and fair judicial systems to ensure that laws are fully respected, with appropriate legal actions taken against violations. That is fine, but equality in front of the law is an illusion. The powerful parties get away with murder because they have the financial resources and legal advisers that allow them to get away with murder, sometimes literally. In putting a case for judicial effectiveness, the Foundation repeats terms like "honest", "fair", "ending discrimination", and "improving human conditions". By design, the free market system is conducive to dishonesty, unfairness, discrimination and deteriorating human conditions. However, "fair" and "honest" have different meanings in the dictionary of free marketeers. Fair prices are unacceptable because they obstruct market forces, whereas a dishonest practice like insider trading is justified as a free market transaction.

3.5.3 *Government integrity*

The Foundation warns of the detrimental effect of the systemic corruption of government institutions by practices such as bribery, nepotism, cronyism, patronage, embezzlement, and graft. Nothing is said about bribery, nepotism, cronyism, patronage, embezzlement, and graft in the private sector. To protect people from government corruption, it is argued, regulation should be kept at minimum. It follows that to prevent corruption in government, the private sector must be more corrupt. Naturally, nothing is said about the ultimate form of corruption, which is regulatory capture, perpetrated by powerful corporate interests against the public at large. It is strange that for the Foundation, the private sector is innocent, the victim of government corruption. Corruption is good if it is perpetrated by the private sector, for example, paying bribes to cut red tape and kickbacks to secure deals. What about lobbying and campaign donations, which are bribes?

3.5.4 *Tax burden*

Tax burden is measured by total tax payments as a percentage of GDP. The underlying idea here is that public-sector spending is wasteful whereas private-sector spending is productive. This is why, according to the Foundation, the government should retain the smallest possible amount of private-sector income by reducing tax rates. When free marketeers call for tax cuts, they mean tax cuts for the 1% and corporate interests (that is, the top marginal income tax rate and the corporate tax rate) on the grounds that the 99% will benefit from job creation and the trickle-down effect.

In 2003, 450 economists, including 10 Nobel Prize laureates, signed a statement opposing the Bush tax cuts (Economic Policy Institute, 2003). They expressed the view that economic growth had not been sufficient to generate jobs and prevent unemployment from rising, but "the tax cut plan proposed by President Bush is not the answer to these problems". The statement made it clear that "passing these tax cuts will worsen the long-term budget outlook, adding to the nation's projected chronic deficits" and that "this fiscal deterioration will reduce the capacity of the government to finance Social Security and Medicare benefits as well as investments in schools, health, infrastructure, and basic research". Moreover, it was suggested that "the proposed tax cuts will generate further inequalities in after-tax income". Those who signed the statement include Nobel Prize winners George Akerlof, Kenneth Arrow, Lawrence Klein, Daniel McFadden, Franco Modigliani, Robert Solow, Joseph Stiglitz, Paul Samuelson and William Sharpe. These economists are certainly not communists, socialists or lefties.

3.5.5 *Government spending*

The Foundation states that "government spending comes in many forms, not all of which are equally harmful to economic freedom", which means that they are all harmful to economic freedom. Government spending on infrastructure, research and development and human capital is not desirable even though it "may be considered investment" (only "may be"). The rationale is that government spending involves a lot of waste. That is right, but the biggest wasteful types of government expenditure are desired by the private sector, particularly military spending and spending on bailing out failed too-big-to-fail firms. On the other hand, private-sector firms indulge in wasteful spending to provide lavish life styles for the CEOs and their cronies, unnecessary advertising and payments to consultancy firms with connections. One has to say that campaign donations and bribes paid to corrupt politicians are not wasteful (from the point of view of the donor)—on the contrary, they represent a high-return investment.

3.5.6　*Fiscal health*

Fiscal health is measured by the budget deficit (or surplus) and public debt. According to the Foundation, the budget reflects a government's commitment (or lack thereof) to sound financial management of resources, which is the advancement of economic freedom. Widening deficits and a growing debt burden, both of which are allegedly direct consequences of poor government budget management, lead to the erosion of a country's overall fiscal health. In a situation like this, the government must take some action to plug the budget gap and keep the lid on public debt. This can be done either by raising taxes, which free marketeers do not like, or by selling public assets through privatization, which free marketeers do like. Thus, if a country is low on fiscal health, it must privatize without a second thought. Naturally, fiscal health should not be restored by reducing military spending because this action has an adverse effect on private-sector war profiteers.

3.5.7　*Business freedom*

Business freedom, as the Foundation sees it, is freedom from regulation, whether regulation is intended for the establishment of a business (licensing) or the governing and supervision of operations. This is because "many regulations hinder business productivity and profitability"—the magical word here is "profitability" (Miller *et al.*, 2020). Regulation should not impinge upon the "free conduct of entrepreneurial activity", the "normal decision-making" and the "price-setting process". One would assume that the "free conduct of entrepreneurial activity" involves pollution, "normal decision-making" involves the confiscation of employee superannuation (*a la* Robert Maxwell) and that the "price-setting process" involves price gouging. Business freedom, *a la* Heritage Foundation, leads to the emergence of monopolies and boom-bust cycles.

3.5.8 Labor freedom

As far as the Heritage Foundation is concerned, labor freedom means both the ability of individuals to find employment opportunities and the ability of businesses to contract freely for labor and dismiss redundant workers when they are no longer needed. The result, according to the Foundation, is enhanced productivity and sustained economic growth. However, there seems to be some contradiction here. A free market was in operation during the Industrial Revolution in Britain. Business owners were able to accumulate wealth while workers struggled and suffered from low wages, no rights and horrible working conditions. Children under the age of 18 were working in mines for more than 12 hours a day. That was labor freedom at its best.

The ability of individuals to find employment is at odds with the ability of businesses to fire at will. When productivity is up, for example as a result of technological innovation, businesses use that to boost profit by reducing the workforce rather than raising wages. Whenever privatization occurs, workers are fired in the name of efficiency while cost cutting is used to boost the salaries, bonuses and golden parachutes of CEOs and their cronies. Governments are not supposed to intervene by imposing minimum wage legislation so that workers are paid less than the minimum wage to the extent that they qualify for food stamps, meaning that businesses are subsidized by taxpayers.

Labor freedom, *a la* Heritage Foundation, means that wealthy entrepreneurs could take advantage of the poor. It means that child labor is fine—it is only immoral but the beauty of free markets is that they have no morals. The United Nations Children's Fund (UNICEF) (2020) estimates that nearly 1 in 10 children are subjected to child labor worldwide, with some forced into hazardous work through trafficking. The Organization suggests that child labor can result in extreme bodily and mental harm, and even death, as well as slavery and sexual or economic exploitation, without schooling and healthcare. Adult labor is abused in sweatshops, factories characterized by unsafe working conditions, mandatory overtime, payment of less than the minimum wage, abusive discipline, sexual harassment, or violation of labor laws and regulations. For the Heritage Foundation, what happens in sweatshops is a non-coercive exchange of labor for pay, in which case it is a legitimate free market transaction.

3.5.9 *Monetary freedom*

Monetary freedom, according to the Heritage Foundation, requires a stable currency and market-determined prices. A stable currency, it is alleged, requires an independent central bank that is unaccountable to anyone. Therefore, some unelected bureaucrats and technocrats can do whatever they like without being held accountable. Look no further than the destructive policy of ultra-low, and even negative, interest rates, which has killed the middle class for the benefit of banks. Independent central banks have been indulged in quantitative easing, which has created housing and stock market bubbles. Inflation is rampant but these independent central banks lie about it. The situation becomes even worse if the independent central bank is a private-sector firm owned by banks, as is the Federal Reserve.

Several arguments can be put forward against central bank independence. To start with, it insulates the conduct of monetary policy from democratic processes when some policy failures can be prevented by political oversight (assuming of course an honest government that does not work for the oligarchy). An independently run monetary policy cannot be reconciled with fiscal policy, giving rise to situations when the two policies pull in opposite directions. Central bank independence produces winners (the 1%) and losers (the 99%)—look no further than what the Covid-triggered quantitative easing has done in the name of reviving the economy. When central bankers are shielded from political oversight, the result could be "technocratic exceptionalism" that can fuel populism. The Economist (2019) still insists that the success of central banks in controlling inflation and interest rates "is threatened by a confluence of populism, nationalism and economic forces that are making monetary policy political again". The fact of the matter is that central banks cannot control inflation and that they lie about it. Yes, they can control interest rates, but they have been abusing this power for the benefit of commercial banks and zombie companies. I find myself in one of these rare moments when I agree with Donald Trump on his attack on the Fed, except that he attacked the Fed for doing the right thing: raising interest rates prior to the advent of COVID-19.

3.5.10 *Trade freedom*

Trade freedom means the absence of restrictions on international transactions including tariffs, export taxes, trade quotas and outright trade bans, as well as non-tariff barriers such as licensing, standard-setting, and other regulatory actions. Free trade, however, may not be suitable all the time everywhere, particularly for developing countries. Historically, the concept of free trade is associated with British imperialism, aiding and abetting corporate Britain to find overseas markets and sources of cheap raw materials. Free trade was the reason for the opium wars against China and the creation of Hong Kong as a foothold for the British Empire in China. The East India Company committed crimes against humanity in the name of free trade. These are issues that will be discussed in detail in Chapter 9.

3.5.11 *Investment freedom*

Investment freedom requires the dismantling of capital controls and abolishing restrictions on foreign ownership. However, many countries found it necessary to reimpose capital controls following the Asian financial crisis and again in the aftermath of the global financial crisis. Sudden capital movements can be detrimental to economic stability, particularly in developing countries. Abolishing restrictions on foreign ownership is convenient for multinationals to acquire privatized public assets in a developing country forced by the IMF to privatize. This is an issue that will be discussed in detail in Chapter 10.

3.5.12 *Financial freedom*

Financial freedom means allowing financial institutions to do as they please without any regulation—again in the name of efficiency, the efficiency of financial markets and the financial system, whatever that means.

However, since the financial sector is the epicenter of corruption and fraud, financial regulation is needed to protect ordinary people from predatory financiers.

3.6 Debunking the Claims of the Heritage Foundation

Miller *et al.* (2020) use the economic freedom index to make some heroic and unsubstantiated claims. They make a number of claims to convey the message that economic freedom, as defined by the Heritage Foundation, is the cause for everything good in our lives and that the lack of economic freedom is the reason of all mishaps. They refer to "far-reaching impacts on various aspects of human development" of economic freedom, which "empowers people, unleashes powerful forces of choice and opportunity, gives nourishment to other liberties, and improves the overall quality of life". They refer to "the undeniable link between economic freedom and prosperity", which is a "striking demonstration of what people can do when they have the opportunity to pursue their own interests within the rule of law". And they refer to "the proven recipe for economic freedom and real human progress".

That is not all. They envisage a "robust relationship between improvements in economic freedom and levels of economic growth". They claim that "the link between economic freedom and overall human development is clear and strong". They claim that "people in economically free societies live longer, have better health, are able to be better stewards of the environment, and push forward the frontiers of human achievement in science and technology through greater innovation". And they claim that "each measured aspect of economic freedom has a significant effect on economic growth and prosperity".

These claims represent how data can be manipulated to provide support for prior beliefs. The figures are sometimes presented as scatter plots of each individual country and when the scatter plot does not work, the "evidence" is presented as bar charts of country groups—it all depends on what tells a good story about the contribution of economic freedom. More importantly, however, correlation does not necessarily imply causation. It is either that they do not know the difference or that they know the difference but choose to ignore it because it is convenient to do so. Let us examine these claims.

The relation between economic freedom and the standard of living is verified by a scatter plot showing high correlation between GDP per capita and the index of economic freedom (correlation coefficient is 0.63). They also use a bar chart showing that average GDP per capita is highest in free countries and lowest in repressed ones. However, the countries run according to neoliberal ideas, which give them high scores of economic freedom, are advanced countries following the Anglo-American tradition. Most of those countries grew and thrived on the exploitation of other people via colonialism. The graphs should be interpreted as such, rather than to imply that economic freedom boosts the standard of living. Conversely, the relation between economic freedom and growth is represented differently—definitely not as a scatter plot because it would show nothing. In this case the relation is examined by looking at average growth in countries gaining economic freedom and those losing economic freedom over the previous 25, 15 and 5 years. Nothing is said about the statistical significance of the difference between means.

The proposition that economic freedom boosts entrepreneurial dynamism (whatever that means) is verified by high positive correlation between the economic freedom index and the Business Environment Pillar Score of the Legatum Prosperity Index (correlation is 0.87). Again, this result is obtained by construction because "entrepreneurial dynamism" is typically found in high GDP per capita countries run according to neoliberal ideas. On the other hand, no scatter plot is presented for the relation between economic freedom and human development. Instead, the results are represented by the average human development index of each country group classified according to the economic freedom index. Oddly, the results show that human development is higher in repressed than mostly free countries. After all, repressed countries include Cuba, which has a higher level of life expectancy than the US.

By using either scatter plots or bar charts of group averages, they show that correlation between economic freedom and environmental performance is highest in free countries, that there is strong positive correlation between economic freedom and global innovation, that correlation is high and positive between economic freedom and democratic governance, and that correlation is also high between economic freedom and social progress (whatever that means). This is cherry picking at its best, but cherry picking is a double-edged source that can be used to support two opposing points of view by using the same dataset.

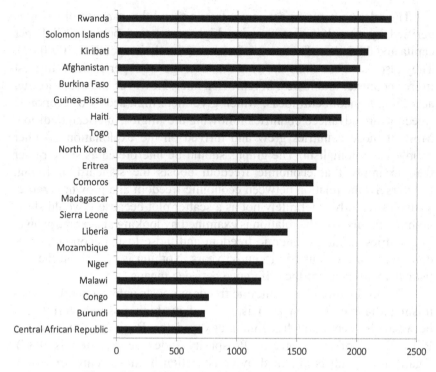

Figure 3.2:   GDP per Capita (US Dollar at PPP Rate)

I will now use the dataset provided by Miller *et al.* (2020) to demonstrate that the opposite can also be true, depending on how the statistics are presented. For this purpose, I will concentrate on the relations between economic freedom, on one hand, and GDP per capita and growth rates, on the other. Starting with GDP per capita, there is no doubt that correlation is high, but this is not a causal effect. Let us look at the lowest 20 countries in terms of GDP per capita as shown in Figure 3.2. Out of these countries, 7 are repressed, 11 are mostly unfree, and one each of moderately free and mostly free. These are the usual suspects. They have low GDP per capita because they are African countries still suffering from decades of exploitation by the free and mostly free "Western" countries. These countries lack the capital and infrastructure necessary for growth. They are famine- and disease-stricken countries, with political instability. One of the countries has been under severe sanctions and another has been going from one war to another as a result of imperialist aggression. The situation is more serious than to be attributed to economic freedom alone.

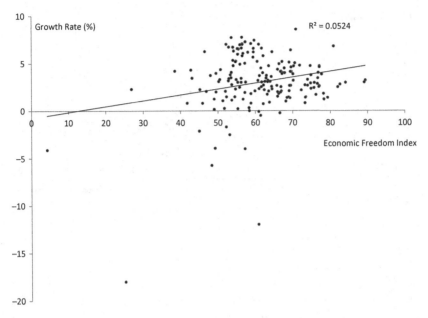

Figure 3.3: Economic Growth as a Function of Economic Freedom (Latest Observation)

Let us now look in more detail at the relation with economic growth. Miller *et al.* (2020) do not report scatter plots in this case because they (the scatter plots) do not serve the purpose, so let us see why. This is shown in Figures 3.3 and 3.4, using two measures of economic growth (last observation and 5 year average). In both cases, correlation is insignificant, which is not surprising because growth depends on a large number of factors—economic freedom may or may not be one of them. This may be the case because a large number of heterogeneous countries are unlikely to produce a pattern. To examine the possibility that correlation may be stronger in certain groups, separate scatter plots are presented in Figure 3.5. Positive correlation appears only in the case of repressed countries, but it is unlikely that growth in these countries will pick up just because they embark on a large-scale privatization program or give foreign investors more rights. After all, the IMF has been using the conditionality "drug" on some of these countries without any tangible result.

In Table 3.2, we can see countries placed in cells defined by the 5 year growth rate and the economic freedom index. Low is the first 33 percentiles, medium is the second 33 percentiles and high is the third

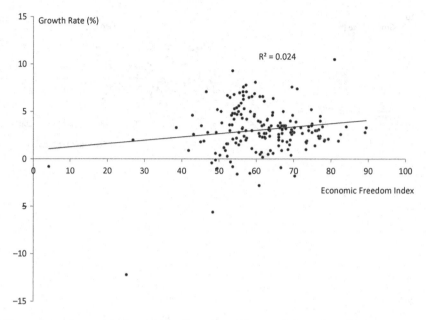

Figure 3.4:   Economic Growth as a Function of Economic Freedom (5 Year Average)

33 percentiles. What we are trying to find out is correspondence between growth and economic freedom, that is, whether or not countries with high (medium or low) growth rates also have high (medium or low) economic freedom indices. The 180 countries in the sample are classified into nine cells ranging between low–low and high–high. We can see that 57 countries only (about 32% of the sample) are classified under high–high, medium–medium and low–low. We can see 20 countries with low economic freedom and high growth. We can also see 26 countries with high economic freedom and low growth. If economic freedom is as important for economic growth as it is portrayed to be by the Heritage Foundation, not so many countries would appear in the low–high and high–low cells.

In Figure 3.6, we can see the top and bottom 10 countries in terms of growth on the latest observation and the 5 year average. If the Heritage Foundation is right about the claim that economic freedom is conducive to growth, then the top 10 must be dominated by the free and mostly free countries, whereas the bottom 10 should be dominated by the repressed and mostly unfree. The distribution of these countries can be found in Figure 3.6. The top 10 countries are dominated by the mostly unfree, that is, the mostly unfree countries have been growing faster than the free,

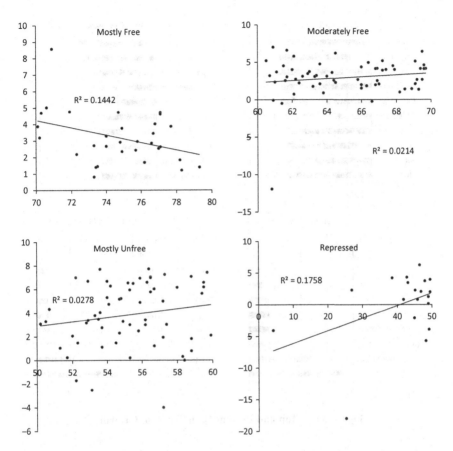

Figure 3.5: Growth as a Function of Economic Freedom (Country Groups)

Table 3.2: Classification of Countries by Growth Rate and Economic Freedom

Economic Freedom Index	5 Year GDP Growth Rate		
	Low	Medium	High
Low	25	15	20
Medium	11	20	29
High	26	22	12

moderately free and mostly free. Ironically, one of the countries in the top 10, when growth is measured as a 5 year average, is repressed (Turkmenistan, with a growth rate of 7.1%). The bottom 10 group is dominated by the repressed countries, which means that these countries

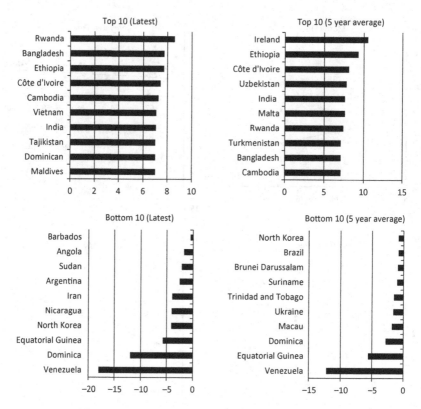

Figure 3.6:   Top and Bottom 10 in Terms of Growth

grow at a lower rate (invariably negative) than countries with higher economic freedom indices. This sounds supportive of the claims made by the Heritage Foundation, except when we take a moment to check these countries as shown in Figure 3.6. They include Venezuela, North Korea and Iran, all of which have been under sanctions and subject to attempts of regime change for a very long time. It is not the lack of economic freedom that is holding growth at bay but rather sanctions and siege imposed on these countries by the free and mostly free countries (one country in particular). The rest of the countries appearing in the bottom 10 have all sorts of problems. One "country" in the bottom 10 is classified as mostly free (Maccau) (see Table 3.3).

Venezuela in particular is at the very bottom of the bottom ten, irrespective of whether growth is measured over 1 year or 5 years. The economic downfall of oil-rich Venezuela, which is seen by some as a

Table 3.3: Classification in Terms of Economic Freedom of Fastest and Slowest 10

	Top 10		Bottom 10	
	Latest	5 year average	Latest	5 year average
Free	0	1	0	0
Mostly Free	1	1	0	1
Moderately Free	1	1	2	2
Mostly Unfree	8	6	3	3
Repressed	0	1	5	4

puzzle, is typically attributed to the lack of economic freedom as a result of the policies adopted by Hugo Chavez and sustained by his successor, Nicolas Maduro. The fact of the matter is that Venezuela's economy has collapsed because of sanctions, destabilization by foreign powers and threats of military invasion. Even worse, on 26 March 2020 (while the world was reeling under the hammer of the Coronavirus) it was announced that the US Department of Injustice charged Maduro with narco-terrorism and drug trafficking, offering a $15 million bounty for his capture (cowboy style). There is no wonder then that Venezuela sits at the very bottom of the list in terms of economic growth.

It is gross oversimplification to relate growth entirely to economic freedom by saying that countries with a higher economic freedom index grow faster than those with low indices. The fact of the matter is that growth is affected by a large number of factors besides economic freedom, government size and free market reform. In a review of the literature, Chirwa and Odhiambo (2016) find that the key determinants of economic growth in developing countries include foreign aid, foreign direct investment, fiscal policy, investment, trade, human capital development, monetary policy, natural resources and reforms, as well as geographic, regional, political and financial factors. In developed countries, the study reveals that the key determinants of economic growth include physical capital, fiscal policy, human capital, trade, demographics, monetary policy, and financial and technological factors. Nothing is said about economic freedom but significant support is found for human capital, which typically requires government spending on health and education.

3.7 The Opposite View: The Work of Richard Wolff

Critics of the free market doctrine, neoliberalism and capitalism are on the increase as we witness crises and grotesque inequality caused by using the free market doctrine as a guideline. One of the most influential critics is the American economist Richard Wolff, who is outspoken (and justifiably so). He often engages in rebuttals of the claims made by the proponents of the free market doctrine, which he typically refers to as "capitalism".

Free marketeers justify their love affair with the market on the basis of efficiency. Wolff (2013) questions the efficiency of capitalism, arguing against any connection between them. For example, he argues that the efficiency obtained through automation contributes to profit while workers are laid off. He attributes the economic and social collapse in Detroit, Cleveland and many other US cities to the relocation of economic activity, not to production inefficiency in those cities. In general, he argues that "efficiency problems did not cause the longer-term economic declines troubling the US and Western Europe". Instead, he suggests that the decision to relocate was not motivated by efficiency but rather by profit, business growth, and market share. He goes on to demonstrate that relocation itself is inefficient because the goods produced elsewhere have to be shipped back in addition to the resources wasted in the process and the pollution (of air, sea and soil) associated with vast transportation networks. Waste of resources also takes the form of abandoned factories, offices and stores. Add to that reduction in the tax base and the consequent reduction in social services, let alone the damage inflicted on people's lives. But then entrepreneurs following the principles of free market do not take into account the social consequences of their actions.

In another piece, Wolff (2020a) shows how COVID-19 debunks the efficiency myth with reference to failure to deal with a pandemic, which requires preparation by stockpiling adequate quantities of test kits, masks, gloves, beds, etc., arguing that it would have been more efficient for the government to produce them. This kind of preparation is not profitable for the private sector. Thus, he concludes that "capitalism does not generate, let alone guarantee efficiency" and that "it's all a mirage of ideological justification". This is how he describes capitalism:

> Capitalism serves capitalists first and foremost. That minority occupies or selects the occupants of most of the dominant positions in society. In

this they are like the masters and lords in slave and feudal societies. In those societies, the self-justification of their dominant minorities concerned their physical, mental, or moral superiority and/or their special relationship to God or Gods. Capitalist societies that broke from slave and feudal predecessors also rejected those systems' self-justifications. Capitalism had to find a different kind of self-justification.

The justification he refers to is efficiency driven by profit maximization. Thus, he argues, "we are all supposed to bow down to capitalism the way our ancestors bowed down to slave masters, feudal lords, and kings".

The rhetoric of free marketeers always contains reference to the unavailability of a viable alternative to capitalism, a proposition that Wolff (2012) challenges brilliantly. This is what he says:

> Really? We are to believe, with Margaret Thatcher, that an economic system with endlessly repeated cycles, costly bailouts for financiers and now austerity for most people is the best human beings can do? Capitalism's recurring tendencies toward extreme and deepening inequalities of income, wealth, and political and cultural power require resignation and acceptance—because there is no alternative?

Wolff argues that capitalism entails and reproduces a highly undemocratic organization of production inside enterprises because private owners establish enterprises and select their directors who decide what, how and where to produce and what to do with the net revenues from selling the output. This small handful of people makes all those economic decisions for the majority of people, who do most of the actual productive work. Free marketeers insist that no viable alternatives exist for this kind of arrangement and that no alternative system could work nearly so well in terms of output, efficiency and labor processes. Then he exposes the falsity of this claim with reference to the Spanish Mondragon Corporation (MC), a stunningly successful alternative to the capitalist organization of production, which consists of many cooperative enterprises grouped into four areas: industry, finance, retail and knowledge. Under this arrangement, the co-op members own and run the enterprise collectively.

While capitalism is definitely an improvement on the previous systems of slavery and feudalism, the three systems share some features. Wolff (2020b) argues that free enterprise does not define capitalism in the sense that it does not distinguish it from slavery and feudalism. Under slavery, the key relationship is that of master and slave, where the slave is the property of the master. Under feudalism, the key relationship links lord and serf by their sworn acceptance of specific obligations, loyalties, and duties to one another. Unlike capitalism, wages do not exist in slave or feudal economic systems. Capitalism is also different in that no person is another person's property. However, the three systems share the characteristic that they all operate in the form of "private" or "free" enterprises in "free" or "unregulated" markets. Wolff (2020b) suggests that "the dualistic employer/employee definition of capitalism suggests affinities with the parallel dualisms of slavery (master/slave) and feudalism (lord/serf)". He further argues that "the employer/employee definition suggests rather that the master/slave and lord/serf dualisms have a modern-day parallel or equivalent in the employer/employee dualism".

3.8 Concluding Remarks

Perhaps it is appropriate to allocate this concluding section to the question of whether or not COVID-19 will change prevailing thinking about the free market doctrine, even though I believe that free marketeers will stick to their guns, come what may. I know of one prominent free marketeer who changed his mind in the aftermath of the global financial crisis and declared that he was wrong. In October 2008, former Federal Reserve Chairman Alan Greenspan told a House Committee that the banking and housing crisis was a "once-in-a-century credit tsunami". When he was asked if his ideology pushed him to make bad decisions, Greenspan said that he found a "flaw" in his governing ideology that has led him to re-examine his thinking (Naylor, 2008).

In the best of times, the free market system generates substantial inequality and inflicts misery and economic destruction on the majority. The system is even more brutal and discriminatory in a crisis, like the health crisis of 2020 and beyond. We have already seen how the crisis has destroyed the welfare of millions, but at the same time, the 1% benefited enormously. This is why the governments of the countries typically preaching the free market system are claiming extraordinary powers to direct economic activity and control markets. This is essential if we are to have any hope of containing the virus and preventing a complete economic collapse. They are talking about the fair pricing, rather than the free market pricing, of the COVID-19 vaccine.

Developing (the preached) countries, on the other hand, have been told for decades by fat men wearing suits and ties and residing in Washington (the IMF's free market gurus) that they do not need any control over their economies and that they should refrain from establishing welfare states. Those fat men tell the finance ministers that free markets deliver milk and honey, but for that they must "reform". If anything, it is the fat men in suits and ties who need to reform their thoughts and stop preaching the free market system.

Will this happen in a post-corona world? I doubt that, and I will take one example of the conservative Australian Treasurer, Josh Frydenberg, who in the midst of the COVID-19 crisis took inspiration from his role models, Margaret Thatcher and Ronald Reagan, suggesting that they "dealt very successfully with the challenges that they faced" and that "they are figures of hate for the left because they were so successful" (Foley, 2020). In response, the *Sunday Morning Herald* (which published the "Frydenberg Declaration") was bombarded with letters, some of which appeared in the 28 July issue. One reader commented by saying the following:

> Treasurer Josh Frydenberg's calls for old nostrums rather than grasping the many innovative ideas available, such as building public housing, turbo-charging renewable energy projects and establishing a living income for all job-seekers not in full-time work, will create winners but many more losers. It's a retreat to ideology when fresh thinking is required.

Another reader said that Thatcher and Reagan were successful at transferring wealth from the poor to the rich. Another said that the duo may have produced stronger economies if a strong economy is measured in terms of the stock market and giant financial corporations, but "if you believe the economy should operate for the benefit of the majority within a cohesive society, then they were an unmitigated disaster with the ramifications still being felt today". Last, but not least, a reader wrote that "instead of channeling his inner Thatcher and Reagan, the Treasurer might think about negative gearing, franking credits and fuel excise subsidies, which collectively cost the taxpayer more than $30 billion a year". That is worthwhile, as far as Frydenberg is concerned, because these benefits go to the rich. With people like him running the financial affairs of a country, I have lost hope. The likes of Josh will always be around to praise Thatcher and Reagan and shout "long live economic freedom".

Chapter 4

The First Commandment: Fiscal Discipline

4.1 Introduction

In his description of the first commandment of the Consensus (that of fiscal discipline), Williamson (1990) starts by saying that "Washington believes in fiscal discipline". To support this proposition, he mentions that "Congress enacted Gramm-Rudman-Hollings with a view to restoring a balanced budget by 1993" and that "presidential candidates deplore budget deficits before and after being elected". He also said that the IMF "has long made the restoration of fiscal discipline a central element of the high-conditionality programs it negotiates with its members that wish to borrow". In reality, successive US presidents have demonstrated insatiable appetite for spending and debt to serve the interests of corporate Washington, particularly the military-industrial complex and Wall Street. Unlike what Williamson said about US presidents disliking deficits, they actually love them. I wonder if he has changed his mind since the early 1990s as the budget deficit and public debt have mushroomed.

Fiscal discipline is definitely one area where Washington does not practice what it preaches. There is nothing new about the IMF demanding and imposing, not negotiating, fiscal discipline, as we saw in Chapter 2. Fiscal discipline is the first commandment for the very simple reason that the IMF has been preaching that to demonize the public sector—after all, Williamson formulated the ten commandments on the basis of the policies imposed by the IMF on borrowing countries (for their own good, of course). Let us start by showing how fiscal discipline is a very clear case of preaching without practicing, at least on the part of political Washington.

4.2 The Meaning of Fiscal Discipline

Williamson (1990) does not sound sure as to what is meant by "fiscal discipline" and what is required to be "fiscally disciplined" as he refers to "differences of view... as to whether fiscal discipline need necessarily imply a balanced budget". One view is that a deficit is acceptable as long as it does not result in a rising public debt-to-GDP ratio. This can only happen if GDP rises by more than the amount of debt needed to finance the deficit or if the deficit is financed by printing money. An even "more relaxed criterion" involves the subtraction of the part of increased debt that has a counterpart in productive public capital formation, simply requiring no increase in the net liabilities of the public sector relative to GDP. Another criterion is that a balanced budget, or a constant public debt-to-GDP ratio, should be a minimal medium-run target and that short-run deficits and surpluses around the target should be used for the purpose of macroeconomic stabilization. Williamson admits, however, that Washington regards this criterion as "too Keynesian", notwithstanding the fact that for Washington "Keynesian" is regarded as a term of abuse because it implies big government.

Problems are associated with the measurement of the fiscal deficit, typically in nominal terms, as the excess of government expenditure over revenue. In the 1980s, the IMF started thinking in terms of "operational deficit", which includes in expenditure only the real component of interest paid on public debt. Tanzi (1989) notes that the IMF has been using the "primary deficit", a concept that excludes all interest payments, because it includes only items that are in principle directly controllable by the authorities. Williamson refers to "questionable practices" that seem to involve understatement of the true deficit, including the exclusion of contingent expenditure and the interest subsidies provided by the central bank, the recording of privatization proceeds as revenues, and the exclusion of the build-up of future liabilities of the social security system.

Therefore, significant differences exist on the interpretation of fiscal discipline. However, Williamson (1990) argues that "there is very broad agreement in Washington that large and sustained fiscal deficits are a primary source of macroeconomic dislocation in the forms of inflation, payments deficits, and capital flight". A fiscal deficit, according to Williamson, arises because of a "lack of the political courage or honesty to match public expenditures and the resources available to finance them". Evidence for lack of fiscal discipline, according to Williamson, is an operational deficit in excess of around 1–2% of GDP unless the excess is used to finance productive infrastructure investment.

4.3 The US Fiscal Deficit

In the fiscal year 2019–2020, which ended on 30 September 2020, the US government spent $6.6 trillion, while revenue was $3.3 trillion, which means that the fiscal deficit was $3.3 trillion, the biggest gap on record. This huge rise in the deficit is due to the massive discretionary spending that came in response to the COVID-19 pandemic. Prior to the onset of the pandemic, it was expected that the deficit would be $1,085 billion in 2020 and $1,192 billion in 2030 (Office of Management and Budget, 2020).

However, the deficit cannot be blamed only on the pandemic because deficit spending is endemic to Washington. In Figure 4.1, we can see the

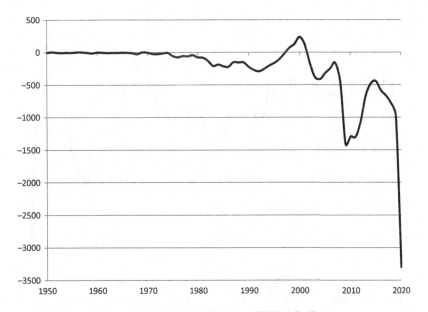

Figure 4.1:   US Fiscal Balance (Billion Dollars)

fiscal balance in billion dollars over the period 1950–2020, showing how things have changed since Williamson wrote about US fiscal discipline in 1990. As a matter of fact, a budget surplus was recorded between 1998 and 2001, until George Bush Junior restored the deficit because he wanted to fight wars, go to Mars and cut taxes (for the rich) at the same time. In 2009, Barack Obama took the deficit to over $1 trillion for the first time as he bailed out failed financial institutions during the global financial crisis. The budget situation improved during the recovery that followed the Great Recession, but Trump took the deficit back to almost $1 trillion in 2019 as a result of increased military spending and tax cuts. The COVID-19 pandemic led to the record deficit of 2020. Figure 4.2 shows a more or less similar trajectory for the fiscal deficit as a percentage of GDP.

We can see clearly that the budget deficit is caused by actions taken for the benefit of corporate Washington and the 1% oligarchy. Deficits are caused by tax cuts, typically intended for lower corporate income tax and marginal tax rates for the super-rich. Deficits are caused by increasing military expenditure, which boosts the incomes of war profiteers, as individuals and corporations. Deficits are caused by rising expenditure to bail out failed companies for the benefit of incompetent executives. One has

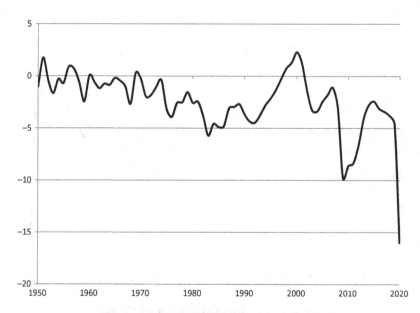

Figure 4.2:   US Fiscal Balance (% of GDP)

to remember that all of these beneficiaries (the super-rich, war profiteers, Wall Streeters, etc.) are big campaign donors.

Even the huge deficit resulting from the fiscal expansion made necessary by COVID-19 mostly benefited the super-rich by boosting the stock market and subsidizing large companies. In April 2020, President Trump signed on a bill for the provision of a $2 trillion relief package to provide cash payments to tens of millions of Americans, immediate relief to small businesses, and expanded unemployment benefits for some of those who are out of work while much of the country was under stay-at-home orders. However, the bill also includes a $500 billion fund to bail out big corporations. Barber and Theoharis (2020) comment on the bail-out fund as follows: "Americans who are desperate for aid from their government could not get it without paying a 25% surcharge to the rich and powerful".

The growing deficit is caused by fiscal profligacy: too much spending relative to tax revenue, and it is also the wrong kind of spending as the lion's share of the "kitty" goes to the military. It is ironic that Washington preaches fiscal discipline, which requires balanced budget when it is in fact less fiscally disciplined in terms of the budget deficit than developing countries that are typically preached to curtail the deficit as a component of IMF conditionality. Figure 4.3 displays some international comparisons in terms of the fiscal balance as a percentage of GDP. We can see that the US is less fiscally disciplined than some impoverished countries such as the Congo, countries that have been in financial trouble (such as Greece) and other countries that are typically accused of being financially undisciplined (such as the "stans", Honduras, Colombia, Mexico and Iran). Why is it that one of the most financially undisciplined countries in the world takes the moral high ground and preaches, via the IMF, fiscal discipline?

This is a remarkable example of preaching without practicing. While a developing country that needs to run a deficit for a transitory period is told not do so by the IMF, the preacher persists in running chronic deficits because of addiction to military spending, the desire to boost the net worth of the one percenters, and commitment to preserving the bonuses of the Wall Streeters. This is an irony of the first commandment.

4.4 The Deficit as an Indicator of Lack of Fiscal Discipline

One would have to wonder whether it is justifiable to worry too much about the fiscal deficit to the extent that deficit implies lack of discipline.

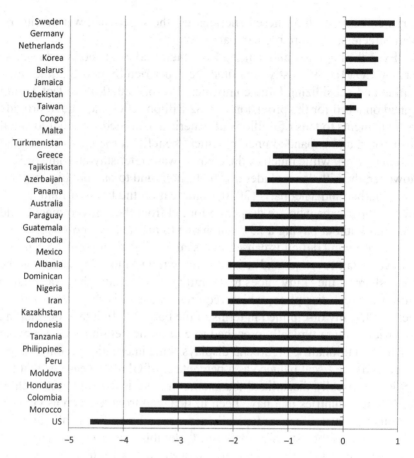

Figure 4.3:   Fiscal Balance as a Percentage of GDP

Whether or not the fiscal deficit is harmful has been debated for a long time. In the early1980s, the US went through what Rauch (1989) calls "fiscal adventurism" when the deficit more than doubled to a startling $185 billion between 1981 and 1984 as Ronald Reagan embarked on a massive military spending spree. At that time, Charles Schultze, who had been the Chairman of the Council of Economic Advisers under President Jimmy Carter, dismissed the proposition that the deficit would cause a crisis, arguing that, with proper macroeconomic management, "there would be no depression, no collapse, no caving in of the economic roof under the weight of the spectacular near-doubling of the national debt in only four years". Rauch (1989) suggests that deficit mongering was unjustifiable by going back to the time of Herbert Hoover in the 1930s. This is what he says:

> In the 1930s Herbert Hoover blamed the budget deficit for prolonging the Depression; in the 1970s people blamed it for inflation. Earlier in this decade people said that the budget deficit would drive up interest rates and abort the economic recovery, and that it would overstimulate the economy and re-ignite inflation; they have accused it of pushing up the dollar, and more recently of making the dollar weak. They have said that it would certainly bring upon us a day of reckoning of one kind or another—a recession, a world financial crash, a big inflation, a crunching of the standard of living. Everybody waited. Nothing happened.

Chakravarty (2018) explains the reasons for believing that a high fiscal deficit is bad for the economy on the grounds that it leads to inflation if it is financed by a monetary expansion and to "crowding out" of private investment if it is financed by borrowing. He goes on to undermine the underlying arguments against deficit spending by suggesting that inflation would be produced by monetary expansion only if output is fixed when demand for goods and services rises—this would happen only if resources are fully employed and factories are running at full capacity. Under these conditions, a fiscal expansion financed by monetary expansion will revive the economy, particularly if it is transitory and the new money is spent on infrastructure rather than importing arms. Even money spent on transfer payments can revive the economy if it is allocated to people with a high marginal propensity to consume, such as the unemployed. A poor country may find itself in a position to run a deficit for the purpose of buying fertilizers, in which case the deficit will pay off in the long run. Almost every government that follows Washington resorted to fiscal expansion and deficit spending to counterbalance the effects of COVID-19.

The proposition, that a high fiscal deficit that is financed by borrowing "crowds out" private investment, is based on the assumption that private investment is always better than public investment. The underlying idea is that a high public demand for loanable funds puts upward pressure on interest rates, consequently reducing private investment. The other implausible assumption in this case is that investment is interest elastic when in fact it is not—this is yet another lesson that we have learned from COVID-19. Moreover, an increase in the demand for loanable funds puts upward pressure on the interest rate only if supply is fixed. On the other hand, a fiscal deficit may "crowd in" private investment when aggregate demand rises as a result of a higher level of government purchases.

Thoma (2011) argues that a fiscal deficit has good, bad and ugly features. The good side is that a fiscal stimulus is more likely to revive the economy than interest rate cuts. The effect may work through pump priming (a fiscal stimulus that prompts private spending). Deficit spending allows countries to buy the infrastructure that they might not be able to afford if it had to be financed all at once, just like households borrow to purchase consumer durables and homes. It is strange that neoliberal economic systems are based on debt—yet, the very same people who glorify this system argue against deficit spending.

The bad, according to Thoma (2011), is crowding out, which happens when the government competes with the private sector for a share of the available loanable funds to finance its deficit spending, but he adds that eventually it hurts economic growth, which depends on private investment. Thoma goes on to make use of the "undisputed fact of life" that "the private sector is more efficient than the public sector", which leads to misallocation of resources. This is a widespread myth (see, for example, Moosa, 2020). At least Thoma admits that "in the case of public goods government can be the more efficient provider, and hence it is not always the case that efficiency falls". The other bad part is the possibility of inflation, which has already been dealt with.

The ugly part, according to Thoma, is the accumulation of debt and the possibility of default. The true ugly part, which for some reason Thoma classifies as "good", is that deficit spending can be used to finance war, even though he qualifies his statement by saying that "whether this is a good or a bad depends upon your view of whether the war is just". A low interest rate environment is ugly because it makes it easy to finance wars of aggression under the pretext of the Cheney doctrine (that the US should attack any country suspected, with a 1% confidence level, of conspiring against it).

In conclusion, Thoma suggests that in the short run, the consequences of deficits are mostly positive when the economy is in a recession because deficit spending can stimulate investment through crowding in when there is little danger that the spending will drive up interest rates or be inflationary due to the large amount of spare capacity in the economy. In the longer run, however, budget deficits can be problematic. Thus, he recommends the use of deficit spending to ease the effects of a recession or avoid making conditions worse by reducing spending or raising taxes before the economy is on better footing. Thus, he notes, "reducing the deficit before the economy is on solid footing can be counterproductive as it could slow the recovery or even cause a setback".

4.5   Washington as a Role Model

The first commandment of the Washington Consensus can hurt developing countries if they are told to balance the budget on an annual basis. It is not the deficit per se but what the deficit is used to finance. And it is not an odd cyclical deficit but rather a chronic deficit that hurts. Washington the preacher has a chronic deficit that is used to finance wars and boost the net worth of the oligarchy. It follows that Washington is not in a position to preach the first commandment.

Washington allows itself to use deficit spending to get out of recession, to get out of crises, and to finance wars of aggression. On the other hand, developing countries under IMF conditionality are denied this privilege but instead they are urged to adopt austerity. Fiscal deficits are not necessarily harmful, so why is it that right-wing economists and free marketeers are totally against deficit spending under any condition? Chakravarty (2018) provides an interesting answer by citing Michael Kalecki as saying "if the government can induce prolonged state of full employment, through fiscal deficit, then it undermines the importance of big business and the hold they have over government policy and an economy". This is why private enterprises can and should indulge in deficit spending but the public sector should not do that. It is the efficiency of the private sector relative to the public sector all over again. This is a point that we will return to when privatization is considered in Chapter 11.

The Heritage Foundation uses "fiscal health" as a component of its economic freedom index, suggesting that fiscal health deteriorates with widening deficits and a growing debt burden, reflecting poor government budget management. However, the very figures provided by the Foundation show no close connection between economic growth and the index of fiscal health. In Figure 4.4, we can see a scatter plot of GDP growth as a 5 year average on the fiscal health index. We can see almost zero correlation and that high scores on fiscal health may be associated with high or low growth. For example, Uzbekistan has a score of 98.9 and a high growth rate of 7.8%. Macau, on the other hand, has a score of 99.9

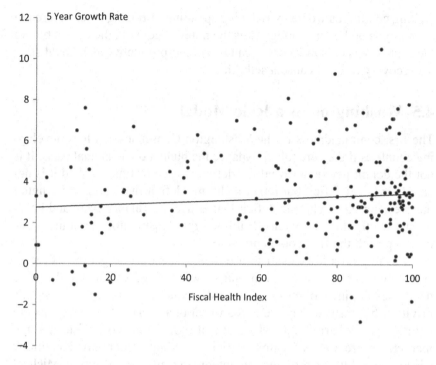

Figure 4.4:   Economic Growth as a Function of Fiscal Health

and a negative growth rate of −1.8%. Paraguay has a low score of 2.8, yet a respectable growth rate of 4.2%. Brazil has a low score of 4.6 and a negative growth rate of −0.8%. In Figure 4.5, we can see that the US has a lower fiscal health index than some countries that are typically told to do something about their fiscal health as part of the IMF conditionality.

According to the first commandment, a fiscal deficit is bad, but it is applied with the attitude of "do as I say", not "do as I do". No distinction is made between structural and cyclical deficit or between a short-run deficit, which may be useful, and a long-run deficit, which can bring about the problem of excessive debt accumulation. No consideration is given to what deficit spending is on: deficit spending to build a dam or to buy fertilizers is rewarding, but nothing can be worse than deficit spending on imported arms. No consideration is given to the principle of the Ricardian equivalence that the economy is little affected by whether a given level of government spending is financed entirely by current taxes or by some feasible combination of taxes and borrowing.

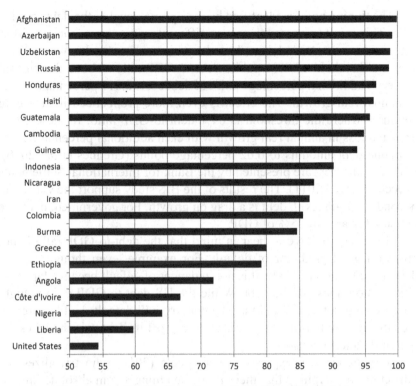

Figure 4.5:   The Heritage Foundation's Fiscal Health Index

4.6 Accumulation of Debt

Perhaps the most serious effect of fiscal deficits is the accumulation of debt. However, as in the case of deficit, debt may be useful—after all, debt is required to finance deficit spending on the infrastructure and fertilizers. The literature on the pros and cons of debt and the optimal level of debt is enormous—so, let us take a look briefly at this literature. In the short run, public debt is a good way for countries to get extra funds to invest in capital formation, which should boost economic growth. Unfortunately, governments tend to take on too much debt because the benefits make them popular with voters. Increasing debt allows political leaders to increase spending without raising taxes. A rising debt-to-GDP ratio indicates that the ability of the underlying country to pay back its debt is diminishing, prompting investors to demand a higher risk premium, thus raising the cost of borrowing.

The tipping point is identified by the optimal level of the debt-to-GDP ratio. This is not an exact science, so different studies have reached different conclusions. A study conducted by economists at the World Bank shows a threshold of 77% public debt-to-GDP ratio—above this threshold, each additional percentage point of debt costs 0.017 percentage points of annual real growth. The effect is even more pronounced in emerging countries where the threshold is 64% debt-to-GDP ratio. In these countries, the loss in annual real growth with each additional percentage point in public debt amounts to 0.02 percentage points (Grennes *et al.*, 2010). Different numbers are presented by the Bank for International Settlements (Cecchetti *et al.*, 2011). The results of the BIS study support the view that, beyond a certain level, debt is a drag on growth. For government debt, the threshold is around 85% of GDP.

However, we have to bear in mind that the debt-to-GDP ratio is not always a good predictor of default. For example, even though Japan's debt-to-GDP ratio is 228%, it is not in danger of default because Japanese citizens hold most of the debt. While the US debt-to-GDP ratio is high, investors are not concerned that the country will default. Unlike Greece, the US can simply print more dollars to pay off its debt, which makes the risk of default rather low.

Another view is expressed by Coppola (2018) who trivializes the impact of debt, arguing that there is no such thing as "an absolute limit to the amount of debt that a government can issue". In this sense, the perceived risk of default makes politicians opt for austerity rather than more debt, in the process failing to restore economies damaged by economic contraction. Instead, Coppola (2018) argues that governments in good standing do not repay debt—rather they refinance it. It follows that what matters is not the debt-to-GDP ratio but rather the debt service cost. Debt can be sustainable if interest payments can be paid comfortably from current income.

The view that debt is not the problem it is portrayed to have been put forward by Lerner (1943) who argued that a government should adjust its deficit so as to set aggregate demand at full employment, thereby eliminating both unemployment and inflation. A policy like this would produce mushrooming debt, but for Lerner this will not necessarily lead to default or inflation. He suggested that default can be avoided by printing money to cover interest payments. In turn, he argued, inflation can be avoided by raising taxes. In essence, Lerner proposed a macroeconomic policy architecture involving money printing to avoid default and taxation to avoid inflation. Leão (2015) proposes a policy prescription that differs from Lerner's in two aspects: it envisions a different way of preventing a very high public debt from ending in default, and it eliminates the burden associated with levying taxes to meet interest payments on debt (in one word, it eliminates the burden altogether).

Cross-sectional evidence using the Heritage Foundation data (Miller *et al.*, 2020) shows no close association between the ratio of debt to GDP and the 5 year growth rate, as shown in Figure 4.6. Overall correlation is statistically insignificant. We can see that a country like Greece, with a debt-to-GDP ratio of 183, has been growing at 0.7% and a country like Bhutan, with a ratio of 103, has been growing at an average rate of 6.1%. On the other hand, Brunei has a ratio of 2.5, yet experiencing a growth rate of −0.9%. But then the Congo has been growing at 5.2% with a ratio of 15.7. A systematic relationship is simply not there—some countries handle their debt properly and others do not.

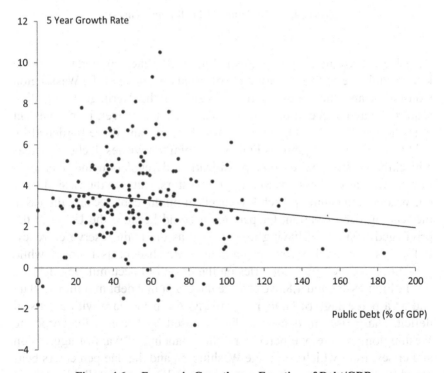

Figure 4.6: Economic Growth as a Function of Debt/GDP

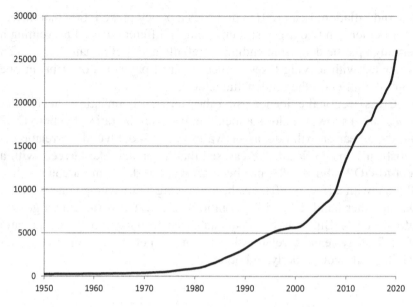

Figure 4.7:   US Public Debt (Billion Dollars)

Like everything else in life, including good wine, "moderation" is the key word. It seems that the principle of fiscal discipline of the Washington Consensus and the index of fiscal health of the Heritage Foundation require the avoidance of debt by all means. This, however, is inconsistent with the fact that developing countries short of capital are burdened by debt to force them to jump as high as Washington wishes. Debt is used as a blackmail instrument to force privatization, deregulation and liberalization, as well as concessions to foreign investors. But like the case of deficit, Washington cannot preach low levels of public debt because the US is the leading debtor nation. Or perhaps it could because the US is in the privileged position of having its currency as the main reserve currency. It follows that the US can accumulate as much debt as it could while preaching to developing countries on the hazard of accumulating debt.

In Figures 4.7 and 4.8, we can see the US public debt in billion dollars and as a percentage of GDP, respectively. As in the case with the fiscal deficit, sharp rises in debt have been caused by tax cuts for corporate Washington and the one percenters, the financing of wars of aggression and crises, from which corporate Washington and the one percenters benefited (the global financial crisis and the COVID-19 crisis). Public debt as

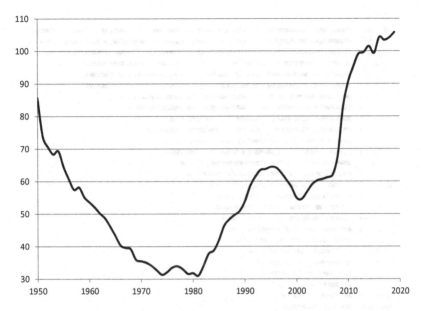

Figure 4.8:   US Public Debt-to-GDP Ratio (%)

a percentage of GDP fell rapidly in the post-World War II period, and reached a low in 1973 under President Richard Nixon. Since then, it has grown consistently, except during the terms of presidents Jimmy Carter and Bill Clinton. Public debt rose during the 1980s, as President Reagan cut tax rates while boosting military spending. It fell during the 1990s, due to declining military spending, higher taxes and the 1990s boom.

In the early 21st century, the ratio of debt held by the public relative to GDP rose again due in part to the Bush tax cuts, increased military spending (caused by the wars in the Middle East) and a new entitlement Medicare D program. Public debt rose sharply in the wake of the 2007–2008 financial crisis, which produced a significant decline in tax revenue and a higher level of spending. During the Obama and Trump years, public debt continued to rise because of the financing of wars, bailing out failed corporations and tax cuts. Then came COVID-19, which caused a rise of a different magnitude. By April 2020, public debt had reached the level of $24 trillion, and by June it was $26 trillion, pushing the debt-to-GDP ratio to 136%. As shown in Figure 4.9, the US has a higher public debt-to-GDP ratio than improvised countries that are typically told to be more fiscally disciplined.

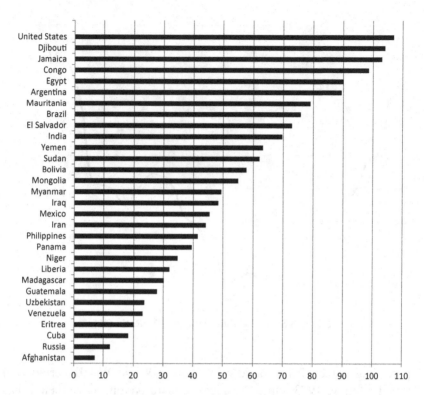

Figure 4.9:   Country Ranking According to Public Debt-to-GDP Ratio

4.7 Fiscal Discipline and Bankruptcy

Two questions are raised in this section: whether the US is fiscally disciplined and whether it is bankrupt. The answer to the first question is in the negative, in the light of the figures we have seen. The view that the US lacks fiscal discipline seems to be held widely. In a letter to *Financial Times*, Willem Thorbecke (Senior Fellow, Research Institute of Economy, Trade and Industry, Tokyo) says the following (Thorbecke, 2017):

The danger to the bond market now, however, is not from inflation. President Donald Trump has increased prospective budget deficits, and these will raise the US trade deficit. Foreigners financing US deficits could resist holding ever-increasing shares of their wealth in US bonds and demand higher interest rates. The recessionary impulse would be immune to expansionary monetary and fiscal policy and would raise unemployment. To prevent this, the US should pursue fiscal discipline and a fairly valued dollar now.

The lack of fiscal discipline on the part of the US federal government is not a new phenomenon—rather, it has been endemic. Back in the 1980s, the Advisory Commission on Intergovernmental Relations (1987) found that while deficit spending reached major economic peacetime proportions only in recent years, it has been a regular feature of federal fiscal policy for the previous 56 years. The Commission called for the implementation of "institutional controls that establish limits on political decisions pertaining to budgetary matters".

It is not only that the US government does not practice fiscal discipline; it practices fiscal profligacy at a pace that makes it comparable to the Roman Empire, which collapsed as a result of profligacy among other factors. As the US public debt reached $22 trillion in 2019, Salter (2019) wrote that "Congress has once again demonstrated its commitment to fiscal profligacy". Profligacy is not only indicated by debt but also by the fiscal deficit and unfunded liabilities for Social Security, Medicare, and Medicaid. Salter argues that "runaway spending has long been a problem at the federal level" and cites the warning of the Government Accountability Office, a non-partisan agency that advises Congress, of "serious economic, security, and social challenges" if deficit spending is not brought under control. Likewise, Boccia (2020) suggests that "Washington's profligacy and lack of a credible commitment to fiscal responsibility also threatens the country's valuable status as the supplier of the world's primary reserve currency: the U.S. dollar". Back in 2013, Schneider (2013) made the following declaration: "It's official. The United States is a profligate nation".

It is even worse than "fiscally undisciplined" and "profligate" because some observers believe that the US is simply bankrupt. If the definition of bankruptcy is insolvency in the sense that liabilities exceed assets, which makes the net worth negative, then the US is definitely bankrupt. In Figure 4.10, we can see the assets and liabilities of the US government as of 30 September 2018 as published by the US Government Accountability Office. We can see that the gap in the balance sheet is $21.5 trillion. This unsustainable position is sustained temporarily because the US is managing to service its debt by borrowing just to pay interest, and because the Federal Reserve keeps printing money.

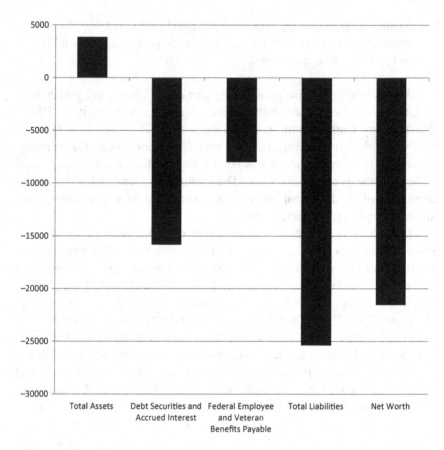

Figure 4.10:   US Government Assets and Liabilities (As of 30 September 2018)

Even without referring to numbers like these, some observers believe that the US is approaching bankruptcy because the printing press of the Fed cannot salvage the situation for ever. This is why DeRensis (2018) talks about the "coming bankruptcy of the American Empire" and cites Senator Rand Paul as saying that "bankruptcy is the Sword of Damocles hanging perilously close to Uncle Sam's neck".

Another measure of bankruptcy is used by Patton (2012) who thinks that the US government has been bankrupt for some time. The measure he uses is what he calls the debt to income ratio, where debt is defined to include the liability from Social Security and Medicare while income is simply tax revenue. Based on the figures available in 2012, Patton estimated the debt-to-income ratio to be somewhere around 5,082%. He asserts that no bank would grant a loan to any individual with a similar debt-to-income ratio—someone would be in a position like this by having 24 credit cards, all of which are up to the limit with an annual income of $75,000.

A prominent economist who has worked extensively on the issue of US bankruptcy, Laurence Kotlikoff, thinks that Uncle Sam is bankrupt. Konish (2018) quotes Laurence Kotlikoff as saying that "the evidence is in front of our eyes that we're bankrupt", asserting that America is bankrupt now, not in the future. Kotlikoff believes that what matters is not the budget deficit or national debt but rather the fiscal gap—the present value of future spending (including debt service) less future tax revenue. Kotlikoff (2011) puts the fiscal gap at a staggering $202 trillion, almost 14 times GDP (Greece, by comparison, has a fiscal gap of about 11 times GDP). He suggests that "to close the US fiscal gap would require raising all federal taxes, immediately and permanently by almost two thirds". Davies and Harrigan (2018) report projections showing that social security will be insolvent in 2034 and Medicare in 2026. They rationalize their prediction in terms of the federal government and its "seemingly insatiable habit of spending money it doesn't have", suggesting that "there isn't really anywhere else in the world that has the amount of money the US government needs to borrow".

4.8 Concluding Remarks

The first commandment of the Washington Consensus is that of fiscal discipline, which is imposed on developing countries for the simple purpose of demonizing the state and the public sector for the benefit of corporate Washington. We have seen that while a preacher must practice what is preached, this rule does not apply to those preaching to developing countries on the benefits of fiscal discipline. This does not mean that fiscal discipline in a true sense is not desirable. It is, however, unlikely that the IMF and World Bank want developing countries to be fiscally disciplined because the objective is to get them so much in debt that eventually they yield to demands for liberalization, deregulation and privatization.

In a Wold Bank document, Schick (1998) describes the basic elements of public expenditure management, which is essential for being fiscally disciplined. These elements are listed as "aggregate fiscal discipline", "allocative efficiency and "operational efficiency". The description of aggregate fiscal discipline requires the budget totals to be the following: (i) the result of explicit, enforced decisions; (ii) they should not merely accommodate spending demands; (iii) the totals should be set before individual spending decisions are made; and (iv) they should be sustainable over the medium-term and beyond. None of these characteristics are valid for the US budget in general and military expenditure in particular—the Pentagon gets what it wants, any time. The rules, roles and information required for enforcing aggregate fiscal discipline cannot be found in the US budget. The World Bank document also specifies the aggregate fiscal discipline problems of some developing countries, including unrealistic budgeting, hidden budgeting, escapist budgeting, repetitive budgeting, cash-box budgeting and deferred budgeting. All of these problems are found in the setting of the US budget.

Developing countries have budgetary problems, not necessarily because of the lack of discipline but because some of them are very poor. Lack of discipline implies that these countries have open access to debt, but they cannot resist accumulating more and more. This is not true. The preacher is not in a position to preach when it is by far less fiscally disciplined than the preached.

Chapter 5

The Second Commandment: Redirection of Public Spending

5.1 The Second Commandment as Described by Williamson

Fiscal discipline requires a reduction of the fiscal deficit and consequently debt. The deficit can be reduced either by boosting revenue (raising taxes) or by cutting expenditure. According to Williamson (1990), Washington prefers expenditure reduction, but, he notes, "it is not clear that this preference is very strong outside of right-wing political circles (including the right-wing think tanks)". This preference comes as no surprise because tax hikes are bad for the rich and good for the poor whereas expenditure reduction is bad for the poor and does not affect the rich. However, corporate Washington does not like declining government orders, particularly for expensive military hardware. Therefore, if expenditure must be cut, it has to be done selectively, targeting mainly health, education and welfare.

The second commandment is about the composition of government expenditure—this is at least how Williamson sees it. It pertains to three major expenditure categories on which views are held strongly: subsidies, education and health, and public investment. According to the second commandment, as portrayed by Williamson, subsidies (particularly "indiscriminate" subsidies) are regarded as "prime candidates for reduction or preferably elimination". This is a typical policy prescription imposed by the IMF on borrowing countries, and it is also the main reason for the eruption of IMF riots. Williamson (1990) justifies this proposition as follows:

> Everyone has horror stories about countries where subsidized gasoline is cheaper than drinking water, or where subsidized bread is so cheap that it is fed to pigs, or where telephone calls cost a cent or so because someone forgot (or lacked the courage) to raise prices to keep pace with inflation, or where subsidized "agricultural credit" is designed to buy the support of powerful landowners, who promptly recycle the funds to buy government paper. The result is not just a drain on the budget but also much waste and resource misallocation, with little reason to expect any offset from systematically favorable effects on income distribution, at least where indiscriminate subsidies are concerned.

Williamson does not mention anything about how the elimination of subsidies creates poverty, hunger and eventually riots—these are the horror stories that he chooses to overlook. The 1977 bread riots in Egypt were caused by the quadrupling over night of the price of bread. In 2003, the IMF recommended the removal of all subsidies in occupied Iraq, even following the devastation inflicted by two military campaigns and years of brutal sanctions (all done to save the Iraqi people from a brutal dictator!). Of course, that came with the call to privatize the oil sector, a lethal combination for the impoverished Iraqi citizens and a lucrative opportunity for the multinationals and oligarchs who would buy the privatized assets and sell the products at market-determined prices that maximize profit. Washington hates subsidies, not because they represent inefficiency or distort the price mechanism, but rather because subsidies benefit the poor. The objective is always to make the poor poorer and the rich richer.

Williamson defends expenditure on education and health on the grounds that they represent investment in human capital. His approval of this kind of expenditure is justified on the grounds that it is beneficial for the "disadvantaged". It is rather strange that expenditure on education and health helps the disadvantaged but subsidies do not. Then it is not clear how the disadvantaged will be helped in the Washington model, given preference for private schools and hospitals. Williamson asserts that "many in Washington believe that expenditures need to be redirected toward education and health in general, and most especially in a way that will benefit the disadvantaged". This sounds good, but it is never put to practice. IMF conditionality, as we have seen, has a negative impact on social spending.

Williamson suggests that "the other area of public expenditure that Washington regards as productive is public infrastructure investment". This is right, but it is at odds with two beliefs held by Washington: the size of the public sector should be limited, and the private sector is more efficient than the public sector. Countries under IMF conditionality typically lack high-quality infrastructure because what comes first is the allocation of funds toward the repayment of debt to the IMF and international bankers. Williamson seems to be happy with the treatment of military expenditure as a high priority area, not because it represents productive investment but because it is a source of lucrative business for the military industry. Go no further than occupied Iraq, which is pouring billions of dollars in the acquisition of arms while the electricity grid is still damaged, more than 17 years after the Bush–Blair "liberation" of the country.

For Williamson, policy reform with respect to public expenditure requires the switching of expenditure from subsidies toward education and health (particularly to benefit the disadvantaged) and infrastructure investment. To his credit, Williamson notes that there are circumstances under which carefully targeted subsidies can be a useful instrument. What happens on the ground, as dictated by Washington through the IMF, is completely different: switching money from health and education toward the military and the payment of accumulated debt. This does not only happen in developing countries blessed by the Washington Consensus, but also in Washington itself.

5.2 The Structure of US Public Expenditure

In this section, it is demonstrated once more that Washington does not practice what it preaches, this time with respect to public expenditure. US public spending consists of mandatory spending and discretionary spending. Mandatory spending, which is required by prior Acts of Congress, covers social security, Medicare, and Medicaid, and other mandatory programs (such as food stamps, unemployment compensation, child nutrition, child tax credits, supplemental security income, and student loans). Interest payments on public debt are not mandatory, but they have to be made to avoid default and maintain faith in the ability of the US government to meet its financial obligations. What we are interested in here, for the purpose of discussing the second commandment, is discretionary spending, which is allocated every year for spending by federal government agencies. The idea is that for Washington to preach the second commandment (of redirecting government expenditure to health, education and infrastructure), one would expect Washington to practice what it preaches, but this is not the case. The majority of US government budget goes to unnecessary and wasteful military spending at the expense of health, education and infrastructure.

Consider Figure 5.1, which shows discretionary spending by government department (agency) in the 2021 budget as reported by Office of Management and Budget (2020). The Department of Defense commands

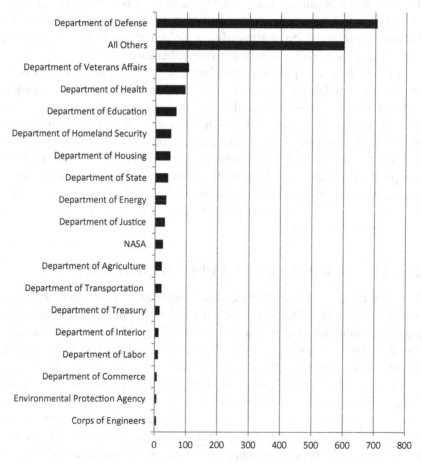

Figure 5.1:   Discretionary Spending by Department (Agency) in the 2021 Budget

the lion's share of the budget, as more is allocated to the Pentagon than all other departments put together. In the 2021 budget, $705 billion is allocated to the Pentagon, consisting of a basic budget of $636 billion and an extra allocation of $69 billion for the "overseas contingency operations" used primarily to finance the operations of the occupation forces in Iraq, Afghanistan and Syria, as well as the drones that bomb weddings and funerals in those countries. In comparison, the Department of Health gets $94.5 billion while the Department of Education receives $66.6 billion. It is not clear where the infrastructure comes in, but irrespective of that, it is too little. Even if the State Department represents diplomacy aimed at averting war, diplomacy gets loose change compared to the huge sums allocated to the war machine.

The fact of the matter, however, is that even the State Department's operations are directed at promoting war for the benefit of the military–industrial complex. The threat of using force against other countries for the purpose of regime change and otherwise is regularly used by diplomats, including the top diplomat (Secretary of State) who is more hawkish than the Secretary of Defense. In Figure 5.2, we can see the true military spending in the 2021 budget as reported by Amadeo (2020). The true military budget is $934 billion, including allocations to the Department of Veterans Affairs ($105 billion), State Department ($44 billion), Homeland Security ($50 billion), National Nuclear Security Administration ($20 billion), and Federal Bureau of Investigation (FBI) and Cybersecurity ($10 billion).

Consider now expenditure on the infrastructure. According to the American Society of Civil Engineers, America's infrastructure is desperately in need of investment. The American Society of Civil Engineers (ASCE) estimates indicate that the US needs to spend some $4.5 trillion by 2025 to fix the country's roads, bridges, dams, and other infrastructure (Thompson and Matousek, 2019). On the other hand, Turner (2019) contends that, by many measures, the infrastructure is in as good a shape as it has been for decades, or even better. Cournoyer (2019) argues that Turner's analysis is admittedly limited as he focuses on the condition of interstate highways, buses and urban rail cars, which are among the most visible public transportation assets. That leaves out a big chunk of other transportation infrastructure, from local roads to subway tracks. She cites Rocky Moretti, the Director of policy and research for TRIP, a transportation research group that often highlights the poor condition of state and federal road networks, as saying that Turner's analysis only skimmed the surface when he looked at the condition of transportation infrastructure.

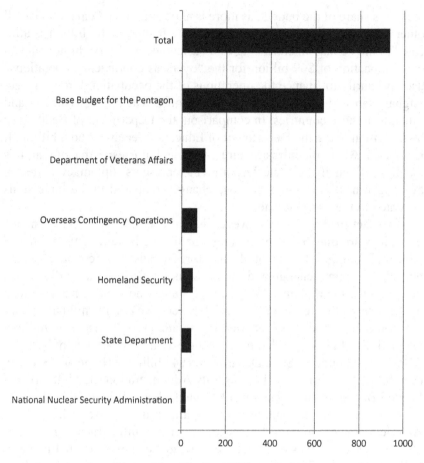

Figure 5.2:   The True Military Budget

At a hearing held on 25 September 2019, the House Budget Committee (2019) heard testimony from expert witnesses on the economic importance of infrastructure, the status and funding needs of American infrastructure, its importance in attracting investment in and building communities, and the need to repair and maintain current transportation, water and other systems while addressing new 21st century challenges. The conclusion reached was as follows: "The United States has been underinvesting in infrastructure for decades, and American families and businesses will reap the economic consequences unless the federal government undertakes a major course correction". Chairman John

Yarmuth said the following: "If we, as a Congress, want to prepare our economy and our nation for a rapidly changing future, we must dramatically improve and modernize our infrastructure".

As for health and education, look again at Figure 5.1 and compare the budgets allocated to the Department of Defense, on the one hand, and the total of what is allocated to the Department of Health and the Department of Education, on the other. The budgets allocated to health and education are no more than 23% of the budget allocated to the Department of Defense, which in any case understates the true size of military spending.

5.3 A Closer Examination of US Military Expenditure

Let us look at the size of military expenditure to answer the question whether or not it is excessive, starting with some data provided by the Stockholm International Peace Research Institute (SIPRI). In Figures 5.3–5.5, we can see a comparison of the top 10 military spenders in terms of total dollar amounts, the world share, and spending

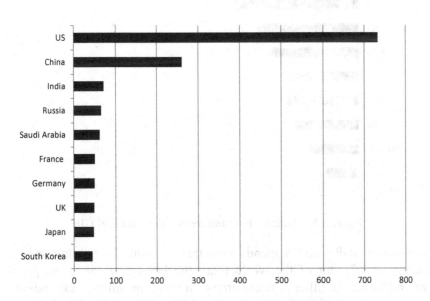

Figure 5.3: Military Expenditure in 2019 (Billion Dollars)

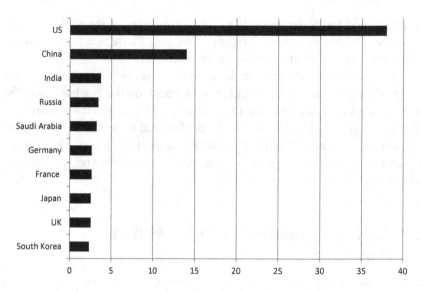

Figure 5.4:　Military Expenditure as a Percentage of World Total

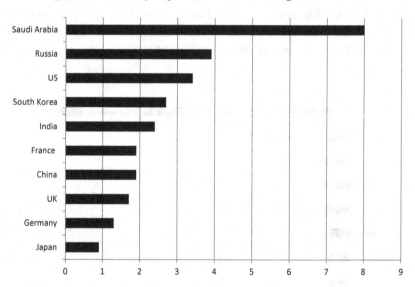

Figure 5.5:　Military Expenditure as a Percentage of GDP

relative to GDP. The US spends more than the other nine countries by a factor of 1.7. Out of the world total, the US spends 38% compared to 36.8% for the other nine countries. In terms of military expenditure as a percentage of GDP, the US comes in third place after Saudi Arabia and Russia. These are two notable exceptions because Saudi Arabia overspends on military hardware by any measure and unnecessarily. Russia, on the other hand, has to respond to NATO's (North Atlantic Treaty Organization) incursion close to its borders. It is noteworthy that NATO troops are closer to the Russian border today than the Wehrmacht was just before the initiation of Operation Barbarossa, which signaled the Nazi invasion of the Soviet Union, on 22 June 1941.

The question that we want to answer here is whether or not US military spending is excessive. According to O'Hanlon (2019), this is a controversial issue, which he attributes partly to "people on both sides of the debate using oversimplified statistics to support their position". Those who think that US military spending is excessive look at it relative to military spending of other countries and to spending by other US federal agencies. On the other hand, those who think that it is not excessive look at the ratio of military expenditure to GDP now compared to what it was during the Cold War. For example, military spending averaged 8–9% of GDP in the 1960s, declining to just under 5% in the 1970s. During the Reagan build-up of the 1980s, it reached 6% before declining somewhat as the Cold War came to an end. O'Hanlon (2019) argues that the right way to make sense of US military spending is to examine what the money is spent on and justifies it on the grounds that "we expect our military to be able to do many things at once". I wonder what he means by "we", since I do not think that this view is shared by the majority of the American people.

The 2018 National Defense Strategy, which was not drawn by "us", mentions the ability of the military to "conduct several missions simultaneously", including the following: maintaining a strong nuclear deterrent; protecting the homeland from attack by missiles, aircraft, terrorists, and others; defeating China or Russia in conventional combat and deterring North Korea while doing so; and sustaining momentum in the "war on terror". This, according to O'Hanlon (2019) is a "much more ambitious agenda than the United States had during most of the 30 years since the Berlin Wall fell, when its main strategic priorities were to be ready for possible two-front war against the likes of Iraq and North Korea". The fact of the matter is that the US has been looking for imaginary enemies to fight, in the process defending the homeland against the aggression of the mighty powers of Iraq, Afghanistan, Libya, Syria, Yemen and Venezuela.

The ability to "conduct several missions simultaneously" seems to be inspired by the neo-cons participating in the Project for the New American

Century (PNAC), a think tank, many of whose members ended up in the administration of George Bush Junior. One of the PNAC's most influential (and notorious) publications was a 90-page report entitled *Rebuilding America's Defenses: Strategies, Forces, and Resources for a New Century*, which was released in 2000 (Project for the New American Century, 2000). According to the report, current levels of military spending were inadequate, forcing policy makers "to try ineffectually to manage increasingly large risks". The true cost of not meeting defence requirements, the authors of the report argued, "will be a lessened capacity for American global leadership and, ultimately, the loss of a global security order that is uniquely friendly to American principles and prosperity".

The report recommended the establishment of four core missions for US military forces: the defence of the American homeland; the fighting and winning of "multiple, simultaneous major theatre wars"; the performance of "constabular duties associated with shaping the security environment in key regions"; and the "transformation of US forces to exploit the revolution in military affairs". The specific recommendations made by the authors of the report included the maintenance of US nuclear superiority, an increase of the active personnel strength of the military from 1.4 to 1.6 million people, the redeployment of US forces to Southeast Europe and Asia, and the selective modernization of US forces. To help achieve these aims, *Rebuilding America's Defenses* advocated a gradual increase in military spending "to a minimum level of 3.5 to 3.8 percent of gross domestic product, adding $15 billion to $20 billion to total defense spending annually".

What the report really means is that the US should use its military power to do as it pleases, initiating wars of aggression of its choice, irrespective of international law, the UN charter and international public opinion—a true manifestation of *Amerika uber alles*. This is sweet music to the ears of the military–industrial complex. What is interesting (actually, ominous), or what Gilmer *et al.* (2004) describe as "most chilling and eerie words", is that the report expresses the view that the underlying process of transformation, even if it brings revolutionary change, is "likely to be a long one, absent some catastrophic and catalyzing event—like a new Pearl Harbor". This is what John Pilger (2002) said about the report, which he refers to as a "document":

> The threat posed by US terrorism to the security of nations and individuals was outlined in prophetic detail in a document written more than two

years ago and disclosed only recently. What was needed for America to dominate much of humanity and the world's resources, it said, was "some catastrophic and catalyzing event—like a new Pearl Harbor" … The attacks of 11 September 2001 provided the "new Pearl Harbor", described as "the opportunity of ages".

The neo-cons described the 11 September attacks as an "opportunity" (not to be missed), in the sense that the event provided a pretext for America to do what it liked. Goodman (2009) explains the appetite for war in terms of the proposition that "the arms industry needs a foreign policy that preserves a level of fear and violence around the globe sufficient to sustain trillion-dollar defense budgets". He also suggests that oil and gas producers need access to energy resources around the globe, hence the need for a strong US military presence in energy-rich regions to support corporate-friendly rulers who suppress populist movements.

The fall of the Soviet Union triggered a tendency to reduce military spending, which the military–industrial complex did not like. That was countered by the emergence of new enemies, such as terrorism. The problem is that terrorism on its own is inadequate for profit maximization because it cannot be fought with expensive military hardware, such as nuclear submarines, giving the need for new enemies at a state level. As a result, new enemies have been created, including rogue states, axes of evil, and countries run by despots who "kill their own people" and the people who "hate our way of life".

Tension with a resurgent Russia and rising China are also convenient. Retired General Richard Cody, a Vice President at L-3 Communications (the seventh largest US military contractor) is quoted as telling shareholders in December 2015 that "the industry was faced with a historic opportunity" following the end of the Cold War, which resulted in a sharp decline in military budgets (Fang, 2016). The opportunity, according to Cody, was raised by a resurgent Russia, in which case, "we know that uptick is coming and so we postured ourselves for it". Fang also quotes Stuart Bradie, the Chief Executive of Kellogg Brown & Root (KBR) (a military contractor with close connection to Dick Cheney), talking about "opportunities in Europe" and highlighting the increase in military spending by NATO countries in response to "what's happening with Russia and the Ukraine".

War profiteers see the escalation of tension as providing new opportunities for boosting weapons sales and endeavor to push the political system, both directly and through industry lobby groups (such as the National Defense Industrial Association) to spend more on military hardware. Pentagon contractor-funded think tanks, such as the Lexington Institute and the Atlantic Council, have also demanded more spending in view of the "Russian threat". The election of Volodymyr Zelenskiy as the president of Ukraine in April 2019 was rather worrying for the military–industrial complex and the Trump administration as there was widespread belief that he would improve relations with Russia to stop the bloodshed in Eastern Ukraine (but that did not happen). William Hartung, director of the Arms and Security Project at the Center for International Policy, has suggested that "Russian saber-rattling has additional benefits for weapons makers because it has become a standard part of the argument for higher Pentagon spending—even though the Pentagon already has more than enough money to address any actual threat to the United States" (Fang, 2016). Hartung (2001) had argued that "if an Eisenhower could not rein in the military lobby, small wonder that Bill Clinton, perceived as a draft-evading child of the 1960s, let the Joint Chiefs have their way".

American exceptionalism has a different manifestation from what we have seen so far. Since the beginning of the 21st Century, America has been in a perpetual state of war, predominantly wars of aggression involving false flags. Another facet of American exceptionalism is that the role played by overlapping war profiteers, the military–industrial complex and the deep state in initiating and encouraging wars. For war profiteers, war is a lucrative cash cow. The damage inflicted on the people of the countries who are unlucky to be on the other side of the war (typically countries that cannot defend themselves against American military might), the devastation is simply a collateral damage or a price worth paying for democracy. According to Charpentier (2017), America has been at war 93% of the time since 1776 (222 out of 239 years), which means that America has only been at peace for less than 20 years since the country's birth. America justifiably fought a legitimate war of liberation against British imperialism, but American wars have been predominantly wars of aggression (particularly in the post-World War II period) or wars fought on false flags.

O'Hanlon (2019) concludes that "the U.S. defense budget is and will remain large relative to budgets of other countries, other federal agencies, and even other periods in American history", which he justifies by saying that US military spending is "modest as a fraction of the nation's economy, at least in comparison with the Cold War era". To make sense of the "defense" budget, one must look more closely at how "defense" dollars are spent. One can only wonder how Russia, with a small fraction of US spending, can stand up to NATO's aggression, and how an impoverished country like North Korea prevents America from taking it the Iraq way.

The fact of the matter is that waste in US military spending is monumental—the Pentagon's "missing trillions" has become a household expression. Lindorff (2018) analyzes the "Pentagon's massive accounting fraud", arguing that "the DoD's leaders and accountants have been perpetrating a gigantic, unconstitutional accounting fraud, deliberately cooking the books to mislead the Congress and drive the DoD's budgets ever higher, regardless of military necessity". Likewise, Turse (2018) wonders what happened to the $500 million, which was sent abroad for international drug wars, while Astore (2018) introduces "the new, super-expensive stealth bomber the US doesn't need". It seems that the Pentagon's job is not to defend the nation but to keep war profiteers happy and prosperous.

A completely different view is put forward by Bandow (2019) who asks the question: "How can a bankrupt republic run the world?" He undermines the pretext of "defending the nation", which he describes as easy because "America has vast oceans east and west and pacific neighbors north and south". Then he goes on to evaluate the risk coming from America's enemies. Russia, he argues, is capable of launching a serious attack on America, but it has no incentive to do so, since the result would be devastating retaliation. China's military is expanding, but it is directed at preventing Washington from dominating the People's Republic at home and in its neighborhood. And while plenty of terrorists are around, terrorism arises mostly "from maladroit U.S. policies that create enemies and make other people's conflicts America's own".

Promiscuous war-making, as suggested by Bandow, does more to accelerate than diminish terrorism. US military spending, according to him, is not intended to defend America, but rather to accomplish a variety of other objectives, such as asserting influence, remaking failed societies, dictating behavior, and promoting American values. One thing Bandow does not mention is the objective of enabling the looters and war profiteers to enrich themselves by confiscating and stealing assets that belong to others, all in the name of the free market. US military spending, he adds, has nothing to do with "protecting America—its territory, people, constitutional system, and prosperity". He concludes that military expenditure is "the price of America's aggressive foreign policy" and the desire to play "global gendarme—or gauleiter, depending upon one's location when America's bombs fall".

Bandow is right in saying that defending America is easy, unless defending America is run according to Dick Cheney's infamous "one percent doctrine", which is used to justify attacking any country that the US does not like on the grounds that any perceived threat to national security can be considered an actual attack on the US. Fein (2014) suggests that "the Cheney moral philosophy would justify attacking any nation that taught its citizens to read because literacy could lead to a mastery of high-energy physics, which could lead to developing a nuclear capability, which could lead to an imminent nuclear attack on the United States". One has to bear in mind that Cheney's Haliburton was one of the biggest beneficiaries of the application of the one percent doctrine to Iraq.

US military expenditure can be cut significantly without jeopardizing the defence of the homeland by following the advice of an American hero, General Smedley Butler, who in the 1930s proposed putting an end to what he called the "war racket" (Butler, 1935). Butler proposed to put an end to the racket by conscripting the directors and executives of armament factories, munitions makers, shipbuilders, airplane builders, and the manufacturers of all the other things that provide profit in war time as well as bankers and speculators. Another step that is necessary to smash the war racket is "the limited plebiscite to determine whether a war should be declared", provided that it is not a plebiscite of all the voters but merely of those who would be called upon to do the fighting and dying. A third step, according to Butler, is to make certain that military forces are deployed for defence only. He suggested, for example, that the ships of the US navy should be specifically limited, by law, to within 200 miles of the US coastline. It is that easy.

Dane (2015) follows Butler by concluding with the slogan "to hell with war". The waste of resources on wars that has nothing to do with defending the homeland is described very well by Dane, who says the following:

> Every hour, taxpayers in the United States are paying $312,500 for cost of military action against ISIS. Every hour, taxpayers in the United States are paying $10.17 million for cost of war in Afghanistan. Every hour, taxpayers in the United States are paying $365,297 for cost of war in Iraq. Every hour, taxpayers in the United States are paying

$10.54 million for total cost of wars since 2001. Every hour, taxpayers in the United States are paying $8.43 million for Homeland Security since 9/11. Every hour, taxpayers in the United States are paying $58 million for the Department of Defense.

The proper way to look at military expenditure and whether it is excessive is to consider the opportunity cost and effectiveness relative to the underlying objective. Excessive military expenditure is justified on the grounds of keeping America's enemies at bay, protecting the homeland and saving lives. If the objective is saving lives, then lives must be saved no matter what the cause of death is. The US lost 58,000 lives in Vietnam, which could have been avoided. Compare this figure with the number of COVID-19 deaths, which surpassed the grim milestone of 300,000 by mid-December 2020. More will die for other health-related reasons as a result of losing medical insurance with the loss of jobs. Thousands of Americans die every year, either because they do not have medical insurance or because they are denied (by insurance companies) access to healthcare on a technicality. Thousands die out of poverty and homelessness. How many lives would be saved by diverting resources away from the Pentagon to health, education and social services?

5.4 Concluding Remarks

Washington is not a role model on how to allocate public expenditure. It cannot be the guardian and custodian of the second commandment of the Washington Consensus. In any case, this commandment does not say that expenditure on health, education and the infrastructure should be financed by diverting resources away from the military. Rather, the commandment calls for the diversion of resources away from subsidies, which would only make hungry people even more hungry, eventually leading to riots, death and destruction.

IMF operations always result in diminishing expenditure on health and education, in which case the second commandment is never put into practice. This commandment (as expressed by Williamson) may, after all, be intended to no more than putting a humanitarian face to the Consensus and perhaps the IMF.

Chapter 6

The Third Commandment: Tax Reform

6.1 The Third Commandment as Described by Williamson

The third commandment of the Washington Consensus is tax reform, which is linked to the objective of boosting tax revenue as an alternative to reducing public expenditure as a remedy for fiscal deficit. At the outset, it must be made clear that the word "reform" should be taken with a big pinch of salt. It is simply change for the benefit of a minority of beneficiaries and profiteers at the expense of the majority.

Williamson (1990) argues that "most of political Washington regards them [tax increases] as an inferior alternative", but "much of technocratic Washington (with the exception of the right-wing think tanks) finds political Washington's aversion to tax increases irresponsible and incomprehensible". I thought that all of the institutions of technocratic Washington are right-wing, in the sense that they think and recommend policy in terms of free market neoliberalism. That is, unless Williamson refers to extreme right-wing think tanks.

Tax reform, according to Williamson (1990), involves the broadening of the tax base and keeping the marginal tax rates "moderate". Tax in this sense is income tax because no tax reformer in the Washington tradition would dare entertain the idea of wealth tax. Tax reform, in the Washington Consensus, is structured in such a way as to benefit the corporate sector and the rich at the expense of the poor—it is a means whereby the rich get richer and the poor get poorer. The objective of broadening the tax base, while keeping marginal tax rates moderate, is to shift more of the tax burden onto middle and low-income households. We often hear about proposals to reduce the corporate tax rate because the business sector creates jobs. We often hear that cutting taxes boosts economic growth, and that the process is self-funding as growth produces a higher level of government revenue. And we often hear that cutting taxes for the rich is good for everyone because of the trickle-down effect (that the tide carries all boats). When applied to developing countries, as recommended by the IMF, the objective of "tax reform" is to enable multinationals to get away with minimal tax payments, if any at all. Nothing is said about closing loopholes in the tax collection system so that a rich person like Donald Trump pays more than $750 in tax for a whole year, as revealed by the New York Times in September 2020 (Buettner *et al.*, 2020).

6.2 The Effect of Taxes on Growth

Tax reduction is justified on the grounds that it boosts growth and creates jobs, leading to even higher tax revenue, which means that tax reductions are self-financing. Let us examine the proposition that higher taxes retard economic growth as firmly believed by the Heritage Foundation (Miller *et al.*, 2020). On the basis of data provided by the Foundation, Figures 6.1 and 6.2 show scatter plots of the 5 year growth rate on income and corporate tax rates. No association whatsoever can be observed. We can see some extreme cases of high growth associated with high tax rates. Ireland has a growth rate of 10.5% and a personal income tax of 41%. Macau has a growth rate of −1.8% and a personal income tax rate of 12%. Bangladesh has a growth rate of 7.1% and a corporate income tax rate of 45%. And Ukraine has a growth rate of −1.6% and a corporate tax rate of 18%.

Sherman (2017) considers the research on the relation between taxes and growth conducted by government departments and agencies, think tanks, academia and private sector companies. He reaches two conclusions: (i) while tax cuts or hikes have some impact, the amount of either spurring or deterring economic growth is often exaggerated and (ii) given that the impact of tax policy is limited, there must be many other drivers of the economy. The US economy, he argues, is much more complex than just a percent change here or there in tax rates. Discussions about tax rates arouse emotions, which is why Sherman suggests that "the proverbial bottom line is that the influence of tax rates isn't as significant as the emotional response to them might suggest".

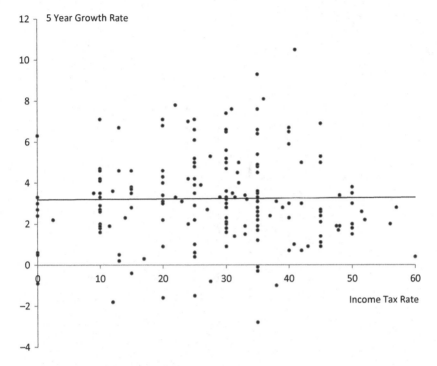

Figure 6.1:   Growth as a Function of the Income Tax Rate

The underlying theory is that tax rate hikes have adverse effects on economic activity through short-run demand-side effects and/or long-run supply-side effects. Short-run demand-side effects arise because lower disposable income leads to lower consumption and/or investment, consequently reducing actual GDP below potential GDP. Long-run supply-side effects arise because potential GDP would decline as a result of behavioral responses to the rise in tax rate, including decreasing labor supply and national savings. However, Fieldhouse (2013) argues that "both short-run demand-side and long-run supply-side growth effects stemming from top tax rate changes are extremely modest". This assertion is supported by the literature, which finds no discernible effect of top tax rate changes on the primary factors driving economic growth. For example, Gravelle and Marples (2011) and Hungerford (2012) find that changes in the top US marginal tax rates have had no statistically significant impact on real GDP growth.

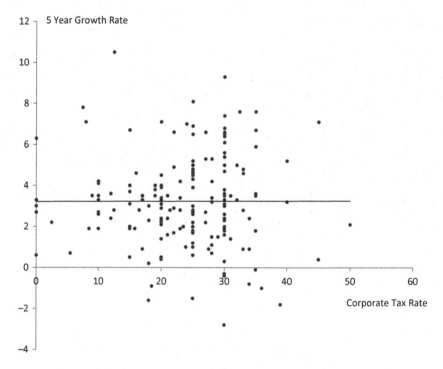

Figure 6.2:   Growth as a Function of the Corporate Tax Rate

Of course, there are exceptions. A free marketeer starting with the prior belief that tax cuts boost growth can, by using the con art of econometrics, find some evidence to support prior beliefs. It is also true that those who dislike tax cuts may use the con art of econometrics to find evidence supporting their prior beliefs. However, if a policy decision on whether or not to cut tax rates is to be taken, then the empirical evidence should be overwhelmingly in favor of this proposition because tax cuts have adverse consequences. McGuire (2019), who talks about the myth that taxes stifle economic growth, makes this point by arguing that "you can cherry-pick studies to show that raising taxes on high earners has a detrimental effect, but the preponderance of studies—and the best ones— find that this will not harm local economies". Further evidence is provided by the Joint Committee on Taxation (2005) that examined the economic effects of reducing marginal tax rates, where it is suggested that "growth effects eventually become negative ... because accumulating federal government debt crowds out private investment". The study concludes that "lowering marginal tax rates is likely to harm the economy over the long run if the tax reductions are deficit financed".

If high taxes are bad for the economy, we should expect robust economic growth during periods characterized by low tax rates, and vice versa. This is not the conclusion reached by Aaron *et al.* (2004) who found that "historical evidence shows no clear correlation between tax rates and economic growth" and that "comparisons across countries confirm that rapid growth has been a feature of both high- and low-tax nations". Allard and Lindert (2006) undertook an extensive examination of the underlying issue in developed countries since the 1960s, analyzing the relation between economic performance and government policy across a wide range of areas, including tax policy, spending policy and regulatory policy in product and labor markets. Their results show that at levels of taxation at or even significantly above those now seen in the US, increasing the ratio of tax revenue to GDP leads to an improvement in economic performance. They explain this result by noting that the additional revenues raised by higher-tax countries are frequently used to undertake growth-promoting activities, such as investment in public education, infrastructure and public health.

For free marketeers, the effect of taxes on economic growth resembles the effect of the brake on the speed of a car. They even argue that tax cuts are self-funded, in the sense that they generate so much growth, leading to growing revenue that more than compensates for the revenue lost through tax cuts. This argument is particularly applicable to income tax on the super-rich and corporate income tax. The idea here is that lower taxes for the rich entrepreneurs and corporations create employment because they put the extra income in productive, employment-generating activity. The fact of the matter is that corporations tend to use the extra cash to buy back their shares and pay the CEOs and their cronies obscene bonuses. The extra cash available for the super-rich goes into the stock market, tax havens and perhaps to pay for trips to the International Space Station at $20 million a piece.

The idea that cutting taxes for the rich benefits the poor is based on the notorious proposition of the trickle-down effect, which is used to justify poverty, inequality and the obscene amounts paid to the CEOs of private-sector firms. The notion of trickle down has been criticized and ridiculed. In the 1992 US presidential election, independent candidate, Ross Perot, called trickle-down economics "political voodoo". In New Zealand, Labour Party MP Damien O'Connor has, in a campaign video for the 2011 general election, described the trickle-down effect as "the rich pissing on the poor". A 2012 study by the Tax Justice Network indicates that wealth of the super-rich does not trickle down to improve the economy, but tends to be amassed and sheltered in tax havens with a negative effect on the tax base of the home economy (Stewart, 2012). Chang (2011) criticizes trickle-down policies, citing examples of slowing job growth in the last few decades, rising income inequality in most rich nations, and inability to provide raising living standards across all income brackets rather than at the top only. Dabla-Norris *et al.* (2015) suggest that if the income share of the top 20% rises, then GDP growth actually declines over the medium term, suggesting that the benefits do not trickle down. In contrast, an increase in the income share of the bottom 20% (the poor) is associated with a higher GDP growth rate.

Opposition to tax cuts and disputing the proposition that they pay for themselves runs across the board, encompassing academics, business people and government officials. Krugman (2007) argues that "supply side doctrine, which claimed without evidence that tax cuts would pay for themselves, never got any traction in the world of professional economic research, even among conservatives". Buffett (2003) commented on the proposed reduction in taxes on dividends by arguing that "when you listen to tax-cut rhetoric, remember that giving one class of taxpayer a 'break' requires—now or down the line—that an equivalent burden be imposed on other parties". In other words, he said, "if I get a break, someone else pays", which means that "government can't deliver a free lunch to the country as a whole". Fukuyama (2008) argues against the proposition that tax cuts pay for themselves, pointing out that "the traditional view was correct: if you cut taxes without cutting spending, you end up with a damaging deficit". He refers to some historical stylized facts: "the Reagan tax cuts of the 1980s produced a big deficit; the Clinton tax increases of the 1990s produced a surplus; and the Bush II tax cuts of the early 21st century produced an even larger deficit".

A big debate erupted on the tax cuts of George Bush Junior, which were introduced between 2001 and 2003 (commonly referred to as the "Bush tax cuts") through the Economic Growth and Tax Relief Reconciliation Act of 2001, and the Jobs and Growth Tax Relief Reconciliation Act of 2003. Kogan (2003) evaluated the claims that the Bush tax cuts of 2001 would boost growth and found "little support for claims made by Administration officials and other proponents of these tax cuts that either the 2001 tax cut or the new 'growth' package would generate substantial improvements in long-term economic growth", that "these tax cuts would have only a small effect on the economy over the long term", and that "the effect is as likely to be negative as positive". On the same issue, the Congressional Budget Office (CBO) (2001) concluded that "the cumulative effects of the new tax law on the economy are uncertain but will probably be small". Likewise, Gale and Potter (2002) found that the effect on long-term economic growth was more likely to be a small negative than a small positive.

Tax cuts do not pay for themselves, and they do not necessarily generate growth. Tax cuts are typically given to those who are already rich and corporations, the parties that (with the help of an army of accountants and lawyers) pay little tax. In a system where grotesque inequality is accepted and justified, the real objective behind tax cuts is to make the rich even richer at the expense of the poor who become poorer. Cutting taxes for the rich and corporations means that the government will have fewer resources to finance the social safety net that benefit the majority. Tax cuts for the rich mean that the middle class, which is becoming increasingly a thing of the past, will pay more than its fair share relative to income.

6.3 The Feasibility of Wealth Tax

The third commandment of the Washington Consensus does not consider the feasibility of introducing a wealth tax. Apparently, this is not "reform" because it affects the welfare of the oligarchy and the one-percenters. Let us look at this issue in a crude manner first, by considering an individual who has amassed $50 billion by digging minerals from the ground and selling them for private profit. This person has this privilege only because his father or grandfather had struck a deal with a corrupt politician who happened to be in power then, a deal that gives the family the right to extract minerals for 100 years in return for paying royalties amounting to a tiny fraction of the profits generated from this operation. In an ideal situation, mineral resources should be under public ownership and the revenues are used for the purpose of being fiscally disciplined. Since this ideal situation cannot be found under the free market system, what is wrong with this person paying a 5% wealth tax? That will only reduce his wealth to $47.5 billion. This amount of tax revenue can be used to find accommodation for every homeless person on the land and more, but for this oligarch it is a small change.

What we see on the ground is exactly the opposite, that is, ordinary middle-class taxpayers subsidizing the super-rich. A large number of the people working for the richest person on earth (with a net worth of $180 billion) qualify for food stamps, which are financed by taxpayers. Khan (2020) suggests that worldwide there is $80 trillion in cash or very liquid cash-like assets, much of which is effectively untaxed. A levy of 2% on this amount would raise $1.6 trillion a year, which is adequate to eliminate world hunger 228 times. Khan also argues that support for wealth taxes is not meant to be an attack on capitalism, arguing that "smart wealth taxes can preserve capitalism in its most sustainable and meritocratic forms by increasing innovation, entrepreneurship and wealth creation, rather than simply wealth preservation".

Let us now consider the merits and demerits of wealth tax. The absence of wealth tax has led to the grotesque levels of inequality we observe today. Wealth inequality is much bigger than income inequality. In 2018, the wealthiest 10% Americans owned 70% of the country's wealth while the richest 1% owned 32%. This is why Bernie Sanders and Elizabeth Warren proposed the imposition of a wealth tax in the run-up to the 2020 presidential election (Kagan, 2020). In 2019, Senator Warren proposed to finance "Medicare for All" by using the proceeds from wealth tax. She had in mind two tax brackets: 2% for people with $50 million or more in assets and 6% for assets above $1 billion. Senator Sanders suggested a 1% tax on wealth over $32 million, gradually rising to 8% for wealth above $10 billion. It is interesting that in 1999, Donald Trump proposed a one-time, 14.5% wealth tax on all people with a net worth of $10 million or more (Kurtzleben, 2019).

Popular support for wealth tax can be seen in the polls. In July 2019, a poll conducted by the New York Times and Survey Monkey revealed that two-thirds of all Americans, including 55% of Republicans, approved a 2% wealth tax on all people with wealth over $50 million (Kurtzleben, 2019). As far as how the people paying wealth tax would feel, opinions are split. On the one hand, 20 self-identified members of the top 0.1% published an open letter in June 2019 calling for a "moderate" wealth tax. On the other hand, there are those who believe that a wealth tax is an attack on the "American dream". *The Daily Telegraph* Editor, Allister Heath, critically describes wealth taxes as "Marxian in concept and ethically destructive to the values of democracies" and that "taxing already acquired property drastically alters the relationship between citizen and state" as accumulated taxes over long periods of time eventually returning wealth to the state (Heath, 2013). According to Heath, it is unethical to force someone who has accumulated wealth through corrupt privatization programs to "donate" a small fraction of his or her wealth to the poor and vulnerable, but it is ethical to see people sleeping on the street or dying because they cannot afford medical fees. In any case, this sounds stranger because free marketeers like Heath do not care about ethics and proudly proclaim that markets have no ethics—they are just "efficient".

The alleged disadvantages of wealth tax are the following: (i) it causes capital flight as the super-rich migrate or send their money to tax havens; (ii) the valuation problem, given that real assets cannot be valued until they are sold; and (iii) the economic freedom argument that wealth taxes are a form of direct asset collection, as well as double taxation, in which case they impinge upon personal freedom and individual liberty. As far as the first point is concerned, the same thing can be said about income tax because high income tax rates motivate tax evasion, which is a criminal offense. Governments strive and cooperate to identify the foreign incomes of their citizens so that they can tax them. In recent years, the US government started pursuing American expatriates to tax foreign incomes and cracking down on tax havens. If this can be done in conjunction with income tax, it can be done in conjunction with wealth tax. The valuation problem is not a problem: we already pay property and land taxes on the basis of valuations as judged by the local authorities. These valuations are typically below the market values of the assets. If that can be done for property and land, it can be done for other assets. In this sense, a wealth tax is an extension of the property and land taxes to other assets like shares, which can be valued more precisely.

The freedom argument is based on a narrow definition of freedom, that is, the freedom of the super-rich not to pay taxes. It is not a double taxation because the super-rich and multinationals have an army of lawyers and accountants who enable them to pay little income and capital gains taxes. Warren Buffet has repeatedly admitted that he pays less tax than his secretary (Isidore, 2013). Wheelwright (2019) identifies five ways whereby Buffett is taxed at a lower rate than his secretary, including the hiring of top accountants to reduce the effective tax rate legally. The proponents of the freedom argument contend that "free nations" (including one "free nation" that houses 25% of the world's prison population) should have no business helping themselves arbitrarily to the personal belongings of any group of its citizens, and that wealth taxes place the authority of the government ahead of the rights of the individual, and ultimately undermine the concept of personal sovereignty. It is strange that we do not hear this argument against bail-outs and bail-ins, which amount to the government helping itself to taxpayers' money (for bail-out) and depositors' money (for bail-in), so that the financial oligarchy pursue their freedom and sovereignty in ripping off the society. It is strange that governments find it acceptable to pass legislation for bail-in but not for wealth tax.

Free marketeers who dislike all sort of taxes, let alone wealth tax, always talk about efficiency. If anything, wealth tax is more efficient than income tax, which favors baby boomers to millennials. Guvenen *et al.* (2019) compare wealth and capital income taxes, suggesting that under capital income taxes, entrepreneurs who are more productive, and therefore generate more income, pay higher taxes whereas under wealth taxation, entrepreneurs who have similar wealth levels pay similar taxes regardless of their productivity. The outcome would be widening the tax base, shifting the tax burden toward unproductive entrepreneurs, and raising the saving rates of productive ones. This reallocation, they argue, boosts aggregate productivity and output. They run a simulation exercise in which the capital income tax is replaced with a wealth tax in a revenue-neutral fashion and find that such a switch delivers a significantly higher average lifetime utility to a newborn (about 7.5% in consumption-equivalent terms). They also find that individuals who are alive at the time of the policy change would, on average, incur large welfare losses if the new policy is capital income tax but would experience large welfare gains if the new policy is wealth tax.

COVID-19 has given rise to calls for the imposition of wealth tax, particularly because the pandemic has affected the poor and vulnerable disproportionately. In South Africa, which has been hit hard by COVID-19, half of the adult population survives with near-zero savings, while 3,500 individuals own 15% of the country's wealth. This is why Chatterjee *et al.* (2020) propose a "progressive solidarity wealth tax", which would allocate the fiscal burden of current interventions on those most capable of paying. Their estimates show that a wealth tax on the richest 354,000 individuals could raise at least $8.3 billion, about 29% of the announced $29.1 billion fiscal cost of the relief package.

Likewise, Collins and Clemente (2020) call for a levy of a one-time pandemic wealth tax on billionaires' windfall gains realized during the pandemic. For example, they suggest that Jeff Bezos, whose wealth increased spectacularly during the pandemic, was worth an estimated $184 billion in August 2020. Under the emergency pandemic wealth tax, Bezos would pay an estimated one-time tax of $42.8 billion and remains the richest person on the planet, with over $140 billion. The wealth of Elon Musk, the CEO of Tesla, nearly tripled during the pandemic to $70 billion in August 2020. He would pay an estimated one-time wealth tax of $27.3 billion and remains 75% richer than he was in March 2020. Mark Zuckerberg, whose net worth was over $88 billion in August 2020, would pay an estimated one-time wealth tax of $22.1 billion. His wealth would be 28% higher than in March 2020. Khan (2020) argues that the ancient Greeks levied the *eisphora* wealth tax on the richest Athenians, particularly during times of war. Since the pandemic and the response resemble a war situation, perhaps there is readiness for a modern day, post-Covid *eisphora*.

The case for wealth tax, irrespective of the details, is strong. The super-rich share the benefits of the infrastructure and government services, financed by the average taxpayer, and benefit from the reverse Robin Hood transfer of wealth from the poor. The wealth tax goes a long way toward the establishment of a fairer, more compassionate society with gains in efficiency. The Washington Consensus does not mention wealth tax because Washington supports the super-rich, not the super-poor.

6.4 Other Avenues for Tax Reform

The third commandment of the Washington Consensus ignores other possible avenues for tax reform. For example, one way to broaden the tax base is to extend GST or VAT to cover financial transactions. As a matter of fact, it does not make any sense not to tax financial transactions when most of these transactions are parasitic, conducted by (or on behalf of) people who can afford to pay extra tax. A better alternative that the Washington Consensus ignores is the imposition of a financial transaction tax (FTT), which is a type of excise tax imposed on trades of financial assets, including stocks, bonds and derivatives. It does not make sense to impose a massive stamp duty on a young couple buying their first home with a massive mortgage. The proponents of FTT highlight its progressivity (the rich pay more), its voluntary nature (don't want to pay? don't trade), and its ability to discourage unproductive high frequency trading. The critics argue that the tax harms savers and investors, reduces economic growth, and fails to raise promised revenue by driving activities to lower taxed areas overseas.

The Institute on Taxation and Economic Policy (2019) presents a strong case for FTT by outlining the benefits that can be reaped by the introduction of FTT, arguing that this tax has the potential to curb inequality, reduce market inefficiencies, and raise hundreds of billions of dollars in revenue. This tax will make it more expensive to trade and reduce the volume of trading. Because financial assets are concentrated in the hands of the wealthiest households, an FTT would be ultimately borne mostly by the wealthy. One has to bear in mind that excessive trading may be unnecessary but it generates commissions for crooked fund managers. By eliminating excessive trading, including high frequency trading, market inefficiencies would be reduced. In terms of revenue generation, the CBO (2018) predicts that a 0.1% tax could generate $777 billion over 10 years, which is equal to the revenue generated by all excise taxes including petrol, tobacco, and alcohol.

The critics argue the tax harms savers and investors, reduces economic growth, and fails to raise promised revenue by driving activities to lower taxed areas overseas. The most prominent opponent is, naturally, the Securities Industry and Financial Markets Association (SIFMA), which has produced a large number of publications and press releases, including *SIFMA Opposes a Financial Transaction Tax*, *FTT: Taxing Your Future*, *The Ramifications of a Financial Transaction Tax*, *FTT: An Unhealthy Proposal*, and *The Facts Don't Support the FTT*. The opposition of SIFMA is understandable, given that it represents securities brokerage firms, investment banking institutions, and other investment firms.

SIFMA is strongly opposed to a financial transaction tax on the grounds that it raises costs to the issuers, pensions and investors who help drive economic growth, negatively impacting those saving for retirement, higher education or to buy a home by reducing savings. Moreover, major economies that have adopted such taxes have had overwhelmingly negative results, including lower asset prices, trading moving to other venues, market dislocation and diminishing liquidity. According to SIFMA, past experience also suggests that it would raise less revenue than supporters often claim. This is rhetoric. Economic growth is not generated by issuers, pensions and investors, but rather by factory workers, miners, health workers and teachers. Those saving for retirement, higher education or to buy a home are hurt by low and negative interest rates, imposed for the benefit of financial institutions. Lower asset prices represent a healthy sign, given that financial assets are typically overpriced. Trading moving to other venues is good because it is the migration of parasitic activities. The proposition that it would raise less revenue than supporters often claim is inconsistent with the estimates of the CBO. I am not sure what "market dislocation" means, but it sounds alarming, which is good for fear mongering.

The Washington Consensus has nothing to say about the tax fraud committed by multinational corporations against host countries, simply because the Consensus is intended to benefit multinationals. They pay little or no tax because corporate income tax is charged on accounting profit, which can be anything by using "creative" (read fraudulent) accounting. Profit is taken to be sales revenue minus all expenses, including operating costs, interest paid on loans, royalties and management fees on intellectual property, and depreciation on capital assets calculated at statutory rates based on their expected lifetimes. One way to avoid tax fraud is to use a cash flow tax that allows the deduction from sales revenue capital and operating costs but not debt interest, royalties and fees paid to affiliated companies for intellectual property. A tax like this, which is relatively simple to administer, removes distortions like the promotion of debt over equity, which undermines economic stability.

6.5 Concluding Remarks

The third commandment of the Washington Consensus, tax reform, calls for a wider tax base and moderate tax rates. Even if we assume that this is what is preached to developing countries by the World Bank and IMF, the commandment does not say anything about other avenues of tax reform such as the introduction of wealth tax and other forms of taxes, as well as combatting tax evasion, which is common among multinationals. Tax evasion is facilitated by various schemes that enable multinationals to avoid paying taxes in countries where they generate huge revenues. Janský and Palanský (2019) estimate that multinationals shift around $420 billion in corporate profits out of 79 countries every year. Why is it that the third commandment says nothing about this malpractice that deprives developing countries of well-deserved tax revenue?

In the section on the wealth tax, we considered an imaginary scenario of what would happen to an oligarch worth $50 billion, accumulated by using concessions to extract natural resources and selling them for private profit. This situation is not totally fictitious because one natural resource rich country has such an oligarch. One day, a brave prime minister dared to propose the introduction of a mining tax to be imposed on the oligarch and mining companies in general. That proposition led to an uproar about this prime minister wanting to destroy the market economy and discourage innovative entrepreneurship. All of a sudden, it came in the news that the prime minister was successfully challenged by his deputy who became the prime minister in a celebration of democracy, since this country is a "Western" democracy. No one knows exactly how that happened, but it is more fact than fiction that the oligarchy played a big role in what was effectively a *coup d'etat*. Had that happened in an African country, "Western" democracies would have condemned the action and called for an urgent Security Council meeting to capture the new prime minister and send him (or her) to the kangaroo court in the Hague. This is how governments look after the oligarchy in the "West". It was an ingenious piece of tax reform that was killed promptly in the name of the free market and for the benefit of the oligarchy.

The last point to be made here is the contradiction between the first commandment of fiscal discipline and the third commandment of tax reform. The Washington Consensus only sees defects that are worthy of "reform" in developing countries. It does not address the issue that the tax code in "Western" countries, which preach tax reform, encourages debt financing, which has an adverse effect on fiscal discipline and makes financial systems susceptible to recurring crises. I wonder why Williamson has not recognized this contradiction. Perhaps he has, but admitting the contradiction amounts to admitting that the ten commandments of the Washington Consensus are rhetorical and do not stand up to rational critique in terms of a theory of non-contradiction.

Chapter 7

The Fourth Commandment: Interest Rate Policy

7.1 Introduction

The fourth commandment of the Washington Consensus calls for the liberalization of interest rates by making them market-determined (rather than determined by the monetary authorities) and the preservation of positive (but moderate) real interest rates. It represents yet another example of a principle that is not adopted by the preachers, as monetary authorities in the preaching countries keep driving interest rates to extremely low levels. It is not only that real interest rates are negative—even nominal interest rates are negative in some preaching countries.

Williamson (1990) identifies two general principles about the level of interest rates that "command considerable support in Washington". The first is that interest rates should be market-determined, which serves the purpose of avoiding "the resource misallocation that results from bureaucrats rationing credit according to arbitrary criteria". This principle is not adopted by Washington and its allies who have been putting downward pressure on interest rates via quantitative easing for the benefit of banks and the corporate oligarchy. It also goes against the subsidization of loans given to the agricultural sector for the purpose of investment in food security. The second principle is that real interest rates should be positive for the purpose of discouraging capital flight and boosting savings. Williamson puts this principle as maintaining positive but moderate interest rates to promote productive investment and avoid the threat of an explosion in government debt. Again, this principle is not adopted by

141

Washington and its allies as we see negative real (and in some cases nominal) interest rates. This is so much the case because governments lie about inflation, which means that real interest rates are more negative than what they appear to be.

Williamson questions the mutual consistency of these two principles and suggests that there is little reason to anticipate a contradiction because "one expects market-determined interest rates to be positive but moderate in real terms". However, he admits that market-determined interest rates may be extremely high, which is what happened in the 1980s. To keep real interest rates down, inflation must rise as nominal interest rates rise, and vice versa. I thought, however, that monetary policy aims at curbing inflation by raising interest rates. If higher nominal interest rates lead to lower inflation, real interest rates will go up, and vice versa. In recent times, central banks around the world justified the objective of driving of interest rates to zero on the grounds of raising the inflation rate to boost economic activity. Williamson seems to be against the practice of segmenting the credit market in the sense of channeling low-cost funds to "priority" sectors. In fact, he seems to be skeptical about the concept of "priority sectors" and argues that "segmented credit markets provide a prime environment for corruption to flourish".

7.2 Market-Determined Nominal Interest Rates

The case for market-determined interest rates is the same as the case for market-determined prices, simply because the interest rate is a price—it is the price of loanable funds or money. According to the loanable funds theory, the interest rate is determined by the demand for and supply of loanable funds. Demand comes from deficit units such as the corporate sector and the government, whereas supply comes primarily from household savings, even though the household sector is also a source of demand for loanable funds.

Figure 7.1 shows the supply of and demand for loanable funds. The equilibrium interest rate is determined by the point of intersection of the supply and demand curves, which gives the equilibrium rate of i_0. However, in no country is the interest rate determined purely by market forces, as central banks determine some policy rates that affect other interest rates such as deposit and lending rates as well as bond yields. For example, the Federal Reserve (the US central bank) determines the federal funds rate (the rate at which banks can lend to each other) and the discount

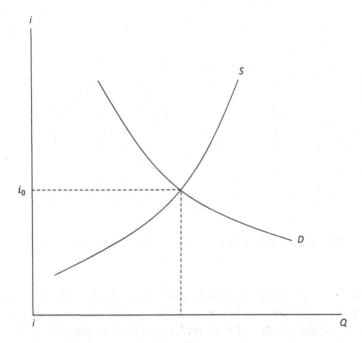

Figure 7.1:   The Equilibrium Interest Rate as Determined by Market Forces

rate (the rate at which banks can borrow from the Fed). Why does Washington preach market-determined interest rates when the Federal Reserve, and other central banks in "Western" countries, have been driving interest rates to record lows and even to negative territory?

Arguments against interference with the forces of supply and demand in the market for loanable funds are the same as those directed at interference with supply and demand in the markets for goods, service and factors of production. If the rate (i^*) is set above equilibrium (i_e), the market will have a surplus of loanable funds, as shown in Figure 7.2. Also shown is what happens when the rate is set below equilibrium, producing a shortage of loanable funds. The first situation is like the case of setting a minimum wage, which creates unemployment (excess supply of labor). The second situation is like the ceiling imposed on rents, which creates a shortage of rental properties. The underlying idea is that the market knows better than a central planner where the price of a commodity should be, and the market knows better than the Fed's Open Market Committee where the interest rate should be.

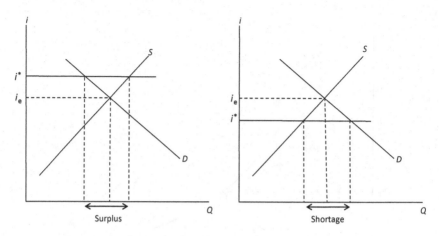

Figure 7.2:   Setting Interest Rate Above or Below Equilibrium

The main argument for market-determined interest rates is that they perform an important role in coordinating people's plans. In this respect, a relevant concept is that of time preference (that is, people's preferences for wanting to make purchases further into the future relative to the near term). When people are focused on the future, they tend to save more (supply more loanable funds) at any given interest rate. According to Cordato (2019), "the interest rate is performing the important function of coordinating the preferences of consumers with the plans of producers through time", which he describes as "part of the marvel of how free markets work and create orderly production decisions that are consistent with people's preferences". Market intervention by the monetary authorities, as Cordato puts it, is "not only arbitrary but disruptive" because "rates that are not reflective of people's time preference, i.e., people's preferences for the present as compared to future goods, will drive a wedge between the desires of savers and entrepreneurs and investors". He cites Frederick von Hayek on how boom and bust business cycles are caused by central bank driven mismatches in the loanable funds market. Cordato (2019) contends that "the Federal Reserve should pull out of the interest rate manipulation business completely" and that "having a Fed whose main job, at least in the eyes of the public, is to set or move interest rates in centrally determined directions makes no more sense than having a powerful government agency determining what should be happening with any other price in the economy".

The arguments against central banks determining interest rates are similar to the arguments against rent control, minimum wages and fair pricing. Rent control, however, offers some benefits. A rent cap would be good for the economy because tenants will have more disposable income to spend on consumer goods, which would help boost small businesses. Tenants will be more able to save, more able to pay for essential items like food and bills, and less likely to get into debt and have to resort to payday loans or seek welfare assistance. This has been so much the case during the COVID-19 pandemic. While a minimum wage does not suit profit-maximizing firms, it has benefits. For example, Leigh and Du (2018) note that "new research indicates that an increase in minimum wages can have important health benefits". Fair pricing is needed when the underlying product is produced by a monopolist and has a low elasticity of demand. In general, arguments against rent control, minimum wages and fair pricing are put forward by free marketeers for the benefit of the oligarchy.

The problem with market-determined interest rates is that these rates may be so high that consumer protection becomes necessary. Under the present environment of ultra-low or negative interest rates, banks pay 0.5% on a deposit or charge depositors for keeping their money with the banks, and yet they charge 20% on credit card bills. Even worse is that market-determined rates enable loan sharks to prey on the poor and vulnerable. For example, Wonga, a high-profile British short-term lender, charges an annual percentage rate (APR) of 4,215% and allows borrowers to roll over loans from one month to the next, meaning that the interest charges can eventually exceed the amount originally borrowed (Insley, 2012). The Economist (2013) argues that "these loans, often taken out by poor people whose fraying finances leave them short of cash at the end of the month, can carry annual rates of several thousand percent".

The argument against the regulation of payday loans, typically based on the free market doctrine, is that regulation amounts to interference with the working of market forces. The main argument against payday loans is that since the providers charge higher interest rates than mainstream financial institutions, they have the effect of depleting the assets of low-income communities. This is a moral issue with deep-rooted historical origins—it is a vivid example of how belief in the power of the market erodes morality. In general, the proponents of payday loans do not like the claims of consumer advocates that payday lenders exploit poor and lower-income customers, prey on their lack of financial sophistication, lead them into chronic borrowing habits at excessively high effective interest rates, and generally take advantage of their weak bargaining position (Lehman, 2003).

Should the central bank avoid intervening in the interest rate determination process, monetary policy will not be used for the purpose of macroeconomic stabilization. Whether or not it is effective, the loss of a policy tool cannot be a good thing. For example, the Reserve Bank of Australia (RBA) changes the cash rate to influence interest rates across the financial system. Changes in interest rates in turn can influence economic activity by affecting saving and investment behavior, household expenditure, the supply of credit, asset prices and the exchange rate. Tight monetary policy (higher interest rates) is used when demand pressure builds up in the economy, reflected in rising prices. Conversely, the RBA can loosen monetary policy to boost economic activity in the face of weak demand. Some central banks use the Taylor rule to adjust interest rates whereby the level of the policy rate is linked to deviations of inflation from its target and of output from its potential (the output gap).

Allowing interest rates to be determined by the market without any intervention by the central bank means that financial resources will be distributed among sectors according to the profitability of investment. If more money is made by investing in the stock market than in agriculture, which is typically the case, then the agricultural sector will be deprived of the financial resources necessary for its development. This can be avoided by subsidizing loans to the agricultural sector, offering low interest loans. In Australia, for example, farmers can apply to the Regional Investment Corporation (RIC) for the Commonwealth's farm business concessional loans, which can be of three types: drought assistance, dairy recovery and business improvement concessional loans. In India, the unexpected withdrawal of the subsidized agriculture gold loans provided by public sector banks has hurt hundreds of farmers who are going through acute financial crisis with the COVID-19 outbreak and the subsequent lockdown across the State of Kerala. Arguing for market-determined interest rates is arguing for failing to support key sectors in the name of the free market.

Market-determined interest rates tend to be volatile, creating interest rate risk, which is difficult to manage in the absence of sophisticated financial markets. Volatility arises because of erratic shifts in the excess demand curve, as shown in Figure 7.3. We start at the equilibrium interest rate 1, which is produced when excess demand 1 is zero (the point of intersection with the vertical axis). When the excess demand curve shifts to 2, the interest rate rises to 2. When excess demand drops to 3, the

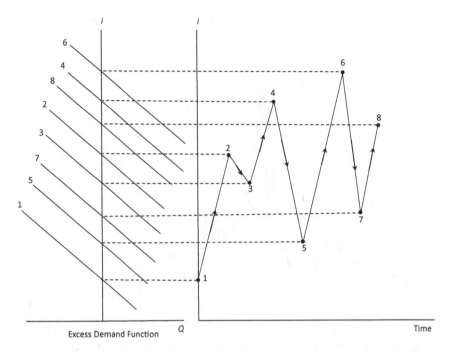

Figure 7.3: **Volatility of Market-Determined Interest Rate**

interest rate declines to 3. The equilibrium interest rate goes up or down as the excess demand curve shifts upwards or downwards. Erratic shifts in the excess demand curve produce volatile interest rates. In 1979, the Federal Reserve shifted from a policy of interest rate targeting to a policy of money supply targeting, leading to a phenomenal rise in (market-determined) interest rates and the recession of the early 1980s. The phenomenal rise in interest rates can be seen in Figure 7.4, which also shows that in the most recent period, interest rates became less volatile as the Federal Reserve intervened more frequently to influence policy rates. Developing countries do not need the headache caused by interest rate volatility—rather, they need subsidized agricultural loans.

The contradiction in the application of the fourth commandment is that in practice, the IMF invariably recommends higher interest rates in response to depreciating currencies, implying that the IMF approves the use of the interest rate as a policy tool. The underlying idea is that high interest rates make domestic currency-denominated deposits and other financial assets more attractive for foreign investors. High interest rates

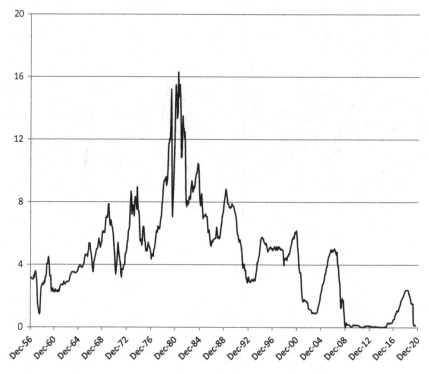

Figure 7.4:   US Three-Month Treasury Bill Rate

are also prescribed to put inflation under control, but they end up worsening the economic downturn. Stiglitz (2002) argues that while high interest rates are intended to control inflation, which may not be a problem to start with, they end up forcing the bankruptcy of countless otherwise productive companies that could not cope with a sudden rise in the cost of funding. Stiglitz also thinks that high interest rates may lead to overvalued currencies, which have to depreciate sooner or later, giving currency traders a one-way bet.

7.3 The Principle of Moderate and Positive Real Interest Rates

The real interest rate is the nominal interest rate adjusted for inflation. The two variables (real and nominal) are related by the Fisher equation, which defines the real interest rate as the difference between the nominal interest rate and inflation. The expected inflation rate is used to calculate the *ex-ante* or expected real interest rate, which is used for investment decision making. The realized inflation rate, on the other hand, is used to calculate the ex-post, or realized real interest rate.

For the real interest rate to be stable, there must be a one-to-one relation between the nominal interest rate and inflation. The two variables should be related as we can see that countries with high inflation or hyperinflation tend to have high interest rates. This is because investors will not hold assets denominated in the currency of a country experiencing hyperinflation unless they are compensated for the loss of purchasing power by a higher nominal interest rate. This may be the case under hyperinflation, but does it hold under moderate-low inflation? In Figure 7.5, we observe the relation between the US three-month Treasury bill rate and inflation, using monthly observations over the period January 1957–July 2020. While the relation is obviously positive, we do not know whether causation runs from inflation to the nominal interest rate (as it is in the Fisher equation) or from the nominal interest rate to inflation when the interest

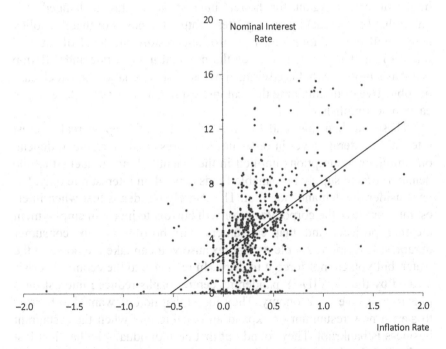

Figure 7.5:   A Scatter Plot of US Nominal Treasury Bill Rate on the Inflation Rate

rate is used as a policy tool. If the direction of causation is unknown, the task of maintaining the real interest rate at a positive but moderate level becomes rather difficult.

Suppose that the moderate level of the real interest rate is 2%. Suppose also that inflation goes up because of a monetary expansion as in the quantity theory of money. If there is any truth to the Fisher equation, the nominal interest rate should adjust automatically, which may work as follows. If inflation is up 1%, the central bank responds by raising the policy rate by one percentage point and commercial banks follow by raising their rates by one percentage point. Only then will the real interest rate be kept at the moderate positive level of 2%. If the central bank does not react, depositors can force banks to raise the deposit rate by reducing savings. This is unlikely to happen because people tend to keep money in the bank rather than under the mattress, and this is why people still hold bank deposits at today's ultra-low interest rates. Furthermore, commercial banks do not always raise or lower their deposit and lending rates according to the moves of the central bank.

Now, suppose that inflation rises because of a cost push factor such as higher oil prices. Again, for the real interest rate to stay unchanged, it is either that banks react by raising rates to attract deposits or that the policy action will put inflation under control and restore the level of the real interest rate. The relation between the nominal interest rate and inflation is not as simple as what is envisaged by the Fisher equation, in which case the objective of maintaining the real interest rate at a moderate level is not easy to accomplish.

These mechanisms, and the very objective of keeping real interest rates at a moderate level in order not to depress real investment, depend on simplistic assumptions implicit in the loanable funds model—that the demand for and supply of loanable funds depend on interest rate only. Let us consider the demand side first. The underlying idea is that when interest rates are low, the corporate sector will borrow to invest in employment creating projects and that consumers will borrow to buy consumer durables. It is not as simple as that because you can take the horse to the water, but you cannot force it to drink. In response to the economic crisis created by the COVID-19 pandemic, central banks reduced interest rates to zero to revive the economy. They found that no one wanted to borrow to start a new restaurant or expand an existing one when the restaurant business is bankrupt. They found out that no individual who had just lost a job wanted to borrow to purchase a new car or a new fridge. They found out that no airline wanted to borrow to buy new planes. The fact of the matter is that this kind of spending depends more on the economic outlook than the interest rate.

Making the real interest rate a policy variable (the objective being to keep it moderately low) is problematic because it is unobservable. Inflation is measured as the percentage change in the consumer price index or another price index. Measurement problems mean that the Consumer Price Index (CPI) does not reflect the true inflation rate, but what is even worse is that governments lie about inflation deliberately in such a way as to report lower inflation figures than they should be. We are repeatedly told that inflation is running at an annual rate of 1.5% or so, presumably because the central bank is doing a good job, and this is why the governor should get a big bonus and a salary raise. However, a visit to the supermarket, hosting a dinner in a restaurant and paying bills for utilities and health insurance show otherwise. If the inflation rate is under-reported, it means that the real interest rate is over-reported.

The view that governments under-report inflation is widespread, for example, Weiner (2019) wonders whether inflation is under control or that "it is just a big lie". Mauldin (2013) suggests that the US Bureau of Labor Statistics (BLS), which compiles the consumer price index, "has engaged in methodological shenanigans over the past couple decades". The result is that the official rate of inflation may be two to four times lower than the actual rate. Governments have strong motives for masking the actual inflation rate and reporting a lower rate instead. These reasons include the following: (i) political gain, as keeping inflation under control sounds good in campaign speeches; (ii) low reported inflation generates big savings for the government because social security payments are adjusted by the inflation rate; (iii) low inflation justifies a policy of low interest rates that governments are pursuing for the benefit of banks and corporate interests; and (iv) low inflation justifies the claim that the destructive and irresponsible policy of quantitative easing is not inflationary.

Some observers believe that inflation is under-reported because the inflation figures are not compatible with the growth of the money supply as predicted by the quantity theory of money and the very definition of inflation that it is a situation where too much money chases too few goods. It also follows from the official definition of inflation adopted by the US Bureau of Labor Statistics that it is "a process of continuously rising prices or equivalently, of a continuously falling value of money" (Boring, 2014). Figure 7.6 shows a big gap between the monetary growth rate and

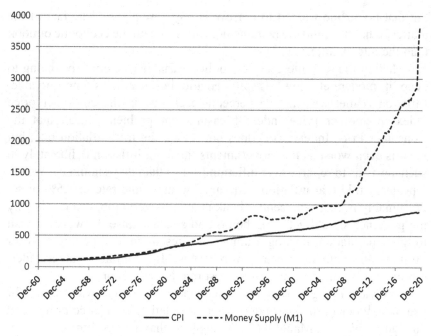

Figure 7.6: The Gap Between Monetary and Price Inflation

the inflation rate in the US. Governments have both the motive and means to manipulate the inflation figures.

The last point to be discussed here is that while Washington and its allies preach the necessity of maintaining real interest rates (which cannot be observed) at a moderately positive level, they are taking deliberate policy action to keep real interest rates extremely negative by pursuing a policy of ultra-low or negative nominal interest rates. This is preaching without practicing at its best. In Figure 7.7, we can see how low nominal interest rates have become, even negative in some cases. By July 2020, nominal short-term interest rates were negative in Japan and Germany and barely above zero in Australia, New Zealand, Korea and the UK. The move toward zero, or away from zero in the wrong direction, has accelerated because policy makers wrongly thought this was a cure for the economic effects of the Coronavirus. In the US, as in Figure 7.8, the real TB rate was at −1.2% in March 2020 as the nominal interest rate was cut to almost zero to combat the Coronavirus. Given that governments underreport inflation, as argued earlier, real interest rates may be even lower in the negative territory. For example, if we take inflation to be represented

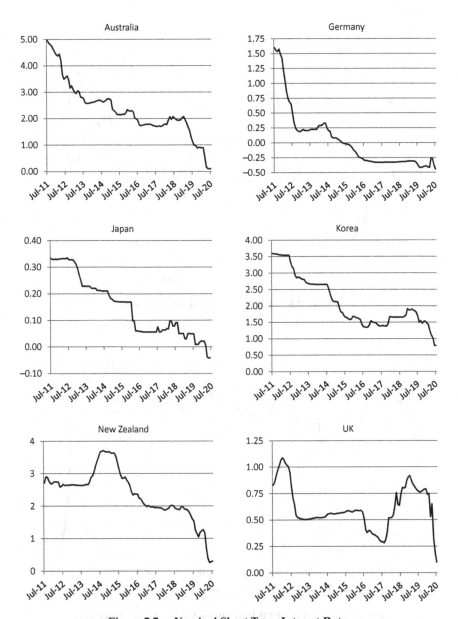

Figure 7.7: Nominal Short Term Interest Rates

by expansion in the M1 money supply, the real TB rate in July 2020 was almost −40% (Figure 7.9). Even if one-tenth of the monetary inflation represents the actual inflation rate, the real rate on the TB rate in July 2020 would be almost −4%.

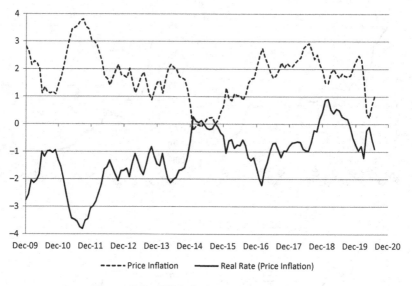

Figure 7.8:   US Inflation and Real TB Rate

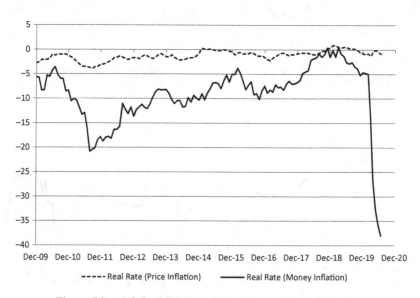

Figure 7.9:   US Real TB Rate (Price Versus Money Inflation)

7.4 Ultra-Low Interest Rates

The policy of ultra-low interest rates, adopted by the governments of the preaching countries, is devastating for prudent savers and retirees who are risk averse and content primarily with the preservation of the purchasing power of their savings. The adverse macroeconomic effect is that low interest rates discourage saving, which is required to finance capital formation and therefore long-term economic growth. The fact of the matter is that Washington and its allies pursue these destructive policies for the benefit of banks and the corporate sector, helping them to finance parasitic activities such as stock buy-backs and venture capital. The minority who hold stocks, including billionaires, benefit because low interest rates boost the stock market by enabling these parasitic activities. Banks benefit from low deposit rates because they can still charge 20% on credit cards. Loan sharks benefit because they can borrow at 2% and lend at 5,000%.

Ultra-low interest rates are supposed to boost the economy when it is contracting. This happens allegedly because companies will borrow to expand productive capacity and employ people, because households will borrow to buy consumer durables, and because savings on mortgage payments will be spent on goods and services. This is nonsense, which has been made very clear during the COVID-19 pandemic. Business investment in capital formation is not interest elastic but rather profit elastic. No business wants to expand unless they expect demand to revive—who wants to borrow to start a restaurant during the pandemic? No household will borrow to buy consumer durables because of an actual or anticipated job loss. The money saved on mortgage payments will not be spent but rather saved because of a potential job loss. What matters for consumption decisions is not the ability to borrow, but rather the economic outlook. Interest rate cuts do not work in this sense.

On the other hand, low interest rates have adverse consequences. They encourage the accumulation of debt for the purpose of financing parasitic activities while prudent savers are penalized and put in a position whereby they have to choose between the erosion of the purchasing power of their capital and exposure to levels of financial risk that they are not comfortable with. Low interest rates create and/or maintain bubbles in financial and property markets, with devastating effects when (not if) they eventually burst. Low interest rates keep zombie companies on life support when it is better for the economy to give them euthanasia. Even worse, low interest rates discourage fiscal discipline by making it more tantalizing for governments to accumulate debt. They also make it cheap to finance wars of aggression.

Another adverse effect of ultra-low interest rates is that the central bank will not be able to respond to an emergency by reducing interest rates, irrespective of whether or not this policy works. In this case, the central bank has to go to the uncharted territory of negative interest rates. Near-zero interest rates could produce misallocation of resources and weak productivity growth. Near-zero interest rates allow less efficient companies to survive, thereby curtailing the "creative destruction" that is critical to support productivity growth. They may even discourage profitable companies from carefully assessing and evaluating investment projects, leading to a less efficient allocation of capital within companies. Ultra-low interest rates may shift the sources of demand in ways that make growth less balanced, less resilient, and less sustainable. Last, but not least, ultra-low interest rates are likely to aggravate income and wealth inequality. This is because low interest rates boost asset prices, not the economy, thus benefiting asset holders at the expense of wage earners. Pension funds and other financial institutions, particularly insurance companies, are unable to make decent real returns on government bonds, in which case they resort to investing in stock and property markets, which are more risky.

For all of these reasons, the Financial Times (2020) argues that "today's ultra-low interest rates are anything but 'natural'" and that "policymakers who have cut rates repeatedly should not be let off the hook so easily". In a letter sent to *Financial Times* in response to this article, Martin Allen stated that "low interest rates are the corollary of rising debt". He suggested that they are not conducive to the accomplishment of the stated objective of boosting the economy, particularly in 2020 and beyond because the current problems in the world economy are the result of the aggregate demand and supply shocks produced by a pandemic.

7.5 Negative Interest Rates

Negative interest rates represent the most dangerous and reckless monetary experiment ever devised by the monetary authorities in "Western" countries. They destroy the entire risk−return system that has been the basis of investing for the last several centuries. The biggest beneficiaries of negative interest rates are banks, which would tax depositors. Under negative interest rates, cash deposited at a bank yields a storage charge, rather than the opportunity to earn interest income. Likewise, banks holding reserves with the central bank will be subject to a storage charge. The underlying idea is that by charging commercial banks to store their reserves at the central bank, banks will be encouraged to lend more, which will not do anything anyway, because households and firms are not willing to borrow when the economic outlook is so bleak.

It is, however, rather silly to suggest that negative interest rates mean that banks will pay borrowers. For example, Johnston (2020) makes the heroic statement that "this [negative rates] means that... some borrowers enjoy the privilege of actually earning money by taking out a loan". Who are those borrowers and how do they differ from other borrowers who do not "enjoy the privilege of actually earning money by taking out a loan"? The same silly argument is made by Wastell (2019) who suggests that "if the RBA introduces negative interest rates, consumers will have to pay a fee to their bank for holding their money in a savings account, while 'earning money' for taking out a loan". A situation like this will be unsustainable because those who get paid for their borrowing will strive to maximize debt. This does not make sense because if a commercial bank pays the central bank a storage fee of 2%, why would it lend at −1% and end up losing 3%? The bank will be better off leaving reserves with the central bank and losing 2% in the process. No bank will lend any money to any borrower, in which case the declared objective of boosting economic activity will not be accomplished.

Wastell (2019) explains how a negative borrowing rate works by saying that borrowers will not receive money into their account *per se*, but instead what they earn is used to subsidize their mortgage repayments. It is truly ludicrous even to refer to "earnings". What the bank will do is that it will offer a "subsidy" of 1% on a mortgage that it would otherwise offer at 4%. Without the subsidy, the bank will charge 4%, anyway. Otherwise, the bank will pay a mortgage holder 1% (the negative interest rate) and charge him or her 4% in fees and commissions. In 2019, a Danish bank called Jyske Bank launched the world's first negative interest rate mortgage, granting mortgages at a negative rate of −0.5%. Under this arrangement, a borrower will make a monthly repayment as usual, but the amount still outstanding will be reduced each month by more than what the borrower has paid (Collinson, 2019). This sounds fine, but banks are not exactly that charitable. Even if they earn 2% on deposits, why would they expose themselves to default risk and pay for that risk? There will never be such a thing as a negative loan rate—the whole thing is a bank scam, and banks are champion scammers.

The fact on the ground is that the prime beneficiaries of negative interest rates are commercial banks because they will still charge interest on loans. They earn 2% by charging depositors, 20% by charging credit card holders and 10% by charging those unfortunate enough to require an overdraft. In mid-August 2020, US banks held $15.6 trillion dollars of deposits, which at a negative interest rate of −2%, would produce $312 billion in bank revenue. The question is: why would anyone want to hold deposits with banks at a negative interest rate? Perhaps security, particularly if the amount is big—in this case, it is like paying for a safety deposit box. The government makes sure that the negative effects of negative rates on banks do not materialize—these effects, as envisaged by Haksar and Kopp (2020), are as follows: (i) the potential impact on bank profitability and (ii) incentive to switch out of deposits into holding cash. There is no wonder, then, that Westpac Chief Economist Bill Evans said in early June 2020 that "the RBA board should use its Tuesday meeting to consider taking the official cost of money into negative territory" (Wright, 2020). That will be good for the profitability of his bank and his bonus.

Negative interest rates, the war on cash and the bail-in legislation are three components of an elaborate government scheme (read "conspiracy") to enrich bankers. Negative interest rates are bound to encourage people to keep money under the bed or in a hole in the ground rather than with banks. This works against the feasibility of bail-in legislation whereby failed banks are allowed to confiscate depositors' money to finance the bonuses and golden parachutes given to the executives who cause the failure in the first place. Well, I should be fair and say that depositors will be given shares in the failed banks, so it is not entirely confiscation, or is it? One can only ask, how much are shares in a failed bank worth? Almost zero, I would say. So, how do governments retaliate against those "irresponsible" depositors who withdraw their money from banks? For one thing, governments are waging a war on cash transactions, not to combat the underground economy (as they claim) but to force people to keep money at banks, so that the money will be confiscated eventually. People are threatened with confinement behind bars if they use cash to settle transactions over a certain value (so much for human rights). But this is not all, as unscrupulous economists acting as "hired guns" have come up with some ingenious proposals to force people to keep money at banks. One idea is to cancel, by a random selection of serial numbers, 10% of the banknotes in circulation. Those who keep money at home will face an expected rate of return of −10% on their cash holdings, in which case they will be better off (or less worse off) by keeping their money with banks at the rate of −2%, hoping that a bail-in will not materialize.

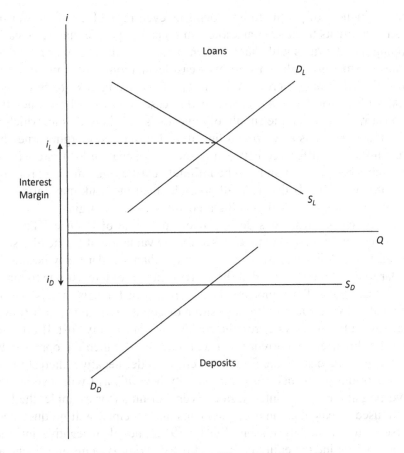

Figure 7.10: Determination of Deposit and Loan Rates

Consider Figure 7.10, which shows the determination of a negative deposit rate and a positive loan rate. In the upper part of the diagram, where the loan rate is determined, D_L and S_L are the demand for and supply of loans curves, respectively. They intersect in a positive territory, producing the loan rate i_L. In the lower part of the diagram, we observe the supply and demand curves for deposits (D_D and S_D, respectively). The demand curve is downward-sloping because even at negative interest rates, people may want to hold deposits for safety (as opposed to keeping cash at home) or because of restrictions on cash transactions or threats to cancel banknotes at random. The more negative the deposit rate, the less the willingness of people to hold deposits even in the face of the war on cash and threats to cancel banknotes. In this case, people may store cash, hoping that the rules will change when sanity prevails again, or they may resort to smuggling the cash to overseas destinations where more sanity prevails. Of course there is also the option of using cash to buy gold, works of art, property or stocks. In this case, the bank determines the deposit rate, at which the supply of deposits is infinitely elastic, which is why the S_D curve is a horizontal line at i_D. The interest margin earned by the bank is the difference between i_L and i_D. A negative loan rate will be untenable because demand will be infinitely elastic (maximizing profit by maximizing debt). If that is at all possible, then the bank may ration the supply of loans while still making a positive interest margin.

Negative interest rates destroy every principle of finance. The time value of money, a concept that is used for the valuation of financial assets, means that a dollar tomorrow is worth more than a dollar today because a dollar today can be invested at the current (positive) interest rate to make more than one dollar tomorrow. Hence, prices of financial assets can be calculated by discounting (at a positive discount rate) future cash flows. Negative interest rates destroy the concept of opportunity cost. If I do not invest a dollar at the current (positive) interest rate, then the opportunity cost of holding cash is the forgone interest. Under negative interest rates, the opportunity cost becomes "opportunity benefit", as I will save by not investing at a negative interest rate. Every formula (for example, the formula used to calculate annuity payments and receipts) will produce perverse results that defy reason. Tan (2019) argues that negative interest rates "undermine the entire premise of our banking systems and financial markets" and that "they distort capital allocation". With negative interest rates, the pricing of options will be distorted, and it will not be possible to calculate the cost of capital correctly. It will be a tough job teaching finance as we know it.

Consider what happens to some international financial operations and pricing conditions with negative interest rates. Covered interest parity (CIP) is a pricing condition whereby the forward rate is determined. The underlying idea is that if the forward rate is inconsistent with covered interest parity, arbitrage will be triggered, which will eventually restore the equilibrium condition. For example, if investors can earn net return by borrowing the domestic currency and investing in a foreign currency while covering the position in the forward market, then equilibrium (indicating the elimination of riskless arbitrage opportunities) will be restored.

That is fine if the domestic currency can be borrowed at 2% and the proceeds are invested in the foreign currency at 5%. If the interest rates on the domestic and foreign currencies are −5% and −2%, respectively, then the operations requires borrowing at −2% and investing at −5%, with a total loss of −7%. Which rational investor wants to do that? The rationale for CIP breaks down in the presence of negative interest rates, in which case it would be impossible to determine forward rates.

Then consider carry trade, the act of borrowing a low interest currency and investing in a high interest currency, hoping that the exchange rate will not move against the investor (depreciation of the currency of investment) by more than the interest rate differential. If the investor can borrow currency A at 2% and invest in currency B at 5%, the investor will make money as long as currency B does not depreciate against currency A by more than 3%. If, on the other hand, the interest rates were −5% and −2%, the investor will only indulge in this operation if they expect currency A to appreciate against currency B by more than 7%. Again, who wants to carry out an operation that promises a definite loss of 7% and an uncertain gain, which is unlikely to materialize? Carry traders, as a matter of fact, act upon the assumption that the exchange rate will not move, so that they earn the interest rate differential. In this case, the interest rate differential that they will "earn" is −7%.

Negative interest rates cannot arise in the loanable funds model because the demand and supply curves cannot intersect in a negative territory. Consider Figure 7.11, which shows the supply and demand curves. At positive interest rates, the supply curve is upward-sloping (BD), implying that more is saved at higher interest rate. When the interest rate is zero, the quantity supplied is zero because the suppliers of funds avoid being exposed to the risk of default when return is zero—this is the basic principle of risk–return trade off. The full supply curve is BDE, with a kink at D. The demand curve is downward-sloping at positive interest rates (AC), but when the rate hits zero, the demand curve becomes horizontal, meaning that it is infinitely elastic at zero interest rate. Hence, the full demand curve is ACF, with a kink at C. In this case, the equilibrium interest rate can only be positive at i_e. When the interest rate is zero, excess demand is represented by the distance CE.

Another possibility is that the demand for loanable funds increases as interest rates become more negative, up to a certain level at which demand becomes infinitely elastic. In this case, the full demand curve is ACGH, which becomes horizontal at the negative interest rate i_1. In this case,

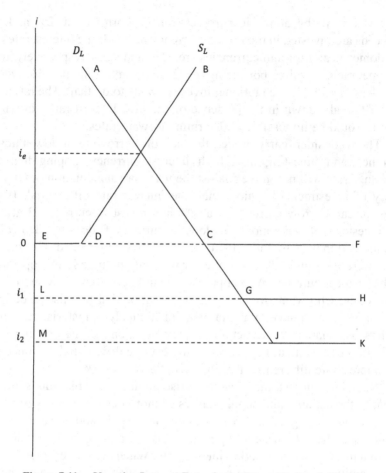

Figure 7.11:   Negative Interest Rates in the Loanable Funds Model

excess demand is represented by the distance GL. Alternatively, demand becomes infinitely elastic at a more negative interest rate (i_2), in which case excess demand is JM. This means that the market cannot be in equilibrium at any negative interest rate.

7.6 Concluding Remarks

The fourth commandment of the Washington Consensus is to let the market determine interest rates while keeping real interest rates at a moderately positive level. This commandment is difficult to implement, particularly targeting the level of the real interest rate, which is unobservable. The relation between the nominal interest rate and inflation is not as simple as what is envisaged by the Fisher equation, in which case the objective of maintaining the real interest rate at a moderate level is not easy to accomplish.

Market-determined interest rates tend to be erratic. They can be too high, thus hurting investors, or too low, thus hurting savers. Central bank intervention is needed to strike a balance between too high and too low rates. Intervention is needed more in developing countries whenever it may be necessary to direct financial resources to certain sectors that are not the most profitable (for example, agriculture as opposed to stock trading). Furthermore, the preachers of market-determined interest rates do not practice what they preach as they are crushing the middle class with ultra-low and negative interest rates for the benefit of banks and corporate interests. By doing that, they are perpetuating an orgy of parasitic activities such as stock buy-backs and venture capital.

I would imagine that free marketeers do not like negative interest rates because they are not market-determined, even though they are extremely profitable for the banking oligarchy. This is one of the cases where government intervention is good and warranted as far as bankers are concerned. However, free marketeers oppose government intervention that prevents bankers from gambling with depositors' money by separating investment banking from commercial banking.

Perhaps it is a good idea for the IMF to follow the lead of Washington and its allies and put into practice the use of negative interest rates in its dealings with poor countries, which would welcome loans at negative interest rates. After all, most of the poor countries endured years of exploitation by imperialist forces, in which case they deserve (as compensation) loans with negative interest rates.

Chapter 8

The Fifth Commandment:
Exchange Rate Policy

8.1 The Fifth Commandment as Described by Williamson

The fifth commandment of the Washington Consensus is that of "competitive" exchange rates. Williamson (1990) expresses the "dominant" view that achieving a "competitive" exchange rate is more important than how the rate is determined. There seems to be some contradiction here: how can we put the exchange rate at a competitive level when we do not know how it is determined? Williamson defines an appropriate level of the exchange rate to be consistent in the medium-run with macroeconomic objectives, which pertains to his concept of the "fundamental equilibrium exchange rate" (Williamson, 1985). Thus, the fifth commandment of the Consensus is about the real exchange rate being at the appropriate level, which is problematical because the real exchange rate (which is defined in more than one way) is unobservable. And no one knows how long the medium run is.

The fifth commandment is allegedly important for a developing country because a competitive real exchange rate is essential for promoting exports. This, according to Williamson (1990), "will allow the economy to grow at the maximum rate permitted by its supply-side potential, while keeping the current account deficit to a size that can be financed on a sustainable basis". He notes that the fifth commandment means that a "competitive real exchange rate is the first essential element of an 'outward-oriented' economic policy, where the balance of payments constraint is overcome primarily by export growth rather than by import substitution". What is the evidence that export growth is more important for the balance of payments than import substitution? How can developing countries compete in the presence of strict regulations about product specification in developed countries' markets? This is probably a reason why Brazilian and other aircraft manufacturers cannot compete with Airbus and Boeing for a slice of the global aircraft market. It is also the reason why Chinese aircraft manufacturers will not have an easy ride. Dismissing import substitution sounds convenient for multinationals seeking markets in developing countries. Free trade, in the Washington tradition, is free in one direction only.

The exchange rate, Williamson argues, "should not be more competitive than that, because that would produce unnecessary inflationary pressures and also limit the resources available for domestic investment, and hence curb the growth of supply-side potential". Thus, he acknowledges implicitly that a competitive exchange rate, which invariably means an undervalued currency, makes imports more expensive. He seems to overlook several factors, including the elasticity of demand for that country's exports, non-price determinants of competitiveness, and the currency of invoicing. If the currency of invoicing is not the domestic currency, the exchange rate becomes irrelevant.

Williamson (1990) notes that the growth of non-traditional exports is dependent not just on a competitive exchange rate at a particular point in time, but also on private-sector confidence that the rate will remain sufficiently competitive in the future to justify investment in potential export industries. Accordingly, it is important to assess the stability of the real exchange rate as well as its level. I would imagine that this means that a requirement of the fifth commandment is to maintain a stable exchange rate, which is "Mission Impossible", particularly for a developed country.

8.2 Exchange Rate Misalignment

It is not clear what a "competitive" exchange rate means, but one would imagine that it is the exchange rate that makes exports competitive in foreign markets. In this sense, a competitive exchange rate implies a weak domestic currency, which is a double-edged sword because a weak currency makes imports more expensive and brings about imported inflation.

This seems to be at odds with the objective of avoiding exchange rate misalignment.

A misaligned exchange rate is inconsistent with current account equilibrium (deficit or surplus). This implies that the domestic currency is neither so strong as to make exports too expensive, nor too weak as to make imports too expensive. In Figure 8.1, we can see the supply and demand curves in the foreign exchange market where demand and supply refer to the domestic currency. E is the exchange rate such that a higher level of E implies a strong domestic currency, and vice versa. Q is the quantity of the domestic currency supplied and demanded. When the exchange rate is at the equilibrium level, E_0, the foreign exchange market is in equilibrium, which corresponds to equilibrium in the current account. This is because demand for the domestic currency is a measure of export earnings whereas the supply of the domestic currency is a measure of import expenditure. At this level, the exchange rate is not misaligned. When the exchange rate is above equilibrium at E_1, the domestic currency is overvalued, thus the exchange rate is misaligned. At this rate, there is excess supply of the domestic currency, which implies

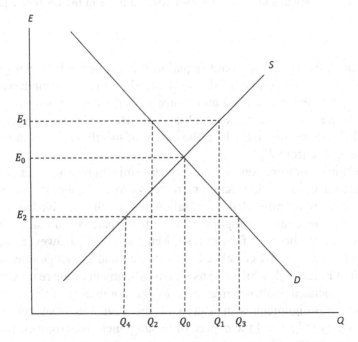

Figure 8.1:   Misalignment of the Nominal Exchange Rate

Figure 8.2:   Nominal and Real Effective Exchange Rates of the US Dollar (2010 = 100)

a deficit in the current account (equal to the difference between Q_1 and Q_2). At E_2, on the other hand, the domestic currency is undervalued, giving rise to excess demand and a surplus in the current account that is equal to the difference between Q_3 and Q_4. Both of the exchange rates E_1 and E_2 are misaligned, where the extent of misalignment is measured by divergence from E_0.

In the literature on exchange rate misalignment, and in the Washington Consensus, misalignment refers to overvaluation or under-valuation in real terms, that is, misalignment of the real exchange rate. Hence, exchange rate misalignment refers to "departures of real exchange rates from equilibrium" (for example, Marston, 1988). However, the real exchange rate is highly correlated with the nominal exchange rate, as can be seen in Figure 8.2, which means that misalignment of the real exchange rate is associated with misalignment of the nominal exchange rate. If, however, misalignment is measured by the deviation from purchasing power parity (PPP) and the degree of misalignment is zero, then the real exchange rate should be constant.

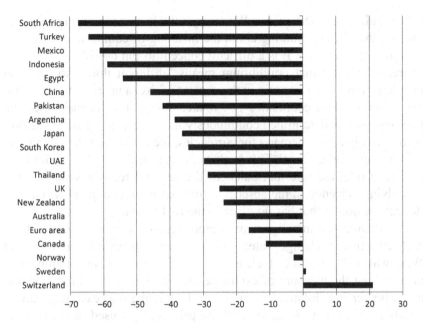

Figure 8.3:   Exchange Rate Misalignment According to Big Mac Index

The Big Mac index, which was developed in 1986 to measure misalignment of bilateral exchange rates, is based on PPP (more precisely, the law of one price). Figure 8.3 displays the July 2020 calculations of the misalignment of bilateral exchange rates against the dollar, where we can hardly see any exchange rate that is not misaligned, with the exception of the Swedish krona. The Swiss franc is overvalued by 21%, whereas the South African rand is undervalued by 67.4%. Presumably, this misalignment results from interference with the forces of supply and demand in the foreign exchange market. By definition, a competitive exchange rate, as required by the fifth commandment, is not market-determined, which is rather strange since the Washington Consensus represents the views of free marketeers.

To measure exchange rate misalignment, we must define the equilibrium exchange rate, which could be either the rate producing a balanced current account or the rate that does not violate the law of one price (LOP). This means that the exchange rate equates common currency prices of identical goods (according to the LOP) or baskets of goods (PPP). However, the concept of "equilibrium" as applied to the exchange rate is rather ambiguous. Driver and Westaway (2004) make this point clear by arguing that "when thinking about the meaning of equilibrium it quickly becomes apparent that it is a difficult concept to pin down". Hence, they express the view that equilibrium means "different things to different people and this is no less true in the context of exchange rates than it is for any other field in economics". A related proposition is that since the exchange rate is determined continuously in the foreign exchange market by the supply of and demand for currencies, the exchange rate will always be at its equilibrium level. This leads to the concept of market equilibrium exchange rate, the rate that balances the demand for and supply of the underlying currency in the absence of official intervention. This is a nice theoretical notion that has no place in the real world.

Exchange rate misalignment is more broadly judged in terms of the real effective exchange rate, which is not observable. Driver and Westaway (2004) make it clear that the literature on misalignment is vague about the measure of exchange rate, whether it is nominal or real and whether it is bilateral or effective. If it is the real exchange rate, a question arises as to the choice of the price indices used to convert the nominal rate into the corresponding real rate. Most theories of equilibrium exchange rates emphasize the real effective exchange rate by using different definitions of the relevant price indices to convert the nominal rate into a real rate. Associated with any given real exchange rate equilibrium is an infinite number of combinations of nominal exchange rates and relative price levels.

Williamson (1990) refers to the concept of "fundamental equilibrium exchange rate". Various concepts of the "equilibrium exchange rate" are used for the purpose of measuring exchange rate misalignment—these concepts (measures) give inconsistent results. The behavioral equilibrium exchange rate (BEER) is the most popular concept. The underlying approach is statistical whereby the real exchange rate is related to fundamentals in a single equation without any underlying theory. A long list of variables appear as determinants of the real exchange rate, including net foreign assets, terms of trade, ratio of total trade to GDP, ratio of consumption to GDP, productivity, interest rates, ratio of outstanding domestic government debt to foreign government debt, ratio of the unit value of exports to the unit value of imports, the relative price of traded to non-traded goods, and so on and so forth. The equilibrium rate is typically calculated by using dubious econometric techniques such as the Johansen test. The outcome can be anything, and any desire can be satisfied.

The fundamental equilibrium exchange rate (FEER) is defined as "an exchange rate that is expected to be indefinitely sustainable on the basis of existing policies" (Cline and Williamson, 2009). This rate, which is supposed to be consistent with medium-term equilibrium, is expected to generate a current account surplus or deficit that matches the country's underlying capital flow over the cycle, assuming that the country is pursuing policies aimed at achieving internal balance as well as it can and that it is not restricting trade for reasons pertaining to the balance of payments. The problems associated with the estimation of FEER are plentiful, for example, Chen (2007) points out that the estimation results are very sensitive to the modification of parameters when a certain hypothesis changes, particularly for developing countries. This is a nice theoretical concept that has no place in reality. No one knows what medium-term equilibrium means and the current account is determined by more than the exchange rate, as we are going to see.

The permanent equilibrium exchange rate (PEER) can be obtained by decomposing the actual real exchange rate into permanent and transitory components, such that the permanent component is taken to be the equilibrium rate. The natural real equilibrium exchange rate (NATREX) is the equilibrium rate produced by domestic economic fundamentals, defined by Stein (1994) as "the rate that would prevail if speculative and cyclical factors could be removed while unemployment is at its natural rate". The desired equilibrium real exchange rate (DEER) is related to FEER—the difference between the two concepts lies in the difference between "optimal" and "desired". The intermediate-term model-based equilibrium exchange rate (ITMEER) is associated with equilibrium that is assumed to be a function of relative current accounts (as a percentage of GDP), relative unemployment, relative net foreign assets to GDP, and the ratio of wholesale to consumer prices.

The difficulty of measuring the extent of exchange rate misalignment can be seen vividly in the debate on whether or not the Chinese yuan is undervalued against the US dollar. This has been the main reason for the US–China trade tension, as China-bashers attribute the US bilateral deficit with China to exchange rate misalignment. Over the past 20 years or so, US politicians and economists have been arguing that "the Chinese currency is undervalued by as much as 40 per cent against the dollar" and that China's exchange rate policy is designed "to depress the value of the yuan and push cheap Chinese goods into US markets" (Wolverson, 2010). For some reason, 40 is the preferred round number used in an *ad hoc* manner by those claiming that the yuan is undervalued. Roubini (2007) agrees with the proposition that the yuan is "grossly" undervalued, suggesting that the Chinese surplus and massive foreign exchange reserves are indicative of exchange rate misalignment. Crockett (2008) refers to a wide agreement that the yuan is undervalued, but he admits that there is little agreement on the size of undervaluation and how to correct it. Goldstein and Lardy (2008) argue that "any reasonable back-of-the-envelope calculation aimed at finding the level of the renminbi that would eliminate China's global current account surplus would generate a large (and growing) estimate of the renminbi undervaluation".

On the other hand, the IMF (2004) concluded that "it is difficult to find persuasive evidence that the renminbi is undervalued". Dunaway *et al.* (2006) found that the choice of the sample period, equation specification, and variable definition can lead to large variations in the results. Chinn *et al.* (2006) cast doubt on the proposition that the yuan is undervalued by suggesting "why the Renminbi might be overvalued (but probably is not)", whereas Wang (2004) noted that the yuan was actually overvalued. Research conducted at Morgan Stanley showed that the yuan was undervalued by one per cent only, a result described by *The Economist* (2007) as "not the answer Congress wants". This variation in the results, and the views based upon them, leads to the inevitable consequence of "cherry-picking".

Enthusiasm for the proposition that the yuan is undervalued has died down, at least according to the views expressed by those who talk economics rather than politics. In July 2018, the IMF declared that "China's yuan is in line with fundamentals" (Reuters, 2018). In March 2019, the Japanese financial firm, Nomura, expressed the view that "the Chinese yuan is probably already overvalued against the US dollar and any efforts by President Donald Trump's team to lock in that level as part of trade negotiations will likely backfire" (Olsen, 2019). The Nomura report considers the underlying issue as a "sticking point for the US, which, despite years of long-term appreciation in the currency, accuses Beijing of keeping it artificially undervalued to boost exports". Coward (2015) examines the JP Morgan real effective exchange rate indices and concludes that "the yuan is probably overvalued by a decent margin". Forsyth (2016) addresses Trump by saying "sorry" because "the Chinese currency is actually way overvalued", arguing that "Trump is wrong on China" and that "even though Beijing has worked mightily to push up its currency, the yuan or renminbi, since then, the billionaire businessman persists in his wrong-headed assertions".

The Economic Times (2019) quotes Julian Evans-Pritchard, senior China economist at Capital Economics in Singapore as saying that based on the real effective exchange rate, the yuan is close to if not slightly stronger than, its long-run average. Yet, amid ongoing US–China trade tension, the US Treasury Department formally designated China a currency manipulator in August 2019. The move came in response to what the Trump administration called China's attempts to "gain an unfair competitive advantage in international trade". At that time, President Trump also stated that China's gradual depreciation of the Renminbi (RMB) is aimed at offsetting the cost of US tariffs on Chinese goods (see, for example, Zumbrun, 2019). The debate carried on in 2020 as the US continued with countervailing investigations into the alleged yuan undervaluation (for example, Global Times, 2020).

Exchange rate misalignment is not exactly a science, but if the extent of misalignment or the equilibrium exchange rate cannot be determined, how is it possible to determine a competitive exchange rate? And then it seems that a country that has what others believe to be a competitive exchange rate runs the risk of being accused of practicing currency manipulation and ends up being on the wrong side of a trade war. No one does that better than Washington.

8.3 Determinants of Competitiveness

The fifth commandment of the Washington Consensus calls for a competitive exchange rate to boost exports as the way to economic prosperity. However, the exchange rate does not exclusively determine price competitiveness, which is the ability to produce goods and services at lower prices than competitors. Farole *et al.* (2010) argue that the term "competitiveness" is used widely and is seemingly intuitive when it is conceptually vague and open to multiple interpretations. Many economists view competitiveness as something experienced only at the firm level and dismiss notions of "national competitiveness" (Krugman, 1996), while others believe the lack of attention to broader national-level notions of competitiveness has been a glaring failure of economic research and policy (Porter, 1990).

Price competitiveness is related to the cost of production, which depends on the factor costs, including labor, raw materials and energy (as well as the exchange rate). The source of price competitiveness could be low wages or abundance of raw materials. Price competitiveness is also affected by the quality of the infrastructure, which determines the cost of transportation. Other relevant factors are imported input prices, economies of scale and taxes, as well as the quality of the financial system and macroeconomic policy. We should also add productivity, which depends heavily on the use of technology, hence expenditure on research and development.

That is not all because competitiveness does not only depend on price. Sharma (1992) notes that the concept of competitiveness is rather complex and requires consideration of a large number of determinants, many of which are not quantifiable. However, he presents a long list of determinants, including the ability to generate exportable surplus, the cost of production, prices prevailing in the domestic and export markets, relative prices of competitors, quality and design of the product, freight and delivery schedules, standards of packaging and aesthetic appeal, the exchange rate and the currency of invoicing, trade policy of the exporting country and the importance of exports to the country. The currency of invoicing is particularly important because if it is not the domestic currency, the exchange rate becomes irrelevant. United Nations Conference on Trade and Development (UNCTAD) (2005) emphasizes the determinants of supply capacity, including domestic transport infrastructure, macroeconomic environment, foreign direct investment, and institutions.

Several empirical studies have been carried out to identify the determinants of competitiveness. Muratoğlu and Muratoğlu (2016) analyze the determinants of export competitiveness in the manufacturing sectors of 12 Organisation for Economic Co-operation and Development (OECD) countries over the period 1999–2010 and find that competitiveness is determined by "conventional variables", including physical capital, labor cost, and infrastructure. They also find that R&D and the share of high-tech exports have positive effects on export competitiveness. Sikharulidze and Kikutadze (2017) examine the competitiveness of 360 Georgian firms and find that those involved intensively in the innovation process record the highest export intensity and that the impact of innovation on exports is sizeable. Porter (1990) notes that competitive advantage is created and sustained through a highly localized process and identifies, as contributors to competitive success, differences in national values, culture, economic structures, institutions, and histories. Tambade *et al.* (2019) identify 30 variables as being "reliable in establishing the potential indicators of competitiveness". Rusu and Roman (2018) find that competitiveness is determined by a variety of factors, including GDP, inflation, trade, labor productivity, labor costs, FDI and tax rate.

The fifth commandment is unimplementable because it is based on a tenuous relation between an unobservable variable (real exchange rate) and another variable that is determined or affected by a large number of variables (competitiveness). It is not exactly like raising or reducing the temperature on a stove to get the desired result of cooking food without burning it.

8.4 The Effect of Devaluation

If the exchange rate is not competitive enough, then devaluation of the domestic currency should make exports more competitive. The fifth commandment is therefore an invitation to indulge in competitive devaluation, which raises the question as to why a trade war has been declared on China, allegedly because it indulges in competitive devaluation. It occurs when one country devalues its currency and other countries respond by devaluing their currencies, resulting in a currency war. As a matter of fact, the very act of devaluing the domestic currency to make exports more competitive is not encouraged. The UNCTAD (2005) argues that the exchange rate has a significant effect on the export performance of the lowest performer because an overvalued currency is seriously detrimental to export performance, while on average a 1% real depreciation could boost exports by 6–10%. However, the UNCTAD makes it clear that "this is not an argument for competitive devaluations of nominal exchange rates".

Is devaluation that effective in making exports more competitive? Let us examine the effect of (nominal) devaluation on the price and quantity of exports and consequently export revenue. The demand for exports by foreigners is a negative function of the price expressed in foreign currency terms. If the exchange rate is expressed as the value in foreign currency terms of one unit of the domestic currency, then the foreign currency price of exports is the product of the exchange rate and the domestic currency price of exports. Assume that the domestic currency price does not change, so that nominal devaluation is equivalent to real devaluation. If demand is elastic, a fall in the foreign currency price of exports resulting from the devaluation of the domestic currency (that is, reducing the exchange rate) produces a more than proportional rise in the quantity

Table 8.1:   Effect of Devaluation With Constant Domestic Price and Elastic Demand

Domestic Currency Price	Exchange Rate	Foreign Currency Price	Quantity of Exports	Export Revenue
10	2.0	20	100.0	2000.0
10	1.9	19	110.0	2090.0
10	1.8	18	121.6	2188.4
10	1.7	17	135.1	2296.5
10	1.6	16	151.0	2415.7
10	1.5	15	169.9	2547.8
10	1.4	14	192.5	2695.0
10	1.3	13	220.0	2860.0
10	1.2	12	253.8	3046.2
10	1.1	11	296.2	3257.7
10	1.0	10	350.0	3500.0

demanded. The result will be a higher level of export earnings (the product of foreign currency price and quantity).

Consider a numerical example, as shown in Table 8.1, where it is assumed that the domestic currency price is fixed at 10 and that the elasticity of demand for exports is −2, so that a 1% decline in the foreign currency price of exports leads to a 2% rise in the quantity of exports. We can see that by reducing the exchange rate (making the domestic currency cheaper), the quantity of exports rises, and so does export revenue. Figure 8.4 shows the demand curve, which represents the quantity of exports demanded as a function of the foreign currency price of exports and export revenue as a function of the exchange rate.

The process seems to work, but only because of two assumptions: elastic demand and no change in the domestic currency price of exports so that nominal devaluation translates into real devaluation. Let us see what happens when the elastic demand assumption is relaxed so that elasticity is −0.9 (that is, a 1% fall in the foreign currency price of exports brings about a 0.9% rise in the quantity of exports). Table 8.2 shows the situation where the quantity of exports rises slowly. Since the quantity demanded rises less proportionately than the price fall, export revenue declines. Figure 8.5 shows the same situation.

Consider now the relaxation of the other assumption, such that the domestic currency price rises in line with inflation, in which case real devaluation is smaller than nominal devaluation. The effect of devaluation

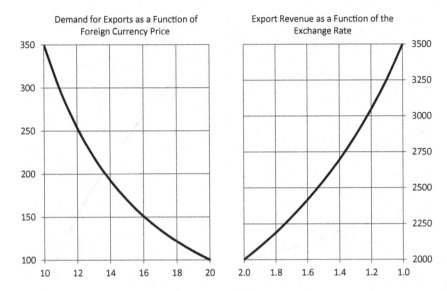

Figure 8.4: Effect of Devaluation on Demand and Export Revenue (Elastic Demand)

Table 8.2: Effect of Devaluation With Constant Domestic Price and Inelastic Demand

Domestic Currency Price	Exchange Rate	Foreign Currency Price	Quantity of Exports	Export Revenue
10	2.0	20	100.0	2000.0
10	1.9	19	104.5	1985.5
10	1.8	18	109.5	1970.1
10	1.7	17	114.9	1953.7
10	1.6	16	121.0	1936.1
10	1.5	15	127.8	1917.2
10	1.4	14	135.5	1896.7
10	1.3	13	144.2	1874.5
10	1.2	12	154.2	1850.1
10	1.1	11	165.7	1823.1
10	1.0	10	179.3	1793.0

on export revenue in the presence of a 4% rise in the domestic currency price of exports is shown in Figure 8.6 under elastic demand. We can see that export revenue rises more slowly when the domestic price of exports rises.

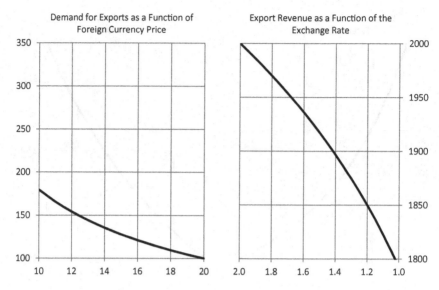

Figure 8.5:   Effect of Devaluation on Demand and Export Revenue (Inelastic Demand)

The effect of devaluation on export revenue is not straightforward. For devaluation to boost export revenue, several conditions must be satisfied. The first is a full (or at least high) pass-through effect from the exchange rate to the foreign currency price of exports, that is, changes in the foreign currency price of exports are proportional to changes in the exchange rate. The second condition is that the volume of exports rises more proportionately than the fall in price to produce a net rise in export revenue. This depends on the elasticity of demand, as we have seen. The third condition is that the supply of exports is infinitely elastic, in the sense that any increase in foreign demand can be met by utilizing excess capacity, that is, exporters must be capable of and willing to accommodate any increase in foreign demand. The fourth condition is that prices and quantities are not affected by factors other than the exchange rate, or at least there are no offsetting effects operating in the opposite direction. We have already seen what happens when the domestic price of exports rises, causing the foreign currency price of exports to rise without a change in the exchange rate. On this issue, Goldberg and Tille (2006) refer to the complications and conditions that impede the materialization of the effect of exchange rate adjustment.

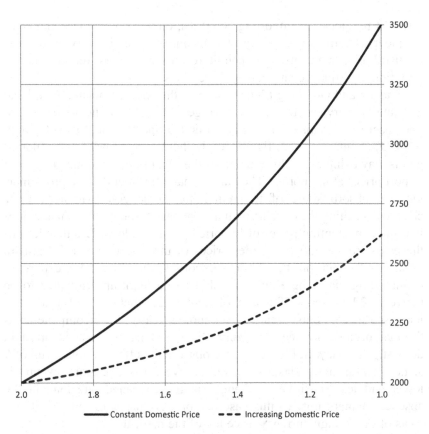

Figure 8.6: Effect of Devaluation on Export Revenue With Increasing Domestic Prices

Let us examine what happens when exchange rate pass-through is incomplete because of distribution mark-ups and profit margins in the destination (foreign) market. In the real world, distribution mark-ups and profit margins create a gap between border prices (domestic prices converted at the current exchange rate) and retail prices (border prices plus mark-ups and profit margins at destination, which are what consumers actually pay). Since these mark-ups are denominated in the currency of the destination market, retail prices become less sensitive to changes in the exchange rate, thus dampening the pass-through effect. The importance of local mark-ups is highlighted by Goldberg and Tille (2006) who point out that "import price sensitivity to exchange rates is not identical to consumption price [that is, retail price] sensitivity" because "after goods arrive at the docks of importing countries, other local services and costs are incurred before the goods reach consumers". They identify the sources of distribution mark-ups as expenditure on wholesalers, retailers, transportation, and finance and insurance services.

Campa and Goldberg (2005) estimate the costs associated with local distribution services to be, on average, 32–50% of the total cost of goods across Organisation for Economic Co-operation and Development (OECD) countries. These figures imply that the retail prices of imported goods may exhibit one-third to half of the sensitivity to exchange rates of import prices at the border. They argue that adjustment of the profit margin can absorb some of the remaining exchange-rate-induced price changes, reaching the conclusion that "the pass-through of exchange rates into the consumption prices of imported goods could be less than half of the pass-through into the border prices of those same goods". Feenstra *et al.* (1998) point out that China's exports to the US and US exports to China going via Hong Kong are subject to a mark-up, estimated to be between 22.4% and 29.8%. Goldberg and Knetter (1997) identify increased foreign outsourcing as yet another reason for incomplete pass-through because it means a decline in the share of costs incurred in domestic currency. In Figure 8.7, we observe the effect of a mark-up of 5 at destination under elastic demand. As we can see, export revenue is lower and less sensitive to changes in the exchange rate than in the absence of mark-ups. In this case, export revenue is calculated on the basis of the foreign currency price net of the mark-up.

Incomplete exchange rate pass-through may also result from changes in the producers' profit margins. Goldberg and Tille (2006) argue that "if the exporters adjust their own profit margins to insulate foreign prices from exchange rate fluctuations, nominal trade balance implications arise purely due to revenue effects of exchange rates on existing quantities of goods traded". Goldberg and Knetter (1997) consider the following real-life example of partial and negative pass-through resulting from changes in the profit margin of producers (exporters). On 5 January 1994, the dollar was worth 113 yen, but by 19 April 1995, it was worth 80 yen. In 1994, a Toyota Celica made in Japan sold in the US for $16,968, but in 1995, it was worth $17,285, a price increase of just 2%. During the same period, the retail price of a large screen SONY Trinitron fell by 15%. The most likely explanation to what happened on that occasion was that Japanese manufacturers reduced their profit margins to offset the effect of the appreciation of the yen on the dollar prices of their products.

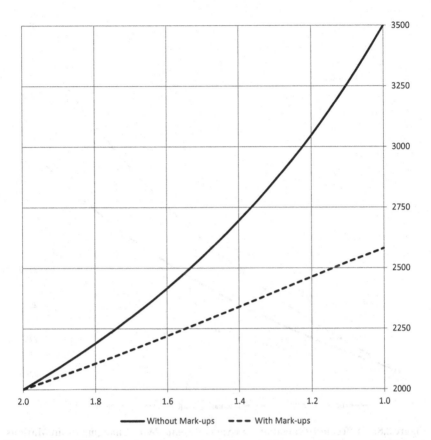

Figure 8.7: Effect of Devaluation on Export Revenue With and Without Mark-Ups

Reduction of profit margins by Chinese firms to preserve market share has been observed in practice, as pointed out by *The Economist* (2010). While the sales of Chinese firms rose by a staggering 42% year-on-year in the first half of 2010, margins were on a protracted slide. Not even seasonal factors, which should have pushed up profit margins by 1.5% in the first half, had any effect. The obvious explanation is that Chinese firms have been reducing profit margins to boost sales. In Figure 8.8, we observe the effect of devaluation on export revenue in the presence of constant and changing profit margins. When the exporter's profit margin is constant, domestic currency devaluation boosts export revenue under elastic demand. This is similar to the base case shown in

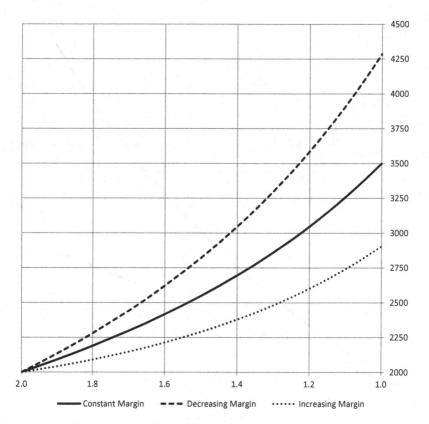

Figure 8.8:   **Effect of Devaluation on Export Revenue With Changing Profit Margins**

Figure 8.4. When the exporter reduces the profit margin every time period, export revenue rises more rapidly. Conversely, when the exporter raises the profit margin every time period, export revenue declines and becomes less sensitive to changes in the exchange rate.

The currency of invoicing is another factor. Page (1981) presents direct evidence indicating that many export goods for a number of industrialized countries are invoiced in the local currency of the buyer rather than the currency of the seller. His estimates show that Japanese firms invoice as much as 62% of all exports in dollars. The empirical work of Grassman (1973) and Page (1977) reveals in general that trades between two advanced countries are typically invoiced in the exporter's currency, but trades between advanced and developing countries are generally invoiced in the advanced country's currency.

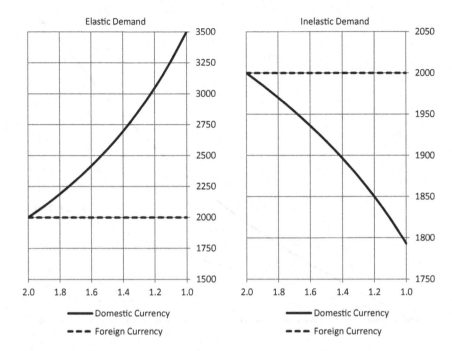

Figure 8.9: Effect of Devaluation on Export Revenue With One Currency of Invoicing

In Figure 8.9, we can see the effect of devaluation on export revenue when the currency of invoicing is the foreign currency rather than the domestic currency under elastic and inelastic demand. When the currency of invoicing is the foreign currency, devaluation has no effect on export revenue because the exchange rate becomes irrelevant. Some intermediate cases can be observed when both currencies are used for invoicing. In Figure 8.10, we can see the effect of devaluation on export revenue under domestic currency invoicing, foreign currency invoicing, and mixed currency invoicing (50–50). We can see that the higher the ratio of foreign to domestic currency invoicing, the less sensitive is export revenue (in foreign currency terms) to changes in the exchange rate.

The use of the dollar as the currency of invoicing in international trade transactions is examined by Goldberg and Tille (2006), who argue that the pass-through effect is important particularly because of the international role of the dollar. They note that the use of the dollar as the currency of invoicing in international trade is consistent with evidence on low

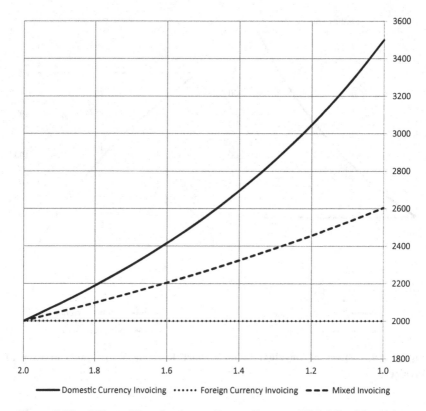

Figure 8.10:   Effect of Devaluation on Export Revenue With Mixed Invoicing

pass-through of exchange rate movements into the import prices of the US and the higher pass-through into the import prices of other countries. A consequence of the international status of the US dollar, they point out, is that "the trade balance effects of exchange rate depreciation can be dramatically different for the United States compared with other countries". Under these conditions, depreciation of the dollar is expected to lead to little change in US demand for imports because the dollar price of imports will not be affected by changes in exchange rates, but the price of US exports will decline in foreign currency terms.

Goldberg and Tille (2006) conclude that "the special international role of the dollar and the related low degree of exchange-rate pass through into US import prices will lead the trade balance response to be primarily through increased quantities of US exports". They attribute the use of the dollar as the currency of invoicing in international trade to the following:

(i) the share of the US market as a destination for world production; (ii) the size of dollar bloc countries outside of the US; (iii) the importance of global trade in commodities and homogeneous goods relative to total trade; and (iv) transaction costs that provide incentive for using the dollar rather than the euro as the currency of invoicing. They suggest that "international trade transactions between other countries and the United States are primarily invoiced in US dollars" and that "more than 99% of US exports and 92% of US imports were invoiced in dollars in early 2003". Countries using their own currencies on part of their sales to the US are the UK, Japan, and some euro area countries. The dollar is used as the currency of invoicing for 48% of Japanese exports compared to 83% for Korea, 90% for Malaysia and 84% for Thailand.

The effect of other factors, such as inflation and growth, may offset the effect of the exchange rate. When everything moves at the same time, which is what happens in an economy as opposed to a lab experiment, there is no guarantee that the exchange rate effect will dominate other factors. For example, a foreign recession reduces the effect of currency devaluation as the demand for exports declines irrespective of changes in the exchange rate. The same happens in the case of a shift in taste against exports. The effect of recession can be seen in Figure 8.11 under elastic and inelastic demand. Without a recession, export revenue rises more rapidly when demand is elastic and falls more slowly when demand is inelastic.

8.5 Fixed Versus Flexible Exchange Rates

An overvalued currency is sometimes blamed on the use of a fixed exchange rate as a nominal anchor to control inflationary pressures, which "translates into a direct loss of price competitiveness for exporting firms" (UNCTAD, 2005). This implies that the use of flexible exchange rates may put the rate at a competitive level. It is not clear whether the competitive level is the equilibrium exchange rate as determined by market forces (correctly aligned) or a misaligned exchange rate that is associated with an undervalued currency. Williamson (1990) does not say how a competitive exchange rate can be determined and he does not mention anything about preference for fixed or flexible exchange rates. This is strange because the Washington Consensus is based on the free market doctrine, in which case preference should be for flexible exchange rates. As far back as 1953, the high priest of free marketeers, Milton Friedman, wrote

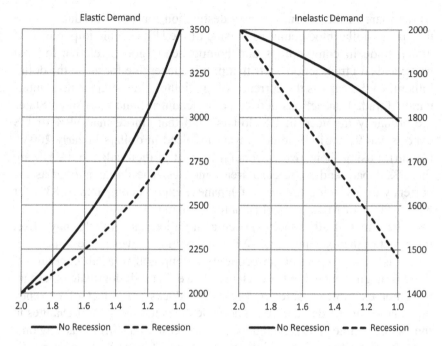

Figure 8.11:   Effect of Devaluation on Export Revenue With Overseas Recession

an influential piece in which he put a strong case for flexible exchange rates (Friedman, 1953; Dellas and Tavlas, 2018).

The proponents of flexible exchange rates claim that adjustment of the balance of payments under this system is smoother and less painful than under fixed rates and that flexible exchange rates move continuously and in small doses to restore equilibrium. Movements of flexible exchange rates are described as small, continuous and determined by market forces. Conversely, movements of fixed exchange rates are large, discrete and triggered by central bank action.

The proponents of flexible exchange rates claim that since they move continuously in reaction to disequilibria in the balance of payments, large and persistent deficits do not arise. This in turn boosts confidence in the international monetary system, resulting in fewer attempts to readjust currency portfolios and producing calmer foreign exchange markets. This is something that we do not observe in practice, simply because the supply of and demand for exports and imports do not depend only on changes in nominal exchange rates, as we have seen. Of course, the proponents of

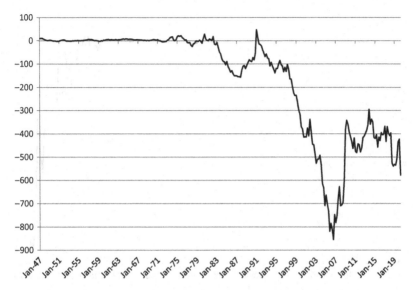

Figure 8.12: US Current Account Balance (Billion Dollars)

flexible exchange rates would argue that a system of perfectly flexible exchange rates has never been tried. However, if their argument is valid, then one would expect a move in the direction of perfectly flexible exchange rates would alleviate the problem of large and persistent deficits.

Nothing can be further away from the truth as can be seen in Figures 8.12 and 8.13, which respectively show the current account balances of the US and UK. Going back to 1947, the US current account was always in close proximity to equilibrium until 1971 when the Bretton Woods system collapsed. In the early 1990s, there was a short episode of surplus resulting from the financial transfers from Saudi Arabia and Kuwait to pay for the first war against Iraq. Ever since, record deficits have been recurring. In the case of the UK, the current account has been in big deficit and highly volatile under flexible exchange rates.

Another argument that is put forward in favor of flexible exchange rates is that liquidity problems do not arise (or at least they are not as acute) under flexible exchange rates because central banks do not hold foreign exchange reserves for the purpose of market intervention. Perhaps, but reserves are not only held for the purpose of foreign exchange market intervention, and because this problem is endemic to

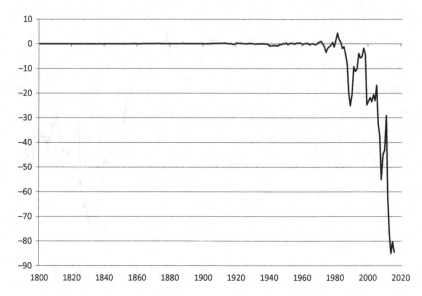

Figure 8.13:   UK Current Account Balance (Billion Pounds)

the post-war dollar-based system. But then take this argument: flexible exchange rates are more conducive to achieving free international trade because this system maintains equilibrium in the balance of payments, which means that tariffs and other trade impediments will not be imposed. This is exactly the opposite to what intuition, the empirical evidence and the facts on the ground tell us. Exchange rate volatility under flexible exchange rates has an adverse effect on international trade. This is one reason why European countries decided to move to fixed exchange rates, starting with the Snake in the Tunnel, moving to the European Monetary System and eventually to the European Monetary Union.

Yet another argument in favor of flexible exchange rates is that they are conducive to policy independence in the sense of allowing a country to follow policies that are different from those of its major trading partners. It is also claimed that, under flexible exchange rates, countries are insulated from what happens in other economies. This means that under flexible exchange rates, the central bank in one country can set the level of interest rates independently of other countries. Again, this is not supported by the facts on the ground: just look at the interest rates of Washington and its allies—they have all converged on zero.

As far as developing countries are concerned, the proponents of flexible exchange rates claim that countries with flexible rates are in a better position to cope with currency crises than those with fixed rates. However, flexible exchange rates are not suitable for small economies with undiversified export bases. For example, in what way are flexible exchange rates useful for oil exporting countries that export one commodity using the US dollar as the currency of invoicing? Furthermore, flexible exchange rates are not appropriate for countries without sophisticated financial systems, as a successful operation of such a system requires developed forward and futures markets. Developing countries do not have developed financial markets.

Flexible exchange rates are inflationary in a general sense, whereas fixed exchange rates provide discipline. Flexible exchange rates cause uncertainty and inhibit international trade and investment because they affect the private sector's decision-making process. They encourage destabilizing speculation, accentuating the appreciation and depreciation of currencies. They are unstable in the sense that small disturbances to exchange rates can grow into extremely large disturbances. With flexible exchange rates, serious balance of payments difficulties could lead to a steep fall in the value of the domestic currency, which could adversely affect price stability and output in the short run.

Irrespective of who is right and who is wrong in this debate, it is not clear where the fifth commandment comes in. Does the maintenance of a competitive exchange rate require the adoption of fixed or flexible exchange rates? If the competitive exchange rate is below equilibrium, then this means that flexible exchange rates should not be adopted by developing countries striving to apply the rules of the Washington Consensus. Furthermore, Williamson (1990) talks about the necessity of the stability of the competitive rate. Again, this sounds as if flexible exchange rates are not desirable, which is inconsistent with the Consensus that hinges on free market pricing.

8.6 Export Growth Versus Import Substitution

The fifth commandment of the Consensus calls for competitive exchange rates to boost exports on the grounds that exports propel growth. Farole *et al.* (2010) argue that "the economic benefits of exporting have a long-established theoretical basis", including the following: (i) static efficiency gains realized by exploiting comparative advantage and improved allocation of scarce resources; (ii) dynamic gains in the more productive export sector engineered by higher competition; (iii) greater economies of scale; (iv) better capacity utilization; (v) dissemination of knowledge; and (iv) technological progress. Furthermore, they suggest that, for developing countries, exports are the main source of hard currency necessary to finance the imports of capital goods, which are an important source of knowledge spillovers.

The literature on heterogeneous firms also emphasizes that exporters on average are more productive, capital-intensive, larger, and pay higher wages than non-exporters. On the other hand, overdependence on commodity exports can contribute to lower long-run growth and it is the way to catching the Dutch disease. Farole *et al.* (2010) refer to the phenomenon of "jobless growth", suggesting that export-driven manufacturing output in East Asia increased by almost 180% in the 1990s, but the associated employment increased by 3% only. Yet, they argue that the East Asian experience of export-led growth provides powerful real-world evidence of the potential for trade to be an engine of growth and poverty reduction. Indeed, despite the steep declines in exports in highly open, export-oriented East Asian economies during the global financial crisis, growth appears to have rebounded more quickly and robustly than in less globally integrated regions.

Despite much effort to boost exports, many developing countries have failed to achieve successful sustainable export-driven growth. Farole *et al.* (2010) suggest that even with the benefit of preferential market access, many developing country exporters face a broad and diverse set of constraints that limit their potential to compete in export markets. The constraints are not necessarily domestic because developed countries put impediments in front of the exports of developing countries. Free trade is free in one direction only, which is developed countries exporting to developing countries but not the other way round. While the growth of trade among developed countries has been encouraged by steadily dropping tariffs and other barriers, the barriers they impose on the manufactured goods of developing countries have not been reduced to the same extent. For example, developed countries put hard-to-meet specifications on the products of developing countries before they are allowed. Thus, a number of export products of particular interest to developing countries are often subject to high import barriers, including non-tariff barriers, such as subsidies, tax breaks, and all forms of protection.

Henson and Loader (2000) explore the impact of sanitary and phytosanitary (SPS) measures in developed countries on developing country exports of agricultural and food products and identify the problems that developing countries face in meeting SPS requirements. Even though agreements negotiated at the World Trade Organization (WTO) are reducing the extent of traditional trade protection measures, such as tariffs and quotas, Mutume (2006) argues that they are being replaced by SPS. For several years in the late 1990s, for example, European countries banned fish from Kenya, Mozambique, Tanzania and Uganda due to concerns about these countries' sanitary standards and control systems. He quotes Trevor Manuel, South Africa's Finance Minister, as saying that "the problem is not that international trade is inherently opposed to the needs and interests of the poor, but that the rules that govern it are rigged in favor of the rich".

Non-tariff measures (NTMs) include a wide range of trade policy measures, such as import quotas, licensing and rules of origin. They also include product-specific requirements, such as quality or content requirements, labeling, testing and certification. Exporters experience obstacles to trade differently, depending on whether they are rigorous requirements, red tape, time spent at customs, certification procedures, arbitrary behavior of officials or informal payments. Tarver (2020) defines a non-tariff barrier as a way to restrict trade using trade barriers in a form other than a tariff. Non-tariff barriers include quotas, embargoes, sanctions, and levies. As part of their political or economic strategy, some countries frequently use non-tariff barriers to restrict the amount of trade they conduct with other countries.

Apart from tariff and non-tariff impediments, exports are blocked by home bias, the tendency of consumers to buy local goods for various reasons. This is so much the case these days where central and local governments run campaigns to encourage preference for local products, even in the name of "patriotism". Plausible explanations for home bias include border costs that make foreign goods more expensive, high elasticities of substitution in consumption, foreign exchange risk, countries finding it easier to engage in domestic trade than international trade, preferences for home goods, weaker distribution networks for imported goods, inherent distrust of foreign products, and the possibility that legal costs are higher when business is done abroad.

At the same time, the Consensus seems to be against import substitution, which makes trade between developing and developed economies free in one direction. The Consensus conveys the advice that exchange rates should be competitive to boost exports, which does not work, while refraining from finding substitutes. The idea behind import substitution is that blocking the imports of manufactured goods can help an economy by boosting the demand for domestically produced goods. The logic, according to Irwin (2020a), is simple: why import foreign-made cars or clothing or chemicals when one could produce those goods at home and employ workers in doing so? Irwin attributes the idea, which goes back centuries in economic thought, to the Argentine economist Raúl Prebisch, who publicized his ideas in Latin America and around the world in the 1950s. Many developing countries adopted import substitution trade strategies after World War II, when economic development was equated with industrialization and capital investment. By the 1980s, however, the idea had fallen out of favor with the rise of the Washington Consensus and its emphasis on free trade.

Import substitution may be coming back as several African countries have recently indicated that they may be embracing it once again. *The Economist* (2020) describes Tito Mboweni, South Africa's Finance Minister, as aspiring to "set up manufacturing to make what we need and stop relying on imports from China". Uganda is trying to discourage imports. Ghana intends to make import substitution a priority. Other countries (such as China, India, and even the US) seek to promote domestic manufacturing and exclude imports from the market. For example, the Trump administration took steps to "reshore" the production of cars, semiconductors, and other manufactured goods to boost American output and create manufacturing jobs.

The views on import substitution of early intellectual leaders in development economics are examined by Irwin (2020b). He argues that while these economists are commonly thought to have issued blanket endorsements of import-substituting policies, he finds that some of them were quite critical of protectionist policies. It appears that even the early supporters of import substitution were aware of the potential downsides to such policies. It is not clear why import substitution necessarily implies protectionism, and even so, why not? This policy was intended to promote industrialization by protecting domestic producers from the competition of imports. Grabowski (1994) is not totally dismissive, arguing that there have been cases of failure and cases of success. Ahmad (1978) contends that if the arguments for abandoning import substitution are to be taken seriously, one must visualize the growth prospects of less developed countries without import substitution. It is difficult to visualize continuing growth in per capita income without a large and growing industrial sector.

The economic performance of the BRICS countries (Brazil, Russia, India, China and South Africa) is examined by Adewale (2017) who argues that import substitution industrialization (ISI) policy helped to catalyze the industrialization process of these five countries and recommends that less developed countries should adopt this form of economic integration and home-grown ISI policy to substitute imports in the short run and embrace liberalization as higher level of industrialization is achieved in the long run.

Export promotion and import substitution are not mutually exclusive—rather, they are complementary. For a country to promote exports, it must have something to export that needs promotion. Oil exporting countries do not need to promote oil because everyone needs oil. For manufactured goods, export promotion needs the production of these goods rather than importing them, which is where import substitution comes in. Complementarity between export promotion and import substitution can be seen in Figure 8.14, where a country has a fixed

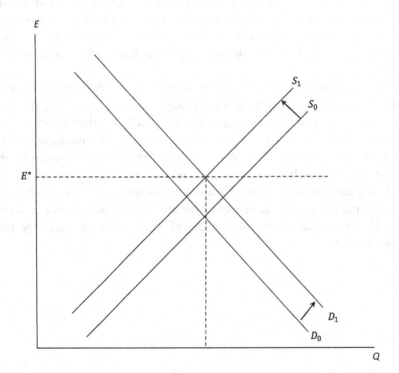

Figure 8.14: The Combined Effect of Import Substitution and Export Promotion

exchange rate at E^* causing excess supply of the domestic currency (hence excess demand for the foreign currency) at the original supply and demand curves, S_0 and D_0. Without resorting to devaluation, which may or may not work, a combination of export promotion and import substitution can be used to eliminate the imbalance in the foreign exchange market (hence in the current account). Export promotion leads to a shift in the demand curve (for the domestic currency) from D_0 to D_1. Simultaneously, import substitution leads to a decline in the supply of the domestic currency, leading to the achievement of equilibrium at the point of intersection of D_1 and S_1.

8.7 Concluding Remarks

The fifth commandment of the Washington Consensus is designed and intended to serve the interests of the oligarchy and corporate Washington. A competitive exchange rate means an undervalued domestic currency, which makes it cheaper for corporate Washington to obtain resources and buy privatized assets. For a number of reasons, devaluation is unlikely to boost exports. The argument against import substitution is intended to give corporate Washington free access to the markets of countries depending on imports.

Problems and contradictions can be observed in the fifth commandment. By definition, a competitive exchange rate, as required by the fifth commandment, is not market-determined, which is rather strange since the Washington Consensus represents the views of free marketeers. The real exchange rate is unobservable, and it can be anything—hence, it cannot be used as a policy variable. A competitive exchange rate implies a weak domestic currency, which is a double-edged sword because a weak currency makes imports more expensive and brings about imported inflation. This seems at odds with the objective of avoiding exchange rate misalignment.

Chapter 9

The Sixth Commandment:
Liberalization of Trade

9.1 The Sixth Commandment as Described by Williamson

Williamson (1990) describes import liberalization as the "second element of an outward-oriented economic policy". In essence, he urges developing countries against a policy aimed at protecting domestic industries from foreign competition so that they have access to imports of intermediate inputs at competitive prices, which is important for export promotion. Doing otherwise, he argues, creates "costly distortions that end up penalizing exports and impoverishing the domestic economy". He urges developing countries against import licensing, which he describes as "the worst form of protection" because of "its massive potential for creating opportunities for corruption". For Williamson and Washington in general, corruption is only rife in developing countries where an import license is granted in return for an envelope containing $5,000. It is not corruption that corporate Washington gets millions of dollars worth of bonuses and golden parachutes from the taxpayer-provided bail-out money, but this is a different issue.

Williamson recommends that if protection is to be pursued, it should be implemented by the imposition of tariffs, so that at least the public purse gets the "rents". He also recommends keeping the distortions to a minimum by limiting tariff dispersion and exempting from tariffs the imports of the intermediate goods needed to produce exports. However, if a country is capable of producing exportable goods, it should be able to produce the intermediate goods required to produce the final goods. And what happens when sanctions are imposed by political Washington? In this age when the sword of sanctions is wielded by Washington against any country that goes out of line (that is, any country that does not say "how high" when Washington says "jump"), the name of the game is self-sufficiency. The fact of the matter is that import liberalization means opening up the markets of developing countries to the exports of the custodians of the Washington Consensus who protect their own markets against foreign competition by various means as we saw in Chapter 8. This is the same mentality that led to imperialism in the 19th century and before. It is the same mentality that led to the destruction of China as a result of the opium wars when a sovereign decision was taken by China to close the door in front of imports of Indian-grown British opium.

The sixth commandment is about free trade, the "free trade ideal". Williamson acknowledges that the sixth commandment is subject to two qualifications: (i) the need to protect infant industries and (ii) the imposition of a "moderate general tariff" if necessary. However, he goes on to say that protection should be "strictly temporary" and that tariffs should be with "little dispersion", whatever that means. He also refers to the issue of timing, that is, whether import liberalization should proceed according to a predetermined timetable or allowing the speed of liberalization to vary endogenously, depending on how much the state of the balance of payments can tolerate.

In a way, therefore, the sixth commandment of free trade makes a lot of sense, except for three problems. The first is that the preachers do not practice what they preach, not now and not when they were at the same stage of development as developing countries. The second is that the benefits of free trade may be exaggerated and that the distribution of the benefits may be skewed in favor of the preachers, not the preached. The third is that free trade is a doctrine that is associated with British imperialism in particular, to the extent that atrocities have been committed to force it on the colonies.

9.2 The Concept of Free Trade

Free trade is defined as a policy whereby the government does not obstruct or interfere with the flows of imports and exports, for example, by applying tariffs to imports and subsidies to exports to change the balance of competitiveness. In other words, free trade is a trade policy that does not restrict imports or exports by using tariffs, subsidies, quantitative restrictions (such as quotas) and non-tariff restrictions. It can also be understood as the free market doctrine applied to international trade. Protectionism is the opposite of free trade, in the sense that the imposition of tariffs and quotas on imports and the provision of subsidies to exports are intended to protect domestic industry. Since the use of protectionist measures is widespread, free trade (like the free market) is an ultimate objective of free marketeers.

Trade liberalization refers particularly to the liberalization of imports in the sense of eliminating quantitative restrictions while using "relatively low uniform tariffs" for the purpose of trade protection. This commandment rests on the proposition that free trade is always beneficial, which is not necessarily true. Free trade requires the following conditions: (i) the abolition of tariffs and other trade barriers (such as quotas on imports or subsidies for producers); (ii) trade in services without taxes or other trade barriers; (iii) the absence of "trade-distorting" policies (such as taxes, subsidies, regulations, or laws) that give some firms, households, or factors of production an advantage over others; (iv) unregulated access to markets and market information; (v) inability of domestic firms to distort markets through government-imposed monopoly or oligopoly power; and (vi) participation in trade agreements that encourage free trade. So, it is all about removing this and that piece of regulation because they "distort" trade—all, of course, for the benefit of big firms from the preaching countries.

In terms of politics, left-wing parties tend to adopt protectionist policies for ideological reasons and because they wish to save jobs at home. Conversely, right-wing parties are predisposed toward free trade policies. For example, Peláez (2008) argues that "left-wing parties tend to support more protectionist policies than right-wing parties". Likewise, Mansfield (2012) suggests that "left-wing governments are considered more likely than others to intervene in the economy and to enact protectionist trade policies". Warren (2008) argues that "certain national interests, regional trading blocks, and left-wing anti-globalization forces still favor protectionist practices, making protectionism a continuing issue for both American political parties". This dichotomy is not necessarily observed in reality because Donald Trump, a protectionist, is certainly no left-wing, but he is a populist. His Secretary of State, Mike Pompeo, has been using carrots and sticks to convince the helpless European countries to buy American gas, not the cheaper and better quality Russian gas.

The value of free trade was first observed and documented in 1776 by Adam Smith in his celebrated work *The Wealth of Nations* (Smith, 1776). He wrote as follows:

> It is the maxim of every prudent master of a family, never to attempt to make at home what it will cost him more to make than to buy…. If a foreign country can supply us with a commodity cheaper than we ourselves can make it, better buy it of them with some part of the produce of our own industry, employed in a way in which we have some advantage.

This statement is based on the concept of "absolute advantage", whereby a country should specialize in the production goods that it can produce more cheaply than other countries and trade with countries that also specialize in the production goods that they can produce more cheaply. This argument was put forward against mercantilism, the dominant view of international trade in the 18th century, which held that a country should amass wealth by exporting more than importing. Instead, Smith argued that all countries gain by producing exclusively the goods in which they are most suited to, trading between each other as required for the purposes of consumption.

The concept of absolute advantage does not address a situation where a country has no absolute advantage in the production of a particular good. This theoretical shortcoming was addressed by the theory of comparative advantage, generally attributed to David Ricardo, who expanded on it in his 1817 book *On the Principles of Political Economy and Taxation* (Ricardo, 1817). He put forward a case for free trade based not on absolute advantage in production of a good, but on the relative opportunity costs of production. A country may have an absolute advantage in the production of two goods but a comparative advantage in the production of one good only. This country should specialize in the production of the good in which it has a comparative advantage, leaving the production of the other good to another country even though it has an absolute advantage.

As an analogy, consider a brain surgeon who is also a good cook: it will be a waste of resources if this brain surgeon divides his time between the hospital where he performs operations and the restaurant where he cooks delicious meals. For the sake of efficiency, he should devote all of his time to the hospital. When a country specializes in the production of whatever good it can produce at the lowest relative cost and trades this good to buy the other goods it requires for consumption, all countries benefit from trade even when they do not have an absolute advantage in the production of anything. While their gains from trade might not be equal to those of a country more productive in all goods, they will still be better off economically from trade than they would be under no trade.

9.3 Free Trade Versus Alternative Doctrines

The proponents of free trade have endeavored to put forward the idea against the alternative doctrines of mercantilism, protectionism, isolationism, socialism and populism. We have already come across mercantilism, which is intended to maximize exports and minimize imports. Mercantilism is thought to be a promoter and enabler of imperialism, prompting the 19th century French economist Claude Frédéric Bastiat (1801–1850) to say "when goods don't cross borders, soldiers will" (Snow, 2010). The underlying idea is that to expand exports, a country may resort to invading another to acquire new markets, which is the essence of Lenin's *Imperialism as the Highest Stage of Capitalism* (Lenin, 1916). These arguments are valid, but this does not mean that free trade leads to peace. Free trade has always been imposed on colonies, the prime example being the opium wars, which ended by forcing China to accept free trade whereby British merchants were allowed to sell opium as they pleased. In this sense, free trade was the freedom of British merchants to indulge in drug trafficking, not the freedom of the Chinese merchants to sell silk to the British. Even worse, it is not even the freedom of the Chinese to preserve their society that was devastated by British-trafficked, Indian-grown opium. The opium wars will be described in detail later on as part of the history of British free trade.

Mercantilism is typically based on the proposition that exports are good and imports are bad. Friedman and Friedman (1997) referred to this way of thinking as a "fallacy", making a very simple and intuitive argument to the contrary. This is what they wrote:

> The truth is very different. We cannot eat, wear, or enjoy the goods we send abroad. We eat bananas from Central America, wear Italian shoes, drive German automobiles, and enjoy programs we see on our Japanese TV sets. Our gain from foreign trade is what we import. Exports are the price we pay to get imports. As Adam Smith saw so clearly, the citizens

of a nation benefit from getting as large a volume of imports as possible in return for its exports or, equivalently, from exporting as little as possible to pay for its imports.

Donald Trump is a champion of mercantilism as he strived to launch trade wars and impose sanctions against most of the rest of the world. The declared reason for the imposition of tariffs against China in particular is the desire, on the part of the US, to reduce or eliminate the bilateral trade deficit on the grounds that a trade deficit is bad for growth and employment. This proposition is supported by (flawed) economic analysis prepared in 2016 by Trump's economic advisers, Peter Navarro (Director of the Office of Trade and Manufacturing Policy) and Wilbur Ross (Secretary of Commerce). In May 2019, Trump tweeted that the imposition of new tariffs on China would make the US "much stronger" and that they would bring far more wealth to the country than a traditional trade deal. He insists that China is far more affected than the US by the imposition of tariffs. Trump got the wrong advice from two economists who told him what he wanted to hear by arguing that imports are bad, just because they have a negative sign in the national income identity. This shows an incredible lack of knowledge of basic macroeconomics.

Protectionism and isolationism are by definition the opposite of free trade. Protectionist policies are advocated on the grounds that they shield the producers, businesses, and workers of the import-competing sector in the country from foreign competitors. However, these policies reduce trade, adversely affecting consumers in general (by raising the cost of imported goods), and harm producers and workers in the export sectors, both in the country implementing protectionist policies and in the countries protected against. This argument makes sense, but it should be considered in terms of costs and benefits rather than being absolute about the benefits of free trade. Isolationism is a category of foreign policies institutionalized by leaders who assert that countries' interests are best served by keeping the affairs of other countries at a distance. One possible motivation for limiting international involvement is to avoid being drawn into dangerous and otherwise undesirable conflicts. However, there is no reason why isolationism and trade are necessarily incompatible. The desire to trade with other countries can actually benefit from non-intervention in the internal affairs of those countries through regime change and pressure to "do as we say or else". The US cannot trade with Venezuela when the Central Intelligence Agency (CIA) is working hard to put a puppet regime headed by the self-declared (or CIA-declared) President, Juan Guido. Normalizing relations and accepting the elected President, Nicolas Maduro, will actually boost voluntary trade. In his masterpiece, *War is a Racket*, General Smedley Butler recommended that the US Navy should not go beyond 200 miles off the US coastline (Butler, 1935).

Socialism is a political, social and economic philosophy encompassing a range of economic and social systems characterized by social ownership of the means of production and workers' self-management of enterprises. Social ownership can be public, collective, cooperative or of equity. While no single definition encapsulates many types of socialism, social ownership is the common element. However, it is not clear why socialism is incompatible with trading freely with the rest of the world. Consider, for example, private versus public ownership of mineral resources. In the "free world", the right to extract minerals and export them for private profit while paying minimal royalties is given to individuals and corporate interests, typically with political connections. In a country like Kuwait, oil resources are owned by the state (hence public ownership), where government-owned companies extract and export oil such that export revenues accrue to the government. In turn, the revenue is used to finance a generous social welfare system. Kuwait was exporting oil freely under a private ownership of oil resources (before the nationalization of the oil sector) and is exporting oil freely under public ownership. It is unlikely that if mineral resources in Australia are transferred to public ownership via nationalization (which is a good idea), then exports of minerals would be affected.

Populism refers to a range of political stances that emphasize the idea of "the people" and often juxtapose this group against "the elite". In other words, it is a political approach that is used to appeal to ordinary people who feel resentment that they are always left behind and disregarded by established elite groups. Populism cannot be positioned on the left–right political spectrum, for example, Donald Trump is a populist on the right whereas Evo Morales is a populist on the left. More recently, however, populism has been associated more with right-wing politicians such as Jair Bolsonaro in Brazil, just like populism was associated with fascism in the 1930s. Rodrik (2018) distinguishes between left-wing and right-wing variants of populism, which differ with respect to the societal cleavages that populist politicians highlight, arguing that the first has been predominant in Latin America and the second in Europe. The feeling that free trade agreements (and globalization in general) steal jobs is the reason why populism is not conducive to free trade.

9.4 Preaching Without Practicing: Sanctions and Trade Wars

Preachers should be role models in the sense that they should practice what they preach. Washington and its allies preach free trade to developing countries, but Washington (particularly Trump's Washington) cannot be further away from free trade as it engages in sanctions and trade wars against the rest of the world. Currently, the Bureau of Industry and Security (BIS) implements US government sanctions against Cuba, Iran, North Korea, Sudan, and Syria pursuant to the Export Administration Regulations (EAR). Several laws delegate embargo power to the President, including the Trading with the Enemy Act of 1917, the Foreign Assistance Act of 1961, the International Emergency Economic Powers Act of 1977, and the Export Administration Act of 1979. Furthermore, several laws prohibit trade with certain countries, including the Cuban Assets Control Regulations of 1963, the Cuban Democracy Act of 1992, the Helms–Burton Act of 1996 (Cuba), the Iran and Libya Sanctions Act of 1996, the Trade Sanctions Reform and Export Enhancement Act of 2000 (Cuba), the Iran Freedom and Support Act of 2006, and the Comprehensive Iran Sanctions, Accountability and Divestment Act of 2010. It is ironic that the names of some of these acts contain words like "assistance", "democracy", "reform", "support" and "freedom" when they inflict death and destruction on the peoples of the countries under sanctions. For example, the Iran Act of 2006 is supposed to support and free the Iranian people from the ruling mullas—in reality, however, the Act has killed thousands of Iranians as pharmacy shelves became progressively empty (and not even the Coronavirus has helped). Perhaps the most appropriate word is "enemy" because this is how the peoples of the sanctioned countries are treated, like enemies. Sometimes sanctions go hand in hand with attempts at regime change and the occasional bombing. And sometimes when sanctions do not work, a full-fledged invasion is seen as the way to bring the country back in line (if in doubt, ask the Iraqis).

Sanctions and embargoes are imposed on a country allegedly to save the people of that country from the brutality of a dictator, but they end up killing more people than the dictator himself. The sanctions imposed on the people of Iraq in the 1990s produced high rates of malnutrition, lack of medical supplies, and diseases caused by polluted water. As a result, some half a million people were killed without affecting the dictator in the least. Denis Halliday was appointed United Nations Humanitarian Coordinator in Baghdad on 1 September 1997, but he resigned in October 1998 after a 34-year career with the UN in order to have the freedom to criticize the sanctions regime, saying "I don't want to administer a programme that satisfies the definition of genocide" (Pilger, 2004). According to a study by Mark Weisbrot and Jeffrey Sachs, the sanctions imposed on Venezuela have deprived the Venezuelan economy of "billions of dollars of foreign exchange needed to pay for essential and life-saving imports", resulting in a staggering 40,000 total deaths in 2017 and 2018. More than 300,000 Venezuelans were put at health risk due to a lack of access to medicine or treatment (Levine-Drizin, 2019). On the effects of the Iranian sanctions while the country is exposed to COVID-19, Hasan (2020) wrote the following:

> The U.S. government is run by sociopaths. How else to explain the Trump administration's callous disregard for the lives of ordinary Iranians in the midst of this global coronavirus crisis? How else to make sense of U.S. officials doubling down in their support for crippling economic sanctions on the Islamic Republic, despite the sheer scale of the suffering?

In reference to Trump, Hasan goes on to say the following: "Imagine being both so cruel and so unreasonable that you make George W. Bush and Dick Cheney look compassionate and reasonable in comparison". On 20 September 2020, the US broke with all other permanent members of the United Nations Security Council and declared unilaterally the reimposition of all UN sanctions against Iran, a move that has no legal basis even according to Washington's close allies (Motamedi, 2020). US Secretary of State, Mike Pompeo, threatened "consequences" for any UN member state that does not comply with the punitive measures, which were lifted under the 2015 nuclear deal and abandoned by the US in 2018.

So much for the sanctions—let us now turn to trade wars, Trump's trade wars, to be specific. On 28 June 2016, presidential candidate Donald Trump was speaking in a campaign rally in Pennsylvania, where he laid out plans to counter the "unfair trade practices" of China and threatened to apply tariffs under sections 201 and 301 of US trade legislation, which he subsequently did. During the same rally, Trump suggested that China's membership of the World Trade Organization enabled the "greatest jobs theft in history". On 3 March 2017, President Trump signed two executive orders, calling for tighter tariff enforcement in anti-subsidy and anti-dumping trade cases, and ordered a review of US trade deficits and their causes. The trade war between the US and China has since escalated to a tit-for-tat confrontation, hurting both countries and the world economy at large.

The justification for Trump's trade plan can be found in a study that was prepared in 2016 by Peter Navarro, then a business professor at the University of California Irvine, and Wilbur Ross, then a private equity investor, both of whom were senior policy advisors to the Trump campaign (Navarro and Ross, 2016). They attribute the decline in the growth rate of the US economy from 3.5% in 1947–2001 to 1.9% since then (in part) to "China's entry to the WTO", which "opened America's markets to a flood of illegally subsidized Chinese imports, thereby creating massive and chronic trade deficits". They go on to explain "how nations grow and prosper by suggesting that GDP growth (and consequently the ability to generate additional income and tax revenue) is "driven" by four factors: consumption growth, growth in government spending, investment growth, and net exports. It follows, according to them, that negative net exports (a deficit in the balance of trade) exert an adverse effect on growth, which means that "reducing this 'trade deficit drag' would increase GDP growth".

The analysis put forward by Navarro and Ross (2016) to justify a trade war is based on a misunderstanding of the national income identity, which is known to anyone who has done economics 101. This misunderstanding can be attributed to the failure to recognize the difference between an identity and a causal relation and between "explaining" and "accounting for". They do not seem to understand why imports have a negative sign in the national income identity, that is, why imports are subtracted from the sum of consumption, investment, government expenditure and exports. Apparently, they believe in something ominous about the negative sign. This is a misinterpretation of the national income identity resting on the flawed reasoning that a higher level of imports implies that goods that might have been produced at home are produced abroad. This misinterpretation leads to the belief that slower growth of GDP is caused by rapid growth of imports. The fact of the matter is that a negative sign is assigned to imports in the national income identity to avoid double counting as imports constitute elements of other components of aggregate expenditure.

While the trade war with China is seen by the Trump Administration as punishment for wrongdoing by China, it has certainly hurt the US. Anderson (2020) explains how Trump's trade with China has hurt the US:

Donald Trump often measures his performance in the White House by how the stock market performs. Unfortunately, by that measure, his trade war with China has failed. New research by economists from the Federal Reserve Bank of New York and Columbia University found U.S. companies lost at least $1.7 trillion in the price of their stocks due to increased U.S. tariffs against imports from China.

The US–China trade war has had a knock-on effect on other countries and the global economy. Some countries may also be impacted indirectly, particularly the important trading partners of the US or China and those that play key roles in their supply chains. Under the leadership of Donald Trump, more and more countries got involved in trade wars. Canada imposed tariffs on $12.6 billion worth of US goods. The EU imposed 25% tariffs on $2.8 billion worth of US goods. The US has been harassing Japan for a "better trade deal". India raised taxes on nuts imported from the US. Turkey tripled tariffs on US goods following the US decision to double its tariffs on steel and aluminum. And Mexico imposed tariffs of up to 25% on US steel, pork, cheese, apples and potatoes.

9.5 The History of British Free Trade

Britain, the inventor of free trade, did not practice free trade during the heyday of the empire on which the sun has set. Chang (2002) describes Britain as being a "pioneer" of activist policies intended to promote its industries, tracing these policies back to the 14th century (Edward III) and the 15th century (Henry VII). He also argues that Britain used trade and industrial policies, involving measures very similar to what countries like Japan and Korea later used in order to develop their industries.

British politicians opposing free trade, such as Prime Minister Benjamin Disraeli, criticized the liberal free trade policies adopted by the Ottoman Empire. In the 1846 Corn Laws debate, Disraeli described the free trade of the Ottoman Empire as "an instance of the injury done by unrestrained competition", arguing that it destroyed what had been "some of the finest manufactures of the world" (Bairoch, 1995). Trade in colonial America was regulated by the British mercantile system through the Acts of Trade and Navigation. Until the 1760s, few colonists openly advocated free trade, in part because regulations were not strictly enforced (New England was famous for smuggling) but also because colonial merchants did not want to compete with foreign goods and shipping (Dickerson, 1951).

However, one has to be fair and say that Britain did fight two wars with China to enforce free trade, Empire style. The first Opium War (1839–1842) was fought between China and Britain, whereas the second Opium War (1856–1860), also known as the Arrow War or the Anglo-French War in China, was fought by Britain and France against China. In each case, the imperialist powers won and gained commercial privileges as well as legal and territorial concessions in China. For many years, Britain shipped Indian cotton and British silver to China, in exchange for Chinese tea and other goods, which were shipped to Britain. In the 18th and early 19th centuries, the balance of trade was heavily in China's favor because British consumers had developed a taste for Chinese tea (as well as other goods like porcelain and silk) whereas Chinese consumers had no taste for British goods. In the late 1700s, Britain tried to alter this balance by replacing cotton with Indian-grown opium. By the 1820s, the balance of trade was reversed in Britain's favor, and it was the Chinese who had to pay for opium with silver. Trade in opium was masterminded by the notorious British East India Company, which invested heavily in growing and processing opium, particularly in the eastern Indian province of Bengal. In fact, the British developed a profitable monopoly over the cultivation of opium that would be shipped to and sold in China.

The Chinese government recognized that opium was becoming a serious social problem, forcing it to ban both the production and the importation of opium in 1800. In 1813, China went a step further by outlawing the smoking of opium and imposing a punishment of beating offenders 100 times. For the British East India Company and the British Empire at large, China was out of touch with "civilized" nations that practiced free trade, which was a convenient excuse for Britain to expand imperial interests in that part of the world. War broke out in November 1839 when Chinese warships clashed with British merchants. In June 1840, 16 British warships arrived at Guangzhou to start a 2-year bombardment of Chinese coastal cities. The first Opium War came to an end in 1842, when Chinese officials signed, at gunpoint, the Treaty of Nanjing, which provided extraordinary benefits to the British, including Hong Kong and a huge compensation to be paid to the British government and merchants. The Treaty of Nanjing provided no benefits for China as the imports of opium resumed rapid growth. In 1856, a second Opium War broke out and continued until 1860, when the British and French captured Beijing and forced on China a new round of unequal treaties, indemnities, and the opening of 11 more treaty ports.

By the power of the gun, the British imposed Empire-style free trade on China and insisted on the "legal right" of British citizens to do what they wanted, wherever they wanted. The British advocated "free trade" and "individual rights", while they were pushing an illegal product (opium) in China. It was so good that the British are until now obsessed with Hong Kong and cannot get over the return of Hong Kong to China in 1997. If at that time, Britain felt that it could win a war against China, as in the good old days, Hong Kong would still be under British rule. But China in 1997 was no Argentina in 1982.

Let us not forget the implicit "free trade agreement" involving Britain, Africa, the Caribbean and America, in a pattern that lasted until the abolition of slavery in 1833. Beginning in the last decade of the 1400s, free trade involved the kidnapping of Africans, cramming them in ships and taking them to the British colonies in the Caribbean and America. The lucrative "triangle of trade" between the west coast of Africa, the Americas and Britain (involving slaves and the goods they were forced to produce) created the first lords of modern capitalism such as John Hawkins, a slave trader, who made a massive fortune in the 1560s. According to Manjapra (2018):

> From the 15th to the 19th centuries, more than 11 million shackled black captives were forcibly transported to the Americas, and unknown multitudes were lost at sea. Captives were often thrown overboard when they were too sick, or too strong-willed, or too numerous to feed. Those who survived the journey were dumped on the shores and sold to the highest bidder, then sold on again and again like financial assets.

According to Eric Williams, a historian of slavery who also became the first Prime Minister of independent Trinidad in 1962, slavery in the British Empire was only abolished after it had ceased to be economically useful (Manjapra, 2018). The triangle of trade involved the export of slaves from Africa to America and the Caribbean Islands, the exportation of raw materials from America and the Caribbean Islands to Britain (including wheat, rice, fish, fur, cotton, timber, tobacco, turpentine, coffee, molasses, rum and sugar) and the exportation of manufactured products from Britain to America.

9.6 The History of US Free Trade

The US indulged in protectionism on a grand scale between the end of the 18th century and 1945 to the extent that Bairoch (1995) describes it as "the homeland and bastion of modern protectionism". In fact, what is known as the "American System" of economics is a mercantilist system. The Republican Party led by Abraham Lincoln strongly opposed free trade and imposed a 44% tariff during the Civil War, in part to pay for railroad subsidies and for the war effort, and to protect favored industries. William McKinley (1892) articulated the stance of the Republican Party as follows:

> Under free trade the trader is the master and the producer the slave. Protection is but the law of nature, the law of self-preservation, of self-development, of securing the highest and best destiny of the race of man. [It is said] that protection is immoral.... Why, if protection builds up and elevates 63,000,000 [the US population] of people, the influence of those 63,000,000 of people elevates the rest of the world. We cannot take a step in the pathway of progress without benefitting mankind everywhere. Well, they say, 'Buy where you can buy the cheapest'.... Of course, that applies to labor as to everything else. Let me give you a maxim that is a thousand times better than that, and it is the protection maxim: 'Buy where you can pay the easiest'. And that spot of earth is where labor wins its highest rewards.

In 1922, Congress enacted the Fordney–McCumber Act, which was among the most punitive protectionist tariffs, raising the average import tax to some 40%. In his 1928 campaign for the presidency, Republican candidate Herbert Hoover promised to raise tariffs on agricultural goods, but after he took office, lobbyists from other economic sectors encouraged him to support higher tariffs across the board. In response to the stock market crash of 1929, protectionism gained strength. Despite a petition from more than 1,000 economists urging him to veto the legislation, Hoover signed the bill into law on 17 June 1930. During the interwar period, economic protectionism took hold in the US, most famously in the form of the Smoot–Hawley Tariff Act, which is believed to be responsible for the prolonging and worldwide propagation of the Great Depression.

The hypocrisy of Washington with respect to free trade has been exposed by Chang (2002), who argues that between the Civil War and the Second World War, the US was literally the most heavily protected economy in the world and notes that the American Civil War was fought on the issue of tariff as much as, if not more, on the issue of slavery (Abraham Lincoln was a well-known protectionist). The Americans, he argues, knew that Britain reached the top through protection and subsidies and therefore that they needed to do the same if they were going to get anywhere. When the US reached the top after the Second World War, it too started "kicking away the ladder" by preaching and forcing free trade to the less developed countries.

9.7 The Pros and Cons of Free Trade: A General Discussion

The proponents of free trade argue that protectionism has a negative effect on economic growth and economic welfare while free trade and that the reduction of trade barriers have a positive effect on economic growth and economic stability. This may or may not be the case, but free traders make this assertion typically without evidence and without qualifications. The fact of the matter is that free trade has merits, but it should not be presented as the only way out and the cure that does not have side effects. More importantly, it should not be imposed on developing countries through IMF conditionality or otherwise.

Krugman (1993) argues that while economists have a notorious reputation for disagreeing about everything, they do agree on the desirability of free trade. He divides the arguments for free trade as narrow economic arguments and broad (political economy) arguments. The basic narrow argument is that if markets were perfect, then *laissez-faire* in general, and free trade in particular, would be Pareto optimal (in the sense that no one can be made better off without making anyone worse off). The problem, which is acknowledged by Krugman, is that since markets are imperfect, the anticipated benefits of free trade do not materialize. However,

Krugman goes on to put forward the theory of domestic distortion as the way out by making it sound as if market imperfection can be dealt with by resorting to free trade. However, he goes on to say that "while the theory of domestic distortion is an effective argument against particular protectionist proposals, it seems somewhat lacking as a positive argument for free trade".

The broad political economy argument for free trade, to which many economists subscribe implicitly, is essentially political: free trade is a pretty good (if not perfect) policy, whereas deviations from it will probably end up doing more harm than good. Krugman presents the following example to illustrate the political economy argument: if two countries impose tariffs unilaterally, the resulting trade war will move them off their contract curve (the set of points representing allocations of two goods between two countries) and leave both countries worse off than if they had adopted free trade policies. In this situation, it would be in their mutual interest to commit themselves to free trade. Without the economic theory of contract curve and asymmetry, we have seen that the trade war between China and the US has hurt both countries. However, this does not mean that countries should be deprived of the right to indulge in one form or another of protectionism if economic justifications exist.

Other prominent economists argue in favor of free trade. Mankiw (2015) suggests that economists reach near unanimity on international trade and traces the economic argument for free trade back to Adam Smith. Poole (2004) distinguishes between economists and the public with respect to their attitudes, describing public support for free trade as "lukewarm" at best because certain groups are adamantly opposed. He then gives examples of reservations about trade: "trade harms large segments of U.S. workers", "trade degrades the environment", and "trade exploits poor countries". However, Lincicome (2018) argues that "recent polls show Americans' support for trade and globalization at or near all-time highs". He concludes that "to the extent there is a protectionist problem in the United States, it originates in our political class, not the American electorate" and that "most Americans generally support freer trade, globalization, and even oft-maligned trade agreements".

On the issue of stability, Caselli *et al.* (2015) also argue against the proposition that openness to international trade aggravates GDP volatility, as trade is conducive to specialization and hence exposure to sector-specific shocks. On the contrary, they suggest that when country-wide shocks are important, openness to international trade can reduce GDP volatility by reducing exposure to domestic shocks and allowing countries to diversify the sources of demand and supply. By using a quantitative model of trade, they assess the importance of the two mechanisms (sectoral specialization and cross-country diversification) and provide what they describe as a "new answer" to the question of whether and how international trade affects economic volatility.

From a theoretical perspective, the benefits of free trade can be understood through David Ricardo's theory of comparative advantage and by analyzing the impact of a tariff or import quota in the supply–demand framework. We have already seen the difference between absolute and comparative advantage. A country has an absolute advantage when it has a productivity edge over other countries in the production of a particular good. A country has a comparative advantage when a good can be produced at a lower cost in terms of other goods. Countries that specialize based on comparative advantage gain from trade. According to the theory of comparative advantage, developed countries have a comparative advantage in capital- and knowledge-intensive industries, such as the professional services sector and advanced manufacturing. Developing countries, on the other hand, have a comparative advantage in basic manufacturing because of low labor costs.

Consider a situation in which two countries, A and B, can produce two goods, X and Y. A has an absolute advantage in producing Y because with its resources it can produce either 2 units of X or 10 units of Y. On the other hand, B has an absolute advantage in the production of X because with its resources it can produce either 8 units of X or 4 units of Y. If they do not trade, they may devote half of their resources to each of the goods. Thus, A will produce 1 unit of X and 5 units of Y, whereas B produces 4 units of X and 2 units of Y. Without specialization and trade, total production is 5 units of X and 7 units of Y. When they specialize and trade, A will produce 10 units of Y and X will produce 8 units of X, that is, a total 8 units of X and 10 units of Y. In Figure 9.1, we can see that total production is maximized at the point (8,10).

Consider now the following situation: A can produce 8 units of X or 10 units of Y, whereas B can produce 6 units of X or 2 units of Y. This means that A has absolute advantage in the production of both X and Y, but it has a comparative advantage in the production of Y because the opportunity cost of producing one unit of Y is 0.8 units of X in A and 3 units of X in B. If they do not specialize and trade, total production will be 7 units of X and 6 units of Y. If they specialize and trade, total

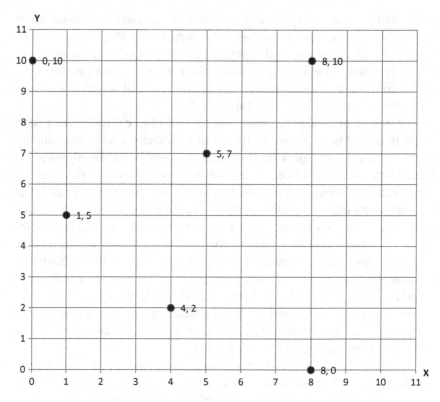

Figure 9.1:   Total Production Under Absolute Advantages

production will be 6 units of X and 10 units of Y. Hence, production will be maximized at point (6,10) in Figure 9.2. Both countries will be worse off if they do not specialize and trade.

In terms of the supply and demand model, a tariff has the same effect as any tax by shifting the supply curve, causing an increase in the domestic price of the good. The higher price boosts domestic production and depresses domestic consumption. As a result, consumers are made worse off because the consumer surplus becomes smaller. Producers are better off because the producer surplus becomes larger. The government also has additional tax revenue. However, the loss to consumers is greater than the gains made by producers and the government, which means that the society will experience a net loss.

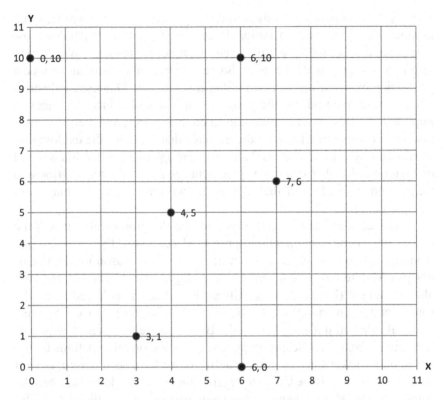

Figure 9.2:   Total Production Under Comparative Advantages

In the real world, we observe selective application of free trade agreements to some countries and the imposition of tariffs on others, which can lead to economic inefficiency through the process of trade diversion. It is economically efficient for a good to be produced by the country which is the lowest cost producer, but this does not always take place if a high cost producer has a free trade agreement while the low cost producer faces a high tariff. Applying free trade to the high cost producer and not the low cost producer as well can lead to trade diversion and a net economic loss.

The economic arguments against free trade center on the assumptions or conclusions of economic theories. The socio-political arguments against free trade are based on the social and political effects that economic arguments do not capture, such as political stability, national security, human rights and environmental protection. For example, some products are important to national security. Countries that allow low wages have a competitive advantage in attracting industry, which may lead to low wages in all countries. Some countries may facilitate low-cost production by allowing pollution of the environment. Domestic industries often oppose free trade on the grounds that it would reduce the prices of imported goods, with a negative impact on their profits and market shares. Socialists oppose free trade on the grounds that it allows the exploitation of workers by capital. Anti-globalization groups oppose free trade based on their assertion that free trade agreements generally do not contribute to the economic freedom of the poor or the working class who may even become poorer.

Some economists advocate free trade on the grounds that it was the reason why certain civilizations prospered economically (for example, Appleby, 2010). It is suggested that trading was the reason for the rise of not just Mediterranean cultures (such as Egypt, Greece and Rome) but also of Bengal (East India) and China. Free trade is believed to be the source of the prosperity of the Netherlands after throwing off Spanish imperial rule and pursuing free trade. But these are all cases of imperialism, ancient and less ancient, imposing free trade on other nations by the sword and musket for their own benefit. As we have seen before, Britain waged two wars to force China to legalize the opium trade and to open the country to British merchants in the name of free trade, which China did not observe. The Dutch might have been slightly less brutal than the Spaniards, but they pursued free trade only for their own benefit at the expense of the people of the colonies. All of these empires committed atrocities while preaching free trade.

9.8 The Pros and Cons of Free Trade: An Itemized List

Let us now examine an itemized list of the pros and cons of free trade. The first perceived advantage of free trade is that it boosts economic growth, but the evidence for this proposition does not stack up. In Figure 9.3, we observe scatter diagrams of GDP growth (measured over 1 year and 5 years) on two measures of free trade: the Heritage Foundation's index of trade freedom and the tariff rate (Miller *et al.*, 2020). We can see that

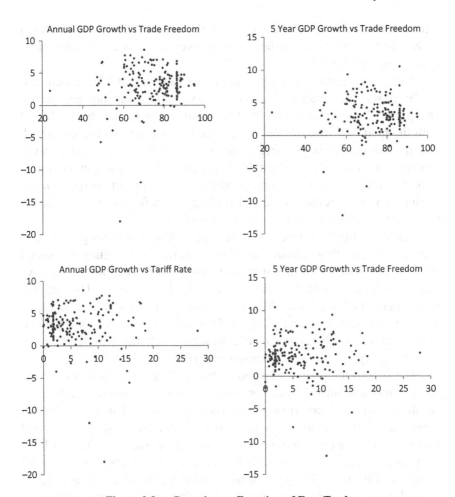

Figure 9.3: Growth as a Function of Free Trade

in all cases the relationship between measures of free trade and growth is flat. Consider the following cases of 5 year growth and the index of trade freedom: Macau, Brunei, Belarus and Greece have high indices ranging between 81.4 and 90 (out of a maximum of 100)—yet, they have recorded growth rates ranging between −1.8% for Macau and 0.7% for Greece. On the other hand, Guatemala has been growing at 3.5% with a trade freedom index of 23.8. Using the tariff rate as a measure of free trade, Brunei and Belarus have recorded growth rates of −0.9% and 0.2% while their tariff rates are 0% and 1.5%, respectively. On the other hand, Costa Rica has a higher tariff rate than any other country—yet, it has been growing at an average rate of 3.5%.

The second perceived advantage of free trade is that it helps consumers by providing cheap imports. In reality, imports are not necessarily cheap and cheap imports may be hazardous. Even though beef infected with the mad cow disease was not cheap, it was a serious health hazard. The third argument is that free trade boosts foreign investment because foreign investors will not establish production facilities in countries imposing trade restrictions. The validity of this proposition rests on the assumption that foreign investment is always beneficial to the host country, which is an issue that we will come back to.

Another perceived benefit of free trade is that it reduces government spending by avoiding subsidies to local industries. This argument rests on another free market proposition that government spending is always bad—this is an issue that we dealt with under fiscal reform. The last perceived benefit of free trade is that it encourages the transfer of technology developed by multinational partners. This sounds more like an argument in favor of foreign direct investment, which we will deal with later. In any case, this alleged advantage does not materialize.

The first of the perceived disadvantages of free trade is that it causes job loss through outsourcing. For example, one of the main objections to North American Free Trade Area (NAFTA) was that it outsourced American jobs to Mexico. This disadvantage pertains mostly to developed countries. As far as developing countries are concerned, free trade allows for poor working conditions, it harms the environment and it forces local firms out of business. For local firms to compete, they may allow children to work under grueling conditions, so that they become more "efficient" and "competitive". In the absence, or a lax implementation, of environmental protection laws, local firms faced with imports may attempt to reduce costs by destroying the environment. Free trade is particularly bad for small firms in small countries.

Free trade and free trade deals create winners and losers. Typically, free trade deals benefit larger corporations already operating across international borders rather than smaller firms, which may be squeezed out by global rivals that enjoy significant economies of scale. The argument could be best put by the political theorist Isaiah Berlin who noted that "freedom for the pike is death for the minnows" (Partington, 2018). Big multinationals benefit from free trade also because it supports the creation of networks of smaller companies in their supply chains. This is why the political decision to sign a free trade deal agreement is influenced by an onslaught of lobbying from powerful vested interests, which means that free trade deals are often simply the result of rent-seeking by politically well-connected parties (corporate Washington). The Transatlantic Trade and Investment Partnership between the US and the EU failed amid widespread public opposition to corporate interests including the US private health industry striving to expand to new markets in Europe.

A total rejection of free trade is presented by Culbertson (1986) who starts his assault by saying as follows:

> Today the evidence should be clear to anyone who wants to look at it: our blind allegiance to free trade threatens our national standard of living and our economic future. By sacrificing our home market on the altar of free trade, we are condemning ourselves and our children to a future of fewer competitive businesses, fewer good jobs, less opportunity, and a lower standard of living. These unacceptable outcomes threaten us in ways that are all related to our practice of free trade.

He goes on to discuss what he calls the "myths of free trade", including the following: (i) comparative advantage governs international trade; (ii) exchange rate adjustments automatically keep foreign trade in balance; (iii) US companies can become competitive through cost cutting; (iv) low-cost goods are efficiently produced goods; (v) all it takes to make free trade work is a level playing field; and (vi) the change to a global economy is inevitable and desirable. He argues strongly against the slogans of "free trade is good" and "protectionism is bad", arguing instead for "replacing sloganeering with pragmatic analysis". To this end, he suggests the following principles: (i) in a world of diverse nations, free trade works perversely, causing destructive competition among nations; (ii) making trade among diverse nations constructive means balancing it and preventing destructive shifts of industries between countries; (iii) to balance its trade and continue its economic growth, a country with a high standard of living and an attractive market will find permanent limitations on imports necessary; (iv) in balancing its trade, the high-income, high-cost country will tie its exports to its imports through trade packages or through exports subsidized from the proceeds of import licenses; (v) countries must manage their trade in ways that meet their particular needs and capabilities; and (vi) national governments have a legitimate and necessary role in arranging constructive international trade.

Unlike Culbertson, Panagariya (2019) talks about "protectionist myths", starting by citing Frédéric Bastiat who noted that the "opposition to free trade rests upon errors, or, if you prefer, upon *half-truths*". Myth one is that developing countries grew the fastest during the period 1960–1973 when they followed inward-looking, import-substitution industrialization policies. Myth two is that industrial policy, including selective protection, was behind the success of East Asian tiger economies. Myth three is that export expansion cannot be credited with catalyzing growth because it followed, rather than led, acceleration in GDP growth. Myth four is that exports were too tiny to have been the engine of growth. Myth five is that the success of Taiwan and South Korea indicates that interventions helped, rather than hurt, growth. While Panagariya (2019) makes convincing arguments to "debunk the myths", one has to remember that what is a myth for one economist is the truth for another. Rodrik (1995) and Chang (2007) make equally convincing arguments to support the propositions that Panagariya considers as myths.

In the final analysis, the goal of business is to realize a higher profit, while the goal of government is to protect its people. Neither unrestricted free trade nor total protectionism will accomplish both. Striking a balance in between is the best option. Countries should be allowed to strike this balance according to their unique conditions. Countries should not be told to adopt free trade or else.

9.9 Concluding Remarks

If free trade is as beneficial as they claim it to be, why is it that "almost all the rest of the developed world today used tariffs, subsidies and other means to promote their industries in the earlier stages of their development" (Chang, 2002, referring to the experiences of Germany, Japan, Korea and Sweden). These facts, Chang argues, must be more widely publicized, not just as a matter of getting history right but also of allowing developing countries to make more informed choices. He calls for the rewriting of the WTO rules to enable developing countries to use tariffs and subsidies for industrial development.

Free trade has some merits, but it should not be imposed across the board. Free trade is portrayed by the proponents as being beneficial, in the sense that a country should specialize in the production of goods in which it has a comparative advantage and trade to obtain other goods. If, as Milton Friedman said, countries should not produce goods that can be produced cheaply by other countries, why is it that the Europeans and Americans do not close down Airbus and Boeing because the Chinese are making aircraft of comparable quality more cheaply? The Commercial Aircraft Corporation of China (COMAC) is developing the C919, a 200-seat narrow-body commercial jet that will compete with the Boeing 737 and Airbus A320. It is very unlikely that this will happen, and the C919 will be fought by declining certification in Europe and the US. Is this not preaching without practicing?

By following the same logic, the Americans should close down their military industry and buy cheaper high-quality weapons from Russia and China. Naturally, this would be foolish because of national security considerations, which is a good argument against free trade. This argument is also valid for civilian goods, such as wheat. Suppose that a country decided, in the name of free trade, not to produce wheat anymore because it is cheaper to buy it from the US and Australia. All of a sudden, this country is put on the list of countries "supporting terrorism" and placed under sanctions, including wheat because wheat can be used to make bread to feed the terrorists. This country will be in a position where its people cannot eat bread, all for the sake of free trade. In this era where sanctions are imposed by Washington and its allies left, right and center, the best way for a country to shield itself from the devastating effects of sanctions is to be self-sufficient. Things are actually going that way, and the trend has been reinforced by COVID-19.

Chapter 10

The Seventh Commandment: Liberalization of Foreign Direct Investment

10.1 The Seventh Commandment as Described by Williamson

The seventh commandment is about foreign direct investment (FDI), which Williamson does not compromise on. He argues that it is "foolish" to limit entry of foreign direct investment because FDI "can bring needed capital, skills, and know-how, either producing goods needed for the domestic market or contributing new exports". One thing that I am sure about is that Kentucky Fried Chicken does not disseminate know-how because Colonel's Sanders's secret formula is still a secret. I do admit, however, that McDonald's has contributed significantly to spreading the skill of hamburger flipping in developing countries. Leaving sarcasm aside, it is not an undisputed fact of life that developing countries must be grateful for FDI. The pros and cons of FDI constitute a debateable topic that will be dealt with in detail later. Williamson also claims that "the main motivation for restricting FDI is economic nationalism, which Washington disapproves of, at least when practiced by countries other than the United States". On this point, he is spot on—this is a clear example of preaching without practicing.

Williamson suggests that "FDI can be promoted by debt–equity swaps", which are encouraged by the US Treasury, the Institute of International Finance, and the International Finance Corporation.

221

According to Williamson, these institutions and organizations are "strongly in favor of debtor countries facilitating debt–equity swaps, on the argument that this can simultaneously further the twin objectives of promoting FDI and reducing debt". This argument is ludicrous because it sounds like paying off debt by selling one's own furniture. Debt–equity swaps work very well for corporate Washington in fulfilling its desire to own, at bargain prices, public assets in debtor countries. The conspiracy starts by providing these countries with loans that they cannot pay back, which they will accept out of desperation. When it is time to pay and they cannot pay, they will receive the following generous offer: "We will forgive debt if you privatize public utilities and give us ownership in return for debt forgiveness". The next thing that the citizens of this country experience is the rise, by a factor of 10, of electricity and water bills.

10.2 An Overview of Foreign Direct Investment

Foreign direct investment is an investment from a party (an individual investor, a company or a government) in one country into a business or corporation in another country with the intention of establishing a lasting interest. The term "lasting interest" is what distinguishes FDI from foreign portfolio investment—in the latter, investors passively hold the securities of foreign companies with a rapid turnover. A foreign direct investment can be made by obtaining a lasting interest or by expanding one's business into a foreign country. It could take the form of mergers, acquisitions or greenfield investment (new projects).

The seventh commandment of the Washington Consensus is to liberalize foreign direct investment, which means giving multinationals (foreign investors in general) a free hand as to what they want to do, simply because FDI is portrayed as being always good for the host country—good in the sense that it leads to economic prosperity. It is just another manifestation of absolutism in the Washington Consensus: FDI is good without any ifs or buts. Even if that is the case, what can developing countries do to encourage FDI, apart from the wholesale privatization of assets and deregulation by abolishing the rules governing the operations of multinationals. We can see that this commandment is related closely to the eighth and ninth commandments of privatization and deregulation.

One has to remember that it takes two to tango. Measures taken by developing countries to attract FDI inflows may be a necessary but not a sufficient condition for attracting FDI. The recent trends show that FDI inflows to developing countries have already reached a peak and now they

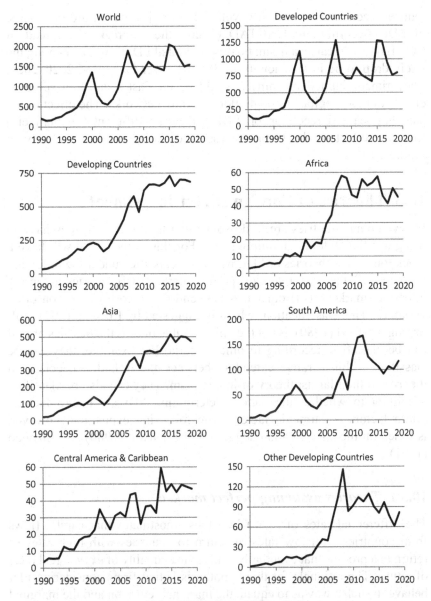

Figure 10.1: FDI Inflows (Billion Dollars)

are either flat or on the decline. This is shown in Figure 10.1 according to statistics published by the UNCTAD. Does this mean that developing countries have to give more concessions to multinationals, particularly now that COVID-19 has already made poor countries even poorer and reduced economic growth in developed countries, which are the source of FDI. According to UNCTAD (2020), the outbreak and spread of COVID-19 will cause a dramatic drop in global FDI flows, estimating the likely drop to be in the vicinity of 30–40% over the period 2020–2021. The primary immediate impact would be on East Asia, with spillover effects to other regions through global supply networks. The effect of the pandemic-caused recession on FDI will be no different (qualitatively) from the effect of the Great Recession of 2009, as shown clearly in Figure 10.1.

10.3 Theories of Foreign Direct Investment

If developing countries are to do something to attract FDI, they have to recognize the factors determining FDI. For this purpose, we will have a quick tour of the theories of FDI, which are classified under the following headings: (i) theories assuming perfect markets; (ii) theories assuming imperfect markets; (iii) other theories; and (iv) theories based on other variables. This classification, which is suggested by Lizondo (1991) following Agarwal (1980), is not the only possible one, as the theories of FDI can be classified according to other criteria. For example, they can be classified within a range extending between the orthodox neoclassical theories to the Marxist theory of imperialism. They can also be classified according to whether the factors determining FDI are macro factors, micro factors or strategic factors. The following exposition, however, is based on the classification suggested by Agarwal (1980) and Lizondo (1991).

10.3.1 *Theories assuming perfect markets*

The differential rates of return hypothesis postulates that capital flows from countries with low rates of return to countries with high rates of return in a process that eventually leads to the equality of *ex ante* real rates of return. The rationale for this hypothesis is that firms considering FDI behave in such a way as to equate the marginal return on and the marginal cost of capital, that is, they invest until the marginal return on capital is equal to the marginal cost of capital. The hypothesis is based on the assumption of risk neutrality, making the rate of return the only variable upon which the investment decision depends. The implication of this hypothesis is that recipient countries compete for FDI by offering high rates of return. High return, however, is not sufficient to attract FDI. Relaxation of the assumption of risk neutrality gives us the portfolio diversification hypothesis, in which risk is another variable upon which the FDI decision is made. The choice among various projects is, therefore, guided not only by the expected rate of return but also by risk. What do developing countries do to make projects less risky?

According to the market size hypothesis, the volume of FDI in a host country depends on its market size, which is measured by the sales of a multinational corporation in this country or by the country's GDP (that is, the size of the economy). This is particularly so for the case of import-substituting FDI. As soon as the size of the market of a particular country has grown to a level warranting the exploitation of economies of scale, this country becomes a potential target for FDI inflows. Needless to say, a country has no control over the size of its economy, but the economy gets bigger via economic growth. This gives rise to a chicken and egg problem. Does the economy grow as a result of FDI or is FDI attracted to growing economies?

10.3.2 Theories assuming imperfect markets

The first of the theories assuming imperfect markets is the industrial organization hypothesis, which says that when a firm establishes a subsidiary in another country, it faces several disadvantages in competing with local firms. These disadvantages emanate from differences in language, culture, the legal system and other inter-country differences. For example, a multinational corporation may have to pay higher wages in the host country than local firms because employment with it is regarded by local workers as being more risky. If, in spite of these disadvantages, the firm engages in FDI, it must have some advantages arising from intangible assets, such as a well-known brand name, patent-protected technology, managerial skills and other firm-specific factors. What this sounds like is that for a country to attract FDI from firms that do not have some advantage is to suppress local firms and prevent them from competing with foreign firms on the basis of the "unfair" advantage of being local. In any case, multinational corporations are so big and powerful that they can obtain concessions from the host government that gives them an advantage over local firms.

According to the internalization hypothesis, FDI arises from actions taken by firms to replace market transactions with internal transactions. For example, if buying oil products on the market is problematical, a firm may decide to buy a foreign refinery. Obviously, this is something that a developing country has no control over, and the only way to entice a foreign firm to buy a refinery is to grant irresistible concessions or privatize and sell at bargain prices.

According to the location hypothesis, FDI exists because of the international immobility of some factors of production, such as labor and natural resources. This immobility leads to location-related differences in the cost of factors of production, such as the locational advantage of low wages. Thus, the level of wages in the host country relative to wages in the home country is an important determinant of FDI. It follows that to attract FDI, a developing country must impose a wage freeze for a prolonged period of time. Another factor that pertains to the labor market is labor disputes, which should have an adverse effect on FDI inflows. The adverse effect on FDI depends on two characteristics of industrial disputes: incidence and severity. In this case, a developing country can attract FDI by making industrial disputes illegal and regarding membership of a trade union a criminal offense. It follows that police brutality would be conducive to the attraction of FDI.

The eclectic theory postulates that three conditions must be satisfied if a firm is to engage in FDI. First, it must have a comparative advantage over other firms arising from the ownership of some intangible assets. Second, it must be more beneficial for the firm to use these advantages rather than to sell or lease them. Third, it must be more profitable to use these advantages in combination with at least some factor inputs located abroad. The first and second requirements are beyond the control of the host country, but the third requirement is under its control. A weak currency and a wage freeze would be useful in this case!

The product life cycle hypothesis postulates that firms indulge in FDI at a particular stage in the life cycle of the products that they initially produce as innovations. Hence, FDI takes place as the cost of production becomes an important consideration, which is the case when the product reaches maturity and standardization. FDI, according to this hypothesis, is a defensive move that is taken to maintain the firm's competitive position against its domestic and foreign rivals. The host country has no control over this factor.

The oligopolistic reaction hypothesis suggests that in an oligopolistic environment, FDI by one firm triggers a similar action by other leading firms in the industry as they attempt to maintain their market shares. Oligopolistic firms may try to counter any advantage that the first firm obtains from FDI by following it with their own FDI in order to maintain a competitive equilibrium. The host country may in this case offer preferential treatment to one oligopolist rather than another!

10.3.3 *Other theories of foreign direct investment*

The internal financing hypothesis postulates that multinational corporations commit a modest amount of their resources to their initial direct investment, while subsequent expansions are financed by reinvesting the profits obtained from operations in the host country. It, therefore, implies the existence of a positive relation between internal cash flows and investment outlays, which is plausible because the cost of internal financing is lower. However, profit repatriation while avoiding taxes is the name of the game for multinational corporations, implying a lack of tendency to reinvest profit. This is particularly true for a company investing in a mine, then leaving when the mine has been depleted, typically with extensive environmental damage. The host country cannot force a multinational firm to reinvest profit for one reason because profit is not declared.

The currency area hypothesis has been put forward to explain FDI in terms of the relative strength of various currencies. The hypothesis postulates that firms belonging to a country with a strong currency tend to invest abroad, while firms belonging to a country with a weak currency do not have such a tendency. In other words, countries with strong currencies tend to be sources of FDI while countries with weak currencies tend to be host countries or recipients of FDI. It follows that this hypothesis is relevant to the fifth commandment of the Washington Consensus, which calls for a "competitive" exchange rate, meaning an undervalued currency. The cost of maintaining an undervalued currency is imported inflation and the effect it has on the cost of living.

The hypothesis of diversification with barriers to international capital flows pertains to the ability of firms to diversify internationally via FDI. For this to be feasible, two conditions must hold: (i) the presence of barriers or costs to portfolio flows that are greater than those associated with direct investment and (ii) investors must recognize that multinational firms provide diversification opportunities that are unavailable otherwise. The implication here is that attracting FDI flows requires, in part, putting obstacles in front of portfolio flows such as restrictions and taxes without imposing similar restrictions on FDI flows.

The Kojima hypothesis is based on the assumption that direct investment provides a means of transferring capital, technology and managerial skills from the source country to the host country. These are in turn taken to be an advantage of FDI that justifies the seventh commandment of the Washington Consensus. As we are going to see later, these advantages are unlikely to materialize—not even to the extent that the host countries benefiting from the recipe of Kentucky Fried Chicken. Managerial skills are not transferred because they are brought from the source countries to run the business and sent back at the end of either a particular assignment or the whole project.

10.3.4 *Theories based on other factors*

Other factors have been used to explain FDI, including political risk and country risk, tax policy, trade barriers, regulation, and strategic and long-term factors. Political risk arises because unexpected modifications of the legal and fiscal frameworks in the host country may change the economic outcome of a given investment in a drastic manner. Sometimes, the wider concept of country risk, which encompasses political risk, is used instead by taking into consideration economic and credit indicators. The implication here is that countries must improve their country risk rankings.

Tax policies are highly relevant as they affect the decisions taken by multinational corporations through three channels. First, the tax treatment of income generated abroad has a direct effect on the net return on FDI. Second, the tax treatment of income generated at home affects the net profitability of domestic investment and the relative profitability of domestic and foreign investments. Third, tax policies affect the relative cost of capital of domestic and foreign investments. This factor pertains to the third commandment of the Consensus, which implies one thing: to attract FDI, host countries must offer tax concessions.

The next factor is trade barriers because FDI, which can be viewed as an alternative to trade, may be undertaken to circumvent trade barriers (such as tariffs). This means that open economies without much restriction on international trade should receive less FDI flows. To attract FDI, therefore, the host country must not indulge in free trade by pursuing protectionist policies. This is in direct contrast with the sixth commandment of the Consensus, which calls for the adoption of free trade.

Regulation is an important factor, which means that for countries to attract FDI, they must give foreign investors a free hand to do as they please. This factor is the essence of the ninth commandment of the Washington Consensus, which calls for deregulation, not only to encourage FDI and trade but also because it is conducive to economic growth as portrayed by free marketeers. Strategic and long-term factors have also been put forward to explain FDI, including the need to develop and sustain a parent–subsidiary relationship, the desire to induce the host country into a long commitment to a particular type of technology, and the economies of new product development. These propositions are portrayed to be beneficial for the host country, but they are first and foremost beneficial for multinationals.

Some theories explain FDI in terms of the willingness of the host country to tolerate pollution. Interaction between the environment and FDI flows takes one of two forms. The pollution haven hypothesis postulates that foreign firms may seek to gain a competitive advantage by relocating their dirty production to countries with lower environmental standards, leading to environmental deterioration in the host country. The pollution halo hypothesis, on the other hand, postulates that foreign enterprises may bring their environmental knowledge and advanced technologies, leading to a clean-up of the environment. This would happen if foreign firms from developed countries are less pollution-intensive than the domestic firms of a developing country. The pollution haven hypothesis is more consistent with observed behavior. If it is valid, then the host country must tolerate high levels of pollution to attract FDI.

Last, but not least, it seems that host countries must become more corrupt to attract FDI. Two competing theories produce opposing predictions of the effect of corruption on FDI. The "grabbing-hand" theory states that corruption resembles a "grabbing hand" that pushes up transaction costs. On the other hand, the "helping-hand" theory states that corruption amounts to an efficient "lubrication" for rigid economic regulation and red tape. It follows that by bribing the host government, multinational corporations could get around regulations or red tape and potentially obtain benefits in terms of profitable contracts, privileged access to markets and subsidies, which would act as an extra incentive for them to engage in FDI (hence, the effect is positive). Hence, corruption is good because it encourages FDI, which is conducive to growth!

10.4 Arguments for FDI

The first argument put forward in support of FDI is that FDI flows continue to expand even when world trade slows down (which would be associated with an overall slowdown) or when portfolio investment dries up. FDI flows tend to be less volatile than portfolio investment flows because FDI represents a long-term commitment to the underlying project. Another observation, made by Goldstein and Razin (2005), is that the ratio of FDI to foreign portfolio investment is higher for developing countries than for developed countries, which makes sense because of the rudimentary state of financial markets and instruments in developing countries.

All of this is fine, except for the first observation that FDI flows continue, come what may. A casual look at Figure 10.1 tells us that FDI inflows are pro-cyclical. They took a big dip in 2009 and they will take a massive decline in 2020–2021. Furthermore, the distinction between the flows of portfolio investment and direct investment may be blurred. Both may involve the purchase of shares in the host country, the only difference being that an investment in shares is considered FDI if the investor has a big stake that enables the exertion of some control, but "big" is a loose word in this respect. If "big" is 15% and less than big is less than 15%, then 14% would represent portfolio investment. Are we supposed to believe that in time of trouble, a portfolio investor would sell the 14% and get out whereas the direct investor would stay just because they have the magical number of 15%?

The second alleged benefit is that FDI involves the transfer of financial capital, technology and other skills desperately needed by developing countries. This is good because technology diffusion and the transfer of capital boost growth in host countries, whereas the provision of training enhances the skills of local workers. However, FDI is often blamed for creating balance of payments problems for the host country because of profit repatriation. FDI does not play an important role in technology diffusion for a number of reasons: (i) inappropriateness of the technology provided as it tends to be too capital-intensive for the host country;

(ii) the availability of cheaper sources of technology; and (iii) R&D activities are concentrated in the multinational corporations' home countries.

The cost of training labor is not large enough to make a significant contribution to the improvement of the skills of local workers. The practices of multinational corporations may be irrelevant to the host country, in which case training is not useful and may even be harmful. Moreover, it is often the case that multinational corporations reserve key managerial and technical positions for expatriates. FDI does not perform the function of providing financial capital adequately because the actual capital flows provided by multinational corporations will not be large if they choose to obtain funds from the local capital market or by borrowing from local banks to avoid foreign exchange risk. Furthermore, the capital contribution of multinational corporations may take non-financial form (for example, they provide goodwill while the local partner provides financial capital). By raising capital locally, multinational corporations crowd out domestic investment, which is perhaps more suitable than foreign investment.

The third perceived benefit is that FDI has a positive effect on income and social welfare in the host country in the absence of distortions caused by protection, monopoly and externalities. If anything, FDI itself creates monopolies, while the failure of the positive effects to materialize is blamed on protection, which is convenient for multinational corporations to do as they please. Multinational corporations exist and operate primarily because of market imperfections, which preclude the conditions under which FDI supposedly boosts welfare. And even if FDI boosts output, it produces some undesirable distributional changes between labor and capital. Furthermore, FDI creates enclaves and foreign elite in the host country and introduces adverse cultural changes. Multinational corporations indulge in the production of luxury goods rather than the basic consumer goods needed in developing countries. Multinational corporations worsen income distribution in host countries and worldwide by paying foreign workers low wages, charging ordinary consumers high (sometimes extortionist) prices, and paying "celebrities" obscene amounts of money for sponsoring their products. They also abuse transfer pricing, depriving host countries of tax revenue. Last but not least, they invariably create a local oligarchy.

As an example, take the operations of US fruit companies in the "banana republics" of Central America. Typically, a banana republic has a large impoverished working class and a ruling-class plutocracy, composed of the business, political and military elites of that society who receive bribes and kickbacks from the likes of the United Fruit Company (White, 1984). In 1910, the founder of the Cuyamel Fruit Company, Sam Zemurray, bought 6,070 hectares on the Caribbean coast of Honduras. In 1911, Zemurray conspired with Manuel Bonilla, an ex-president of Honduras (1904–1907), and the American mercenary General Lee Christmas, to overthrow the civil government of Honduras and install a military government that was friendly to foreign businessmen (that is, friendly to FDI). The campaign was successful as Miguel R. Dávila (1907–1911) was replaced by General Manuel Bonilla (1912–1913). The US State Department justified regime change by suggesting that President Dávila was too politically liberal and a poor businessman whose management had indebted Honduras to Britain, which was unacceptable according to the Monroe Doctrine (see, for example, Euraque, 1996).

The fourth perceived benefit of FDI is that it boosts employment in the host country by setting up new production facilities, by stimulating employment in distribution, and by acquiring and restructuring ailing firms. It is also likely to have a positive effect on productivity if (i) it is export-promoting and (ii) the underlying conditions allow the installation of plants designed to realize economies of scale. However, the domination of a developing country by a multinational corporation may be detrimental to growth through a lower rate of capital accumulation, greater incidence of undesirable practices and adverse effect on competition. FDI can reduce employment through divestment and closure of production facilities. FDI leads to an increase in wage inequality in the host country and to a worsening of market concentration, as well as the possibility of monopolistic or oligopolistic practices.

Let us now examine some cross-sectional figures of FDI, GDP growth and GDP per capita as published by the Heritage Foundation (Miller *et al.*, 2020). In Figure 10.2, we observe data on 182 countries, the variables being FDI inflows as a percentage of GDP (%), FDI per capita (in dollars), the latest 1 year GDP growth rate (%), the latest average 5 year growth rate (%) and GDP per capita on a PPP basis (in thousands of dollars). In all cases, GDP growth rate or GDP per capita are measured on the vertical axis whereas the FDI variable is measured on the horizontal axis. In none of the scatter plots do we find any indication that GDP growth or GDP per capita is positively related to FDI inflows.

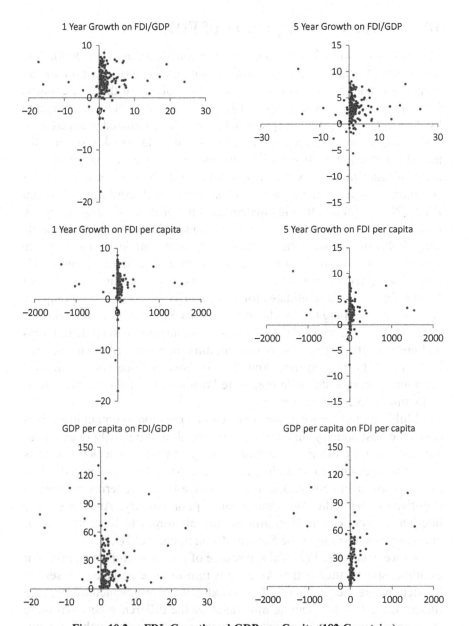

Figure 10.2: FDI, Growth and GDP per Capita (182 Countries)

10.5 Adverse Consequences of FDI

FDI, which for some is a symbol of new colonialism, may lead to the loss of sovereignty and a compromise of national security. Multinational corporations are known to interfere with the politics of the host country, for example, the Chilean coup of 1973 (the Chilean 9/11) was instigated by AT&T. In 1953, the US (presumably the CIA) initiated a covert mission to overthrow the Guatemalan government under Jacobo Arbenez for the sake of the humble banana. The process began by accusing the government of Guatemala of being "communist", which is (or at least was) a common pretext to launch a war of aggression. According to William Blum (2004), intervention in Guatemala is the product of lobbying by the United Fruit Company, which had significant holdings within Guatemala and felt threatened when the Guatemalan government decided to compete with the company. Numerous officials, such as President Eisenhower's Under-Secretary of State (and formerly Director of the CIA) Walter Beedle Smith, were candidates for an executive position in the company while he was helping to plan the intervention (Blum, 2004). The coup was successful, which enabled the United Fruit Company to keep its holdings and preserve its profits. This is how multinationals contribute to the welfare of the host countries. And this is how political (and military) Washington cooperates with corporate Washington for the "noble cause" of looting helpless countries.

Multinational corporations are often in a position to obtain incentives (from the host country) in excess of their needs and typically in excess of the benefits they bring to the host country (and this is exactly what is behind the seventh commandment of the Washington Consensus). They are very powerful negotiators, likely to strike favorable terms in bilateral negotiations with the government of a poor country. And they have intelligence services, navies, armies, and air forces to back them up if necessary—not to forget the Security Council and NATO.

As we have seen, FDI is also a source of pollution and corruption. For example, spent batteries that Americans turn in to be recycled are sent to Mexico, where the lead inside them is extracted by crude methods that are illegal in the US. FDI can be motivated by the difference between more stringent domestic environmental regulation and comparatively lax regulation in the FDI destination country. The "helping-hand" theory, which describes the relation between FDI and corruption in the host country, states that corruption provides the "lubrication" needed to deal with rigid economic regulation and red tape. In the free market language, bribery allows supply and demand to operate, in the sense that under competitive bidding for a government procurement contract, the highest briber wins while the lowest-cost firm can afford the highest bribe.

It seems therefore that FDI is a double-edged sword, far away from being always benign. The seventh commandment of the Washington Consensus is designed for the benefit of multinational corporations by providing unlimited access to cheap labor and other resources as well as open markets. The cost to the host country could be enormous. If corruption can be justified in the name of efficiency, then any adverse consequence of FDI for the host country can be justified, including the killing of hundreds of thousands in the Chilean 9/11 and the poisoning of thousands of peasants in Bhopal, India, by a foreign direct investor who literally got away with murder.

10.6 Concluding Remarks

Like everything else in the Washington Consensus, FDI is portrayed as being always good, beneficial and the conduit to economic prosperity. This is not true because FDI may be beneficial, but it can also be harmful. Thus, FDI should be evaluated in terms of costs and benefits rather than accepting the attractiveness of FDI as an undisputed fact of life.

No one presents a better case against FDI than Cohen (2007), who argues that "only the most rabid proponents deny the potential for MNCs and FDI to inflict costs and harm on large numbers of people and countries". He looks at multinational corporations in terms of "their demonstrable threat to a country's overall economic growth and prosperity as the result of the inherent conflict between their single-minded pursuit of profits and the interests of the host country's population". The offenses committed by, and the products of the activities of, multinational corporations (the main source of FDI in developing countries) include bribing regulators, tax avoidance, reduced competition, price collusion, diminished union and worker negotiating leverage, increased pollution, and increased capital outflows in the form of profit remittances. This makes one wonder why Williamson (1990) thinks that it is "foolish" to limit entry of foreign direct investment.

Chapter 11

The Eighth Commandment: Privatization

11.1 The Eighth Commandment as Described by Williamson

Williamson (1990) starts his description of privatization by talking about debt–equity swaps, which he seems to like on the grounds that they "involve no monetary pressure when the equity purchased by the foreign investor is bought from the government, in the course of an enterprise being privatized". I am not sure what he means by "monetary pressure", but pressure is always involved because debt–equity swap occurs when a debtor cannot pay—it is like foreclosure by a bank on the home of a customer who fails to meet three mortgage payments, and it is like someone forced to sell his car and furniture to pay debt. Williamson describes debt–equity swap as "one attraction seen in privatization", except that he does not say attraction for whom.

One of the benefits of privatization, as seen by Williamson, is that "privatization may help relieve the pressure on the government budget, both in the short run by the revenue produced by the sale of the enterprise and in the longer run inasmuch as investment need no longer be financed by the government". This argument, which is invalid theoretically and empirically, was used to justify the wholesale privatization program of John Howard's government in the 1990s Australia. Yes, privatizing a private hospital will save the government millions in running costs, but will taxpayers be better off? Unlikely, because someone bitten by the neighbor's dog will no longer get free treatment—rather, this person will have to pay $500 for the treatment in a private hospital. The consequences can be dire if the victim presents the bill to the neighbor who owns the dog. When the neighbor refuses to pay, dispute erupts and it may end in violence in the form of shooting or stabbing (this has actually happened). This kind of privatization can also push people into private health schemes that they cannot afford. Williamson also forgot to say that the savings made by the government and the proceeds of the privatization can be used to cut taxes for the rich in accordance with the third commandment.

The main rationale for privatization, according to Williamson, is "the belief that private industry is managed more efficiently than state enterprises, because of the more direct incentives faced by a manager who either has a direct personal stake in the profits of an enterprise or else is accountable to those who do". At the very least, he argues, "the threat of bankruptcy places a floor under the inefficiency of private enterprises, whereas many state enterprises seem to have unlimited access to subsidies". Whose belief is this? Is it the belief of the minority beneficiaries from privatization or the belief of the general public that stands to lose? Senior managers in private firms are only accountable to themselves, and waste in the private sector may take the form of obscene payments to the CEO and his or her inner circle. Huge bonuses paid to the CEO of a company that sees its stock price sliding is a waste. Rewarding a CEO for losing $5 billion rather than the anticipated $10 billion is a waste. Paying a CEO who has just destroyed his or her company a golden parachute of $160 million is a waste. This talk about the alleged efficiency of the private sector compared to the public sector is nonsense. We will come back to this point later on.

Williamson points out that "this belief in the superior efficiency of the private sector has long been an article of faith in Washington", which is not surprising because Washington represents and fights for the interests of the oligarchy. Following the enunciation of the Baker Plan in 1985, it became an official US policy to promote privatization in foreign countries by using carrots and sticks. The IMF and the World Bank have since been encouraging privatization in Latin America and elsewhere, but this comes naturally because the two international financial institutions represent and fight for corporate interests. When Iraq was invaded and occupied in 2003, the plan (encouraged by the IMF) was to privatize immediately everything under the sun. It was, of course, to the benefit of the Iraqi people that Washington wanted to make Iraqi public enterprises more efficient by privatizing them!

Williamson goes on to say that "the lack of a strong indigenous private sector is one reason that has motivated some countries to promote state enterprises", but the fact of the matter is that those countries are forced to privatize by several means, including IMF conditionality, debt–equity swaps, military occupation and the installation of puppet regimes. In the 1990s, Russia was transformed from a super-power to an impoverished third-world country by the puppet regime of Boris Yeltsin who initiated the "great grab", the massive privatization program that created the Russian oligarchy. Leaders of third-world countries who do not privatize or denationalize enterprises are doomed—examples are plentiful: Nicolas Maduro, Evo Morales and Lula da Silva (among the living) and Fidel Castro, Mohammad Mosaddeq and Salvador Allende (among the dead). For Williamson, failure or refusal to privatize state enterprises has a "nationalistic motivation and hence commands little respect in Washington". Who has allowed Washington to be the judge and jury on matters of economic efficiency? Who cares if rejecting privatization commands little respect in Washington? And why is it that "economic efficiency" is imposed by all necessary means, including invasion and regime change? This is the freedom to choose at its best.

One has to give Williamson the credit for admitting that the public sector is not always inferior to the private sector and that under certain circumstances public ownership is preferable to private enterprise (such as public transport or in the presence of environmental spillovers). He summarizes his view by suggesting that "privatization can be very constructive where it results in increased competition, and useful where it eases fiscal pressures". Privatization does not lead to competition but rather to monopolies or oligopolies (for example, the privatization of utilities). Again, I would say that foreclosure eases the fiscal pressure of having to meet mortgage payments. If this is a benefit, then the cost is homelessness.

11.2 An Overview of Privatization

Privatization is the transfer of a government-owned (state-owned) businesses, operations, or assets to the private sector. It occurs when public ownership becomes private ownership. While the origin of the word "privatization" is attributed to Drucker (1969), Bel (2006) argues that this attribution is incorrect and that the terminology of privatization played an evolving role in German economic policy from the 1930s through the 1950s. Drucker actually used the term "reprivatization" following his negative appraisal of the managerial capabilities of the public sector, describing the government as a "poor manager" and "not a doer". The word "reprivatization" is used on the grounds of giving back to private sector executive responsibilities that had been private before the public sector took them over through nationalization and municipalization starting in the last decades of the 19th century. Privatization, according to Drucker, is putting things right.

The history of privatization goes back to Ancient Greece, when governments contracted out their operations to the private sector. In the Roman Republic, most of government services and operations were performed by the private sector, including tax collection, the provision of army supplies (military contractors), and construction. However, state-owned enterprises were also in operation. During the Renaissance, most of Europe was practicing feudalism, at a time when the Ming dynasty in China was privatizing manufacturing industry. In Britain, the privatization of common lands occurred from 1760 to 1820, preceding the Industrial Revolution.

The first mass privatization program of the 20th century occurred in Nazi Germany during the period 1933–1937, covering a diversified set of sectors, including steel, mining, banking, public utilities, shipyards, shiplines and railways. Privatization became very popular in the 1980s as a result of the triumph of neoliberalism and the free market doctrine. Kagami and Tsuji (2000) argue that the 1980s and 1990s are characterized by the "great crusade of market forces against large governments" when the notion of "small government" was introduced by the Anglo-American alliance and enforced by the World Bank and IMF. As a result, privatization became widespread in Latin America where public enterprises providing public services were rapidly sold off to the private sector, including water management, transportation and telecommunication. In the 1990s, Russia witnessed the "great grab", the massive and most corrupt privatization program in history. According to Stuckler *et al.* (2009), the Russian program caused a high mortality rate owing to the loss of employment and the healthcare that went with it. Privatization programs in Latin America were almost as corrupt as the Russian program, creating a powerful oligarchy and grotesque inequality.

The transfer of ownership from the private sector to the public sector can be implemented by using several methods. The first is the use of initial public offerings (IPOs) whereby newly issued shares in the privatized firm are sold to the public in a primary market transaction. Subsequently, the newly issued shares are traded on the stock exchange as the public enterprise becomes a shareholding company. The second method is asset sale privatization or asset divestiture to a strategic investor, typically implemented by an auction or through a trust agency established by the government. On 17 June 1990, the government of East Germany established a *Treuhandanstalt* to privatize East German public enterprises (*Volkseigene Betriebe*) prior to the German reunification. Voucher privatization is another method, involving the distribution of vouchers, which represent part ownership of an enterprise to all citizens, usually for free or at a minimal price. Privatization from below involves the start of new private businesses in formerly socialist countries.

The choice of the privatization method is influenced by the availability or otherwise of a fairly developed stock market, as well as political and firm-specific factors. In developing and transition countries, the preferred method is direct asset sales to a few investors, partly because of the unavailability of developed stock markets. This method also enables corruption and cronyism, which is the name of the game, since privatization is essentially a reverse-Robin-Hood transfer of wealth from the poor to the rich. Voucher privatization was used mainly in the transition economies of Central and Eastern Europe (such as Russia, Poland, the Czech Republic and Slovakia). Bennett *et al.* (2007) identify three methods of privatization used in Russia and the Czech Republic: privatization by sale, mass privatization, and mixed privatization.

11.3 The Effects of Privatization

The effects of privatization have been debated extensively. Literature surveys conducted by Nellis and Kikeri (2002), Megginson and Netter (2001) and the OECD (2003) show that privatization improves efficiency consistently if industries are competitive with well-informed consumers and that the more competitive the industry, the greater the improvement in output, profitability and efficiency. However, privatized public enterprises typically end up as oligopolies that may collude against customers who are not informed at all. Customers are informed only to the extent that they know what the oligopolists want them to know (which is anything that boosts sales). They suggest that the efficiency gains lead to a one-off increase in GDP and, through improved incentives to innovate and lower costs, tend to boost economic growth. These papers reach rosy conclusions about privatization because two of them are conducted by the staff of two organizations that preach privatization, the World Bank and the OECD. However, Birdsall and Nellis (2002) identify winners and losers by assessing the distributional effects of privatization. They write the following:

> While most technical assessments classify privatization as a success, it remains widely and increasingly unpopular, largely because of the perception that it is fundamentally unfair, both in conception and execution. We review the increasing (but still uneven) literature and conclude that most privatization programs appear to have worsened the distribution of assets and income, at least in the short run.

It seems that the proponents of privatization talk about efficiency in the sense that profit maximization requires the minimization of waste to operate at the lowest possible cost. Let us look at this matter intuitively by considering a recently privatized firm, taken away from public ownership and given to the oligarchy with a good connection to the government. I am talking about something like the relationship between the Russian oligarchy and Boris Yeltsin in the 1990s when he "donated" the property of the Russian people to the oligarchy in return for helping him win his second election. In the spirit of the free market, that was a highly successful transaction and a mutually beneficial deal.

Anyway, how will efficiency evolve in a newly privatized firm? The new CEO will fire 20,000 workers in the name of efficiency, while giving himself or herself a $30 million annual salary in addition to all of the perks that go with it, including a bonus that is independent of performance, a promised golden parachute, a private jet and helicopter rides to the golf course for recreation after "hard work". Members of the CEO's inner circle will also be paid high salaries and enjoy perks to the extent that the saving on the wage bill obtained by firing 20,000 workers will be offset by lavish executive pay. Workers who are fortunate enough to keep their jobs will have to accept pay cuts (again in the name of efficiency) and work longer hours under deteriorating conditions. To enhance efficiency, the firm starts cutting corners for the purpose of reducing costs. The waste produced by operations can go in the atmosphere, rivers and lakes instead of being treated because waste treatment is costly and inefficient. Efficiency is enhanced through tax evasion. The increase in efficiency is achieved at massive social costs, including unemployment, poverty, inequality and environmental degradation.

Privatization is an exercise in corruption, large-scale corruption as those with political connections gain large wealth, just because they have connections. Still, the proponents of privatization suggest that daily petty corruption is larger without privatization and that corruption is more prevalent in non-privatized sectors (for example, Nellis and Kikeri, 2002). This proposition is not supported by the facts on the ground as we observe the massive fraud committed by financial institutions against ordinary people. It is common to observe the capture of the political elite by large private-sector corporations that indulge in lobbying with impunity and expect favors in return for their campaign donations (let alone bribery, intimidation and blackmail). Look no further than the revolving door between the US government, on the one hand, and financial and "defence" corporations on the other. This is corruption on a grand scale, the kind of corruption that leads government to steal taxpayers' and depositors' money to bail out or bail in failed financial instructions (some of that money typically goes to cover the golden parachutes of the departing CEOs and the lavish pay of the new CEOs). It is ludicrous to suggest that the private sector is not corrupt or that it is less corrupt than the public sector. Martimort and Straub (2006) show that private ownership could open the door to more corruption.

Public dissatisfaction with and resentment of privatization are crucially affected by the degree of corruption. Privatization in Latin America has invariably experienced increasing push-back from the public. This is how Martimort and Straub (2006) describe the situation in Latin America:

> By the early 2000s there is in most Latin American countries a strong and rising public discontent with the outcome of privatization, a decline in private investors' interest and an often open defiance from newly elected governments. By now, the optimistic mood of the 1990s is largely forgotten, and some even question the validity of the privatization paradigm that once was a cornerstone of reforms in the region. Talks of renationalization are even sometimes heard.

They demonstrate public dissatisfaction with privatization by referring to the results of Latinobarómetro, a survey of public opinion that has been conducted on an annual basis in several Latin American countries since 1995. As of 2003, negative views of privatization ranged from 53% in Honduras to 83% in Argentina for a Latin American average above 67%. Furthermore, negative opinions had increased significantly since 1998, going, for example, from below 50% to 83% in Argentina, from 38% to 75% in Bolivia, and from 48% to almost 73% in Peru.

It is not only Latin America and Eastern Europe where public dissatisfaction, even outrage, is observed. In Australia, where the government is typically pro-privatization, irrespective of which of the two major parties is in power, a public inquiry was conducted into the wholesale privatization program that was initiated by Prime Minister John Howard in the mid-1990s (Hetherington *et al.*, 2016). The report, based on submissions, identifies the most significant consequences of privatization, proposes seven principles and makes 12 recommendations. The principles are the following: (i) citizens have a right to well-resourced and capable governments delivering quality public services paid for through a just tax system; (ii) quality, rather than cost, is the best measure to judge who has the capacity to deliver services; (iii) privatization should not be presented as providing greater choice to citizens when it removes the choice to continue using existing government services; (iv) privatization should not be seen as a means of making savings by lowering the quality of services provided or by reducing the wages and employment conditions of workers; (v) whether government-funded services are provided in the public or private sphere, the community must be able to hold governments accountable for those services; and (vi) all privatized services should be completely transparent to the public. These principles are valid, but they do not govern privatization in Australia or anywhere else. Privatization involves collusion between corrupt politicians, aspiring for lucrative private-sector jobs post public service, and the oligarchy (domestic and foreign) that wants to accumulate wealth at the expense of depriving people of their right to tax-funded public services.

The proponents of privatization would dismiss this report on the grounds that it calls for a "nanny state", a derogatory term that conveys the view that a government or its policies are overprotective or interfering unduly with personal choice. In a nanny state, the government behaves like a nanny, where politicians and bureaucrats act as if they know more about how we should live and run our lives, including the management of our health. For example, Blanco (2017) explains why liberty and the nanny state are incompatible. He refers to "state paternalism", the notion that "government should regulate what its people can do, essentially deciding what is best for us". State paternalism, he argues, "operates under the guise of protecting people from themselves using government power; but it always ends in the destruction of liberty, responsibility, and solidarity". It is invariably the case that free marketeers (or at least some of them) complain about government intervention in health and education but not about dragging ordinary citizens to unnecessary tax-financed wars.

Public revolt against privatization can be explained in terms of the concept of "double movement". Karl Polanyi emphasized the societal concerns of self-regulating markets through this concept, arguing that whenever societies move toward increasingly unrestrained, free market rule, a natural and inevitable societal correction emerges to undermine the contradictions of capitalism (Polanyi, 1944). This was the case in the 2000 Cochabamba protests, which took place in Cochabamba, Bolivia's fourth largest city, between December 1999 and April 2000 in response to the privatization of the city's municipal water supply company Sociedade de Investimento e Gestão (SEMAPA). The wave of demonstrations and police violence was described as a public uprising against water prices (see, for example, Olivera, 2004).

The public inquiry into the consequences of privatization in Australia identifies eight sectors where things have become worse as a result of privatization: electricity, aged care, child care, hospitals, child protection, disability, prisons, and vocational education and training. The case of private prisons is rather interesting as the report identifies the consequences of privatizing prisons as follows: (i) diminishing quality and performance of contracted prison services; (ii) contracts that fail to secure the effectiveness and efficiency of private prisons; (iii) cost to the public sector when rectifying problems created by private company failures; (iv) reduction in prison education to assist in rehabilitation; and (v) reduction in staffing numbers and pay conditions. It is even worse because the inmates are used as slave labor. Shahshahani (2018) tells the story of a 24 year old inmate of a private detention center in Georgia (US) who was placed in solitary confinement because he complained about the delay of his $20 paycheck. He was paid 50 cents an hour, which is the market price of inmate labor, and this is why corporate Washington loves free market pricing. In a magnificent speech, Chris Hedges (2017) said the following about private prisons in the US:

> Our system of mass incarceration is not broken—it works exactly the way it is designed to work. The bodies of poor people of color do not generate money for corporations on the streets of our deindustrialized cities but they generate 40 or 50 thousand dollars a year if we lock them in cages and that is why they are there.... One million prisoners now work for corporations inside prisons as modern day slaves, paid pennies on the dollar without any rights or protection. They are the corporate state's ideal workers.

The fact of the matter is that no civilized society should have private schools or private hospitals, let alone private prisons. However, these are now facts of life, the result of what Hedges calls the "corporate coup":

> Corporations are legally empowered to exploit and loot. It is impossible to vote against Goldman Sachs and Exxon Mobile. The pharmaceutical and insurance industries are legally empowered to hold sick children hostage while their parents frantically bankrupt themselves trying to save their sons or daughters. Banks are legally empowered to burden people with student loans that cannot be forgiven by declaring bankruptcy. The animal agricultural industry is legally empowered to charge those who attempt to publicize the conditions in the vast factory farms where diseased animals are warehoused for slaughter, with a criminal offence. Corporations are legally empowered to carry out tax boycotts.

This is the kind of economic freedom that the Heritage Foundation and free marketeers in general talk about. It is the freedom of corporate entities and the oligarchy to do as they please to enrich themselves.

11.4 Arguments for Privatization

For the proponents of privatization, everything is rosy because of the magic of the almighty market: lower prices, improved quality, more choices, less corruption and less red tape. I can only see higher and persistently rising prices and deteriorating quality in privatized higher education and healthcare, to say the least. More choices cannot be provided by oligopolists who tend to collude against consumers. I can only see rampant corruption in the parasitic operations of private-sector financial institutions, which are run by oligarchs who commit fraud (let alone crime) with impunity. Non-financial private-sector firms commit fraud by selling goods that are different from what is advertised and commit crime by selling things that can hurt us and by polluting the environment. Less red tape also means that profit-maximizing firms can do whatever they can, without any restrictions, to achieve the noble objective of maximizing profit, irrespective of societal considerations.

Let us now look at the pros of privatization as perceived and put forward by the advocates. The first argument is that state-run industries tend to be bureaucratic and that a political government may only be motivated to improve a function when its poor performance becomes politically sensitive. There is no reason whatsoever why state-run industries are inherently bureaucratic. If private-sector firms improve functions to maximize profit, politicians should strive to improve functions to be re-elected. The second argument is that private-sector firms have a greater incentive to produce goods and services more efficiently to boost profit. This so-called "efficiency" may be achieved at a staggering social cost in terms of unemployment, inequality, environmental damage, fraud and criminal activity. For free marketeers, the society is an externality that simply distorts market flows and rationality.

A strange argument is that of specialization, that is, private-sector firms can specialize, but public-sector firms cannot. Well, British Airways was as specialized before privatization as after privatization, and the same applies to British Rail. Private-sector firms are supposed to improve things regularly, whereas the government may put off improvements due to political sensitivity and special interests. Yes, the government may put off building a new airport runway for serious environmental considerations. Private-sector firms put off improvements when they do not have the financing or when they anticipate a recession.

In terms of accountability, the managers of private-sector firms are accountable to the few sitting on boards of directors, whereas the managers of public companies are more accountable to the broader community. What is wrong with being accountable to the broader community? This means that public companies take into account the social costs and benefits of any decision they make, unlike the managers of private firms who consider private costs and revenues only. Those managers do what they do to maximize their own personal gains, not even the gains of the shareholders, let alone workers. Another argument pertains to civil-liberty concerns as a company controlled by the state may have access to information that may be used against individuals who disagree with their policies. It is a well-known fact that private-sector firms with access to information cooperate to the full extent with intelligence agencies. Edward Snowden has told us that something like this actually happens in reality.

It is also argued that the government tends to run enterprises for political goals rather than economic ones. This means, for example, that irrespective of profit (and for the sake of votes), the government provides health, education, banking and telecommunications to remote rural areas, even though these operations are not profitable. I assume that "economic goals" pertain to profit maximization. Free marketeers argue that public-sector firms lack market discipline. What discipline did the market provide for major financial institutions that went under in 2008, the likes of Merrill Lynch and Lehman Brothers? The executives of the likes of Merrill and Lehman strive to maximize their personal gains by maximizing exposure to risk, hoping that the market goes their way. However, they know that if the market goes the other way, they will be fired with golden parachutes that will maintain lavish life styles forever. The failed firm can then claim the too-big-to-fail status, which will put it back in business as usual under the foresighted leadership of a new CEO who could have been fired with a golden parachute by another firm. The new CEO would eventually get another golden parachute from his new appointment. The doomsday cycle continues in this manner, inflicting misery on ordinary people who have to endure job losses and austerity. For the foresighted leaders of private-sector firms, it is all about short-termism and making a "quick buck"—it cannot be further away from discipline.

Some pro-privatization gurus argue that even natural monopolies should be run by the private sector because governments can use legislation to deal with anti-competitive behavior. This does not sound right because those who believe in the power of privatization also believe in deregulation. According to them, the government should not tell companies to refrain from exploiting consumers or polluting rivers. An outrageous claim made to support privatization is that ownership of, and profits generated by, successful enterprises tend to be dispersed and diversified, which stimulates capital markets and promotes liquidity and job creation. This argument is essentially for the concentration of wealth and inequality, implicitly using the notorious trickle-down effect. It means that the oligarchs who amass wealth out of privatization tend to invest their money in projects that employ people. Well, go no further than the Russian oligarchs who ended up smuggling their money to tax havens including London, the world capital of financial fraud.

The advocates of privatization claim that nationalized industries are prone to interference from politicians for political or populist reasons. This intervention takes several forms: making an industry buy supplies from local producers, forcing an industry to freeze its prices, increasing its staffing to reduce unemployment, or moving its operations to marginal constituencies. It is rather strange that actions like these are regarded as "political" or "populist" rather than giving priority to societal needs instead of profit maximization. Buying supplies from local producers is essential in the pursuit of an expansionary fiscal policy aimed at taking the economy out of recession, and in ordinary times to support local job creation, because it is not only the private sector that generates jobs. Is it not better to freeze prices than increase them ahead of the inflation rate to maximize profit? Is increasing staffing worse than firing 20,000 employees so that the CEOs and their cronies get huge bonuses for doing nothing? Is not moving operations to marginal constituencies conducive to regional development, even though it is not conducive to profit maximization?

The very objective of profit maximization is taken to be an argument for privatization because profit is made by enticing consumers to buy their products in preference to those of their competitors or by reducing costs. Persuading consumers to buy things they do not need through wasteful advertising expenditure is hardly commendable. It is like the companies making bombs and rockets convincing the government, through lobbying and bribery, to go to war in the name of defending the homeland. Akerlof and Shiller (2015) argue that "free markets, as bountiful as they may be, will not only provide us with what we want, as long as we can pay for it; they will also tempt us into buying things that are bad for us, whatever the costs". They suggest that as long as profit can be made, markets (or the entrepreneurs working according to the free market principles in pursuit of self-interest) will deceive us, manipulate us and prey on our weaknesses, tempting us into purchases that are bad for us. As for cutting costs, this can be achieved easily by creating unemployment, corruption, crime and environmental damage.

Privatization is supposed to be good for everyone because it is conducive to economic growth, assuming of course that the benefits of growth are realized by everyone, which is hardly the case. The Russian privatization program of the 1990s (the heist of the century) had dire consequences for the Russian economy. The seizure of assets by the oligarchs at bargain prices deprived the government of the financial resources that could have been used to jump-start the economy. The oligarchs refrained from putting money into their companies, which could have stimulated the economy and created jobs. Instead, they were more inclined to sell off anything of value, convert assets into dollars, and smuggle those dollars out of the country, depriving the Russian economy of growth-spurring financial resources. Joseph Stiglitz, as quoted by Hays (2016), identified the following effects of privatization on the Russian economy: (i) the economic incentives encouraged asset stripping rather than wealth creation; (ii) Russia's human capital in technical and scientific areas was wasted; and (iii) the large, relatively equal middle class had its livelihood taken away. By 1998, the Russian economy (measured by GDP) had shrunk by 44%.

The empirical evidence on the effect of privatization on economic growth is mixed, which is convenient. The effect has been found to be positive, negative and neither, depending on the mode of privatization and the underlying country or region. Those finding positive effects include Plane (1997), Barnett (2000), Boubakri *et al.* (2009) and Koyuncu (2016). Those finding negative effects include Cook and Uchida (2003) and Naguib (2012). The fact of the matter is that we do not need "manufactured" empirical evidence to argue that privatization can be detrimental to growth when the explanations put forward by free marketeers for the positive effect of privatization on growth are weak, rhetorical and counterfactual.

Privatization has negative consequences for growth because it results in unemployment, it involves corruption, it is corrosive for human capital (as well as social capital and social cohesion in general), and it leads to the concentration of wealth—none of these consequences are conducive to growth. Furthermore, privatization deprives the government of the sources of revenue needed to finance investment in infrastructure and human capital. Privatization intensifies the financialization of the economy, which is bad for growth. Last, but not least, when the oligarchs smuggle funds abroad, they divert away financial resources that can otherwise be used to finance capital formation. Claiming that privatization boosts economic growth is ideological rhetoric that is counterfactual and implausible.

The privatization of social services and utilities is justified in terms of three factors: (i) lack of government resources; (ii) low-quality public provision; and (iii) pressure to liberalize the economy. Mehrotra and Delamonica (2005) argue that "compulsions of various kinds have tended to drive the growing role of the private sector in social services in developing countries, rather than any particular merits that flow intrinsically from private provision of social services". The first two of these explanations, however, are implausible. The lack of resources argument is not valid because even if funds are available, they are misdirected and because utilities generate revenue. The argument that the water provided by the private sector is better than the water provided by the public sector can be dismissed by considering what has happened to the water of Flint, Michigan, after privatization. The third explanation is plausible—in reality, however, it is pressure from the oligarchy to loot public assets.

11.5 Arguments Against Privatization

The adverse consequences of privatization are identified in *Taking Back Control: The Community Response to Wholesale Privatisation in Australia* (Hetherington *et al.*, 2016). The report identifies dire consequences at a sectoral level. The consequences of the privatization of electricity are job losses, inflated bills for consumers, service disconnections, outflow of profit, reduction in research and maintenance, reduced investment in apprenticeships (which has been pronounced in the telecom sector and railways), and loss of accountability and transparency. In the area of aged care, the consequences have been reduction in care hours, reduction of staffing and skill mix, and erosion of pay and conditions for staff. Barwick (2020) describes the privatization of aged care in Australia as follows:

> In a shameful breach of the trust of Australians, successive federal governments have handed control of our aged care sector to large, unaccountable "vultures" which extort and exploit our elderly relatives, extracting profit from the country while avoiding tax.

These dire consequences of privatizing aged care are not only confined to Australia, for example, Moberg (2014) tells the following story about a nursing home in Michigan:

> The state operates a nursing home for veterans in the town. Until 2011, it directly employed 170 nursing assistants, but also relied on 100

assistants in the same facility provided by a private contractor. The state paid its direct employees $15 to $20 an hour and provided them with health insurance and pensions. Meanwhile, the contractor started pay for its nursing assistants at $8.50 an hour—still billing the state $14.99—and provided no benefits for employees. This led to high worker turnover, reduced quality of care, and heavy employee reliance on food stamps and other public aid.

In the area of child care, going by market forces has created an over-supply in regional areas and an undersupply in rural and metropolitan areas. Other consequences are the following: 0–2 year age groups have a shortage of places and long waiting lists due to higher staff costs, lower wages for child care workers, and lower quality of care. The privatization of hospitals has produced limited government control over quality, poor contracting management, cost blow-outs, and decline in quality of services to the public. Again, these consequences are not only confined to Australia because privatization is the reason why basic health outcomes are worse in the US than in Cuba, even though Cuba, which has a totally public healthcare system, has a fraction of the US per capita healthcare expenditure. Fung (2012) cites a report of the Institute of Medicine in which the following is stated about the private healthcare system in the US:

> 30 cents of every medical dollar goes to unnecessary healthcare, deceitful paperwork, fraud and other waste. The $750 billion in annual waste is more than the Pentagon budget and more than enough to care for every American who lacks health insurance... Most of the waste came from unnecessary services ($210 billion annually), excess administrative costs ($190 billion) and inefficient delivery of care ($130 billion).

In the area of disability, the Australian report identifies the adverse consequences as loss of the right to choose services, loss of a public disability safety net for people with complex needs, fears of service cutbacks and deterioration of quality care, lack of accountability, and reduced pay for workers. In the area of vocational education and training, the consequences have been the demise of the internationally respected technical and further education (TAFE) system, the emergence of fraudulent and predatory behavior (including the targeting of vulnerable people, leaving them with debts they cannot pay), poor quality education, less access to more capital-intensive courses, and cut of services to regional areas.

We can see clearly that the common denominations are higher prices, lower wages and deteriorating quality.

This has been so much the case with the corporatized Australian sector of higher education, which is now in the doldrums because of COVID-19, as the main customers (Chinese students) are not coming. Once upon a time, when governments viewed higher education as an investment rather than a cost, universities were well funded with taxpayers' money. At that time, academics ran the show and a vice chancellor was typically a brilliant scholar who got paid a salary loading of no more than 10% of the professorial salary. The standard of graduates was extremely high and the academic staff enjoyed job satisfaction. With the corporatization of universities, a vice chancellor became a CEO with a seven figure salary, a bonus for the performance of those who actually do the work, and a big entourage of suit-and-tie bureaucrats with fancy job titles. On a more junior level of the bureaucracy, there has been a significant increase in the number of employees called "senior managers". Students have become customers and the customers are always right, so the standard went down to make customers happy (in particular, weak students who should not have been admitted in the first place). A massive amount of wasteful advertising is used to attract customers, irrespective of whether or not they are qualified to be customers. The fees charged for a piece of paper that does not enhance employability have been skyrocketing. Where are the efficiency, lower prices and higher quality promised by the gurus of privatization?

Let us now look at an itemized list of the cons of privatization. A privatized firm will never subordinate the profit motive to social objectives, irrespective of the rhetoric about corporate social responsibility. In terms of accountability, the public has less control and oversight of private companies even though their operations may bring about serious societal outcomes. State-owned companies can be used as instruments to further social goals for the benefit of the nation as a whole. Public companies can be made more easily to adhere to the social obligation to those who are less able to pay or to regions where the service is unprofitable. Market failure makes it necessary that public companies run natural monopolies and provide public goods, both of which are caused by market failure. The profit made by public companies (which is not maximized at any cost) can be used to finance social welfare.

The production of goods with low elasticity of demand should never be left to a profit-maximizing firm. One such example is pharmaceutical companies that charge extortionist prices for drugs and pay their executives obscene salaries and bonuses. Millions of people die because they cannot afford to pay $1,000 for a pill or an injection. The public sector should be in charge of goods with low elasticity of demand, or at least they should be produced by a firm organized as a cooperative setup. Profit maximization by pharmaceutical companies is an objective that is accomplished at the expense of the misery of ordinary people.

Common sense tells us that privatization leads to poverty, joblessness, reduced wages and benefits, and products with inferior quality. Dagdeviren (2006) finds results that do not lend much support to the arguments that privatization contributes to the efforts of poverty alleviation through various channels, such as efficiency, job creation and revenue generation for government. A report published by *In the Public Interest* (2014) concludes that in most cases, privatization leads directly to cutbacks in government investment in skill development and to reductions in workers' pay and benefits. In turn, workers have less income to invest in their households, their children and their neighborhoods, leaving individuals and their communities poorly served in the present and ill prepared for the future. Holland (2014) dismisses the promises made by the advocates of privatizing public services that "the magic of the free market will result in better services for fewer tax dollars". Time and again, he argues, those ideological claims run headlong into reality because private companies have to turn profit, which means cutting corners, paying lower wages and often failing to provide quality goods and services.

The worst kind of privatization is the privatization of war, when private contractors and mercenaries are hired to do the killing of people in defenseless countries invaded by the very countries that preach privatization. This trend (fueled by the dominance of neoliberal thinking, with its emphasis on the free market doctrine) has led to the emergence of enormous opportunities for private military and security companies (PMSCs) to thrive and prosper. Surowiecki (2004) suggests that while the US Army used to be one of the most self-contained organizations in the government and possibly the world, it now relies heavily on the private sector. Tasks that used to be reserved for army engineers, like coordinating communication networks over a battlefield, are now performed by private telecommunications companies. The term "logistical support" covers the provision of services, including catering, laundry and haircuts. During the occupation of Iraq, these tasks were performed by KBR, which charged the Pentagon millions of dollars in return. According to Surowiecki (2004), "a full one half of all defense jobs are now manned by private sector employees". The growth of private contracting can be observed not only in the military but also in the CIA, National Security Agency (NSA) and the Department of Homeland Security (DHS), where private contract employees outnumber government employees. Their activities include protecting military personnel and assets, training and advising armed forces, maintaining weapons systems, interrogating detainees and, on occasions, fighting. Most of the torturers involved in monstrosities against detainees in Iraq were private-sector employees, psychopaths who enjoy inflicting pain on others without being held accountable.

The hazard of privatizing violence in war zones has been illustrated clearly by the repeated human rights abuses perpetrated by mercenaries, including the indiscriminate killing of civilians and torture. In 2007, contractors from Blackwater, a notorious PMSC, massacred 17 civilians in Baghdad. The British company ArmorGroup, now owned by G4S, was the focus of a US Senate inquiry in 2010 because of its operations in Afghanistan, facing allegations that their recruits threatened to attack Afghan Ministry of Defence personnel. In Somalia, security company Saracen International was supposedly training "anti-piracy" forces, but according to the UN, the company violated arms embargoes in 2011 while arming and training militias. Erik Prince, the founder of Blackwater, wants to go even further, suggesting that the war in Afghanistan should be led by an American viceroy (a mercenary) who would report directly to Trump (Prince, 2017). The same rationale is presented: the private sector is more efficient, even in the conduct of war. It is more efficient in torture and committing crimes against humanity because it is motivated by insatiable greed.

It is going well for private military contractors even under COVID-19—for one thing, the pandemic has not made any difference for those engaged in the conduct of war, threats of war, and attempts at regime change. In September 2020, the Washington Post reported that the Pentagon had redirected most of its $1 billion in pandemic funding to military contractors. The Coronavirus Aid, Relief, and Economic Security (CARES) Act, passed by Congress in March 2020, granted the Pentagon $1 billion to deal with the Coronavirus, but the funds were diverted to obtain military supplies, including jet engine parts, body armor, uniforms and other military needs, as if the almost trillion dollars allocated to the war machine is inadequate (Greg and Torbati, 2020).

11.6 Concluding Remarks

Privatization, we are told, promotes competition and eliminates corruption. In reality, however, the opposite is true because the beneficiaries of privatization collude and commit fraud to maximize their net worth to the detriment of the rest of the society. Privatization aggravates the financial burdens of the public at large as a result of the use of monopolistic or oligopolistic pricing. Privatized firms tend to abuse market power in the name of profit maximization and free market pricing.

We are often told by the oligarchs, and the corrupt politicians who look after them, that privatization is good for all of us because the government is inherently inefficient and because people working for the government have low IQs and do not know how to run a successful business. Some politicians claim that those working for the public sector are not as smart as those working for the private sector, even at the risk of admitting that they have low IQs. Naturally, when these politicians get out of public service and join the private sector in appreciation of their services to the private sector, they do it not only for money but also to boost their IQs. The government is expected to subsidize the allegedly more efficient privatized firms in order to fulfill its obligations to the society.

Privatization enriches the politically connected few who secure lucrative deals and acquire public assets at bargain prices—in the process, public interest is sacrificed for private profit. This is true, particularly in developing countries where privatization is rushed on advice from the Washington establishment, using carrots, sticks or seriously violent means. Private sector executives have no compunction about adopting profit-making strategies or corporate practices that make essential services unaffordable or unavailable to large segments of the population. Except for the custodians, promoters and enablers of the Washington Consensus, it is erroneous to presume that public ownership is always problematical. Yes, public firms are not problem-free, but the solution is not to privatize them—rather, the solution is to identify and solve the problems.

Perhaps the best closing remark to close this chapter is Barwick's (2020) description of privatization. This is what she says:

> Privatisation is not about more efficient delivery of public services—it is a mechanism to loot nations and concentrate profits into the hands of a select few, an extension of the corporatist (a.k.a. fascist) merger

between governments and megabanks which caused the economic breakdown and financial crisis now sweeping the globe.

These are truly words of wisdom from a conscientious person who has endeavored to expose this kind of neofascism. The world would be a better place for most of us if elected politicians were motivated by the needs of the majority rather than the wild desires of a minority of oligarchs.

One last issue that deserves mentioning here is the role played by consultancy firms, as described by Bailey (2000) who uses the term "art of consultancy". These firms always put a case for privatizing public firms and sustaining privatized firms, even where they are inefficient on a whole range of criteria. They are effectively participants in the revolving door activity between politicians and large corporations. Privatization (with its establishment of oligarchies) is anti-democratic because it leads to the concentration of power in those who consolidate their position by donations to existing political parties that in turn feel the need for a *quid pro quo*. Privatization is a form of social welfare for the most well-off group in society. That they feel entitled to this and have a rapacious need to maintain their position means that governments will become more and more authoritarian.

Chapter 12

The Ninth Commandment: Deregulation

12.1 Introduction

Deregulation is the removal or reduction of restrictions on the operations of individuals and companies. Posner (1999) defines deregulation as "the removal or reduction of comprehensive controls over particular industries", the regulated industries, while recognizing that all industries are regulated to a greater or a lesser extent. Deregulation often takes the form of eliminating a regulation entirely or altering an existing regulation to reduce its impact. Measures of deregulation may include one or more of the following: (i) reducing restrictions on conduct; (ii) removing outdated, inconsistent, or otherwise unnecessary rules; (iii) eliminating particular disfavored regulatory impacts; and (iv) boosting competition in a regulated market. Raso (2017) suggests that the first is most likely to attract the greatest effort from agencies while the third receives the most public attention.

Three broad reasons can be presented for deregulation. The first reason is that the underlying regulation is no longer effective, in the sense that it no longer produces socially desirable outcomes. For example, the deregulation of the US airline industry in 1977 was motivated by the desire to get rid of a system of price and route regulation that was impeding the industry's growth. The second reason is ideology, which explains why wholesale deregulation took off on both sides of the Atlantic as a result of the advent of Reaganism–Thatcherism in the early 1980s, justified intellectually by the teachings of Milton Friedman and Fredrick von Hayek. The third reason is that a regulated industry might seek to bring about deregulation through lobbying and campaign donations. For example, the Glass–Steagall Act, also known as the Banking Act of 1933, was signed into law by President Franklin Roosevelt on 16 June 1933 to separate investment and commercial banking as an emergency response to the massive bank failures that had occurred during the Great Depression. In 1999, the powerful banking lobby managed to extract Bill Clinton's signature to abolish the Act.

Deregulation is advocated on the grounds that it stimulates economic activity by eliminating restrictions for new businesses to enter the market, which would hamper competition and consequently innovation. Arguably, companies benefit from deregulation because they do not need to channel resources to compliance, using those resources in the productive activity of developing new products for the benefit of consumers. Deregulation, however, may drive small firms out of business, thus creating monopolies (Citibank is one such example). Deregulation may not work in the consumers' best interests, for example, the removal of the regulation requiring banks to hold cash reserves is not in the interest of bank customers. Another adverse consequence of deregulation is that it allows companies to be opaque and fraudulent.

Donald Trump has turned out to be a champion deregulator, which is not surprising given his background as a business tycoon. In October 2016, Republican presidential nominee Donald Trump declared that as many as 70% of federal agency regulations could be eliminated if he was elected in November, just hours after an adviser announced that the candidate would seek to cut 10% (Reuters, 2016). Trump, who blamed regulation for stifling business, told a crowd at a town hall event in New Hampshire that regulations for the environment and safety would remain. In January 2017, Trump slammed the Dodd–Frank Act, describing it as a "disaster" and promised to "do a big number" on it soon. He suggested that the financial overhaul went too far, blaming excessive regulation for making it "virtually impossible" for small and medium-sized businesses to get loans from banks (Egan, 2017). He has since dismantled regulation systematically in fields including the environment, education, housing, agriculture, labor, health, and finance (for a complete listing, see Brookings, 2020). It is ironic, however, that Trump is a deregulator, except when it comes to his enemies. In May 2020, he threatened "big action" against Twitter, accusing social media platforms of silencing conservatives, and vowed to "strongly regulate, or close them down, before we can ever allow this to happen" (Rampell, 2020).

12.2 The Ninth Commandment as Described by Williamson

Deregulation is described by Williamson as "another way of promoting competition"—"another" presumably means in addition to privatization. However, deregulation may boost the monopolistic powers of big firms when they can do what they like in the absence of restrictions on their operations. They find it easier, in the absence of regulation, to make it prohibitively expensive for new firms to enter the industry. Go no further than what happened in the US banking sector following the abolition of the Glass–Steagall Act in the 1990s. Concentration, in terms of the percentage of assets held by the largest banks, has increased at a tremendously high rate. In Figure 12.1, we can see the percentage of assets held by the top five banks between the 1930s, when the Glass–Steagall Act was implemented, and the time of the global financial crisis. The rise was spectacularly rapid following the abolition of the Act. In Figure 12.2, we can see the percentage of assets held by the largest five banks between 1995 and 2017 as a result of financial deregulation.

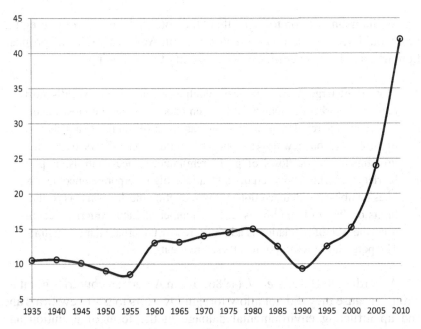

Figure 12.1:   US Banking Concentration (Assets Held by Largest Three Banks)

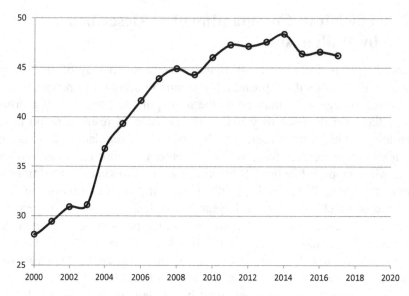

Figure 12.2:   US Banking Concentration (Assets Held by Largest Five Banks)

Williamson goes on to argue that "the potential payoff from deregulation would seem to be much greater in Latin America". On this proposition, he cites Balassa *et al.* (1986) as saying the following:

> Most of the larger Latin American countries are among the world's most regulated market economies, at least on paper. Among the most important economic regulatory mechanisms are controls on the establishment of firms and on new investments, restrictions on inflows of foreign investment and outflows of profit remittance, price controls, import barriers, discriminatory credit allocation, high corporate income tax rates combined with discretionary tax-reduction mechanisms, as well as limits on firing of employees.... In a number of Latin American countries, the web of regulation is administered by underpaid administrators. The potential for corruption is therefore great.

According to Balassa *et al.* (1986), Latin American countries got it all wrong because they did not allow foreign investors to start new firms and end up inflicting environmental damage in the form of pollution and deforestation. This is why Jair Bolsonaro of Brazil has done a good job by killing the Amazon rainforests in the name of deregulation. Apparently, he did not learn from the experience of Ecuador where Chevron dumped more than 16 billion gallons of toxic waste water into the rainforest, leaving local people suffering from a wave of cancers, miscarriages, and birth defects. Those countries also got it wrong by putting restrictions on the likes of Chevron to repatriate profit without paying taxes. For Balassa *et al.* (1986), regulation and deregulation cover almost everything, including price controls, import barriers, credit allocation, corporate income tax rates, and corruption. They talk in the very spirit of the Washington Consensus.

For Balassa *et al.* (1986), regulation is conducive to corruption, which means that deregulation kills corruption. They seem to forget that deregulation in the "West" is invariably the result of lobbying and regulatory capture, both of which represent sophisticated and more effective forms of corruption than passing an envelope containing $5,000, as they do in Latin America and the rest of the third world. Williamson himself argues that the regulation of economic activity on a case-by-case basis "provides opportunities for corruption" and "discriminates against small and medium-sized businesses". In the spirit of the Washington Consensus, corruption is fine because it is good for the business of foreign direct investors, as we have seen. As for local small and medium-sized businesses, they are likely to be crushed and forced out of business by liberalization and deregulation, the very prescriptions of the Washington Consensus.

12.3 Arguments for Regulation

Regulation in general is needed to preserve social values and environmental standards—otherwise, the law of the jungle will prevail in a polluted environment. Pollution is good for profit maximization because when firms are allowed to dispose of their toxic waste, they will save on the cost of waste treatment and become more efficient. However, this kind of efficiency is socially undesirable, at least from a public health perspective. It is not clear why free marketeers oppose regulation when they expect the government to enforce property rights and the rule of law, which represent regulation. Markets depend on government regulation for their stability, which is what gives rise to long-term co-evolution of the state and markets in capitalist societies. This is what has been happening since the advent of the Industrial Revolution.

Regulation is needed in cases of market failure caused by monopoly, externalities, public goods, asymmetric information, etc. These are basic principles that students of economics learn at an early stage of their study of the "dismal science". Regulation is required for the attainment of collective desires as judged by a significant segment of the society. The problem here is that the 1% powerful minority does not like to go by the collective desires of the 99% majority because the minority is only motivated by profit maximization. Regulation is required to deal with the problem of irreversibility that a certain type of conduct from current generations can result in outcomes from which future generations may not recover at all. Even though the proponents of deregulation argue that regulation stifles competition, regulation may actually create a level playing field and boost competition (for example, by ensuring that new electricity providers have competitive access to the national grid). Unlike the rhetoric, the oligarchy does not like competition and often indulges in anti-competitive behavior for the sake of maximizing profit—hence regulation is bad. Regulation is needed to maintain quality standards for services (for example, by specifying qualification requirements for service providers). Profit maximization can be achieved by cutting corners and swindling consumers, and this is why regulation is needed to protect consumers from fraud.

On the last point, consider the observation that some supermarket items sell for more per unit in larger sizes. In the absence of legislation requiring them to display unit prices on the products, supermarkets can generate more profit from large items than small items by (i) selling a big product for more than the number of units multiplied by the unit price and/or (ii) reducing the product size (the number of units) at the same price. In both cases, these are easier to hide in a big product than a small one. In fact, reducing the product size at the same price has been a common practice. Greenwood (2018) expresses this situation eloquently by saying that "all around you, all the time, many consumer products are growing lighter, thinner, less substantial—all while maintaining the same price". She also has the following to say:

> It's probably happened to you in a supermarket aisle, or maybe at home while making a favorite family recipe. You'll notice something odd—a can of tomato soup seems to hold less than it did, or the tuna used to be enough for three sandwiches, not two. It might dawn on you in the bathroom, where last month the household went through twelve rolls of toilet paper, up from the usual 9 or 10.

This is not a new phenomenon but rather an old practice. In the early 1960s, the Committee on the Judiciary (1961) published a report in which the following question was raised: "how badly have consumers been fooled?". The report makes it quite clear that "if per-ounce cost as well as the unit cost were stamped on the package, the consumer would have no difficulty in making comparisons". Regulation is required for the provision of sufficient information (for example, about the features of competing goods and services) and for ensuring wide access to services (for example, ensuring that poorer areas where profit margins are low are provided with electricity and health services).

In addition to these general arguments, specific kinds of regulation may be advocated on more specific grounds. For example, financial regulation is intended to preserve financial stability and protect consumer savings from excessive risk taking by financial institutions. Environmental regulation is intended to prevent environmental degradation (arising, for example, from high levels of tourist development) and to respond to apprehension regarding environmental pollution and standards (such as the regulation of the disposal of hazardous materials).

12.4 Arguments Against Regulation

Like the arguments for, the arguments against regulation may be general or situation-specific. The first argument is that some forms of regulation are seen as imposing unnecessary "red tape" and other restrictions on the smooth operation of businesses. As a result, adverse economic consequences materialize. This is true to a certain extent: some red tape is totally unnecessary, but for the proponents of regulation, anything and everything is unnecessary red tape. It is not a matter of having or not having regulation, but rather the extent and quality of regulation. The second argument against regulation is that regulatory agencies may be captured by the regulated industries, which would lead to diminishing competition, thus failing to serve the public interest. Regulatory capture is widespread, but it does not provide a reason for dismantling regulatory agencies in the name of enhancing competition. Regulatory capture is a form of corruption that can and should be dealt with. Appointing someone from Goldman Sachs to be the US Treasury Secretary is simply ludicrous, and it should not be allowed. The revolving door between the government and the corporate sector should be closed or regulated. Regulatory capture must be regulated—hence, this is an argument for, not against, regulation.

Deregulation enthusiasts also argue that an extreme form of regulation is government-owned and operated firms, which are allegedly inefficient. This issue was dealt with in the previous chapter on privatization. The efficiency of the private sector relative to the public sector is simply a myth perpetuated by right wingers. Simms (2013) dismisses the alleged superiority of the private sector by writing the following:

> Private sector dynamism versus public sector inefficiency has been a dominant political narrative of the last few decades. It has supplied the excuse for upheaval in many of the public services that we rely on. Yet from healthcare costs to train company subsidies, evidence of private sector superiority is thin. The public sphere in its broadest sense—including voluntary, mutual, cooperative, and social enterprise models—can be more efficient and more effective.

The allegation that the private sector is inherently more efficient than the public sector is put forward by privatization enthusiasts to justify the privatization of public enterprises or at least the outsourcing of some to the private sector. This proposition is not supported by casual empiricism or formal empirical evidence. For example, Hodge (1996) reviews 129 reports and case studies, and finds that outsourcing works well in some cases and badly in others. Stone (2013) suggests that many studies claiming the benefits of outsourcing do not take into account the broader economic and social cost of outsourcing.

Deregulators dismiss the notion of market failure as a misguided proposition that is wrongly used to justify regulation. However, the issues of public goods and externalities represent market failure that requires regulation and state provision of public goods. This is known to anyone with a minimal knowledge of economics. As free marketeers, deregulators deplore government intervention, including attempts to correct market failure, on the grounds that it may lead to an inefficient allocation of resources. This is called government failure, which (according to free marketeers) may be (or is) more severe and costly than market failure. It is not clear to me how the imposition of restrictions on a polluting firm leads to an inefficient resource allocation. Free marketeers seem to think that allowing private-sector firms to pollute with impunity leads to an efficient allocation of resources.

One facet of market failure is market power, which is used to justify regulation. Deregulators argue that market power tends to be undermined with the passage of time by competitive or technological change. This does not happen in reality where monopolists and oligopolists prevail (look no further than Google). Another argument against regulation is that government intervention creates more problems than it is supposed to solve because regulators may be incapable of accurate predictions, lacking any reliable ability (or true incentive) to gather and evaluate the vast amount of information that guides a free market. What prediction is needed to tell a polluter not to dispose of toxic waste in the river or to prevent the likes of Bernie Madoff from swindling people? What prediction is needed to regulate corruption? The implication of this argument is that regulators are not smart enough to be as good predictors as those running private-sector firms like the geniuses who brought ruins to Merrill Lynch, Bear Stearns, Lehman Brothers, and the Royal Bank of Scotland.

It is not clear how regulation impedes competitiveness and raises prices when regulatory measures are taken to break up monopolies and big firms. Regulation is problematical, deregulators argue, because it disrupts the working of the free market system and the associated price mechanism. The free market system brings ruins to most people, in which case the disruption of this system is desirable from a societal point of view. They also argue that regulatory legislation may provide privileges to special interests, but this is corruption that should not be allowed and needs regulatory measures to control.

Some of the anti-regulation arguments have been used by the pro-regulation camp. For example, consider the argument that regulation empowers certain groups and provides to certain individuals. The move toward free markets (hence deregulation) in Victorian England gave already-privileged people more privileges by transferring land from public to private ownership. It is more intuitive to suggest that deregulation rather than regulation is associated with the redistribution of wealth and power from the majority to a minority. Deregulation of the financial sector has created an elitist group of highly paid, low-IQ, and greedy bankers and financiers whose contribution to human welfare was the devastation inflicted by the global financial crisis (let alone the Jeffrey Epstein fiasco). These bankers yearn for free banking, but when they are in serious trouble, they call on the government to save them under the notorious pretext of being too big to fail.

A wave of unfettered deregulation can only be rationalized on ideological grounds, but ideology is blind to the facts on the ground. Like everything else, deregulation is not good under all circumstances and not all kinds of regulation are necessary or effective. For example, the prohibition of alcohol in the 1920s America was good only for gangsters and thugs. In this case, regulation created monopolies run by gangs, but that did not prevent people from drinking at monopoly prices. It is all about striking balance between the underlying costs and benefits. For deregulators, regulation has costs but no benefits.

As stated in the introduction to this chapter, Trump has been a champion deregulator whose Council of Economic Advisers has its own set of arguments for deregulation. In a report entitled *The Growth Potential of Deregulation*, the Council of Economic Advisers (2017) describes "excessive" regulation as "a tax on the economy, costing the US an average of 0.8 percent of GDP growth per year since 1980" (for them any regulation is "excessive"). The usual set of arguments are presented against regulation: "It is making us less competitive"; "It is costly, with much of the burden falling on small businesses and entrepreneurs"; "It perpetuates inequality, hurting the most vulnerable the hardest"; and "Occupational licensing can be a form of regulation that creates barriers to entry and makes workers less mobile". The fact of the matter is that deregulation creates corporate giants that kill competition and small business. It is counterfactual and ludicrous to suggest that regulation is conducive to inequality, when exactly the opposite is true. Inequality has been on the rise as a result of the wave of financialization that followed the abolition of the Glass–Steagall Act in 1999. Deregulation creates billionaires, which is good for billionaires, but not for the rest of the society, given that the trickle-down effect is a mirage.

The report claims that "the Administration's continued deregulatory policies will drive continued economic growth". On the assumption that the savings produced by deregulation are used to finance research and development spending, it is suggested that deregulation boosts growth. The report notes that "if a country deregulates enough to move from the most-regulated quartile to the least-regulated quartile, its annual rate of growth could increase as much as by 2.3 percentage points". This claim, which involves a degree of precision that can only be found in physics, is similar to the claim made by Beard *et al.* (2011) who find that reducing the total budget of all US federal regulatory agencies by 5% produces 1.2 million private sector jobs each year and that firing one regulatory agency staff member creates 98 jobs in the private sector. These quantitative results sound ridiculous, most likely produced by extensive data mining motivated by an ideological anti-regulation stance. Naturally,

Beard *et al.* (2011) do not tell us anything about the mechanism whereby the firing of a regulator leads to job creation. I suppose that McDonald's monitor the news about regulatory agencies and hire more burger flippers when they hear that a regulatory agency has just fired some 10 people. It is even better if these regulators are hired by McDonald's.

The view that deregulation boosts growth is repeated by Coffey *et al.* (2020) who, like Beard *et al.* (2011), provide precise estimates of the effect of deregulation on growth. Their empirical results show that regulatory restrictions have had a net effect of dampening economic growth by approximately 0.8% per annum since 1980. They suggest that "had regulation been held constant at levels observed in 1980, our model predicts that the economy would have been nearly 25 percent larger by 2012", which means that regulation cost the US economy $4 trillion in terms of lost GDP between 1980 and 2012 (that is, $13,000 per capita). Results like these are easily obtainable by using the con art of econometrics to provide support for a prior belief. The same set of data can be used to obtain results showing that regulation has benefited the US economy by producing $3.5 trillion (or any number for that matter) worth of extra output. By the way, results like these are typically irreproducible, which can be convenient.

Let us examine the relation between economic growth (GDP growth measured over one year and as a 5 year average) and some measures of deregulation as reported by the Heritage Foundation (Miller *et al.*, 2020). These measures include three indices for business freedom, labor freedom, and investment freedom, all taking values in the range 0–100. Figure 12.3 shows that irrespective of the measure of deregulation, the relation with growth is obscure in a sample of 158 countries. When the 5 year growth rate and the index of business freedom are classified into low, medium, and high (according to the first, second, and third 33% percentiles), we find that only 57 countries out of 158 fall in the low–low, medium–medium, and high–high cells. The high freedom–low growth cell contains 25 countries, meaning that these countries have been experiencing low growth even though they have high levels of business freedom.

12.5 Arguments for and Against Environmental Regulation

Unregulated markets cannot protect the environment because it encompasses public goods (such as clean air) whose values are not well reflected

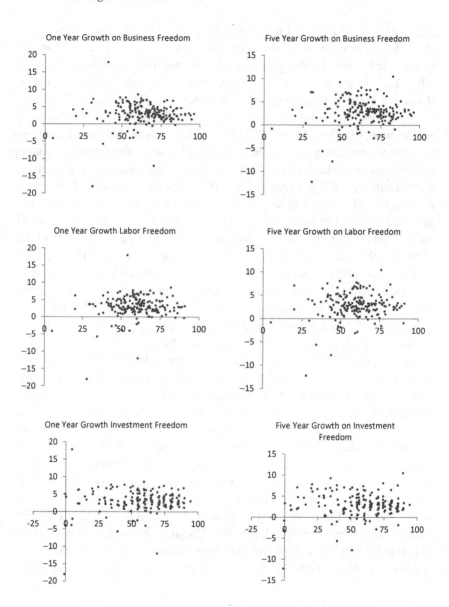

Figure 12.3:   Economic Growth as a Function of Deregulation-Driven Freedom

by market processes. Environmental regulation is required to ensure efficient production of goods and services from a finite supply of non-renewable resources. Environmental regulation pays off in terms of the value gained by preserving non-renewable natural resources and by avoiding costs elsewhere in the economy. Environmental regulation motivates firms to adopt more efficient means of production because they tend to be environmentally friendly. Environmental regulation may put a drag on economic growth, but a high GDP per capita does not compensate for breathing polluted air. However, there is no reason why a clean environment cannot go hand in hand with economic growth. Pollution is an externality that must be dealt with through government intervention. In this sense, the adverse effects of environmental regulation are often exaggerated. Environmental regulation forces markets to reckon with the true costs of doing business. When polluters are told to spend on waste disposal or taxed, they are in effect forced to take into account social as well as private costs.

Deregulators put forward a number of arguments against environmental regulation, even though they (like all of us) do not like to breathe polluted air, swim in a polluted river, or suffer the effects of soil pollution. The effects of air, water, and soil pollution (exposure to carbon dioxide, methane, nitrous oxide, sulfur dioxide, lead dust, etc.) on the human species have been identified by Moosa and Ramiah (2014) as the following: coughing, wheezing, shortness of breath, a tight feeling around the chest, nausea, vomiting, collapse, convulsions, coma, blindness, rapid breathing, high heartbeat rate, clumsiness, emotional upsets, fatigue, dizziness, depersonalization, euphoria, sensation detachment, nausea, slurred speech, lower IQs, short attention spans, learning disabilities, hyperactivity, impaired physical growth, hearing and visual problems, stomach aches, irritation of the colon, kidney malfunction, anemia, leukemia, and brain damage. Of course, we should not forget about the ultimate destruction of life: death.

Deregulation enthusiasts suggest that the (almighty) market is in a better position than the government to solve environmental problems. But then for free marketeers, the market is better than the government at anything. The market is supposed to work like this: the customers of a polluting firm recognize that the firm is polluting the environment (not sure how that happens) and boycott the firm, forcing it to reduce its activity or do something about the pollution it causes. By the time this happens (if at all), the environment would have already suffered significant damage.

Another argument is that environmental regulation is motivated by populist sentiment rather than actual hazards—it is always the Greens and environmentalist hooligans who use fear mongering to reduce the bonus given to the CEO of a polluting firm. This claim is counterfactual because environmental disasters are very common. Lakritz (2019) describes the nine deadliest human-made disasters in the past 50 years, including the Seveso disaster (1976), Love Canal (1978), the Bhopal gas leak (1984), Exxon Valdez oil spill (1989), and Asbestos in Libby (1990). The Bhopal gas leak killed thousands of impoverished Indians because, guided by the free market doctrine, the CEO of the polluting company was trying to cut costs and be more efficient.

Environmental regulation is allegedly compromised by the tendency to adopt harsh standards without seeking solid evidence on the underlying cause and effect. Perhaps, but in matters of life and death, it is always better to err on the side of caution. Free marketeers suggest "free market environmentalism" as the way out, expressing the view that environmental disputes can be settled by voluntary action and common-law rights. This means that polluters will eventually stop polluting as a result of a law suit that takes place after pollution-caused cancer takes its toll on the community. Deregulators argue that since deregulation has worked well in the areas of transport and utilities, there is no reason to believe that environmental deregulation will not work. But then who said that deregulation has worked in transport and utilities? British rail provided better service than the countless private companies running the service currently. And who said that deregulation has worked in utilities, given that customers are charged extortionist prices and offered crooked deals?

For free marketeers, environmental regulation kills jobs and hurts the economy (and reduces the bonuses paid to the CEOs and their cronies). The fact remains that environmental regulation aiming at pollution control saves lives. The adverse effects of environmental regulation on the bottom lines of "fat cats" should be the least of our concerns. This is why for some, the real question is not how to resolve the conflict between economic and environmental goals, but rather how to get more environmental protection for less money—that is the efficiency of environmental regulation. The opponents of environmental regulation effectively say that people are to be allowed to pollute, but should a dispute arise, courts will deal with the matter. "Pollute if you can afford it" sounds like "kill if you can afford it"—in both cases, "if you can afford it" means "if you can get away with it".

Back to Donald Trump, a champion of deregulation in general and environmental deregulation in particular. Not many people realize that Trump abolished 28 acts of environmental regulation in his first three years in office. This can be done very easily when deregulators are appointed to run regulatory agencies, such as the Environmental Protection Agency. Table 12.1 lists the acts that have disappeared under

Table 12.1:   Environmental Regulation Acts Abolished by Trump

Number	Act
1	National Environmental Policy Act
2	Endangered Species Act
3	Clean Water Act
4	National Historic Preservation Act
5	Migratory Bird Treaty Act
6	Migratory Bird Conservation Act
7	Clean Air Act
8	Archaeological Resources Protection Act
9	Paleontological Resources Preservation Act
10	Federal Cave Resources Protection Act
11	Safe Drinking Water Act
12	Noise Control Act
13	Solid Waste Disposal Act
14	Comprehensive Environmental Response, Compensation, and Liability Act
15	Archaeological and Historic Preservation Act
16	Antiquities Act
17	Historic Sites, Buildings, and Antiquities
18	Farmland Protection Policy Act
19	Coastal Zone Management Act
20	Federal Land Policy and Management Act
21	National Wildlife Refuge System Administration Act
22	National Fish and Wildlife Act
23	Fish and Wildlife Coordination Act
24	Administrative Procedure Act
25	River and Harbors Act
26	Eagle Protection Act
27	Native American Graves Protection and Repatriation Act
28	American Indian Religious Freedom Act

Trump's presidency. If the motivation for abolishing these acts is boosting economic growth, then one cannot help think that Trump and his advisors believe that the following, among others, hamper growth: drinking clean water, avoiding noise, protecting farmland, preserving wildlife, and preserving native American graves. We will have to wait a few years to find out how much in output will be added to American GDP as a result of abolishing acts that allegedly inflicted damage on the US economy.

12.6 Financial Regulation

Financial regulation can be justified on several grounds, one of which is the objective of maintaining financial stability. If corruption and fraud cause financial boom and bust, regulation against malpractices and fraudulent behavior in the financial sector can contribute to financial instability. Another motive for financial regulation in general is consumer protection, for example, protecting the public from those selling junk bonds as AAA securities. Transparency International (2015) suggests that "corruption in the banking sector has manifested itself in many scandals involving money laundering, rate rigging, and tax evasion, all of which undermine the public's trust in financial institutions".

Excessive risk taking with other peoples' money is fraud. As Dewatripont and Freixas (2012) put it, "it has been noted that risk taking is intrinsically involved in the business of banking and that this can lead to unethical conduct at the expense of the public interest". Some free marketeers argue against regulation because it is easy to circumvent, choosing to overlook the fact that Bernie Madoff managed to engage in fraudulent activity on a massive scale for such a long time only because regulators turned a blind eye to what he was doing.

Corruption in the financial sector is not a new phenomenon—it is certainly not a phenomenon of the 20th or 21st century. Misconduct and criminal behavior are entrenched in financial operations and transactions. In 1721, formal investigations exposed a web of deceit, corruption, and bribery that led to the prosecution of many of the major players in the crisis following the South Sea bubble of 1720, including both company and government officials. Many members of parliament took bribes in the South Sea Company stock and traded in the stock on insider information (Painter, 2006). Financial fraud goes even further back as Chakrabarty (2013) talks about finance-related fraud around 300 BC.

The extent of corruption on Wall Street is best described by Snyder (2010) as follows:

> If you ask most Americans, they will agree that the financial system is corrupt. It is generally assumed that just like most politicians, most big bankers are corrupt by nature. But the truth is that the vast majority of Americans have no idea just how corrupt the U.S. financial system has become. The corruption on Wall Street has become so deep and so vast that it is hard to even find the words to describe it. It seems that the major financial players will try just about anything these days—as long as they think they can get away with it. But in the process they are contributing to the destruction of the greatest economic machine that the planet has ever seen.

Corruption is more rampant in the financial sector than in other sectors of the economy because the commodity traded in the financial sector is money, which makes it more tantalizing to commit fraud. Moreover, fraud in the financial sector can be very difficult to detect, given that "financial innovation" has created so much complexity that, together with the so-called "creative accounting", makes the detection of fraud a rather difficult task. Hutton (2010) argues that London and New York have become the centers of an international financial system in which the purpose of banking is to make money out of money, and here the complexity of the "innovation" allows extensive fraud and deception.

Corruption is a cause of financial instability and crises. The results of a 1986 FDIC survey show that criminal misconduct by insiders was a major contributing factor in 45% of bank failures (Sprague, 1986). The last three major crises (the savings and loan crisis, the subprime crisis, and the global financial crisis) were caused predominantly by greed-driven fraud and corruption. In its final report on the crisis, the FCIC (2011) uses variants of the word "fraud" over 150 times to describe what led to the crisis. One of the conclusions reached by the Commission is that "there was a systemic breakdown in accountability and ethics". This is what the Commission had to say:

> We witnessed an erosion of standards of responsibility and ethics that exacerbated the financial crisis. This was not universal, but these breaches stretched from the ground level to the corporate suites. They resulted not only in significant financial consequences but also in damage to the trust of investors, businesses, and the public in the financial system.

Mortgage fraud was not the only form of fraud that led to the eruption of the global financial crisis as fraud took many shapes and forms. Investors were led to believe that mortgage-backed securities were high-quality assets. Financial institutions collected commissions from CDOs, then from CDO-squared based on the original CDOs. A particular insurance company sold billions of dollars worth of insurance policies against default without having the money to meet claims (or the knowledge required to estimate the risk embodied in the underlying securities). Investors were persuaded to buy junk securities by an institution that knew with a high degree of confidence that those securities would lose value overnight and then that same institution took a bet on the collapse. Does anyone not agree that this is a scandal of monumental dimensions?

Regulatory capture is widespread in the financial sector as banks and major financial institutions bend the rules for their private benefit by using high-level bribery, lobbying, and influence peddling. Green and Nader (1973) suggest that capture is enhanced by the exchange of personnel, arguing that "a kind of regular personnel interchange between [regulatory] agency and industry blurs what should be a sharp line between regulator and regulatee, and can compromise independent regulatory judgment". Regulatory capture played a big role in the advent of the global financial crisis. According to Kaufman (2009), capture was the main reason for the systemic failure of oversight, regulation, and disclosure in the financial sector.

Why is corruption rampant in the finance industry? Partnoy (2010) provides an answer to this question by suggesting that it is the absence of fear of punishment. For example, regulators were tipped off to the fraud committed by Bernie Madoff, but nothing happened for a long time, either because regulators did not understand the tip or because they did not have the political will to bring a case against him. Partnoy makes it clear that "in financial markets, the question of whether an action is morally wrong is typically irrelevant; the relevant consideration is profit". What is important to remember is that fraud in the financial sector is not a phenomenon that is associated with "few rotten apples"—rather, it is endemic, entrenched in the very culture that governs behavior in the financial sector.

12.7 Good Regulation Versus Bad Regulation

The debate on regulation has been centered on the choice between a free market (economy) and a regulated market (economy). However, the debate should be about good regulation versus bad regulation. Regulation is needed, but bad and unnecessary regulation should be avoided. Bad regulation is bad for economic growth, but good regulation is good for economic growth. In this section, the good regulation versus bad regulation debate is reviewed with particular reference to financial regulation.

The global financial crisis has taught us a lesson the hard way, the lesson that corruption, fraud, and greed are rampant in the finance industry and that these should be regulated to avoid another crisis. The financial oligarchs should never be given a free hand to do as they please, and this is where regulation comes in. Alan Greenspan, the former chief of the Federal Reserve System, once said that there is no need for the regulation of fraud because if a stock broker indulges in fraudulent activity, he will be recognized by the financial community and no one will deal with him (Roig-Franzia, 2009). Obviously, the victims of Bernie Madoff do not sympathize with this view. But while Greenspan has since changed his mind about the charm of the free market, some "die-hard" free marketeers still advocate the idea that free markets provide the only salvation.

The real question, particularly in the aftermath of the global financial crisis, is not whether or not financial regulation is needed, but whether a particular set of regulatory measures are good or bad. In other words, the debate should be about the distinction between good regulation and bad regulation. However, this issue is hardly dealt with, perhaps because of the extreme view expressed by free marketeers that no regulation is good regulation and any regulation is bad regulation, which triggers a debate on more regulation or more deregulation. The proposition that the debate should be about good regulation versus bad regulation seems to be assuming increasing acceptance, even by the general public. The debate should be about the quality and not (or not only) about the quantity of regulation.

There is no question that regulation is a mixed blessing. Regulation serves a vital role in improving social, environmental, and economic standards. Regulation defines and enforces property rights, which are the basis for economic exchange. But regulation also gives government bureaucrats the power to flex their muscles on ordinary people. The dark side of regulation is that it may be used to serve the interest of a small minority at the expense of the majority, which typically occurs under regulatory capture. Even well-intentioned regulation can bring problems of its own. This is why the costs associated with regulation have to be balanced against potential benefits. In general terms, good regulation should produce benefits that outweigh the costs.

Attempts have been made to identify the characteristics of good regulation. Banks (2003) lists the following characteristics: (i) it must have a sound rationale and be shown to bring a net benefit to society; (ii) it must be better than any alternative regulation or policy tool; (iii) it must be robust to errors in the assumptions underlying it; (iv) it should not be immortal in the sense that it should be dismantled when it is no longer required; (v) it should state (*ex ante*) what it is going to do and establish verifiable performance criteria; (vi) it should be clear and concise; (vii) it must be enforceable; and (viii) it needs to be administered by accountable bodies in a fair and consistent manner. Likewise, Thomadakis (2007) argues that "good regulation must start with a clear understanding of the objective—and this necessitates a trilateral dialogue between regulators, the regulated community, and the beneficiaries of regulation". For him, "good regulation serves the public interest through supporting ongoing confidence in processes, such as the market process, in which the public participates in activities, such as auditing, on which the public relies". He also identifies some criteria for good regulation: necessity, transparency, proportionality, effectiveness, and flexibility. D'Arcy (2004) suggests another list of criteria for good regulation: fair (applied equally), simple, inexpensive, enforceable, targeted, and proportional.

Good financial regulation is any regulation that helps reduce the incidence of financial crises and provides consumer protection from rampant corruption in the finance industry. Because corruption contributes to the advent of financial crises, good regulation combats corruption and protects the vulnerable without imposing excessive costs on the society. Good regulation should have a positive balance in terms of costs and benefits. Bad regulation, on the other hand, can be bad because it represents capture, which may take the form of erecting barriers to maintain the competitive position of existing firms.

It has been argued that distinguishing between good regulation and bad regulation is not an exact science, which makes it rather difficult to judge a piece of regulation as good or bad. Furchtgott-Roth (2000) writes the following on this issue:

> Chemists use precise tests to detect and identify the component elements of different substances. Physicists have methods to examine objects, both large and small. Biologists can discern much information about the basic building blocks of life from genetic material. Scientists have many techniques to answer fundamental questions about the world, but can

those techniques enable them to distinguish a good government regulation from a bad one? Labeling some regulations "good" and others "bad" may seem simple, but what distinguishes one from the other?

However, two criteria can be used to determine whether a piece of regulation is good or bad, particularly financial regulation. If the objective of regulation is to combat fraud and corruption, then the first criterion is its effectiveness in doing so. The second criterion is that the regulation pays off in terms of costs and benefits. Each piece of regulation has arguments for and against, which means that a good regulation must have more arguments for than against. Examples of good regulation are the regulation of payday loans and insider trading, both of which are fraudulent activities that are justified in terms of the free market doctrine. Examples of bad regulation are the regulation of short selling and high-frequency trading. Short selling exposes fraud and incompetence, and no one should tell anyone not to buy now and sell two seconds later.

12.8 Concluding Remarks

The ninth commandment of the Washington Consensus is that of deregulation, as the preachers urge developing countries, or force them, to deregulate, to give corporate Washington a license to loot. The preached countries are told that deregulation does wonders, as it leads to more competition, lower prices, innovation, more jobs, and robust growth. The arguments put forward in favor of deregulation are intended to serve the interests of multinationals seeking to establish footholds in developing countries and for the benefit of a minority of local oligarchs who are loyal to the preaching countries.

As serious as this topic is, there is no harm in ending up with a humorous representation of the benefits and consequences of deregulation as portrayed by Brinson (2011) who lists 10 unforeseen effects of deregulation. Number 10 is "Bye, Bye Jobs", in reference to job losses following the deregulation of railways and airlines. Number 9 is "Down and Out on the Farm", citing how people in rural areas were affected by the deregulation of railways (cancellation of non-profitable routes to remote rural areas). Number 8 is "Face the Music", that is, the control of commercial radio stations means that "no matter where you tune in, you're likely to hear the same songs". Number 7 is "Try Me! No, Me!", that is, deregulation has put us in a situation where we are bombarded with direct mail and telemarketers trying to get us to choose one thing or another. Number 6 is "How much do we know?", that is, the Telecommunications Act of 1996 had the unforeseen effect of limiting the news and information we receive.

Back to airlines in Number 5, which is about "Peanuts". Brinson (2011) says the following about the good old days when flying was fun:

> Remember the good old days, when you got a full meal when flying? When flight attendants were plying you with drinks at every turn? Now, you might be in danger of starving, with nothing but a small pack of peanuts or pretzels and a tiny cup of soda or water on a cross-country journey.

That is true—these days you pay extra for extra leg room, luggage, meals, and entertainment (and you would not dare ask for another glass of wine, even in business class). Number 4 is "Remote Decontrol", which is about the rising prices of cable television. Number 3 is "Can You Hear Me Now?", which is about how deregulation spawned the proliferation of smart phones, and with it, new industries producing apps and other features (texting while driving has been one negative consequence). Number 2 is "Going Bust", that is, some companies go belly-up even though deregulation is intended to help them. As a result of the lack of restraint, deregulated industries run wild, waging war against each other. Number 1 is "Crash!", in reference to how financial deregulation caused the global financial crisis.

Deregulation is convenient for multinationals working in developing countries because they can pollute the environment with impunity. On 29 September 2020, it was announced that Rio Tinto was facing accusations that a mine it had abandoned in Papua New Guinea two decades ago is leaking poisonous waste into rivers (BBC News, 2020). This is not an isolated incident. While multinational corporations do what it takes to maximize profit, those living in poor countries bear the burden by inhaling polluted air, drinking dirty water, and eating contaminated food.

Rich countries can punish polluters, but poor countries cannot do that. The US demanded and obtained a $20 billion fund from BP to meet claims for economic losses and environmental costs from the Gulf of Mexico oil spill. The US can do that because it is a powerful host country, and BP had little choice but to yield, given political pressure and public anger. Developing countries are host to multinationals that typically poison the environment and cause immense loss of life and property, but multinationals are more powerful than developing countries, in which case they get away with murder. Had the BP incident occurred in the Bay of Bengal rather than the Gulf of Mexico, BP would have got away by paying $2 million, if anything at all. Khor (2010) suggests that developing countries should be able to adopt a "polluter pays" scheme.

Those who oppose regulation and call for deregulation do not mention pro-business regulation, which is more conspicuous in the financial sector. Bail-out is a pro-business regulation as the government channels taxpayers' money to save failed institutions. Bail-in is a pro-business regulation that allows failed banks to confiscate depositors' money. The war on cash, whereby anyone using cash above a certain limit is put behind bars, is a pro-business regulation intended to force people to keep their money with banks so that banks can confiscate the money if and when they fail. Low and negative interest rates represent a pro-business regulation that allows the corporate sector to engage in the parasitic activities of stock buy-backs and venture capital, and to allow banks to charge customers for looking after their deposits while charging them 20% for credit cards. The situation is truly tragic, at least for 99% of the population.

Chapter 13

The Tenth Commandment: Property Rights

13.1 Introduction

According to Williamson (1990), "there is general acceptance that property rights do indeed matter". This is right, and it is probably why the Industrial Revolution started in Britain not because of technology, but because of the establishment of a sophisticated system of property rights. This is why no Industrial Revolution took place in ancient China when they had the technology of the time.

However, there is a dark side to property rights, a concept that emerged at the time of imperialism. European imperialism used property rights to claim ownership to whole countries and their resources (and people). King Leopold of Belgium claimed property rights to vast regions of the Congo. The East India Company claimed property rights to vast areas of East Asia. Britain until now claims property rights to the Falklands. White settlers claimed property rights to farms and fertile land in Rhodesia and South Africa. Oligarchs claim property rights to the minerals that are supposed to belong to the people at large. Slave owners claimed property rights to slaves. Multinationals claim property rights to privatized assets that they acquired cheaply through extortion and bribery.

Property rights in the Washington Consensus are not about a system that is used to protect a family home from intruders, but rather they are used to protect the interests of the oligarchs and multinationals from the rightful owners of the same property rights. The tenth commandment works very well with the commandments of privatization, deregulation and liberalization to accomplish the objective of "liberalize, deregulate and privatize".

13.2 An Overview of Property Rights

The term "property right" refers to the right of an owner of a property (a good or an asset) to use the property for consumption and/or income generation (use rights). A property right also implies the right to transfer the property to another party in the form of a sale, gift, or bequest (transfer rights). A property right typically conveys the right to contract with other parties by renting, pledging, or mortgaging the property or by allowing other parties to use it. Free marketeers refer to private property rights, implying the ability of the owner to exclude others from using the property. Some economists argue that the poor lack easy access to the property mechanisms that could legally fix the economic potential of their assets so that they could be used to produce, secure, or guarantee greater value in the market (Besley and Ghatak, 2009). This implies that property rights are key to economic development.

Alchian (2008) defines property rights as "theoretical socially-enforced constructs in economics for determining how a resource or economic good is used and owned". The bundle of rights includes the following: (i) the right to use the good; (ii) the right to earn income from the good; (iii) the right to transfer the good to others, alter it, abandon it, or destroy it (the right to ownership cessation); and (iv) the right to enforce property rights. Property ownership may be public, common, or private.

Public property (also known as state property) is a property that is publicly owned, but its access and use are managed and controlled by a government agency or an organization granted such authority (an example is a national park or a state-owned enterprise). Common property or collective property is a property that is owned by a group of individuals such that access, use and exclusion are controlled by the joint owners. Private property is both excludable and rival. Private property access, use, exclusion and management are controlled by the private owner or a group of legal owners.

Property rights affect economic activity via several channels. The first is the risk of expropriation, the fear that property may be confiscated, which discourages investment in productive assets. The second channel is the cost of protecting property, which diverts resources away from productive activity. The third channel is that the absence of property rights does not allow the exploitation of gains from specialization and trade, for example, by renting or leasing the property. The fourth channel is that the absence of property rights precludes the possibility of using the property to support other transactions, for example, as collateral.

Besley and Ghatak (2009) use casual empiricism to show that property rights are associated with economic welfare measured in terms of GDP per capita. First, they show positive correlation between GDP per capita and a measure of property rights provided by the International Country Risk Guide, which is the risk of appropriation (measured on a scale of 0–10, where 10 means less risk). The scatter diagram shows positive correlation, which is most likely spurious. Rich countries with high levels of GDP per capita have more developed systems of property rights than countries with low GDP per capita. It is not necessarily the case that property rights have led to higher levels of GDP per capita. They also show negative correlation between the ease with which individuals can register their property (provided by the World Bank) and GDP per capita. Accordingly, they conclude that improving property rights is associated with economic development. However, they acknowledge the ambiguity of the direction of causation, suggesting the possibility that economic development induces a switch to improved property rights, as opposed to property rights facilitating economic development.

This kind of evidence can tell us anything. Consider Figure 13.1, which shows scatter plots of GDP growth rates (1 year and 5 years) on the

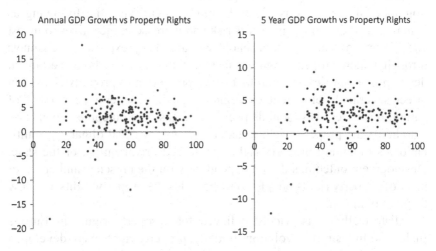

Figure 13.1:   Growth as a Function of Property Rights

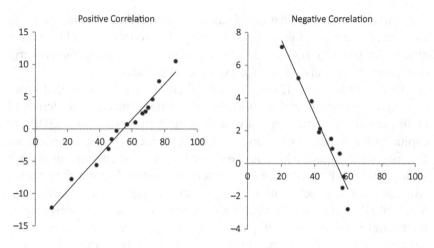

Figure 13.2:   5 Year Growth as a Function of Property Rights (Selected Countries)

property rights index provided by the Heritage Foundation, which assumes values ranging between 0 and 100 (Miller *et al.*, 2020). Obviously, we cannot see any correlation, positive or negative, simply because growth depends on more than property rights. In Figure 13.2, we see scatter plots of 5 year growth on the property rights index, using selected groups of countries. For some countries, correlation is highly positive; for others, it is highly negative.

Denison and Klingler-Vidra (2012) have produced an annotated bibliography of the property rights literature, identifying the following as benefits: (i) reduction in investors risk and increase in incentives to invest and (ii) improvements in household welfare. They explore the channels through which property rights affect growth and household welfare in developing countries and find that better protection of property rights can affect several development outcomes, including better management of natural resources. This sounds peculiar because the outcome depends on who holds the property right to natural resources: local oligarchy, multinationals obtaining property rights via forced privatization, or the state. Development outcomes do not depend only on the presence and enforcement of property rights but also on who holds the property rights and how they are obtained.

Historically, it is widely believed that property rights in Europe fueled the Industrial Revolution. Initially, property rights were developed during the Middle Ages, but those rights went to the ruling monarchies that confiscated private property while imposing arbitrary taxes and refused to pay their debts. Following the English Civil War of 1642–1646 and the Glorious Revolution of 1688, shifts of political power away from the Stuart monarchs led to the strengthening of property rights of both land and capital owners, setting the stage for the Industrial Revolution. This is an example of how political power can be enhanced by property rights and the creation of an oligarchy. North *et al.* (2006) argue that property rights originate to facilitate elites' rent-seeking activities. In a historical study of medieval England, for instance, North and Thomas (1971) find that the dramatic development of English land laws in the 13th century resulted from elites' interests in extracting rent from land ownership after a sudden rise in land prices in the 12th century.

No one can deny the importance of property rights for developing countries. The problem is that the concept is used to protect the oligarchy and multinationals operating in developing countries. They are not meant to be about the protection of the society as a whole against predatory foreign investors and confiscators of property. It is never about public property but rather about private property. And again, the principle of preaching without practicing is valid for property rights. For centuries, imperialist countries (now preaching property rights) confiscated property from its rightful owners and used property rights to protect their unlawful acquisitions, typically by the sword and gun. Property rights should not be maintained without looking into how they were acquired.

13.3 Property Rights as an Invention of Imperialism

European imperialist powers have historically used property rights to "legalize" their forceful acquisitions of assets and resources in the countries they invaded. The indigenous population was never protected by property rights. Schmidhauser (1992) refers to "several major families of law as a concomitant of military conquest, colonial aggrandizement, and/or economic penetration—the attributes of legal imperialism".

King Leopold of Belgium personally held the property rights to rubber plantations as a private enterprise in the so-called Free State of Congo, which could not have been further away from being free. Concessions were allocated to private companies. In the north, the Société Anversoise was given 160,000 square kilometers, while the Anglo-Belgian India Rubber Company (ABIR) was granted a comparable territory in the south. The Compagnie du Katanga and Compagnie des Grands Lacs were given smaller concessions in the south and east, respectively. His Majesty kept some 250,000 square kilometers of territory for himself under the "crown domain", which was added to the territory he already controlled under the "private domain".

Property rights were maintained by sheer brutality. In the concessionary territories, the private companies that had purchased concessions (property rights) from the Free State administration were able to use virtually any available means to boost production and profits without any intervention from the state (this is "deregulation"). Two companies, ABIR and Anversoise, were particularly harsh in treating Congolese workers. Those who refused to work were coerced, dissenters were beaten and whipped, hostages were taken to ensure prompt collection, and punitive expeditions were sent to destroy villages that refused to provide slave labor. Apparently, they held property rights to humans as well.

Wherever the imperialists landed they confiscated property from the indigenous population and claimed property rights of their own. Columbus claimed the new world to the Spanish crown. The Spaniards claimed property rights to the gold and silver of South America while butchering the original holders of the property rights. The same happened in Australia. The same happened in North America. The same happened in Africa. And the same happened in East Asia and the Middle East. In an act of illegal transfer of property rights, the British Empire granted Palestine to private settlers in accordance with the Balfour Declaration of 1917. Britain and France used the Sykes–Piccot Agreement of 1916 to grant themselves property rights in Iraq, Jordan, Lebanon and Syria. By the power of the gun, Britain granted itself property rights in the Falkland Islands and Hong Kong, choosing to keep the former and abandon the latter because they knew they could win a war against Argentina but not against China. The list is endless.

Modern-time imperialism is no different. The imperialist powers that bombed Libya back to the Stone Age are fighting among themselves for property rights where property is the Libyan oil fields. American troops are in Syria for the sole purpose of claiming property rights to Syrian oil as a prelude to stealing it—they will most likely leave when they have stolen all of the oil. In January 2020, at a Wisconsin rally, Donald Trump took pride in his decision to retain troops in eastern Syria to control oil fields there (Brennan, 2020). This is not only a violation of the property rights of the Syrian people but also a war crime according to international law, which Trump does not recognize. Then of course there is the property right to the earth minerals in Afghanistan. The US Geological Survey began exploring the mineral resources of Afghanistan following the invasion of the poor country. The aerial surveys determined that Afghanistan may hold 60 million tons of copper, 2.2 billion tons of iron ore, and 1.4 million tons of rare earth elements such as lanthanum, cerium and neodymium, as well as significant quantities of aluminium, gold, silver, zinc, mercury and lithium. Presence in Afghanistan is motivated by the availability of property rights to grab.

13.4 Settlements and Slavery

The imperialist expansion in Africa and the New World was accompanied by massive land confiscation and transfer of property rights by force from the indigenous population to the civilian settlers coming from imperialist countries. Perhaps the cases of South Africa and Zimbabwe are the most paramount in this respect. In South Africa, the Natives Land Act of 1913 decreed that natives were not allowed to buy land from whites and vice versa. Exceptions had to be approved by the Governor-General. The native areas left initially totaled less than 10% of the entire land mass of the Union, which was later expanded to 13%. Yet, in August 2018, Donald Trump tweeted a message of support for South Africa's "hard-pressed white farmers" (Frum, 2018).

According to a 2017 land audit by the South African government, 72% of the country's arable land remains in the hands of whites, who account for fewer than 10% of the total population (Clark, 2019). Since the ruling African National Congress came to power in 1994, under the leadership of Nelson Mandela, one of its central undertakings has been to relieve this disparity. For the likes of Trump, the transfer of property rights in one direction by force is tolerable, but making things right is intolerable.

Bond (2008) argues that "Africa remains disempowered on fronts ranging from trade to direct investment" as the continent hosts some of the world's worst cases in terms of poverty and inequality. Yet, the looting of Africa is not new and dates back many centuries to the point at which value transfers began via appropriation of slave labor and slave trade. Then, precious metals and raw materials were extracted by forceful colonialist methods, followed by a declaration of property rights. In recent decades, wealth extraction through imperialist relations has intensified, and some of the same kinds of primitive looting tactics are now once again in place throughout the entire continent.

In Zimbabwe, thousands of white farmers were forced from their farms, sometimes violently, between 2000 and 2001 under a government program of land reform. The origin of this story goes back to 1895 when Southern Rhodesia was occupied by the British South Africa Company (associated with the master imperialist Cecil Rhodes), following the subjugation of the Matabele (Ndebele) and Shona nations. More than 3,000 white soldiers who assisted in the BSAC takeover of the country were given land grants of 1,200 hectares (3,000 acres) or more—as a result, black people living on the land became tenants. In 1930, the Land Apportionment and Tenure Act displaced Africans from the country's best farmland, restricting them to unproductive and low-rainfall tribal-trust lands and high-rainfall areas for white ownership, which gave rise to cases of black people being excluded from their own land (forceful transfer of property rights). White settlers were attracted to Rhodesia by the availability of tracts of prime farmland that could be purchased from the state at bargain prices.

The property rights of slave traders were a fantastic privilege, allowing them to kidnap Africans in coastal raids and ship them to America where the rights were transferred to the highest bidders. About 12 million Africans were shipped across the Atlantic over a span of 400 years between the 16th and 19th centuries when slavery was abolished (Lovejoy, 1989). The transfer of property rights took place after a public sale that was advertised in advance. In 1835, the British government borrowed the equivalent of £300 billion in today's money from the Rothschilds to finance "slave compensation" following the abolition of slavery. The compensation money went exclusively to the owners of slaves who had lost their "property" and property rights.

A major reason for the American Civil War between the Union and Confederate armies was the long-standing controversy over slavery, which had an economic dimension. The agricultural south depended on slaves working in the fields to generate income, which means that the abolition of slavery would have cut their profit margins significantly and deprived them of property rights. Southerners (even those who did not own slaves) viewed any attempt by the federal government to limit the rights of slave owners over their "property" as a potentially catastrophic threat to their entire economic system. Slaves were a property and the slave owners held the property right to that property.

13.5 Property Rights of Oligarchs and Multinationals

Multinationals and the oligarchs claim property rights to privatized assets that they acquire cheaply through extortion and bribery (and sometimes through invasion and occupation). Once they obtain these property rights, they demand protection, which is provided by "reform" under the Washington Consensus.

In the early 1990s, the then Russian President Boris Yeltsin, the darling of the "West", launched an aggressive privatization program that was a bonanza for the oligarchs who enjoyed the transfer of property rights from ordinary Russians who at one time had employment and healthcare as a results of the public ownership of the privatized assets. Property rights were transferred to the oligarchs at a rate of about 800 a month in rigged auctions that allowed the oligarchs to acquire public assets for a fraction of what they were worth. When Putin tried to reverse the grab of property rights by renationalizing privatized public assets, he was demonized. The Washington Consensus is intended to defend the property rights of the oligarchs, not those of ordinary people. The same applies to multinationals that acquire the rights to privatized public assets under duress.

13.6 Intellectual Property Rights

Intellectual property rights include patents, copyright and industrial design right. A patent is a form of right granted by the government to an inventor or their successor-in-title, giving the owner the right to exclude others from making, using, selling, offering to sell, and importing an invention for a limited period of time in exchange for the public disclosure of the invention. Industrial design rights protect the visual design of objects that are not purely utilitarian. An industrial design consists of the creation of a shape, configuration or composition of pattern or color, or combination of pattern and color in three-dimensional form containing aesthetic value.

Intellectual property rights can be justified on the grounds that a person has a natural right over the labor and products produced by their body, which means that appropriating these products is viewed as unjust. Another argument is that a society that protects private property is more effective and prosperous than societies that do not. This means that intellectual property rights are intended to maximize social utility. Yet another argument is that by being a creator of something, one is inherently at risk and vulnerable for having their ideas and designs stolen and/or altered.

That is fine. The author of a book should receive royalties as people pay to acquire the book, and there is no reason to set a time limit on the receipt of royalties. However, it is a different story when a pharmaceutical company comes up with a drug and prices it beyond the reach of most people to maximize profit, knowing that the demand for the drug is inelastic because the alternative is certain death. Take, for example, COVID-19 where the world is desperate for a vaccine. Where is morality if a company comes up with a vaccine and puts a price tag of $300 a shot? That is immoral because it is beyond the reach of a large number of people even in rich countries. It is also inefficient from a public health perspective because COVID-19 is a pandemic, which means that leaving out people from poor countries means that the virus will keep on orbiting the planet. How many people would have been saved by making the AIDS pills available at a reasonable price?

Furthermore, some observers reject the very notion of intellectual property. The Founder of the Free Software Foundation, Richard Stallman, argues that although the term "intellectual property" is in wide use, it should be rejected altogether because it "systematically distorts and confuses these issues, and its use was and is promoted by those who gain from this confusion" (Stallman, 2018). He asserts that the term "operates as a catch-all to lump together disparate laws [which] originated separately, evolved differently, cover different activities, have different rules, and raise different public policy issues". He goes on to argue that it creates bias by confusing these monopolies with ownership of limited physical things, likening them to property rights. Likewise, Boldrin and Levine (2008, 2009) prefer to use the term "intellectual monopoly" as a more appropriate and clear definition of the concept, which they argue, is very dissimilar from property rights. They further argue that "stronger patents do little or nothing to encourage innovation", mainly explained by its tendency to create market monopolies, thereby restricting further innovations and technology transfer.

Free software activists have criticized the implied analogy with physical property (like land or a vehicle), arguing that such an analogy fails because physical property is generally rivalrous while intellectual works are non-rivalrous (that is, if one makes a copy of a work, the enjoyment of the copy does not prevent enjoyment of the original) (see, for example, Doctorow, 2008). A similar argument is that unlike the situation with tangible property, there is no natural scarcity of a particular idea or information: once it exists at all, it can be reused and duplicated indefinitely without such reuse diminishing the original. Kinsella (2001) rejects the notion of intellectual property on the grounds that the word "property" implies scarcity, which may not be applicable to ideas.

Maney (2015) explains how patents kill innovation and hold tech companies back. Kinsella (2010) argues that "people are literally dying because Fabrazyme is in short supply and the sole, monopolistic manufacturer, Genzyme, can't make enough quickly enough–and no one else is permitted to make it due to the patent". He criticizes what he calls the "intellectual propagandists" who "callously, arrogantly, and smugly retort that without patents, Genzyme would never have invented the drug in the first place", which would have resulted in the death of 20,000 rather than 5,000 people. He goes on to say the following:

> So saving 15,000 (I'm guessing at the numbers) is better than none, right? So the ones who die have no complaint about the patent system, since without it they'd die anyway. What a chilling mentality; and of course there is no reason to think drugs would not be invented absent patents.

The history of innovation and patenting is rife with example after example of the occurrence of near-simultaneous invention, but the first to file (or invent, depending on the jurisdiction) gets the monopoly. Without patents, they would all be able to take products to market, and they would all benefit from the accumulated body of human knowledge that they had no role in producing. Patent holders build on the insights and discoveries of others from the past, and in the future, people will build on the discoveries being made now. What is wrong with this?

Patents are seen as granting monopoly power, which can be very dangerous, particularly in some industries producing essential goods such as the pharmaceutical companies. Emanuel (2019) explains excessively high drug prices in the US in terms of the federal government granting drug companies a monopoly through patents and Food and Drug Administration (FDA) marketing exclusivity, arguing that "when you give a company a monopoly, they're going to raise prices until raising the prices reduces their margin". As a solution, he recommends regulation, which is against the ninth commandment, by saying that monopolies should be regulated and that "every other country in the world [apart from the US] regulates drug prices, typically through some formal process of negotiation".

Intellectual property is used for tax evasion by multinationals through profit shifting. The OECD (2017) estimates the lost annual tax revenues as a result of this activity to be in the range of $100–240 billion. This massive tax evasion is realized by the following: (i) using IP royalty payment schemes to shift profit from higher-tax locations to lower-tax locations; (ii) using the same to overcome EU withholding tax protections; (iii) using fraudulent accounting to create intangible assets that can be expensed against taxation in certain IP-beneficial regimes; and (iv) using fraudulent accounting to maximize the effect of corporate relocations to low-tax regimes.

13.7 Concluding Remarks

Washington and its allies, the countries that preach property rights to developing countries, indulge in massive transfer of property rights from the general public to the oligarchy and corporate interests through privatization, bail-out and bail-in. Privatization is effectively the transfer of property rights to public assets to the private sector. Bail-out is the transfer of property rights to public funds from the public to failed corporate interests. Bail-in is the coercive transfer of property rights to personal deposits from depositors to failed banks by allowing them to confiscate the deposits of private citizens. I wonder why free marketeers think that the government is a bad thing when governments look after corporate interests in the name of being "business-friendly". Oligarchs like corrupt politicians who help them enrich themselves in return for some rewards in one form or another. They hate honest politicians who go by the mandate of serving the people at large.

One particular type of property right is patents, a subject that has triggered considerable debate. In 1742, Benjamin Franklin invented a new type of stove, for which he was offered a patent. He refused it, arguing in his autobiography that because "we enjoy[ed] great advantages from the inventions of others, we should be glad of an opportunity to serve others by any invention of ours" (*The Economist*, 2014). This is something that does not happen these days because it is not conducive to profit maximization.

Patent laws, as applied to pharmaceuticals, are the most damaging. Hlomani (2020) suggests that "the era of the AIDS pandemic offers important insight into how patent laws can be complicit in the loss of lives". Likewise, Shulman (2001) argues that "in AIDS-stricken Africa, the enforcement of Western drug patents is a needless death sentence for millions". This debate has come back, but it is about the current COVID-19 pandemic and the provision of vaccines. One way or another, vaccines should be somehow made available to all, which brings in the issue of patents. The opponents of patents argue that the patent system will inhibit access to the vaccine for those who cannot afford it. The proponents argue that without the incentives for innovation provided by the patent system, a vaccine may not be developed in a timely fashion, if at all.

Pharmaceutical companies should be able to cover the cost of developing the vaccine and make some profit. The patent system should not be used by a company to maximize profit and pay the CEO a bonus of $25 million. Granting a patent long enough for the company to make some reasonable profit is fine, but the ultimate objective should be to make the vaccine available to all. This is not a matter of patents only—it is also a matter of public spending priorities and international development aid.

Chapter 14

Epilogue

14.1 Recapitulation

In 1989, an international economist, John Williamson, coined the term "Washington Consensus" and constructed a list of ten policy recommendations that reflect the common thinking and practice of the international financial institutions based in Washington DC as well as the US Treasury and think tanks. For years before Williamson came up with his list, the International Monetary Fund and the World Bank had been imposing these types of policies on the developing countries requiring loans from the two institutions. Variants of these policies have been incorporated in the conditionality provisions attached to the IMF and World Bank loans and the adjustment programs imposed on borrowing countries. The ten policy recommendations are invariably based on the free market doctrine and neoliberalism, even though Williamson tells us every now and then that his list differs from what the Washington free marketeers would like to see. In practice, however, the difference is subtle, as Williamson's list does not differ significantly from the principles on which the IMF operates and what the rest of Washington thinks.

In this book, the ten policy recommendations on Williamson's list are called the ten commandments. When they are written like the Ten Commandments, they read as follows:

1. Thou shalt be fiscally disciplined.
2. Thou shalt redirect thy public spending.
3. Thou shalt reform thy tax system.

4. Thou shalt liberalize thy interest rates.
5. Thou shalt make thy exchange rate competitive.
6. Thou shalt liberalize international trade.
7. Thou shalt liberalize foreign direct investment.
8. Thou shalt privatize thy public assets.
9. Thou shalt deregulate thy economy.
10. Thou shalt strengthen property rights.

The ten commandments of the Washington Consensus boil down to one commandment: in the name of thy God, *laissez-faire*, and for the benefit of multinationals and the oligarchy, thou shalt liberalize, deregulate and privatize. The hidden agenda behind the Consensus is startling. Fiscal reform is intended to keep the lid on the public sector, shift the tax burden to the middle class and give multinationals and the oligarchy tax concessions. Interest and exchange rate "reforms" are intended to make it cheaper for multinationals to acquire public assets in developing economies. The liberalization of foreign trade implies open markets for multinationals without the need to use armies and navies as in the case of 19th century imperialism. The liberalization of foreign direct investment means giving multinationals concessions to do as they please, and own assets in any sector without exceptions. Privatization amounts to the disposal of national wealth by selling public assets at bargain prices to multinationals, allowing them to own utilities, mines, hospitals and other enterprises producing goods and services that are essential to well-being. Deregulation means giving multinationals a free hand, allowing them to pollute without limits, pay less than minimum wages and charge extortionist prices for goods and services characterized by inelastic demand. Strengthening property rights means that foreign investors who acquire public assets are protected from renationalization. It is all for the benefit of multinationals and the oligarchy.

The policy recommendations implied by the ten commandments have been preached or imposed on developing countries by political, technocratic and corporate Washington using a number of approaches. The first approach is to bomb the country that refuses to obey the ten commandments back to the Stone Age, then invade it and impose the commandments. In May/June 2003, the occupation authority in Baghdad was recommending, on advice from the IMF, shock therapy involving the removal of subsidies (second commandment) and the privatization of everything under the sun (eighth commandment), including (of course) the oil sector. This approach may be called the Pentagon Consensus or the NATO Consensus. The second approach is to engineer a regime change by taking out (preferably assassinating) the elected president and replacing him or her with a puppet president who obeys the ten commandments. This approach may be called the CIA-MI6 Consensus (or the Five-Eye Consensus) which was successful in Iran in 1953, temporarily successful in Bolivia in 2020, and unsuccessful in Cuba despite decades or relentless work. This approach is currently followed in Venezuela to replace the elected president with a self-declared president backed by political and corporate Washington. The third approach is the most common, involving the use of the carrots and sticks embodied in conditionality and adjustment programs of the IMF and World Bank. The fourth approach is to train economists in the tradition of Milton Friedman and Fredrick von Hayek and put them in senior positions in the finance ministries of the underlying countries. This approach worked quite well, particularly in Latin America.

In this book, the ten commandments were discussed critically, identifying problems in principles and implementation. The first problem is that the preachers do not practice what they preach, adopting instead the attitude of "do as I say, not as I do". Political Washington preaches fiscal discipline, even though it is the world champion in fiscal profligacy. Another example is that the preachers do not obey the fourth commandment of market-determined interest rates as they drive interest rates artificially into negative territory. The second problem is that some of the recommendations are not implementable. How would any country have a competitive exchange rate (meaning an undervalued currency) when no one knows what the equilibrium exchange rate is? The third problem is that some of the recommendations are pure propaganda used to put a human face on the Consensus. The second commandment of redirection of public expenditure to health and education is not encouraged by the IMF, whose operations curtail social spending.

The fourth problem is the portrayal of the people of the country to be beneficiaries of the "reform" when the real beneficiaries are the oligarchy and multinationals. The tenth commandment of property rights is, on paper, a good recommendation to protect people's property, but it is intended mainly to protect the assets grabbed unfairly or illegally by the oligarchy and multinationals. The fifth problem is that of contradiction between some of the commandments. For example, the first commandment of fiscal discipline is inconsistent with the third commandment of tax reform if tax reform means adopting a tax system, as in the preaching countries, that encourages the accumulation of debt.

14.2 A Better Alternative: The Beijing Consensus

The way forward is to adopt a new international financial system and a new system of international relations. We have already seen that the Chinese model of international economic relations is working well, in which case the Beijing Consensus (BJC) has outperformed the Pentagon Consensus, the NATO Consensus, the CIA-MI6 Consensus and the Washington Consensus. Although the Washington Consensus is less brutal than the NATO Consensus and the CIA-MI6 Consensus, the preachers of the Consensus have made so many promises that could not be fulfilled. The case of Argentina is a perennial example, as described by Önis (2004): "The country strictly conformed, perhaps more so than any other 'emerging market', to the advice of the [IMF]", however after surging in the early 1990s and then beginning to "lose momentum", the end result was "complete collapse".

A number of developing countries that have tried both the Washington Consensus and the Beijing Consensus seem to prefer the latter. Instead of prescribing rigid recommendations for the problems of developing countries, the Beijing Consensus is pragmatic, exhibiting the same degree of pragmatism that has propelled economic development in China. The Beijing Consensus recognizes the need for flexibility in solving problems, emphasizing ideals such as equitable development and a "peaceful rise". According to Ramo (2004):

> China is writing its own book now. The book represents a fusion of Chinese thinking with lessons learned from the failure of globalisation culture in other places. The rest of the world has begun to study this book.

While the Washington Consensus prescribes the same strict and homogeneous "reforms" to nearly all developing countries, the Beijing Consensus recognizes the need for a unique approach according to each nation's specific challenges. The Beijing Consensus recognizes the idea that self-determination is important for development, unlike the Pentagon, NATO, CIA-MI6 doctrines. Lyman (2005) argues that "China's investments are attractive to Africans... because they come with no conditionality related to governance, fiscal probity or other of the concerns that now drive western donors". Unlike "Western" countries, China does not seek to impose its own priorities on partner countries. Yes, the Beijing Consensus is a better alternative than the Washington Consensus.

The Beijing Consensus is based on the Chinese model of development and international relations. Compare this with the American model of international relations whereby the internal affairs of far-away countries are considered a threat to the national security of the US, which makes it necessary to take military action against those countries. Here, I am not talking about the build-up of weapons of mass destruction by dictators who "kill their own people". I am talking about the desire of people in faraway countries to have multiple sons and daughters—yes, that is a threat to US national security. In 1974, the US National Security Council under Henry Kissinger produced a classified 200-page study, *National Security Study Memorandum 200: Implications of Worldwide Population Growth for US Security and Overseas Interests* (NSSM 200). The study, which was declassified in 1989, identified 13 "key countries" in which "special U.S. political and strategic interests" existed. The targeted countries were the following: India, Bangladesh, Pakistan, Nigeria, Mexico, Indonesia, Brazil, the Philippines, Thailand, Egypt, Turkey, Ethiopia and Colombia. The recent resurgence of interest in this document can be attributed to the belief of some that COVID-19 is a conspiracy intended to reduce world population.

US security interests were seen (by the authors of the report) as threatened by demographic and political realities in developing countries, particularly the age structure in high-fertility countries with large numbers of young people. A major US security interest concerned access to "reserves of higher-grade ores of most minerals", and the terms for exploration and exploitation of those resources. The study advised that civil disturbances affecting the "smooth flow of needed materials" would be less likely to occur "under conditions of slow or zero population growth". The document called for "integrating population factors in national plans, particularly (within) health services, education, agricultural resources and development" while relating "population policies and family-planning programs to major sectors of development: health, nutrition, agriculture, education, social services, organized labor, women's activities, and community development". This sounds like the Washington Consensus.

Like free trade, Washington learned this idea from the previous master, Britain. In 1944, King George VI created the Royal Commission on Population "to consider what measures should be taken in the national interest to influence the future trend of population". According to the Commission, Britain was gravely threatened by population growth in its colonies, since "a populous country has decided [*sic*] advantages over a sparsely-populated one for industrial production". The Commission warned that the combined effects of increasing population and industrialization in the colonies "might be decisive in its effects on the prestige and influence of the West", affecting particularly "military strength and security" (Brewda, 1995). If this is how the custodians of the Washington Consensus feel about developing countries, can anyone imagine that they are serious about prosperity in the former colonies?

Naturally, political Washington is very unhappy about the rise of the Beijing Consensus. Mike Pompeo, the former US Secretary of State, visited developing countries forging economic ties with China on the basis of the Beijing Consensus to tell the leaders of those countries that they were making a big mistake by going that way. In late October 2020, he was on a visit to Sri Lanka, which has been ratcheting up its relationship with China. In a meeting with the President of Sri Lanka, Pompeo described the Chinese government (invariably referred to as the Chinese Communist Party) as a "predator", and suggested that, as a result of the deals struck with China, Sri Lanka was compromising its sovereignty and independence. The Sri Lankan president told Pompeo that his country would "remain neutral" (Mauldin and Shah, 2020; Aljazeera, 2020). I suppose that Sri Lanka may, as a result, be put on the list of countries supporting terrorism or become exposed to the US Treasury Consensus (sanctions)—even worse, it could be the Pentagon and CIA Consensus.

14.3   A Better Alternative: Rodrik and the Keynesians

Rodrik (2006) has proposed what is called the "augmented" Washington Consensus by adding ten more principles to the ten commandments. Unfortunately, however, some of these principles are no different from any principle based on neoliberal thinking, even though some of them add a humanitarian character to the Consensus. Three of the ten added principles are the establishment of social safety nets, targeted poverty reduction and "prudent" capital-account opening. However, free market principles can still be found in flexible labor markets and independent central banks. While the non-independence of central banks has led to hyperinflation in many countries (as a result of politicians putting pressure on central bankers to expand the money supply), leaving unaccountable central bankers to do what it takes to please corporate interest is also hazardous. Like everything else in life, "moderation" is the keyword.

On the other hand, Marangos (2014), who argues that the Washington Consensus is identified as a "neoliberal manifesto", suggests a Keynesian alternative to the Consensus. The proposal emphasizes state interventionist policies, the excessive priority given to price stability instead of full employment, recycling the country's savings back into the domestic economy in coordination with industrial policy and domestic financial regulation, supporting policies that aim at a stable and permanently low level of interest rates and the direction of credit to specific parts of the economy, regulation of foreign banks and reinforcement of fair competition, and the role of globalization in development and capital controls.

The proposal put forward by Marangos (2014) is based on the proposition that Keynesians reject the Washington Consensus because it involves the imposition of strict free market neoclassical policies on developing countries. Hence, he describes "reforms" guided by the Consensus as "unrealistic and unpractical" because they amount to a "one-size-fits-all" policy, concluding that the Consensus is "inappropriate". He reformulates the ten commandments by suggesting that the first commandment of fiscal discipline must include provisions for boosting domestic savings and stabilizing domestic inflation. Public expenditure priorities in the second commandment must include provisions for stabilizing the real economy through Keynesian policies and for improved educational opportunities. Under tax reform comes a proposal to introduce property taxation as the major source of revenue and the elimination of tax loopholes, as well as taxing income earned on flight capital. The fourth commandment becomes "financial liberalization" involving the targeting of a low inflation rate and the strengthening of prudential supervision. Property rights include land reform and microcredit. Unfortunately, nothing in terms of change is suggested in the areas of privatization, deregulation and foreign direct investment.

An eleventh commandment is suggested by Marangos (2014) under the heading "institution building". This proposal includes a role for the state in maintaining effective institutions, as well as providing public goods, internalizing externalities, correcting income distribution, maintaining decent infrastructure, a stable and predictable macroeconomic, legal and political environment, and a strong human resource base. Reforms under this heading include reforming the judiciary, education and civil services, building a national innovation system, modernizing the market institutional structure and institutional reform in the financial sector.

14.4 A Better Alternative: Reforming the International Monetary System

Other alternatives can be sought in terms of reforming the international monetary system, which was born in 1944. Together with the enforcers of the Washington Consensus, the World Bank and the International Monetary Fund, the system was born as integral components of the Bretton Woods Conference, which was held to design the post-war international monetary system. Varoufakis (2016) suggests that an alternative to this system may be found in the original proposal put forward by Keynes at the conference, which witnessed a clash of two men and their visions: Harry Dexter White, representing the US Treasury, and John Maynard Keynes, representing the British Treasury. Given the rising star of the US and the fading British Empire at that time, White's proposal won the day. Keynes proposed the idea of a global central bank, the International Clearing Union (ICU), and an international currency, which he called the "Bancor", with the objective of keeping the global economy in balance. Keynes recognized that it was not only debtor countries that were dangerous for stability, but that creditor countries were at least equally responsible. He also proposed the establishment of a global sovereign wealth fund that could be used to finance investment in capital formation.

Keynes's proposal is discussed by George (2007) from a global justice perspective. She looked not only at the financing of trade through the ICU and the Bancor but also at Keynes' original plans for an International Trade Organization (ITO). Unlike the WTO, which evolved in its place, the ITO charter recognized the UN, including the Universal Declaration of Human Rights. It emphasized full employment, social and economic progress and labor standards, and mandated cooperation with the International Labour Organisation. The charter was used to formulate plans for sharing skills and technology and to permit poorer countries to use government aid and intervention for development and to protect their infant industries. The ITO charter outlawed the practice of subsidizing products on foreign markets at ultra-low prices, which means that the massive agricultural policies handed by rich countries to their farmers would not be used to outcompete developing country farmers. Speculative capital flows would be penalized by the ICU, helping to prevent the economies of developing countries from becoming subject to the whims of speculators.

Anti-globalization sentiment has been rampant owing to the observed fate of the developing countries told to follow the Washington Consensus. Bello and Feffer (2009) argue for the virtues of deglobalization by suggesting the following:

> The current global downturn, the worst since the Great Depression 70 years ago, pounded the last nail into the coffin of globalization. Already beleaguered by evidence that showed global poverty and inequality increasing, even as most poor countries experienced little or no economic growth, globalization has been terminally discredited in the last two years. As the much-heralded process of financial and trade interdependence went into reverse, it became the transmission belt not of prosperity but of economic crisis and collapse.

Naturally, "deglobalization" is a scary word as far as free marketeers are concerned. They do not want to see the possibility of replacing neoliberal globalization with more localized economies that are more compatible with ecological and social justice. Deglobalization implies that production should be intended primarily for local rather than export markets. Under this system, trade policy and industrial policy (including subsidies, quotas and tariffs) would be used to protect local markets from destruction by corporate-subsidized commodities and strengthen local manufacturing industry. Measures would be taken for land and income redistribution to create vibrant local markets and local sources of financial investment. Not only is investment to be directed toward "environmentally congenial" technology, economic growth is de-emphasized while the quality of life is brought to the fore. Social equity and environmental equilibrium are seen as going hand in hand.

14.5   What Is Worse Than the Washington Consensus?

The Washington Consensus is based on what Gürdeniz (2020) describes as the "neoliberal disaster". This is how he describes neoliberalism:

> Neoliberalism created a society of individualists, consuming without thinking. The masses looked the other way during the bloody interventions in Afghanistan, Iraq, Libya and Syria, wars conducted either to access energy and raw material resources or to create new markets. Most did not question their governments, submitting to the artificial threat of terror. While the weak states disintegrate in political bloodbaths, the vigorous elites of financial-capital have supported the growth of a universal middle class racked with consumer debts.

What is worse than the Washington Consensus is something to the right of the Consensus where the public sector is eliminated completely. Consider a world with private everything: courts, police, army, national guard, fire brigade, navy, air force, intelligence services and roads, all of which operate without any restrictions because regulatory agencies will also disappear. This is the world that anarcho-capitalists aspire for. Anarcho-capitalism is a political philosophy and economic theory that advocates the elimination of centralized states in favor of free markets and private property. In the absence of the state, anarcho-capitalists would argue, the society tends to self-regulate through participation in the free market (Morris, 2008).

This vision is exposed by Kosanke (2010) who puts forward a case for an "unobstructed market". He defends the value of advertising, emphasizes the necessity of risk for progress, and stresses the importance of non-compulsory insurance. He promotes the abolition of various "state evils", particularly antitrust legislation, transnational subsidies, compulsory licensing, censorship, and fair prices. These points deserve some remarks. Advertising is aimed at manipulating consumers so that they buy things they do not need—even things that make them sick or kill them. Risk is necessary for progress, but abolishing compulsory car insurance is recklessness. Abolishing antitrust legislation leads to the rise of monopolies, which (ironically) he does not like. Abolishing fair prices means that people will die because they cannot afford healthcare, given that public hospitals are "state evils".

Kosanke (2010) explains the danger of a "distorted price system", the "futility of regulation", the failure of collectivism to deal with catastrophe, and the inefficiency of monopoly. A distorted price system means that the producers of a necessary product with a low elasticity of demand can charge any price they want, irrespective of the social consequences. The futility of regulation implies no limit to what corporations can do to maximize profit, including the abuse of human rights. He objects to price controls, the minimum wage, collectivist unions, and full employment, arguing instead for "legitimate free trade" and competition with respect to prices, wages and employment. Full employment is unlikely to be achieved, but this does not mean that the unemployed should be condemned to poverty, homelessness or death, which makes it necessary to have a "state evil" called "social safety net". He praises private security markets, even though these markets lead to grotesque inequality and financial crises that are typically followed by devastating recessions. He praises the "economic law of supply and demand", even though economics, unlike physics, does not have laws. He rebukes taxation because it is used to finance "state evils" such as health and education.

However, he is absolutely right in criticizing the "CIA/DEA involvement in international drug smuggling", which "illustrates the inevitable hypocrisy of prohibition". He is right in condemning war, reflexive obedience to authority, tribalism, pro-war propaganda, the military draft, and the military–industrial complex. These are the true state evils. Still, what he suggests in general is to go further right than the Washington Consensus and its neoliberal foundation. Some of the suggestions are unethical, to say the least, and they only consider private costs and revenues. He seems to defend selfishness and individualism, and condemns altruism and compassion.

I am not sure how the world that anarcho-capitalists aspire for is supposed to work. Will someone whose house is on fire calling the fire brigade be asked to state his subscription number? If this person does not have a subscription, will the fire brigade refuse to respond? I suppose that the ready answer would be that the next-door neighbor who has a valid subscription would call the fire brigade to put out the fire in the first person's home to avoid the eventuality of catching fire. Will each billionaire have a police force and an army, but the rest of people will have no protection against burglary, kidnapping and murder? How does the private market work in this case? This sounds like a world run by Mafia bosses—it is certainly worse that the Washington Consensus.

14.6 The Hazard of Economic Extremism

Any model of economic development should strike a balance and avoid extremes. Neoliberalism, with unshaken belief in the magic of the market is an extreme, just like communism is an extreme. Privatization is not good always and under any circumstances. Deregulation can be harmful, even though cutting red tape is useful. Foreign direct investment can be useful, but it should be regulated. Subsidies may be needed as a component of the social safety net. Public ownership can be useful. Fair pricing may be needed in the case of goods and services with inelastic demand. More importantly, however, extreme measures should not be imposed on other countries by telling them that this is the only way out or by threatening them with deprivation from IMF and World Bank loans.

I have seen a comic representation of economic systems in terms of what happens to the owner of two cows (http://www.cowries.info/funstuff/language/cows.html). Under communism, the state takes the two cows and gives the owner some milk. Under fascism, the state takes both cows and sells the owner some milk. Under socialism, the owner is expected to give one of the cows to the neighbor. Under unfettered capitalism, however, ownership of cows is restricted to the oligarchy. People work for the oligarchy by milking the cows and then use the wages to buy milk from the oligarchs. Under financialized capitalism, this is what happens:

> You have two cows. You sell three of them to your publicly listed company, using letters of credit opened by your brother-in-law at the bank, then execute a debt/equity swap with an associated general offer so that you get all four cows back, with a tax exemption for five cows. The milk rights of the six cows are transferred via an intermediary to a Cayman Island Company secretly owned by the majority shareholder who sells the rights to all seven cows back to your listed company. The annual report says the company owns eight cows, with an option on one more.

This is the kind of system that the Washington Consensus promotes. This system has inflicted extensive damage on the custodians of the Washington Consensus, except for corporate Washington. Developing countries could do without it.

A compassionate system is what we should look for, where the state makes sure that those who cannot afford to buy milk are given milk until they can afford to buy it. Nothing is wrong with the state doing that, but everything is wrong with a state that is run by corrupt politicians looking after corporate interests at the expense of the majority of people. As an example, look no further than the policy of negative interest rates and the declared war on cash, let alone bail-ins and bail-outs.

14.7 COVID-19 Has the Last Word

Perhaps COVID-19 will create a new world in so far as international relations are concerned. Gürdeniz (2020) notes that "Covid-19 has reminded the world that the public sphere is vital in an environment where profit-oriented capitalism has pushed the population to abandon social morality". On the other hand, he argues, "China has managed to remain strong morally and economically, providing a stable model for the 21st century". COVID-19 has changed thinking in such a way as to favor self-sufficiency, which has also been aided by the sanctions imposed by Washington left, right and center.

Pope Francis has presented his blueprint for a post-COVID-19 world, covering a vast number of issues from fraternity and income inequality to immigration and social injustice, with a scathing description of *laissez-faire* capitalism (Poggioli, 2020). In a document released in October 2020, he denounced what he described as "this dogma of neoliberal faith" that "resort[s] to the magic theories of 'spillover' or 'trickle'" and suggested that "the marketplace cannot resolve every problem". A good economic policy, he said, "creates jobs—it doesn't eliminate them".

COVID-19 is likely to put an end to the American era sooner rather than later. The pandemic has shown that the US cannot even help itself, let alone others. America's global image has been tarnished, even destroyed, by aggression against countries such as Venezuela and Iran, depriving them of humanitarian supplies as they struggle to deal with the pandemic. The pandemic has shown the importance of the public sector, as demonstrated by China—with its strong centralized state structure, it turned out to be the state most prepared for the pandemic or any other catastrophic scenario. Gürdeniz (2020) is hopefully right in thinking that "the Washington Consensus is taking its last breaths as a result of the pandemic crisis". It is unlikely, however, the custodians of the Washington Consensus will give in without a fight. Let us hope at least that the fight will not be a war erupting between a declining power and a rising power as predicted by the Greek philosopher and war historian, Thucydides, more than 2,000 years ago.

Addressing officials in developing countries, I would like to put forward three brand new commandments. First, beware of "reform" based on the neoliberal manifesto of the Washington Consensus. Second, if the fat guys in suits and ties arriving from Washington tell you that you need reform, tell them that they need reform. Third, explore alternatives to the neoliberal manifesto that the fat guys are payed handsomely to promote for the benefit of corporate Washington.

References

Aaron, H.J., Gale, W.G. and Orszag, P.R. (2004). Meeting the revenue challenge, in Rivlin, M. and Sawhill, I. (eds). *Restoring Fiscal Sanity*, Washington, DC: Brookings Institution Press.

Adewale, A.R. (2017). Import substitution industrialisation and economic growth—Evidence from the group of BRICS countries, *Future Business Journal*, 3, 138–158.

Advisory Commission on Intergovernmental Relations (1987). *Fiscal Discipline in the Federal System: National Reform and the Experience of the States*, July. Available at: https://library.unt.edu/gpo/acir/Reports/policy/a-107.pdf.

Agarwal, J.P. (1980). Determinants of foreign direct investment: A survey, *Weltwirtschaftliches Archiv*, 116, 739–773.

Ahamed, L. (2014). *Money and Tough Love: On Tour with the IMF*, London: Visual Editions.

Ahmad, J. (1978). Import substitution—A survey of policy issues, *Developing Economies*, 16, 355–372.

Akerlof, G.A. and Shiller, R.J. (2015). The dark side of free markets, *The Conversation*, 21 October. Available at: https://theconversation.com/the-dark-side-of-free-markets-48862.

Alchian, A.A. (2008). Property rights, *New Palgrave Dictionary of Economics* (second edition), London: Palgrave.

Aljazeera (2020). Pompeo Slams 'Predator' China on Sri Lanka Trip, 28 October.

Allard, G.J. and Lindert, P.H. (2006). Euro-productivity and Euro-job since the 1960s: Which institutions really mattered, *NBER Working Papers*, No. 12460.

Allison, J.A. (2012). *The Financial Crisis and the Free Market: Why Capitalism is the World Economy's Only Hope*, New York: McGraw-Hill.

Amadeo, K. (2020). US military budget, its components, challenges, and growth, *The Balance*, 20 March. Available at: https://www.thebalance.com/u-s-military-budget-components-challenges-growth-3306320.

Anderson, S. (2020). Trump's trade war cost U.S. company stock prices $1.7 trillion, *Forbes*, 1 June.

Appleby, J. (2010). *The Relentless Revolution: A History of Capitalism*, New York: Norton.

Astore, W.J. (2018). Meet the new, super-expensive stealth bomber the US doesn't need, *The Nation*, 4 June.

Bailey, G. (2000). *Mythologies of Change and Certainty in Late Twentieth Century Australia*, Melbourne: Australian Scholarly Publishing.

Bairoch, P. (1995). *Economics and World History: Myths and Paradoxes*, Chicago: University of Chicago Press.

Bakalar, N. (2008). Rise in TB is linked to loans from I.M.F., *New York Times*, 22 July.

Balassa, B., Bueno, G.M., Kuczynski, P.P. and Simonsen, M.H. (1986). *Toward Renewed Economic Growth in Latin America*, Washington: Institute for International Economics.

Bandow, D. (2019). How can a bankrupt republic run the world? *Daily Breeze*, 2 January.

Banks, G. (2003). The good, the bad and the ugly: Economic perspectives on regulation in Australia. Available at: http://www.pc.gov.au/news-media/speeches/cs20031002/cs20031002.pdf.

Barber, W.J. and Theoharis, L. (2020). The evil tucked into the $2 trillion coronavirus stimulus bill, *Time*, 2 April.

Barnett, S. (2000). Evidence on the fiscal and macroeconomic impact of privatization, *IMF Working Papers*, No.130.

Barro, R.J. and Lee, J.W. (2005). IMF programs: Who is chosen and what are the effects? *Journal of Monetary Economics*, 52, 1245–1269.

Bartlett, B. (2013). Financialisation as a cause of economic malaise, *New York Times*, 11 June.

Barwick, E. (2020). Aged care is a public good, not a cash cow, *Australian Alert Service*, 7 October, 5–6.

Basu, L. (2019). The 'Washington Consensus' is dead. But what should replace it? *Open Democracy*, 13 April.

Baxter, L.G. (2011). Capture in financial regulation: Can we channel it toward the common good? *Cornell Journal of Law and Public Policy*, 21, 175–200.

BBC News (2020). *Rio Tinto: Mining Giant Accused of Poisoning Rivers in Papua New Guinea*, 29 September.

Beard, T.R., Ford, G.S., Kim, H. and Spiwak, L.J. (2011). Regulatory expenditures, economic growth and jobs: An empirical study, *Phoenix Center Policy Bulletin*, No. 28.

Bel, G. (2006). Retrospectives: The coining of "Privatization" and Germany's national socialist party, *Journal of Economic Perspectives*, 20, 187–194.

Bello, W. and Feffer, J. (2009). The virtues of deglobalization, *Foreign Policy in Focus*, 3 September.

Bennett, J., Estrin, S. and Urga, G. (2007). Methods of privatization and economic growth in transition economies, *Economics of Transition*, 15, 661–683.

Benson, J.S. (2001). The impact of privatization on access in Tanzania, *Social Science & Medicine*, 52, 1903–1916.

Besley, T. and Ghatak, M. (2009). Reforming property rights, *Vox*, 22 April.

Biddle, C. (2014). *The Causes of War and Those of Peace*, 2 October. Available at: https://www.theobjectivestandard.com/2014/10/causes-war-peace/.

Birdsall, N. and Nellis, J. (2002). Winners and losers: Assessing the distributional impact of privatization, *Center for Global Development Working Papers*, No. 6.

Birdsall, N., De la Torre, A. and Caicedo, F.V. (2010). The Washington consensus: Assessing a damaged brand, center for global development, *Working Paper 213*.

Black, W. (2011). *How the Servant Became a Predator: Finance's Five Fatal Flaws*, 25 May. Available at: http://www.huffingtonpost.com/william-k-black/how-the-servant-became-a_b_318010.html.

Blanco, B. (2017). Why liberty and the nanny state are incompatible, *Foundation for Economic Education*. Available at: https://fee.org/articles/why-liberty-and-the-nanny-state-are-incompatible/.

Blum, W. (2004). *Killing Hope: U.S. Military and CIA Interventions Since World War I*, Monroe (Maine): Common Courage Press.

Boccia, R. (2020). *At $23 Trillion, the U.S. National Debt Already Exceeds the Size of the U.S. Economy*, 31 January. Available at: https://www.heritage.org/debt/commentary/23-trillion-the-us-national-debt-already-exceeds-the-size-the-us-economy.

Boldrin, M. and Levine, D.K. (2008). *Against Intellectual Monopoly Archived 2017-12-06 at the Wayback Machine*. Cambridge: Cambridge University Press, 2008.

Boldrin, M. and Levine, D.K. (2009). *Intellectual Property Rights and Economic Growth in the Long-Run*. Available at: http://levine.sscnet.ucla.edu/papers/aea_pp09.pdf.

Bond, P. (2008). The looting of Africa, in Lechini G. (ed), *Globalization and the Washington Consensus: Its Influence on Democracy and Development in the South*, Buenos Aires: Consejo Latinoamericano de Ciencias Sociales.

Boring, P. (2014). If you want to know the real rate of inflation, don't bother with the CPI, *Forbes*, 3 February.

Boubakri, N., Smaoui, H. and Zamiti, M. (2009). Privatization dynamics and economic growth, *Proceedings of Annual London Conference on Money, Economy and Management*, 9–10 July 2009, London: Imperial College.

Brautigam, D. (2009). *The Dragon's Gift: The Real Story of China in Africa*, Oxford: Oxford University Press.

Brennan, D. (2020). Trump says U.S. troops stayed in Syria 'Because I Kept the Oil', *Newsweek*, 15 January.

Brewda, J. (1995). Kissinger's 1974 plan for food control genocide, *Schiller Institute*, 8 December. Available at: https://archive.schillerinstitute.com/food_for_peace/kiss_nssm_jb_1995.html.

Brinson, L.C. (2011). *10 Unforeseen Effects of Deregulation*. Available at: https://money.howstuffworks.com/10-effects-of-deregulation.htm.

Brook, Y. (2016). *Free Market*, 13 November. Available at: http://serious-science.org/free-market-7407.

Brookings (2020). *Tracking Deregulation in the Trump Era*. Available at: https://www.brookings.edu/interactives/tracking-deregulation-in-the-trump-era/.

Buettner, R., McIntire, M., Craig, S. and Collins, K. (2020). Trump paid $750 in federal income taxes in 2017: Here's the math, *New York Times*, 29 September.

Buffett, W. (2003). Dividend voodoo, *Washington Post*, 20 May.

Buncombe, A. (2019). US sanctions on Venezuela responsible for 'Tens of Thousands' of deaths, *The Independent*, 26 April.

Butler, S. (1935). *War is a Racket*. Available at: https://www.ratical.org/ratville/CAH/warisaracket.pdf.

Campa, J. and Goldberg, L. (2005). Exchange rate pass-through into import prices, *Review of Economics and Statistics*, 87, 679–690.

Carrier. D. (2016). Roberto Saviano: London is heart of global financial corruption, *The Guardian*, 29 May.

Caselli, F., Koren, M., Lisicky, M. and Tenreyro, S. (2015). Diversification through trade, *CEP Discussion Papers*, No. 1388.

CBO (2001). *The Budget and Economic Outlook: Update, August*. ftp://ftp.cbo.gov/30xx/doc3019/EntireReport.pdf.

CBO (2018). *Impose a Tax on Financial Transactions*, 13 December. Available at: https://www.cbo.gov/budget-options/2018/54823.

Cecchetti, S.G., Mohanty, M.S. and Zampolli, F. (2011). The real effects of debt, *BIS Working Papers*, No. 352.

Center for Global Development (2007). *Does The IMF Constrain Health Spending in Poor Countries? Evidence and an Agenda for Action*. Available at: https://www.cgdev.org/files/14103_file_IMF_report.pdf.

Chakrabarty, K.C. (2013). Fraud in the banking sector—causes, concerns and cures, *National Conference on Financial Fraud*, New Delhi, 26 July. Available at: http://www.bis.org/review/r130730a.pdf.

Chakravarty, M. (2018). The fiscal deficit: What is so bad about it? *CBGA Blog*, 9 July.

Chang, H.J. (2002). *Kicking Away the Ladder: Development Strategy in Historical Perspective*, London: Anthem Press.

Chang, H.J. (2007). *Bad Samaritans: Rich Nations, Poor Policies and the Threat to the Developing World*, London: Random House Business Books.

Chang, H.J. (2011). *23 Things They Don't Tell you about Capitalism*, New York: Bloomesbury Press.

Charpentier, A. (2017). *The U.S. has been at War 222 out of 239 Years*, 19 March. Available at: https://freakonometrics.hypotheses.org/50473.

Chatterjee, A., Gethin, A. and Czajka, L. (2020). Coronavirus: Why South Africa needs a wealth tax now, *The Conversation*, 28 April.

Chen, J. (2007). Behavioral equilibrium exchange rate and misalignment of Renminbi: A recent empirical study. *Paper presented at the 6th International Conference on the Chinese Economy*, 18–19 October, Paris.

Chinn, M.D., Cheung, Y.W. and Fujii, E. (2006). *Why the Renminbi Might be Overvalued (But Probably Isn't)*, Madison: University of Wisconsin.

Chirwa, T.G. and Odhiambo, N.M. (2016). Macroeconomic determinants of economic growth: A review of international literature, *East European Journal of Economics and Business*, 11, 33–47.

Clark, C. (2019). South Africa confronts a legacy of apartheid, *The Atlantic*, 3 May.

Clark, J.R. and Lee, D.R. (2011). Markets and morality, *Cato Journal*, 31, 1–25.

Cline, W.R. and Williamson, J. (2009). *Estimates of Fundamental Equilibrium Exchange Rates*, Washington, DC: Peterson Institute for International Economics.

Coffey, B., McLaughlin, P. and Peretto, P. (2020). The cumulative Cost of Regulations, *Review of Economic Dynamics*, 38, 1–21.

Cohen, S.D. (2007). *Multinational Corporations and Foreign Direct Investment: Avoiding Simplicity, Embracing Complexity*, Oxford: Oxford University Press.

Cohen-Setton, J. (2016). *The New Washington Consensus*, 3 June. Available at: https://www.bruegel.org/2016/06/the-new-washington-consensus/.

Collins, C. and Clemente, F. (2020). It is time to levy a one-time pandemic wealth tax on billionaires' windfall gains, *Market Watch*, 20 August.

Collinson, P. (2019). Danish bank launches world's first negative interest rate mortgage, *The Guardian*, 14 August.

Committee on the Judiciary (1961). *Hearings before the Subcommittee on Antitrust and Monopoly*, Washington, DC: US Government Printing Office.

Cook, P. and Uchida, Y. (2003). Privatization and economic growth in developing countries, *Journal of Development Studies*, 39, 121–154.

Coppola, F. (2018). Everything you've been told about government debt is wrong, *Forbes*, 17 April.

Cordato, R. (2019). Interest rates should be set by the market, not the fed, *John Locke Research Brief*, 2 December.

Council of Economic Advisers (2017). *The Growth Potential of Deregulation*, 2 October.

Cournoyer, C. (2019). How bad is America's infrastructure crisis? Maybe not as bad as it seems, *Governing*, 12 February.

Coward, B. (2015). Is the Chinese Yuan undervalued or overvalued? *Advisor Perspectives*, 19 August.

Craig, E. (1998). *Routledge Encyclopaedia of Philosophy*, London: Taylor & Francis.

Crockett, A. (2008). Commentary, in Goldstein, M. and Lardy, N. (eds). *Debating China's Exchange Rate Policy*, Washington, DC: Peterson Institute for International Economics.

Culbertson, J.M. (1986). The Folly of Free Trade, *Harvard Business Review*, September.

Cushen, J. (2013). Financialisation in the workplace: Hegemonic narratives, performative interventions and the angry knowledge worker, *Accounting, Organizations and Society*, 38, 314–331.

D'Arcy, B.J. (2004). What is good regulation? Concepts and case studies for control of point and diffuse source pollution, *Proceedings of the 2004 WISA Biennial Conference*, 2–6 May, Cape Town.

Dabla-Norris, E., Kochhar, K., Suphaphiphat, N., Ricka, F. and Tsounta, E. (2015). Causes and consequences of income inequality: A global perspective, *IMF Staff Discussion* Note, June.

Dagdeviren, H. (2006). Revisiting privatization in the context of poverty alleviation: The case of Sudan, *Journal of International Development*, 8, 469–488.

Dane, L. (2015). Blood Money: These companies and people make billions of dollars from war, *The Daily Sheeple*, 24 March.

Davidson P. (2007). *Interpreting Keynes for the 21st Century*, London: Palgrave Macmillan.

Davies, A. and Harrigan, J. (2018). *The Federal Government is Bankrupt, Foundation for Economic Education*, 13 June.

Dellas, H. and Tavlas, G.S. (2018). Milton friedman and the case for flexible exchange rates and monetary rules, *Cato Journal*, Spring/Summer 2018, 361–377.

Denison, M. and Klingler-Vidra, R. (2012). *Annotated Bibliography for Rapid Review on Property Rights, Economics and Private Sector Professional Evidence and Applied Knowledge Services* (*EPS PEAKS*). Available at: https://partnerplatform.org/?tcafmd80.

DeRensis, H. (2018). The coming bankruptcy of the American empire, *Mises Institute*, 21 November. Available at: https://mises.org/power-market/coming-bankruptcy-american-empire.

Dewatripont, M. and Freixas, X. (eds). (2012). *The Crisis Aftermath: New Regulatory Paradigms*, London: Centre for Economic Policy Research.

Dickerson, O.M. (1951). *The Navigation Acts and the American Revolution,* Philadelphia: University of Pennsylvania Press.

Doctorow, C. (2008). "Intellectual Property" is a Silly euphemism, *The Guardian,* 21 February.

Dorfman, J. (2016). Ten free market economic reasons to be thankful, *Forbes,* 23 November.

Dreher, A. (2006). IMF and economic growth: The effects of programs, loans, and compliance with conditionality, *World Development,* 34, 769–788.

Driver, R.L. and Westaway, P.F. (2004). *Concepts of Equilibrium Exchange Rates, Bank of England Working Papers,* No. 248.

Drucker, P.F. (1969). *The Age of Discontinuity,* New York: Harper & Row.

Dunaway, S., Leigh, L. and Li, X. (2006). How robust are estimates of equilibrium real exchange rates? The case of China, *IMF Working Papers,* No. 06/220.

Economic Policy Institute (2003). *Economists' Statement Opposing the Bush Tax Cuts,* 3 April. Available at: https://www.epi.org/publication/econ_stmt_2003/.

Economic Times (2019). *How Does China Manage the Yuan, and what is its Real Value?* 9 August.

Egan, M. (2017). Trump pledges to 'Do a Big Number' on Dodd-Frank wall street reform, *CNN Business,* 30 January.

Emanuel, E.J. (2019). Why are drug prices so high in the United States? *Rand Review,* 30 May.

Epstein, G.A. (2002). Financialisation, rentier interests, and central bank policy, working paper, *Department of Economics and Political Economy Research Institute (PERI).* University of Massachusetts, Amherst.

Euraque, D.A. (1996). *Reinterpreting the Banana Republic: Region and State in Honduras,* 1870–1972, Chapel Hill, NC: University of North Carolina Press.

Falk, A. and Szech, N. (2013). Morals and markets, *Science,* 340, 707–711.

Fang, L. (2016). U.S. defense contractors tell investors Russian threat is great for business, *The Intercept,* 20 August. Available at: https://theintercept.com/2016/08/19/nato-weapons-industry/.

Farole, T., Reis, J.G. and Wagle, S. (2010). Analyzing trade competitiveness a diagnostics approach, *World Bank Policy Research Working Papers,* No. 5329.

FCIC (2011). *The Financial Crisis Inquiry Report,* Washington, DC: U.S. Government Printing Office.

Feenstra, R.C., Hai, W., Yao, S. and Woo, W.T. (1998). The U.S.-China bilateral balance: Its size and determinants, *Paper presented at the UNDP-HIID Conference on China's Integration into the Global Economy,* 17 January. Available at: http://www.econ.ucdavis.edu/working_papers/98-9.pdf

Fein, B. (2014). Attacking Syria: A war of aggression? *Huffington Post,* 23 January.

Ferguson, N. (1998). *The House of Rothschild: Money's Prophets 1798–1849*, New York: Viking Press.

Fieldhouse, A. (2013). A review of the economic research on the effects of raising ordinary income tax rates, *EPI-TCF Issue Briefs*, No. 353.

Financial Times (2020). *Today's Ultra-Low Interest Rates Are Anything But 'Natural'*, 20 August.

Foley, M. (2020). Treasurer's inspiration from thatcher, Reagan has merit: Economists, *Sunday Morning Herald*, 26 July.

Forsyth, R.W. (2016). Sorry, Trump, but chinese currency is actually way overvalued, *Barron's*, 6 April.

Foster, V., Butterfield, W., Chen, C. and Pushak, N. (2009). *Building Bridges: China's Growing Role as Infrastructure Financier for Sub-Saharan Africa*, Washington, DC: The World Bank.

Friedman, M. (1953). The case for flexible exchange rates, in *Essays in Positive Economics*, Chicago: University of Chicago Press.

Friedman, M. (1962). *Capitalism and Freedom*, Chicago: University of Chicago Press.

Friedman, M. and Friedman, R.D. (1979). *Free to Choose: A Personal Statement*, New York: Harcourt Brace Jovanovich.

Friedman, M. and Friedman, R.D. (1997). The case for free trade, *Hoover Digest*, No. 4.

Frum, D. (2018). The dangerous myths of South African land seizures reactionaries on either side of the Atlantic are empowering one another, *The Atlantic*, 30 August.

Fukuyama, F. (2008). The fall of America, Inc, *Newsweek*, 3 October.

Fung, B. (2012). How the U.S. health-care system wastes $750 billion, *The Atlantic*, 8 September.

Furchtgott-Roth, H.W. (2000). The art of writing good regulations, *Federal Communications Law Journal*, 53. Article 2. Available at: http://www.repository.law.indiana.edu/fclj/vol53/iss1/2.

Gale, W.G. and Potter, S.R. (2002). An economic evaluation of the economic growth and tax relief reconciliation act of 2001, *National Tax Journal*, March.

Gandásegui, M.A. (2008). Global processes and its effects on latin America: Polycentric vs perturbed worlds, in Lechini G. (ed). *Globalization and the Washington Consensus: Its Influence on Democracy and Development in the South*, Buenos Aires: Consejo Latinoamericano de Ciencias Sociales.

George, S. (2007). Now is the time to rediscover John Maynard Keynes's revolutionary ideas for an international trade organisation and adapt them to rebalance the world's economies in the 21st century, *Global Policy Forum*, January.

Gilmer, G., Schwartz, E. and Areen, M. (2004). War profiteering in Iraq: Corporate contracts, private military companies, and the national resource curse, *EDGE Final Paper*, 1 June.

Glennie, J. (2009). The case for real aid, *New Internationalist*, 1 September.

Glennie, J. (2011). What comes after the Washington consensus? *The Guardian*, 9 February.

Global Coalition for Social Protection Floors (2017). Statement to the IMF on the findings of the evaluation report and the IMF's approach towards social protection, 25 October. Available at: http://www.socialprotectionfloorscoalition. org/2017/10/statement-to-the-imf-on-the-findings-of-the-evaluation-report-and-the-imfs-approach-towards-social-protection/.

Global Times (2020). *China Wants US to Stop Countervailing Probes over 'Yuan Undervaluation'*, 23 July.

Goldberg, L. and Tille, C. (2006). International role of the dollar and trade balance adjustment, *Occasional Paper 71*, Group of Thirty, Washington, DC.

Goldberg, P.K. and Knetter, M.M. (1997). Goods prices and exchange rates: What have we learned? *Journal of Economic Literature*, 35, 1243–1272.

Goldstein, I. and Razin, A. (2005). Foreign direct investment vs foreign portfolio investment, *NBER Working Papers*, No. 11047.

Goldstein, M. and Lardy, N. (2008). China's exchange rate policy: An overview of some key issues, in Goldstein, M. and Lardy, N. (eds). *Debating China's Exchange Rate Policy*, Washington, DC: Peterson Institute for International Economics.

Goodman, L.C. (2009). *War Profiteering Ain't Physics*, 19 May. Available at: http://inthesetimes.com/article/20097/war-profiteering-aint-physics.

Gorton, G.B. (2010). *Slapped by the Invisible Hand: The Panic of 2007*, Oxford: Oxford University Press.

Grabowski, R. (1994). The failure of import substitution: Reality and myth, *Journal of Contemporary Asia*, 24, 297–309.

Grassman, S. (1973). A fundamental symmetry in international payments, *Journal of International Economics*, 3, 105–16.

Gravelle, J. and Marples, D. (2011). *Tax Rates and Economic Growth, Congressional Research Service*. Available at: http://www.fas.org/sgp/crs/misc/R42111.pdf.

Gray, J. (2009). *False Dawn: The Delusions of Global Capitalism* (revised edition), London: Granta Publications.

Green, M. and Nader, R. (1973). Economic regulation vs. competition: Uncle Sam the monopoly man, *Yale Law Journal*, 82, 876.

Greenwood, V. (2018). What makes downsizing so hard to swallow? *BBC Worklife*, 18 May. Available at: https://www.bbc.com/worklife/article/20180510-the-food-you-buy-really-is-shrinking.

Greg, A. and Torbati, Y. (2020). Pentagon used taxpayers money meant for masks and Swabs to make jet engine parts and body armor, *Washington Post*, 22 September.

Grennes, T., Caner, M. and Koehler-Geib, F. (2010). Finding the tipping point— when sovereign debt turns bad, *World Bank Policy Research Working Papers*, No. WPS5391.

Guirguis, A. and Howarth, D. (2020). COVID-19: Government bans price goug-ing, exploitative exports of personal protective equipment, *National Law Review*, 13 April.

Gupta, S., Dicks-Mireaux, L., Khemani, R., McDonald, C. and Verhoeven, M. (2000). Social issues in IMF-supported programs, *IMF Occasional Papers*, No. 191.

Gupta, S. and Shang, B. (2017). *Public Spending on Health Care under IMF-Supported Programs*. Available at: https://blogs.imf.org/2017/03/09/public-spending-on-health-care-under-imf-supported-programs/#more-17249.

Gürdeniz, G. (2020). *Covid-19 and the End of the Washington Consensus*, 1 April. Available at: https://uwidata.com/9548-covid-19-and-the-end-of-the-washington-consensus/.

Guvenen, F., Kambourov, G., Kuruscu, B., Ocampo-Diaz, S. and Chen, D. (2019). Use it or lose it: Efficiency gains from wealth taxation, *NBER Working Papers*, No. 26284.

Haksar, V. and Kopp, E. (2020). How can interest rates be negative? *Finance and Development*, March.

Haley, J.A. (2017). Sovereign debt restructuring: Bargaining for resolution, *CIGI Papers*, No. 124.

Halper, S. (2010). *The Beijing Consensus: How China's Authoritarian Model will Dominate the Twenty-First Century*, New York: Basic Books.

Harcourt, B.E. (2011). *The Illusion of Free Markets: Punishment and the Myth of Natural Order*, Cambridge (MA).: Harvard University Press.

Harper, T. (2019). *The Chinese Model in Africa and its Wider Challenge*, 27 August. Available at: https://theasiadialogue.com/2019/08/27/the-chinese-model-in-africa-and-its-wider-challenge/.

Hartung, W.D. (2001). Eisenhower's warning: The military industrial complex forty years later, *World Policy Journal*, 18 (spring).

Harris, L. (2003). *Trading and Exchanges*, Oxford: Oxford University Press.

Hasan, M. (2020). The coronavirus is killing Iranians. So are Trump's brutal sanctions, *The Intercept*, 18 March.

Hausmann, R. (2016). *Overdosing on Heterodoxy Can Kill You*, 30 May. Available at: https://www.project-syndicate.org/commentary/heterodox-economics-venezuela-collapse-by-ricardo-hausmann-2016-05?barrier=accesspaylog.

Hays, J. (2016). *Russian Privatization and Oligarchs*. Available at: http://fact-sanddetails.com/russia/Economics_Business_Agriculture/sub9_7b/entry-5169.html.

Heath, A. (2013). A wealth tax would be ethically wrong and economically destructive, *The Telegraph*, 19 February.

Hedges, C. (2017). *Speech*. Available at: https://www.youtube.com/watch?v=Ycuw9Cvh6W4.

Henson, S. and Loader, R. (2000). Barriers to agricultural exports from developing countries: The role of sanitary and phytosanitary requirements, *World Development*, 29, 85–102.

Hertz, N. (2004). *The Debt Threat*, New York: Harper Collins.

Hetherington, D., Law, A. and Henderson, Y. (2016). *Taking Back Control: A Community Response to Privatisation*. Available at: https://d3n8a8pro 7vhmx.cloudfront.net/cpsu/pages/1573/attachments/original/1508714447/ Taking_Back_Control_FINAL.pdf?1508714447.

Hlomani, H. (2020). Patents kill patients: A case for the future of Covid-19 treatment, *The Mandela Rhodes Foundation*, 13 July. Available at: https://www. mandelarhodes.org/ideas/patents-kill-patients-a-case-for-the-future- of-covid-19-treatment/.

Hodge, G.A. (1996). *Contracting out Government Services: A Review of International Evidence*, Melbourne: Montech Pty Ltd.

Holland, J. (2014). How a bogus, industry-funded study helped spur a privatization disaster in Michigan, *Moyers on Democracy*, 17 July.

Horowitz, E. (2013). How pharmaceutical ads distort healthcare markets, *Psychology Today*, 15 April.

House Budget Committee (2019). *Strong Infrastructure and a Healthy Economy Require Federal Investment*, 22 October. Available at: https://budget.house. gov/publications/report/strong-infrastructure-and-healthy-economy-require- federal-investment.

Hungerford, T. (2011). Changes in the distribution of income among tax filers between 1996 and 2006: The role of labor income, capital income, and tax policy, *Congressional Research Service*. Available at: http://taxprof.typepad. com/files/crs-2.pdf.

Hutton, W. (2010). Now we know the truth: The financial meltdown wasn't a mistake—it was a con, *The Guardian*, 19 April.

IEO (2003). *Fiscal Adjustment in IMF-Supported Programs*, Washington, DC: IMF Independent Evaluation Office.

IGM (2012). *Price Gouging*, 2 May. Available at: https://www.igmchicago.org/ surveys/price-gouging/.

IMF (2004). People's republic of China: 2004 article IV consultation, *Country Report*.

IMF (2016). *Conditionality*. Available at: http://www.imf.org/en/About/Factsheets/ Sheets/2016/08/02/21/28/IMF-Conditionality.

Insley, J. (2012). GE money refuses mortgages to payday loan borrowers, *The Guardian*, 13 July.

Institute of Medicine (2012). *Best Care at Lower Cost: The Path to Continuously Learning Health Care in America*. Available at: http://www.iom.edu/ Reports/2012/Best-Care-at-Lower-Cost-The-Path-to-Continuously-Learning- Health-Care-in-America.aspx.

Institute on Taxation and Economic Policy (2019). *Benefits of a Financial Transaction Tax*, 28 October. Available at: https://itep.org/benefits-of-a-financial-transaction-tax/.

Irwin, D.A. (2020a). *Import Substitution is Making an Unwelcome Comeback*, Washington, DC: Peterson Institute for International Economics.

Irwin, D.A. (2020b). The rise and fall of import substitution, *Peterson Institute for International Economics Working Papers*, No. 20–10.

Isidore, C. (2013). Buffett says he's still paying lower tax rate than his secretary, *CNN Business*, 4 March.

Ismi, A. (2004). *Impoverishing a Continent: The World Bank and the IMF in Africa*, Halifax: The Halifax Initiative Coalition.

ITPI (2014). *Race to the Bottom: How Outsourcing Public Services Rewards Corporations and Punishes the Middle Class*, 3 June.

Jahn, B. (2005). Kant, Mill and Illiberal legacies in international affairs, *International Organization*, 59, 177–207.

James, K.C. (2020). Introduction, in Miller, T., Kim, A.B. and Roberts, J.M. (eds). *2020 Index of Economic Freedom*, Washington, DC: The Heritage Foundation.

Janský, P. and Palanský, M. (2019). Estimating the scale of profit shifting and tax revenue losses related to foreign direct investment, *International Tax and Public Finance*, 26, 1048–1103.

Jensen, N. (2004). Crisis, conditions, and capital: The effect of international monetary fund agreements on foreign direct investment inflows, *Journal of Conflict Resolution*, 48, 194–210

Johnson, S. and Boone, P. (2010). The doomsday cycle, *Vox*, 22 February.

Johnston, M. (2020). How negative interest rates work, *Investopedia*, 17 March.

Joint Committee on Taxation (2005). *Macroeconomic Analysis of Various Proposals to Provide $500 Billion in Tax Relief*, JCX-4-05, 1 March. Available at: http://www.house.gov/jct/x-4-05.pdf.

Kagami, M. and Tsuji, M. (2000). *Privatization, Deregulation and Economic Efficiency*, Cheltenham: Edward Elgar.

Kagan, J. (2020). Wealth Tax, *Investopedia*, 6 March.

Kaufman, D. (2009). Corruption and the global financial crisis, *Forbes*, 27 January.

Kentikelenis, A. (2015). Bailouts, austerity and the erosion of health coverage in southern Europe and Ireland, *European Journal of Public Health*, 25, 365–366.

Kentikelenis, A., Stubbs, T. and King, L. (2016). The IMF has not lived up to its own hype on social protection, *The Guardian*, 25 May.

Kentikelenis, A., King, L., McKee, M. and Stuckler, D. (2014). The international monetary fund and the ebola outbreak, *Lancet Global Health*, 3(2), e69–70.

Kentikelenis, A., King, L., McKee, M. and Stuckler, D. (2015a). The international monetary fund and the ebola outbreak, *Lancet Global Health*, 3, 69–70.

Kentikelenis, A., Stubbs, T. and King, L. (2015b). Structural adjustment and public spending on health: Evidence from IMF programs in low-income countries, *Social Science & Medicine*, 126, 169–176.

Kentikelenis, A., Stubbs, T. and King, L. (2016). IMF conditionality and development policy space, 1985-2014, *Review of International Political Economy*, 23, 543–582.

Khan, I. (2020). Here's how a revamped wealth tax could fuel the COVID recovery, *World Economic Forum*, 3 August.

Khan, M.S. and Sharma, S. (2001). IMF conditionality and country ownership of programs, *IMF Working Papers*, No. 01/142.

Khor, M. (2010). The double standards of multinationals, *The Guardian*, 25 June.

Kiger, P.J. (2019). *How Venezuela Fell from the Richest Country in South America into Crisis*, 9 May. Available at: https://www.history.com/news/venezuela-chavez-maduro-crisis.

Kinsella, S. (2001). Against intellectual property, *Journal of Libertarian Studies*, 15, 1–53.

Kinsella, S. (2010). When patents kill: Genzyme's patent-protected, life-saving drug, *Christian Science Monitor*, 13 December.

Kogan, R. (2003). Will tax cuts ultimately pay for themselves? *Center on Budget and Policy Priorities*, 3 March.

Komlik, O. (2015). *What is Financialisation? Marxism, Post-Keynesianism and Economic Sociology's Complementary Theorizing, Economic Sociology and Political Economy*, 31 January. Available at: http://economicsociology.org/2015/01/31/what-is-Financialisation-marxism-post-keynesianism-and-economic-sociologys-complementary-theorizing/.

Konish, L. (2018). An economist thinks US is bankrupt: What it means for retirement, *CNBC*, 10 September.

Kosanke, J. (2010). *Instead of Politics*, Charleston (SC): CreateSpace

Kotlikoff, L. (2011). How close is America to Fiscal crisis? *The Economist*, 11 February.

Koyuncu, J.Y. (2016). Does privatization affect economic growth? An evidence from transition economies, *Anadolu University Journal of Social Sciences*, 16, 51–57.

Krishnan, G. (2016). *Exposing The IMF and World Bank—Organizations that are Systematically Controlling and Crippling the World Economy Through Neoliberalism*, 15 May. Available at: https://www.linkedin.com/pulse/exposing-imf-world-bank-organizations-controlling-economy-krishnan.

Krugman, P. (1993). The narrow and broad arguments for free trade, *American Economic Review*, 83 (Papers and Proceedings), 83, 362–366.

Krugman, P. (1996). Making sense of the competitiveness debate, *Oxford Review of Economic Policy*, 12, 17–25.

Krugman, P. (2007). *The Conscience of a Liberal*, New York: Norton.

Kurtzleben, D. (2019). How would a wealth tax work? *NPR*, 5 December.

Lakritz, T. (2019). The 9 deadliest manmade disasters in the past 50 years, *Insider*, 1 June.

Langness, D. (2016). *Greed, Commerce and Self-Interest: The Real Causes of War*, 21 March. Available at: https://bahaiteachings.org/greed-commerce-and-self-interest-the-real-causes-of-war.

Leão, P. (2015). Is a very high public debt a problem? *Levy Economics Institute, Working Papers*, No. 843.

Lechini, G. (2008). Introducción, in G. Lechini (ed). *Globalization and the Washington Consensus: Its Influence on Democracy and Development in the South*, Buenos Aires: Consejo Latinoamericano de Ciencias Sociales.

Lehman, T. (2003). In defense of payday lending, *The Free Market*. Available at: http://mises.org/freemarket_detail.aspx?control=454.

Leigh, J.P. and Du, J. (2018). Effects of minimum wages on population health, *Health Policy Brief*, 4 October. Available at: https://www.healthaffairs.org/do/10.1377/hpb20180622.107025/full/.

Lenin, V.I. (2016). *Imperialism, The Highest Stage of Capitalism*. Available at: https://www.marxists.org/archive/lenin/works/1916/imp-hsc/index.htm.

Lerner, A. (1943). Functional finance and the federal debt, *Social Research*, 10, 38–51.

Levine-Drizin, G. (2019). Sanctions are economic warfare, *In These Times*, 30 May.

Lindorff, D. (2018). The pentagon's massive accounting fraud exposed, *The Nation*, 27 November.

Lincicome, S. (2018). The "protectionist moment" that wasn't: American views on trade and globalization, *Free Trade Bulletin*, No. 72.

Lizondo, J.S. (1991). Foreign direct investment, in international monetary fund, determinants and systematic consequences of international capital flows, *IMF Occasional Papers*, No. 77, 68–82.

Loewenson, R. (1995). Structural adjustment and health policy in Africa, *International Journal of Health Services*, 23, 717–730.

Lovejoy, P.E. (1989). The impact of the atlantic slave trade on Africa: A review of the literature, *Journal of African History*, 30, 365–394.

Lyman, P.N. (2005). China's rising role in Africa, *Council on Foreign Relations*.

Mancini, D.P. and Henderson, R. (2020). CureVac vows 'ethical margin' on price of Covid-19 Vaccine, *Financial Times*, 16 August.

Maney, K. (2015). How patents kill innovation and hold tech companies back, *Newsweek*, 25 February.

Manjapra, K. (2018). When will britain face up to its crimes against humanity? *The Guardian*, 29 March.

Mankiw, N.G. (2015). Economists actually agree on this: The wisdom of free trade, *New York Times*, 24 April.

Mansfield, E. (2012). *Votes, Vetoes, and the Political Economy of International Trade Agreements*, Princeton: Princeton University Press.

Marangos, J. (2014). A Keynesian alternative to the Washington consensus policies for international development, *International Journal of Trade and Global Markets*, 7, 67–85.

Marshall, A.G. (2014). IMF, world bank, giant consultants admit the storm is coming, *World of Resistance Report*, 26 July. Available at: https://truthout. org/articles/world-of-resistance-report-imf-world-bank-giant-consultants-admit-the-storm-is-coming/.

Marston, R.C. (1988). Misalignment of exchange rates: Effects on trade and industry, in Marston R.C. (ed). *Misalignment of Exchange Rates: Effects on Trade and Industry*, Chicago: University of Chicago Press.

Martimort, D. and Straub, S. (2006). Privatization and corruption, *Working Paper*.

Martinez, M.A. (2009). *The Myth of the Free Market: The Role of the State in a Capitalist Economy*, Sterling (VA): Kumarian Press.

Mauldin, J. (2013). *Is the Government Lying to us About Inflation? Yes!*, 22 March. Available at: https://www.mauldineconomics.com/outsidethebox/is-the-government-lying-to-us-about-inflation-yes.

Mauldin, W. and Shah, S. (2020). Pompeo visits Sri Lanka as it deepens China relationship, *Wall Street Journal*, 28 October.

McArdle, M. (2011). Capital gains: Are members of congress guilty of insider trading—and does it matter? *The Atlantic*, November.

McGuire, T. (2019). Do high local taxes really hurt economic growth? *Kelogg Insight*, 26 June.

McKinley, W. (1892). Speech on October 4, 1892 in Boston, *William McKinley Papers*, Washington: Library of Congress.

McKinnon, R.I. (2010). China in Africa: The Washington consensus versus the Beijing consensus, *International Finance*, 13, 495–506.

Meadowcroft, J. (2019). The economists and the general, *Features Magazine*, 30 May.

Megginson, W.L. and Netter, J.M. (2001). From state to market: A survey of empirical studies on privatisation, *Journal of Economic Literature*, June 2001.

Mehrotra, S. and Delamonica, E. (2005). The private sector and privatization in social services: Is the Washington consensus 'Dead'? *Global Social Policy*, 5, 141–174.

Mill, J.S. (1848). *Principles of Political Economy with Some of their Applications to Social Philosophy*, London: John W. Parker.

Miller, T., Kim, A.B. and Roberts, J.M. (2020). *2020 Index of Economic Freedom*, Washington, DC: The Heritage Foundation.

Moberg, D. (2014). Privatizing government Services doesn't only hurt public workers, *In These Times*, 6 June.

Moosa, I.A. (2020). *Controversies in Economics and Finance: Puzzles and Myths*, Cheltenham: Edward Elgar.

Moosa, I.A. and Ramiah, V. (2014). *The Costs and Benefits of Environmental Regulation*, Cheltenham: Edward Elgar.

Morris, A. (2008). Anarcho-Capitalism, in Hamowy, R. (ed.). *The Encyclopedia of Libertarianism*, Thousand Oaks (California): SAGE.

Motamedi, M. (2020). US claims UN sanctions on Iran reinstated. The world disagrees, *Aljazeera News*, 20 September.

Moyo, D. (2010). *Dead Aid: Why Aid Makes Things Worse and How There Is Another Way for Africa*, London: Penguin.

Muchie, M. (2008). The impact of the Washington consensus on democratic stability: The case of Ethiopia, in Lechini G. (ed). *Globalization and the Washington Consensus: Its Influence on Democracy and Development in the South*, Buenos Aires: Consejo Latinoamericano de Ciencias Sociales.

Muratoğlu, G. and Muratoğlu, Y. (2016). Determinants of export competitiveness: Evidence from OECD manufacturing, *Journal of Economics and Political Economy*, 3, 111–118.

Mutume, G. (2006). New barriers hinder African trade, *African Renewal*, January.

Naguib, R.I. (2012). The effects of privatization and foreign direct investment on economic growth in Argentina, *Journal of International Trade and Economic Development*, 21, 51–82.

Naim, M. (1999). Fads and fashion in economic reforms: Washington consensus or Washington confusion? *Foreign Policy Magazine*, 26 October.

Nash, R. (1993). *The Economic Way of Thinking Part 3: The Free Market System, Foundation for Economic Education*, 1 December. Available at: https://fee.org/articles/the-economic-way-of-thinking-part-3-the-free-market-system/.

Navarro, P. and Ross, W. (2016). *Scoring the Trump Economic Plan: Trade, Regulatory, & Energy Policy Impacts*. Available at: https://assets.donaldjtrump.com/Trump_Economic_Plan.pdf.

Naylor, B. (2008). Greenspan admits free market ideology flawed, *NPR*, 24 October.

Nellis, J. and Kikeri, S. (2002). Privatisation in Competitive Sectors: The Record to Date, *World Bank Policy Research Working Papers*, No. 2860.

North, D.C. and Thomas, R.P. (1971). The rise and fall of the manorial system: A theoretical model, *Journal of Economic History*, 31, 777–803.

North, D.C., Wallis, J.J. and Weingast, B.R. (2006). A conceptual framework for interpreting recorded human history, *NBER Working Papers*, No. 12795.

O'Hanlon, M.E. (2019). Is US defense spending too high, too low, or just right? *Brookings*, 15 October.

OECD (2003). *Privatising State-Owned Enterprises: An Overview of Policies and Practices in OECD Countries*, 18 November.

OECD (2017). Inclusive framework on BEPS, *Background Brief*, January.

Office of Management and Budget (2020). *A Budget for America's Future*, 10 February. Available at: https://www.whitehouse.gov/wp-content/uploads/2020/02/budget_fy21.pdf.

Olivera, O. (2004). *Cochabamba: Water War in Bolivia*, New York: South End Press.

Olsen, K. (2019). China's Yuan 'may already be overvalued' and is set to move lower, Nomura says, *CNBC*, 11 March.

Önis, Z. (2004). Argentina, the IMF, and the limits of neo-liberal globalization: A comparative perspective, *Review of International Affairs*, 3, 375–392.

Ooms, G. and Schrecker, T. (2005). Expenditure ceilings, multilateral financial institutions, and the health of poor populations, *The Lancet*, 365, 1821–1823.

Ostry, J.D., Loungani, P. and Furceri, D. (2016). Neoliberalism: Oversold? *Finance and Development*, June.

Oxfam (2002). Death on the doorstep of the summit, *Oxfam Briefing Papers*, No. 29.

Page, S.A.B. (1977). Currency of invoicing in merchandise trade, *National Institute Economic Review*, 33, 1241–1264.

Page, S.A.B. (1981). The choice of invoicing currency in merchandise trade, *National Institute Economic Review*, 98, 60–72.

Painter, A. (2009). The Washington consensus is dead, *The Guardian*, 11 April.

Painter, R. (2006). *Ethics and Corruption in Business and Government: Interdependence and Adverse Consequences*, University of Chicago Law School, Fulton Lectures.

Palasat, G. (2001). *IMF's Four Steps to Damnation, The Guardian*, 29 April. Available at: https://www.theguardian.com/business/2001/apr/29/business.mbas.

Panagariya, A. (2019). Debunking protectionist myths: Free trade, the developing world, and prosperity, *Economic Development Bulletin*, No. 31.

Partington, R. (2018). Is free trade always the answer? *The Guardian*, 13 August.

Partnoy, F. (2010). *Infectious Greed: How Deceit and Risk Corrupted the Financial Markets*, London: Profile Books.

Patton, M. (2012). Is America bankrupt? *Forbes*, 23 July.

Peet, J. (1992). *Myths of the Political-Economic World View from Energy and the Ecological Economics of Sustainability*, Washington, DC: Island Press.

Peláez, C. (2008). *Globalization and the State* (Volume II): *Trade Agreements, Inequality, the Environment, Financial Globalization, International Law and Vulnerabilities*, New York: Palgrave MacMillan.

Petsoulas, C. (2001). *Hayek's Liberalism and its Origins: His Idea of Spontaneous Order and the Scottish Enlightenment*, London: Routledge.

Pilger, J. (2002). John Pilger reveals the American plan, *New Statesman*, 16 December.

Pilger, J. (2004). Why we ignored Iraq in the 1990s, *New Statesman*, 4 October.

Pitt, M. (1993). Analyzing human resource effects: Health, in Demery, L., Ferroni, M.A. and Grootaert, C. (eds.). *Analyzing the Effects of Policy Reforms*, Washington, DC: World Bank.

Plane, P. (1997). Privatization and economic growth: An empirical investigation from a sample of developing market economies, *Applied Economics*, 29, 161–178.

Poggioli, S. (2020). Pope Francis laments failures of market capitalism in blueprint for post-COVID World, *NPR*, 4 October.

Polanyi, K. (1944). *The Great Transformation*, New York: Farrar & Rinehart.

Poole, W. (2004). Free trade: Why are economists and noneconomists so far apart? *Federal Reserve Bank of St. Louis Review*, 86, 1–6.

Porter, M. (1990). *The Competitive Advantage of Nations*, New York: Free Press.

Posner, R.A. (1999). The Effects of Deregulation on Competition: The Experience of the United States, *Fordham International Law Journal*, 23, 7–19.

Prince, E.D. (2017). The MacArthur model for Afghanistan, *Wall Street Journal*, 31 May.

Project for the New American Century (2000). *Rebuilding America's Defenses: Strategy, Forces and Resources for a New Century*. Available at: http://truthandarttv.com/RebuildingAmericasDefenses.pdf.

Przeworski, A. and Vreeland, J. (2000). The effect of IMF programs on economic growth, *Journal of Development Economics*, 62, 385–421.

Ramo, J.C. (2004). *The Beijing Consensus*, London: Foreign Policy Centre.

Rampell, C. (2020). Trump is all about deregulation—except when it comes to his enemies, *Washington Post*, 29 May.

Raso, C. (2017). What does "Deregulation" actually mean in the Trump era? *Brookings Center on Regulation and Markets*, 1 November.

Rauch, J. (1989). Is the deficit really so bad? *The Atlantic Monthly*, February.

Reuters (2016). *Donald Trump Says 70% of Federal Regulations 'Can Go'*, 7 October. Available at: https://fortune.com/2016/10/07/donald-trump-business-regulations/.

Reuters (2018). *IMF Says Dollar Over-valued, Chinese Yuan in Line with Fundamentals*, 25 July.

Ricardo, D. (1817). *On the Principles of Political Economy and Taxation*, London: John Murray.

Rickards, J. (2016). Behind the scenes of the monetary agency that is just as powerful as the military and CIA, *The Daily Reckoning*, 4 August. Available at: http://www.businessinsider.com/the-imf-is-just-as-powerful-as-the-military-and-cia-2016-8?IR=T.

Rodrik, D. (1995). Getting interventions right: How South Korea and Taiwan grew rich, *Economic Policy*, 20, 55–107.

Rodrik, D. (2006). Goodbye Washington consensus, hello Washington confusion? A review of the world bank's economic growth in the 1990s: Learning from a decade of reform, *Journal of Economic Literature*, 44, 973–987.

Rodrik, D. (2011). *The Great Divergence, the Other Way Around*, 21 July. Available at: https://rodrik.typepad.com/dani_rodriks_weblog/2011/07/the-great-divergence-the-other-way-around.html.

Rodrik, D. (2018). Populism and the economics of globalization, *Journal of International Business Policy*, 1, 12–33.

Roig-Franzia, M. (2009). Credit crisis cassandra: Brooksley born's unheeded warning is a eefuel 10 years on, *Washington Post*, 26 May.

Romer, P. (2020). The dismal kingdom: Do economists have too much power? *Foreign Affairs*, March/April 2020.

Rothschild, K.W. (1947). Price theory and oligopoly, *Economic Journal*, 57, 299–320.

Roubini, N. (2007). Why China should abandon its dollar peg? *International Finance*, 10, 71–89.

Rowden, R. (2009). *The Deadly Ideas of Neoliberalism: How the IMF has Undermined Public Health and the Fight Against AIDS*, New York: Zed Books.

Rusu, V.D. and Roman, A. (2018). An empirical analysis of factors affecting competitiveness of C.E.E. countries, *Economic Research*, 31, 2044–2059.

Ryan, C.R. (1998). Peace, bread and riots: Jordan and the international monetary fund, *Middle East Policy*, 6, 54–66.

Salter, A.W. (2019). Fiscal profligacy: A failure of congress and the people, American institute for economic research, 13 June.

Schick, A. (1998). *Contemporary Approach to Public Expenditure Management*, Washington, DC: World Bank.

Schmidhauser, J.R. (1992). Legal imperialism: Its enduring impact on colonial and post-colonial judicial systems, *International Political Science Review*, 13, 321–334.

Schneider, H. (2013). Yes, America is profligate, *Washington Post*, 12 January.

Sen, K. and Koivusalo, M. (1998). Health care reforms and developing countries: A critical overview, *International Journal of Health Planning and Management*, 13, 199–215.

Shahshahani, A. (2018). Why are for-profit US prisons subjecting detainees to forced labor? *The Guardian*, 17 May.

Sharma, O.P. (1992). Export competitiveness: Some conceptual issues, *Foreign Trade Review*, 27, 107–119.

Sherman, B. (2017). Tax rates and economic growth: Is there really a correlation? *Forbes*, 17 October.

Shulman, S. (2001). In Africa, patents kill, *MIT Technology Review*, 1 April.

Sikharulidze, D. and Kikutadze, V. (2017). Innovation and export competitiveness: Evidence from Georgia firms, *European Journal of Economics, and Business Studies*, 8, 131–137.

Simms, A. (2013). *The Private Sector is more Efficient than the Public Sector.* Available at: https://b.3cdn.net/nefoundation/78cfe0444c38b5b9d0_3hm6i yth8.pdf.

Sirico, R.A. (2012). *Defending the Free Market: The Moral Case for a Free Economy*, Washington, DC: Regnery Publishing.

Skidelsky, R. (2009). *Keynes: The Return of the Master*, London: Allen Lane.

Sky News (2009). *Prime Minister Gordon Brown: G20 Will Pump Trillion Dollars into World Economy*, 2 April.

Smith, A. (1776). *The Wealth of Nations*, New York: The Modern Library (Random House).

Snow, N. (2010). If goods don't cross borders..., *Foundation for Economic Education*, 26 October. Available at: https://fee.org/resources/if-goods-dont-cross-borders/.

Snyder, M. (2010). *11 Examples of How Insanely Corrupt the US Financial System has Become*, 13 April. Available at: http://endoftheamericandream. com/archives/11-examples-of-how-insanely-corrupt-the-u-s-financial-system-has-become.

Somers, M. and Block, F. (2014). *The Return of Karl Polanyi, Dissent*, Spring. Available at: https://www.dissentmagazine.org/article/the-return-of-karl-polanyi.

Sprague, I.H. (1986). *Bailout: An Insider's Account of Bank Failures and Rescues*, New York: Basic Books.

Stallman, R.M. (2018). Did you say 'Intellectual Property'? It's a seductive mirage, *Free Software Foundation*, 15 December. Available at: https://www. gnu.org/philosophy/not-ipr.en.html.

Stein, J.L. (1994). The natural real exchange rate of the US dollar and determinants of capital flows, in Williamson, J. (ed). *Estimating Equilibrium Exchange Rates*, Washington, DC: Institute for International Economics.

Stewart, H. (2012). Wealth doesn't trickle down—it just floods offshore, *The Guardian*, 22 July.

Stiglitz, J. (2002). *Globalization and its Discontents*, New York: Norton.

Stiglitz, J. (2004). The post Washington consensus, *The Initiative for Policy Dialogue*. Available at: http://policydialogue.org/files/events/Stiglitz_Post_Washington_Consensus_Paper.pdf.

Stiglitz, J. (2010). *Free Fall: America, Free Markets, and the Sinking of the World Economy*, New York: Norton.

Stone, C. (2013). Pursuing 'efficiency' in the public sector: Why privatisation is not necessarily the answer, *The Conversation*, 2 April.

Stubbs, T. and Kentikelenis, A. (2017). *How years of IMF Prescriptions have Hurt West African Health Systems*, 23 February. Available at: http://the

conversation.com/how-years-of-imf-prescriptions-have-hurt-west-african-health-systems-72806.

Stubbs, T., Kentikelenis, A. and King, L. (2016). Catalyzing aid? The IMF and donor behavior in aid allocation, *World Development*, 78, 511–528.

Stuckler, D. and Basu, S. (2009). The international monetary fund's effects on global health: Before and after the 2008 financial crisis, *International Journal of Health Services*, 39, 771–781.

Stuckler, D., King, L. and Basu, S. (2008). International monetary fund programs and tuberculosis outcomes in post-communist countries, *PLoS Med*, 5, 1079–1090.

Stuckler, D., King, L. and McKee, M. (2009). Mass privatisation and the post-communist mortality crisis: A cross-national analysis, *Lancet*, 373: 399–407.

Stuckler, D., Basu, S. and McKee, M. (2011). International monetary fund and aid displacement, *International Journal of Health Services*, 41, 67–76.

Surowiecki, J. (2004). Army, INC, *The New Yorker*, 12 January.

Tambade, H., Singh, R. and Modgil, S. (2019). Identification and evaluation of determinants of competitiveness in the Indian auto-component industry, *Benchmarking: An International Journal*, 26, 922–950.

Tan, C. (2019). The downside of negative interest rates, *American Century Investments*, September.

Tanzi, V. (1989). Fiscal policy and economic restructuring in Latin America, Paper presented at a conference on the economic reconstruction of Latin America at the Fundação Getúlio Vargas, Rio de Janeiro (7–8 August).

Tarver, E. (2020). Nontariff barrier, *Investopedia*, 26 July.

The Economist (2007). Misleading misalignment, 21 July.

The Economist (2010). Where are the profits? 11 December, 68.

The Economist (2013). Cap and trade: A Modern proposal with ancient roots, 30 November.

The Economist (2014). Patents that kill, 8 August.

The Economist (2019). *The Independence of Central Banks is Under Threat from Politics*, 13 April.

The Economist (2020). *How Manufacturing Might Take off in Africa*, 11 June.

Thoma, M. (2011). Government deficits: The good, the bad, and the ugly, *CBS News*, 22 May.

Thomadakis, S.B. (2007). What makes good regulation, *IFAC Council Seminar*, Mexico City, 14 November.

Thompson, C. and Matousek, M. (2019). America's infrastructure is decaying—here's a look at how terrible things have gotten, *Business Insider*, 26 February.

Thorbecke, W. (2017). Fiscal discipline is now required from the US, *Financial Times*, 11 December.

Transparency International (2015). Incentivising integrity in banks, *Working Paper*. Available at: http://www.transparency.org/whatwedo/publication/incentivising_integrity_in_banks.

Turner, M.A. (2019). Local transportation policy and economic opportunity, the Hamilton project, *Policy Proposal 2019-03*, January.

Turse, N. (2018). The pentagon sent $500 million abroad for international drug wars. What happened next is a mystery, *The Nation*, 8 February.

Turshen, M. (1999). *Privatizing Health Services in Africa*, New Brunswick: Rutgers University Press.

UNCTAD (2005). *Determinants of Export Performance*. Available at: https://unctad.org/en/docs/ditctab20051ch2_en.pdf.

UNCTAD (2020). Impact of the Covid-19 pandemic on global FDI and GVCs: Updated analysis, *Investment Trends Monitor*, March 2020.

UNICEF (2020). *Child Labour*. Available at: https://www.unicef.org/protection/child-labour.

Varoufakis, Y. (2016). Imagining a new Keynesian Bretton woods, *World Economic Forum*, 6 May.

Wang, T. (2004). Exchange rate dynamics, in Prasad, E. (ed). *China's Growth and Integration into the World Economy: Prospects and Challenges*, IMF Occasional Papers, No. 232.

Washington Post (2009). A conversation with John Williamson, *Economist*, 12 April.

Wastell, R. (2019). *Negative Interest Rates: Is it Time to Bury your Money?* 16 August. Available at: https://www.ratecity.com.au/home-loans/mortgage-news/negative-interest-rates-time-bury-money.

Warren, K. (2008). *Encyclopedia of U.S. Campaigns, Elections, and Electoral Behavior*, New York: SAGE Publications.

Weiner, G. (2019). *Low Inflation in 2019—Is it Just a Big Lie?* 29 March. Available at: https://supersavingtips.com/low-inflation-big-lie/.

Weldon, D. (2016). *The IMF, the Neoliberal Agenda and the World We've Built*, 27 May. Available at: https://medium.com/bull-market/the-imf-the-neoliberal-agenda-and-the-world-weve-built-9e411b3de0a0#.zf8b55jg2.

Wheelwright, T. (2019). *5 Ways that Billionaire Warren Buffett Pays a Lower Tax Rate than His Secretary*, 30 August. Available at: https://www.entrepreneur.com/article/338189.

White, R.A. (1984). *The Morass: United States Intervention in Central America*, New York: Harper & Row.

Williamson, J. (1985). The exchange rate system, *Policy Analyses in International Economics*, No. 5. Washington: Institute for International Economics.

Williamson, J. (1990). What Washington means by policy reform, in Williamson, J. (ed). *Latin American Adjustment: How Much Has Happened?* Washington: Peterson Institute for International Economics.

Williamson, J. (1993). Democracy and the Washington consensus, *World Development*, 21, 1332–1333.

Williamson, J. (2000). What should the world bank think about the Washington consensus? *World Bank Research Observer*, 15, 251–264.

Williamson, J. (2002). Did the Washington consensus fail? Outline of remarks at CSIS. Washington, DC: Institute for International Economics, 6 November.

Williamson, J. (2003). An agenda for restarting growth and reform, in Kuczynski, P.P. and Williamson, J. (eds.). *After the Washington Consensus: Restarting Growth and Reform in Latin America*, Washington: Institute for International Economics.

Williamson, J. (2004). The strange history of the Washington consensus, *Journal of Post Keynesian Economics*, 27, 195–206.

Wolff, R.D. (2012). Yes, there is an alternative to capitalism: Mondragon shows the way, *The Guardian*, 25 June.

Wolff, R.D. (2013). Capitalism efficient? We can do so much better, *The Guardian*, 17 March.

Wolff, R.D. (2020a). COVID-19 exposes the weakness of a major theory used to justify capitalism, *Counterpunch*, 9 July.

Wolff, R.D. (2020b). Many terms that are frequently used to describe capitalism simply don't hold up under scrutiny, *Counterpunch*, 28 July.

Wolverson, R. (2010). Confronting the China–US economic imbalance, *Council on Foreign Relations*, 18 February. Available at: http://www.cfr.org/publication/20758/confronting_the_chinaus_economic_imbalance.html.

Woodroffe, J. and Ellis-Jones, M. (2000). States of unrest: Resistance to IMF policies in poor countries, *World Development Movement Report*. Available at: http://www.wdm.org.uk/cambriefs/DEBT/unrest.htm.

Worstall, T. (2011). The Washington consensus works, *Forbes*, 22 July.

Wray, L.R. (2011). Lessons we should have learned from the global financial crisis but didn't, levy economics institute of Bard college, *Working Paper*, No. 681, August.

Wright, S. (2020). Go below zero: RBA urged to take rates negative for economic boost, *Sydney Morning Herald*, 2 June.

Zumbrun, J. (2019). Why the U.S. labeled China a currency manipulator and what it means, *Wall Street Journal*, 6 August.

Index

Printed in the United States
by Baker & Taylor Publisher Services

Printed in the United States
by Baker & Taylor Publisher Services